A THEORY OF PRECEDENT

A Theory of Precedent

From Analytical Positivism to a Post-Analytical Philosophy of Law

by

RAIMO SILTALA

·HART·
PUBLISHING
OXFORD – PORTLAND OREGON
2000

Hart Publishing
Oxford and Portland, Oregon

Published in North America (US and Canada) by
Hart Publishing c/o
International Specialized Book Services
5804 NE Hassalo Street
Portland, Oregon
97213-3644
USA

Distributed in the Netherlands, Belgium and Luxembourg by
Intersentia, Churchillaan 108
B2900 Schoten
Antwerpen
Belgium

Hart Publishing Ltd is a specialist legal publisher based in Oxford, England.
To order further copies of this book or to request a list of other
publications please write to:

Hart Publishing Ltd, Salter's Boatyard, Oxford OX1 4LB
Telephone: +44 (0)1865 245533 or Fax: +44 (0)1865 794882
e-mail: mail@hartpub.co.uk
www.hartpub.co.uk

British Library Cataloguing in Publication Data
Data Available
ISBN 1 84113–123–7 (cloth)

Typeset by Hope Services (Abingdon) Ltd.
Printed in Great Britain on acid-free paper
by Biddles Ltd, Guildford and King's Lynn.

". . . the unlimited right to ask any question, to suspect all dogmatism, to analyze every presupposition, even those of the ethics or the politics of responsibility."

Jacques Derrida, *On the Name*, 28.

Acknowledgments

I am indebted to a great many colleagues, advisors and friends in the field of law and jurisprudence, but only a few of them can be mentioned here: Professor Neil MacCormick, my distinguished opponent at the official thesis defence on 3 October 1998, for the highly insightful, critical and learned comments he then made on "why cases have *rationes* and what these are"; Professor Aulis Aarnio, the supervisor of my doctoral thesis, for the inspiration he initially gave me to take up the challenge of legal theory and Wittgenstein, and for teaching me the state of the art of analytical jurisprudence; Professor Hannu T. Klami, for his learned and perceptive comments on the original manuscript, for our many discussions on jurisprudence, and for providing me with all the facilities I needed during the lengthy research work; Professor Kaarlo Tuori, for his invaluable comments on the rational reconstruction of some of the basic tenets of modern legal thinking and the multi-layered structure of law; Professor Martti Koskenniemi, for his insightful comments on the methodological framework and the Derrida-inspired Introduction and final chapters of this book; and Justice Jukka Kemppinen, for his good advice in all matters of judgment, for providing the translation of J.L. Borges' *Del rigor en la ciencia*, and for being a friend.

I am grateful to the following private foundations for the generous financial support I received for my study on precedents: Emil Aaltonen Foundation, Hilkka and Otto Brusiin Foundation, Ella och Georg Ehrnrooth Stiftelse, Finnish Cultural Foundation, Oikeustieteen tutkimussäätiö, and Oskar Öflund Foundation. I wish to thank Richard Hart at *Hart Publishing Ltd.* for accepting my thesis in its novel, high-standard series on legal philosophy and Glynis Dyson for her invaluable help in copy-editing the manuscript and Andrew Halpin for preparing the index. Finally, I would like to express my deep gratitude to my parents, Laura and Tatu Siltala, to whom this book is dedicated, for always encouraging me in my scholarly and other aspirations; Tuija for her all-encompassing affection, love and support; and our two lovely daughters, Anna and Pomeliina, for teaching me the most valuable things in life.*

Raimo Siltala
Helsinki, January 2000

* The present book is based on my doctoral thesis which was defended in public on 3 October 1998. Professor Neil MacCormick acted as the officially nominated opponent at the thesis defence. On MacCormick's comments on the thesis, see D. N. MacCormick, "Raimo Siltala, *A Theory of Precedent: From Analytical Positivism to A Post-Analytical Philosophy of Law*, Opponent's Review" (1998) *Oikeus* 424. My *lectio praecursoria*, entitled "The Quest for the Ultimate Premises of the Law", was published in (1998) *Oikeus* 420. Since the thesis defence, several structural, stylistic and other changes have been effected throughout the text.

Abbreviated Contents

Acknowledgments vii

Part A: How to Do Things with Precedents

1 Frame of Analysis 3
2 The Concept of a Legal Norm: Legal Rules and Principles 41
3 A Theory of Precedent Ideology 65
4 Confrontations 109
5 Theory and Practice of Precedent-Following 121

Part B: A Theory of the Multi-Level Structure of Law

6 Towards a Rule of Law Ideology for Precedents 151
7 Discourse-Theoretical Frame of Law: *Ratio* and *Auctoritas*, and the Felicity Conditions of Legal Adjudication 179
8 The Quest for the Final Premises of Law—I: The Infrastructures of Legal Norm Constitution 197
9 The Quest for the Final Premises of Law—II: The Infrastructures of Judicial Signification under Precedent-Following 233
10 Summary 249

Bibliography 269
Index 279

Contents

Acknowledgments vii

Part A: How to Do Things with Precedents

1 *Frame of Analysis* 3

1. Wróblewski on the Three Ideologies of Judicial Decision-Making 3
   - 1.1 Ideology of bound judicial decision-making 3
   - 1.2 Ideology of free judicial decision-making 4
   - 1.3 Ideology of legal and rational judicial decision-making 5
2. Ross on a Judge's Normative Ideology 6
3. Hart on the Rule of Recognition 8
4. Object of Inquiry: Precedents and Precedent-Following 10
5. Object of Inquiry Redefined: Theoretical and Philosophical Premises of the *Ratio* of a Case, as Derived from the Multi-Level Structure of Law 14
6. Legal Systemic Frame: Precedents in the Civil Law and Common Law Context 15
7. Theoretical Frame of Reference: From Analytical Positivism to a Post-Analytical Philosophy of Law 17
8. Auxiliary Frame of Reference: Derrida, the Critical Legal Studies and Deconstruction 22
9. Questions on Method: From Analytical Model Construction to a Radical Questioning of the Ultimate Premises of Law ("... up against the limits of language") 29
10. Objections and Refutations 34

2 *The Concept of a Legal Norm: Legal Rules and Principles* 41

1. The Idea of Strong and Weak Legal Imputation 41
2. Dworkin's Challenge to Legal Positivism 43
3. Summers on the Categories of Legal Formality 47
4. Legal Principles Redefined as Norms with Low Legal Formality 49
5. Rules, Principles, and Background Reasons of Law 54
6. Legal Rules and Legal Principles/Policies in the Context of Precedents 58

3 A Theory of Precedent Ideology 65

1. Terminological Definitions 65
2. The Models of Precedent Ideology 67
   - 2.1 Fragments of a judge's precedent ideology 67
   - 2.2 General outline of the models of precedent ideology and their relation to Wróblewski's ideologies of judicial decision-making 76
3. The Realm of Predetermined Meanings: Judicial Reference 78
4. A Lawgiver, Dressed in Robe: Judicial Legislation 80
5. In Search of the Prior Court's Original Intentions: Judicial Exegesis 84
   - 5.1 Reconstructing the *ratio* from the normative premises of a prior decision 85
   - 5.2 Facts treated as material by the prior court 87
6. An Interplay of Similarity and Dissimilarity in Precedent-Following: Reasoning by Analogy and Distinguishing 91
7. Systemic Construction of Underlying Reasons from a Prior Court Decision or Line of Decisions 96
   - 7.1 Evolvement of legal systematicity in Dworkin's theory of law 96
   - 7.2 "[T]he best constructive interpretation of past legal decisions" 97
8. Rejudging a Prior Court Decision: Judicial Revaluation 102
9. Axiological and Teleological Background Reasons of Law: Judicial Consequentialism and Rightness Reasons in Judicial Decision-Making 105
10. The Judgment Intuitive: "by feeling and not by judgment" 107

4 Confrontations 109

1. Operative Precedent-Norm Conception 109
2. Deontic Mode: Degree of Legal Formality Involved 110
3. Systemic Statics of Precedent-Following: Degree of Systematicity in a Set of Precedents 110
4. Systemic Dynamics of Precedent-Following 111
   - 4.1 Systemic dynamics, I: legal source doctrine and other factors which exert influence on the binding force of the *ratio* of a case 111
   - 4.2 Systemic dynamics, II: degree of binding force of the *ratio* of a case 114
5. Method of Argumentation Adopted in a Precedent Ideology 115
6. Techniques of Departure from a Precedent 116
7. Theoretical Rationale of a Precedent Ideology 117

5 *Theory and Practice of Precedent-Following* 121

1. Judicial Exegesis with Formally Defined *Ratio Decidendi* (United Kingdom) 121
2. A Flexible System of Substantive Rules under Legal Pragmatism (United States/State of New York) 123
3. Divergence of Official Action and Professional Self-Understanding of the Judiciary (France) 127
4. A Flood of Discordant Precedents under Mutually Inconsistent Theoretical Premises (Italy) 128
5. A Free-Floating System of Outweighable and Formally Binding Reasons (Federal Republic of Germany) 132
6. Judicial Positivism under a Perplexed Relation of a Case's Headnote and the Whole of Judicial Reasoning (Finland) 135
   - 6.1 Preliminary outline of the precedent ideology adopted by the Finnish Supreme Court of Justice 135
   - 6.2 The doctrine of judicial headnotes, defined as equal with the *ratio decidendi* of a case 137
   - 6.3. A critique of headnote-oriented judicial positivism 141
   - 6.4 The author's preference: case-to-case reasoning by analogy and distinguishing 142
7. Conclusion: From Pure Types of Precedent Ideology to the Law in Action in Precedent-Following (A Tale of Grasshoppers, Beehives and Anthills) 143

Part B: A Theory of the Multi-Level Structure of Law

6 *Towards a Rule of Law Ideology for Precedents* 151

1. Prologue: Surface-Structure Level of Operative Precedent-Identification and Precedent-Following 151
2. General Outline of the Multi-Level Theory of Law and Its Relation to Tuori's Conception of Law 152
   - 2.1 The three levels of law, presented in the form of a diagram 152
   - 2.2 Tuori on the multi-layered structure of law 155
   - 2.3 Confrontations with Tuori's theory of law 157
   - 2.4 Relations between the levels of law: condition of possibility, professional morality of aspiration, and relation of restructuring 158
3. Reframing the Ideological Premises of Precedent-Following 160
   - 3.1 Fragments of a judge's precedent ideology reconsidered 160
   - 3.2 A formal definition of the rule of precedent recognition 163
4. A Rule of Law Ideology for Precedents? 165

4.1 Fuller, *The Internal Morality of Law* 165
4.2 Six facets of a rule of law ideology for precedent-following 168

5. The "View from the Bench": A Rule of Law Ideology for Precedents Contested by the Bad Faith Argument 175

7 *Discourse-Theoretical Frame of Law:* Ratio *and* Auctoritas, *and the Felicity Conditions of Legal Adjudication* 179

1. The Discourse-Theoretical Identity of Law under Analytical Positivism 179
2. The Axiomatic Ground of Legal Discourse: *Ratio* and *Auctoritas* 179
   2.1 The concept of legal validity 182
   2.2 The concept of legal rationality 183
3. Felicities and Infelicities of Legal Discourse 185
   3.1 J.L. Austin on misfires and abuses of speech acts 185
   3.2 Alexy on the meta-rules of rational legal discourse 187
   3.3 Claim to correctness, claim to authority, and pursuit of legitimacy 189
4. The "View from the Bench" Revisited: The Felicity Conditions of Legal Adjudication and the Quest for Empirical Legitimacy 192
5. Limits of the Discourse-Theoretical Frame of Law: Meta-Rules, Speech Acts and Social Institutions 195

8 *The Quest for the Final Premises of Law—I: The Infrastructures of Legal Norm Constitution* 197

1. Prologue: How Long Is the Standard Metre? 197
2. The Infra-Structures of Legal Norm Constitution: The Constitutive *A Priori* of Law 201
3. The Final Validity Ground of Law: Validity of Legal Validity 204
   3.1 Validity in Kelsen's *Pure Theory of Law* 205
   3.2 Validity based on a moral and/or political validity conception: Peczenik and MacCormick on the final validity ground of law 211
   3.3 Validity based on normative validity itself: Aarnio and the theory of legal autopoiesis on the final validity ground of law 212
   3.4 The inherent limits of the legal positivist frame 214
4. Rationality of Legal Rationality: The Ultimate Ground of Legal Justifiability 215
   4.1 Wróblewski and MacCormick on the final premises of legal rationality 215
   4.2 From the meta-rules of legal rationality to a Wittgensteinian form of life: Aarnio and Peczenik on the final premises of legal rationality 217

5. Recognition of the Rule of Recognition 221

6. Norm/Fact Character of the Ultimate Rule of Recognition 221

6.1 Between Kelsen and Borges: Is the ultimate rule of recognition a norm or a fact? 221

6.2 A shift from ontology to epistemology: external statements of fact and internal statements of validity 226

7. Conclusion: Is There a "Standard Norm" for Law? 229

9 *The Quest for the Final Premises of Law—II: The Infrastructures of Judicial Signification under Precedent-Following* 233

1. Prologue: "an infallible paradigm of identity"? 233

2. *Différance* ("this almost nothing of the unpresentable") 235

3. Syntagmatic and Paradigmatic Dimensions of Language, and the *A Priori* of a Discourse Formation 238

4. An Outline of the Four Paradigms of Judicial Signification under Precedent-Following and Related Judicial Imagery 239

5. Ascription of Meaning-Content to the *Ratio* of a Case under the Four Paradigms of Judicial Signification under Precedent-Following 242

5.1 Legislative paradigm of precedent-following: self-referentiality and the reproduction of original identity 242

5.2 Dispute-solving paradigm of precedent-following: contextual sense-differentiation by an incessant interplay of deferral/distancing 243

5.3 Systemic paradigm of precedent-following: sense-differentiation by privileging the latent signification structure beneath the manifest precedent-norm or reasons formulation 244

5.4 Extra-legal paradigm of judicial adjudication: production of radical dissimilarity by displacement of the legal premises 245

6. In Conclusion: *Différance* and Other Infrastructures of Judicial Signification under Precedent-Following 246

10 *Summary* 249

1. How to Read Precedents 249

2. From Analytical Positivism to a Deconstruction of Law 255

3. Conceptual Analytics of Precedent-Norm Formation, Presented in the Form of a Triangle (or "Iceberg") 260

4. Theory and Practice of Precedents 262

5. Reading the Law/Skating on Thin Ice 264

Bibliography 269

Index 279

Part A

How to Do Things with Precedents

1

Frame of Analysis

1. WRÓBLEWSKI ON THE THREE IDEOLOGIES OF JUDICIAL DECISION-MAKING

Jerzy Wróblewski has distinguished three distinct ideologies of judicial adjudication: the ideology of *bound* judicial decision-making; the ideology of *free* judicial decision-making; and the ideology of *legal and rational* judicial decision-making.[1] By means of the typology he is then able to classify the great schools of legal thought under three main headings.

1.1 Ideology of bound judicial decision-making

The ideology of bound judicial decision-making is the outcome of *political liberalism*, which aims at safeguarding the rights of an individual citizen against the state and other citizens, and *legal positivism*, as exemplified by, e.g., the English school of analytical jurisprudence and John Austin, the German School of *Begriffsjurisprudenz*, and the French *école exégètique*.[2] The formal values of liberty, legal certainty, legal security, and stability and consistency in law application are regarded as the highest values to be protected by the state under the valid rules of law.[3] Under such premises, law is conceived of as a closed, consistent and complete system of general and abstract norms of statutory origin, as enacted by Parliament. Statutory norms and formally valid enactments of a lower hierarchical status are, moreover, the only formally acknowledged source of law. As Wróblewski wrote:[4]

> "The ideology of bound judicial decision-making has a very simple doctrine of the 'sources' of law and it can be summarised briefly: the unique primary source of law is a statute in the formal sense of this term; decisions have to be based on statutory rules."

The law-creating role of the judge is held at bay by reference to Baron de Montesquieu's well-known *dictum*, to the effect that "judges are only the mouth which proclaims the formulation of law".[5]

[1] J. Wróblewski, *The Judicial Application of Law* (Kluwer, 1992), 270, 273–314. On Wróblewski's notion of reconstruction, see ibid., 266–7.

[2] On the ideology of bound judicial decision-making, see ibid., 273–83.

[3] Ibid., 278, 280.

[4] Ibid., 291. Cf. H. Kelsen, *Pure Theory of Law* (Peter Smith, 1989), 233: "According to a positivistic theory of law, the source of law can only be law".

[5] Wróblewski, above at n. 1, 274, 276. Cf. Baron de Montesquieu, *L'esprit des lois*, 404 (Book XI, ch. 6): "*Mais les juges de la nation ne sont, comme nous avont dit, que la bouche qui prononce les paroles de la loi; des êtres inanimés qui n'en peuvent modérer ni la force ni la rigueur*".

Today such extreme formalism in judicial decision-making is often taken as a textbook example of legal fiction, although there are still some remnants of it in the French system of adjudication.[6] A somewhat more realistic interpretation of the ideology of bound judicial decision-making would admit of a judge's limited discretionary powers, as either deliberately delegated to the courts by Parliament or as brought into effect in the mutual interaction of rapid social change and the flexible legal standards laid down by the legislator. Thus, Hans Kelsen argued that the application of a statutory or any other legal norm by necessity requires some discretion on part of the judge.[7] Hart, in turn, pointed out that, because of the open-textured character of linguistic concepts and legal rules, judges need to exercise some overtly rule-creating discretion on the "grey", penumbral areas of a legal rule's semantic coverage.[8]

In Wróblewski's classification, however, neither Kelsen nor Hart would count as true representatives of the ideology of bound judicial decision-making, because of the said discretionary powers granted to judges. But neither do they easily qualify as representatives of the third category, the ideology of legal and rational judicial decision-making. The Polish author himself admits that the three-fold classification of the ideologies of judicial decision-making is not clear-cut at the boundaries, due to its status as a set of reconstructions of judicial decision-making.[9] In actual jurisdiction, a full-scale enforcement of the ideology of bound judicial decision-making would, of course, be extremely rigid and blind in the face of social injustice. The belief in the formal completeness of law at the point of its inception and the denial of the interpretive powers of the judiciary might also require some intellectual self-sacrifice on the part of judges and other legal professionals alike.

1.2 Ideology of free judicial decision-making

Wróblewski's ideology of free judicial decision-making is an expression of the revolt against legal formalism, as inspired by the shortcomings of legal positivism of the nineteenth century. The ideology of free judicial decision-making comprises various intellectual movements such as François Gény's *libre recherche scientifique* in France, the *Freirechtslehre* or *Freirechtsbewegung* (i.e. Free Law Movement) in Germany, sociological jurisprudence and the realist movement in the United States, and the *Führerstaat* ideology of Nazi Germany in the 1930s.[10]

[6] See M. Troper, C. Grzegorczyk and J. Gardies, "Statutory Interpretation in France", in D.N. MacCormick and R.S. Summers (eds), *Interpreting Statutes: A Comparative Study* (Dartmouth, 1991), 203–4, 211. Cf. M. Troper and C. Grzegorczyk, "Precedent in France", in MacCormick and Summers, ibid., 107, where it is said that the judges are supposed to exercise, not "judicial power", but only a "jucidial function".

[7] Kelsen, above at n. 4, 233–6.

[8] H.L.A. Hart, *The Concept of Law* (Clarendon Press, Oxford, 1961), 124–8, 200.

[9] Wróblewski, above at n. 1, 267.

[10] On the ideology of free judicial decision-making, see Wróblewski, ibid., 284–304, and on its general description and theoretical justification, see ibid., 284–94.

Moreover, it may be taken to refer to any judicial ideology in which the role of the judge is emphasised, and the role of the legislator is belittled, in the creation of valid legal norms. As adherents of the ideology of free judicial decision-making Wróblewski mentions Gény, Ehrlich, Kantorowicz, Heck, Schmitt, and Bülow, among others.

The ideology of bound judicial decision-making was said to be connected with the ideas of political liberalism. No parallel, uniform background rationale can be pointed out for the ideology of free judicial decision-making, with the one exception of national socialism and the ideas put forth by the legal scholars of the *Third Reich*.[11] Rather, what is common to all the various traits of free judicial decision-making is their critical attitude towards the formalist premises of legal positivism and the ideology of bound judicial decision-making. The profound changes which have taken place in the legislative techniques in the twentieth century may have, in part, contributed to the birth of such judicial anti-formalism. An increased use of general clauses in legislation has denoted a more or less open delegation of norm-creating power from the legislator to the courts of justice,[12] and the general belief in the formal values of legal positivism may also have waned among citizens. Instead of the formal characteristics of law, the ideology of free judicial decision-making underscores the dynamic character of jurisdiction, its responsiveness to the problems of the real world "out there".

Apart from statutory rules, Wróblewski enumerates the following value-laden sources of law which are acknowledged by the ideology of free judicial decision-making: legal practice, social rules, social facts and social regularities, evaluations of facts connected with law, evaluation of other facts, sources of evaluations, and evaluations in general.[13] Wróblewski also comments briefly on the American doctrine of the "hunch", or an irrational, emotion-based evaluation of the concrete facts at hand and the judge's intuitive legal response to it;[14] but his main emphasis is on the European free law doctrine. Despite his rather severe criticism, Wróblewski still deems the ideology of free judicial decision-making to be better grounded than the bound alternative.[15]

1.3 Ideology of legal and rational judicial decision-making

The third alternative, the ideology of legal and rational judicial decision-making, is given a somewhat laconic treatment by the Polish legal philosopher, even though it is the one he himself opts for.[16] Wróblewski defines this

[11] Ibid., 297.

[12] On a critical account of the impact of such general clauses, see J.D. Hedemann, *Die Flucht in die Generalklauseln: Eine Gefahr für Recht und Staat* (JCB Mohr, Tübingen, 1993).

[13] Wróblewski, above at n. 1, 292–3.

[14] Ibid., 290.

[15] Ibid., 300–1.

[16] Ibid., 305–14. At 311–13, some attention is given to socialist legal systems as examples of the ideology of legal and rational judicial decision-making. Subsequent changes in society though, have turned such considerations to address issues of legal history.

alternative, as the terminology reveals, with reference to the two formal values of legality and rationality in judidial adjudication. Legality denotes conformity with the requirements of the law in force, while rationality concerns the internal and external premises of legal justification.[17] By means of the outward justification of a judicial decision, i.e. by reference to the epistemic and axiological premises of adjudication, the legality of a judicial decision can be displayed in open terms.

The ideology of legal and rational judicial decision-making is said critically to analyse—or, rather, critically to deviate from—the two other ideological alternatives, thus being situated in the middle ground between bound and free ideologies of legal adjudication. Such a judicial ideology avoids both the *ultra-rationalistic fallacy* of strictly bound judicial decision-making and the *irrationalistic fallacy* of entirely free judicial decision-making.[18] It is less constrained *vis-à-vis* prevalent legal source material than the model of formally bound law application, since it leaves room for the use of judicial evaluations as "a necessary element of judicial heuresis and justification".[19] However, in contrast to the model of entirely free law application, legal and rational judicial decision-making does not approve of the conception of judge-made law, i.e. the creation of general and abstract legal rules by the courts. Finally, Wróblewski points out that no ideology of judicial decision-making is able to draw the conceptual boundaries of legality in judicial law application, as that task is left for legal doctrine to fulfil.[20] One might perhaps say that no rule or meta-rule can determine its own terms of application in an exhaustive manner.[21]

2. ROSS ON A JUDGE'S NORMATIVE IDEOLOGY

In his empiricism-inspired[22] book, *Om ret og retfærdighed* (*On Law and Justice*), the Danish legal philosopher, Alf Ross, argued for the adoption of a moderate prediction theory in legal science, to the effect that an insight into the

[17] Wróblewski, above at n. 1, 307–311; Wróblewski, "Informatics and Ideology of Judicial Decision-Making", in *Informatica e diritto* (1984), 119–20.

[18] Wróblewski, above at n. 1, 306.

[19] Ibid., 310.

[20] Ibid.

[21] Cf. L. Wittgenstein, *Philosophische Untersuchungen—Philosophical Investigations* (Basil Blackwell, Oxford, 1967), § 85 (pp. 39–40/39^e–40^e); Hart, above at n. 8, 123.

[22] "The leading idea of this work is to carry, in the field of law, the empirical principles [of science] to their ultimate conclusions": A. Ross, *On Law and Justice* (University of California Press, 1958), IX. Yet, as Markku Helin has convincingly argued, there are some specifically hermeneutics laden elements at the very core of Ross' conception of law. The idea of using legal norms as a "*tydningsskema*", i.e. a scheme of interpretation, in qualifying a set of social phenomena as legally relevant, plus the adoption of a judge's normative source ideology in predicting the future outcomes of judicial adjudication, self-evidently cannot be reduced to the basic postulates of logical empiricism, strictly defined. The idea of understanding valid legal norms as *tydningsskema* is no doubt derived from Hans Kelsen. See M. Helin, *Lainoppi ja metafysiikka* (Suomalaisen lakimiesyhdistyksen julkaisuja, Helsinki, 1988), 162–3 ff.

normative ideology internalised by the judge[23] will make it possible for a legal scholar to make predictions on the future course of adjudication.[24] The validity of a legal norm, D, is defined with reference to the outcome of such a prediction: "the real content of the assertion 'A = D is valid law' is a prediction to the effect that D under certain conditions will be taken as the basis for decisions in future legal disputes".[25] As a consequence, assertions of legal validity can have only the status of probability assertions, i.e. statements concerning the greater or lesser probability that a given norm or other legal source material will be part of the normative ideology upon which a judge will draw when giving a ruling on the facts of a novel case. Knowledge gained of such normative premises of adjudication will then provide a legal scholar with a normative *scheme of interpretation*[26] by reference to which a coherent and meaningful reading may be given of certain legally qualified social phenomena, and of the judges' conduct specifically.[27]

Since a modern legal system is not just vast in volume but also in a continuous state of change, the content of a judge's normative ideology will have to be approximated by the prevalent legal source doctrine in the legal system concerned.[28] Equipped with an insight into the normative ideology internalised by the judges, the outcome of future legal adjudication may—"with considerable certainty", as Ross put it—be predicted by the collective efforts of legal science.[29] Ross underscores the fact that the content of such a source ideology is norm-descriptive, not norm-expressive, i.e. not a collection of legal norms but a doctrine concerning such norms.[30] Since there can be no direct access to a judge's state of mind at the moment of judicial decision-making, the idea of such norm-descriptivity must be read in the sense of *rational reconstruction* or normative abstraction only, in approximation of the specific legal premises that were, in fact, operative in the judge's mind. Like Hart in his account of the

23 In the Danish original "*den normative ideologi der besjæler dommeren*": A. Ross, *Om ret og retfærdighed* (Nyt nordisk forslag, 1953), 56. Since the English translation is not always entirely accurate, the Danish original edition will be used as the primary reference here.

24 Ross, ibid., 56–7; cf. Ross, above at n. 22, 43.

25 Ross, above at n. 22, 75. Cf. "*Gældende dansk ret kan herefter bestemmes som den normative ideologi der faktisk er virksom, eller må tænkes virksom, i dommerens sind, fordi den opleves af ham som socialt forbindende or derfor effektivt efterleves*" (Ross, ibid., 47).

26 In Danish: "*tydningsskema*": Ross, ibid., 47 ff. Cf. Kelsen, *Reine Rechtslehre: Einleitung in die rechtswissenschaftliche Problematik* (Scientia Verlag, 1994), 4–7 ("*Die Norm als Deutungsschema*").

27 Ross, above at n. 23, 47–8.

28 Ibid., 90 ff.

29 Ross, above at n. 23, 56–7: "*Retsvidenskaben beskæftiger sig med den normative ideologi der besjæler dommeren. Kendskab til denne ideologi (og dens tolkning) sætter os derfor i stand til med betydelig sikkerhed at forudberegne det retsgrundlag, hvorpå visse fremtidige afgørelser vil blive truffet, og som altså vill figurere i domspræmisserne. Men hvilket forhold består der mellem præmisserne og konklusionen, der naturligvis er det vi virkelig er interesseret i at kunne forudberegne?*" Cf. Ross, above at n. 22, 43.

30 Cf. Kelsen's dichotomy of *Rechtsnormen*/*Rechtssätze*, or legal norms and legal sentences concerning such norms, in Kelsen, *Reine Rechtslehre. Mit einem Anhang: Das Problem der Gerechtigkeit* (Verlag Franz Deuticke, Wien, 1960), 73–7, esp. 75.

judges' rule of recognition in a modern legal system,[31] Ross makes room for less than fully perfected legal source material within the scope of a judge's normative ideology. For Ross, the pertinent legal sources are an "aggregate of factors which exercise influence on the judge's formulation of the rule on which he bases his decision". Instantly applicable legal rules lie at one end of the spectrum of legal source material available to a judge, while mere "ideas of legal inspiration" lie at the other.[32]

When analysing the content of a judge's normative ideology, Ross uses the two terms, i.e. an individual judge and the courts of justice in totality, interchangeably, since the concept of a legal system is said to necessitate the supra-individual and, therefore, a more or less converging character of the normative ideology internalised by the judges in question. Purely idiosyncratic motives which, *per definitionem*, do not find support in the legal source doctrine, cannot be incorporated in the concept of a legal system without turning it into a scattered collection of individual, potentially incompatible decisions of a *Kadi-Justiz*.[33] Still, Ross makes the concession that judge-specific, idiosyncratic factors do, in fact, exert influence on the outcome of legal adjudication, and—notwithstanding the essentially collective, supra-individual character of the law and judges' legal source ideology—the idiosyncratic factors affecting a judge's decision-making "must be considered by anyone interested in forecasting a concrete legal decision".[34] If the impact of judge-specific, idiosyncratic motives is to be duly taken into account by legal science, while their significance is denied and ruled out from the officially acknowledged set of normative premises of adjudication, the final outcome of analysis will be precariously close to Duncan Kennedy's bad faith argument which will be considered at length at the end of chapters 6 and 7.

3. HART ON THE RULE OF RECOGNITION

Hart defined the legal system as a union of two kinds of rules: primary rules of obligation, and the secondary rules of recognition, change, and adjudication:[35]

> "There are therefore two minimum conditions necessary and sufficient for the existence of a legal system. On the one hand those rules of behaviour which are valid

[31] Hart, above at n. 8, 98.

[32] Ross, above at n. 23, 92; Ross, above at n. 22, 77.

[33] On the notion of *Kadi-Justiz*, see M. Weber, *Wirtschaft und Gesellschaft* (JCB Mohr, Tübingen, 1972), 486 and 563–4.

[34] The English translation of Ross' *Om ret og retfærdighed* states that the non-legal factors influencing a judge's decision-making "must be considered by anyone interested in forecasting a concrete legal decision": Ross, above at n. 22, 36. The Danish original is, however, interestingly somewhat ambiguous in this respect, to the effect that the idiosyncratic factors affecting a judge's decision-making "*må tages i betragtning*". It may be read either in the sense that such factors *must*, or that they *may*, be taken into account by legal science: Ross, above at n. 23, 49.

[35] Hart, above at n. 8, 113.

> according to the system's ultimate criteria of validity must be generally obeyed, and, on the other hand, its rules of recognition specifying the criteria of legal validity and its rules of change and adjudication must be effectively accepted as common public standards of official behaviour by its officials."

Thus, apart from primary rules of *obligation*, a legal system consists of: secondary rules of *change*, which confer power on certain authorities to enact, alter or derogate the valid rules of obligation; secondary rules of *adjudication*, which lay down the formal procedure to be observed when primary rules of obligation are applied and enforced in the courts of justice; and the rule, or rules, of *recognition* with reference to which the valid rules of obligation are identified as valid law by the judges and other law-applying officials. This definition of the legal system, however, would seem to be in flat contradiction to Hart's original intention, in *The Concept of Law*, of not providing a definition of law at all.[36] To "save the phenomena", Hart's definition of a legal system might be read in the sense of a cluster definition or a paradigm, instead of a standard definition of a concept.[37] A cluster definition does not require that all of its characteristic features are present at the same time, but a sufficient set of such factors will do. A paradigm, in turn, is a model to be followed to a greater or lesser extent. Hart's idea of judicial semantics, as outlined in terms of a "core of settled meaning" and a "penumbra of doubt", would seem to fit adequately into such an approach.[38]

The rule of recognition is accepted by judges and other law-applying officials as a criterion for the identification of the primary rules of obligation.[39] Hart, however, seems to ignore the fact that secondary rules of change and adjudication must somehow also be identified before they can be duly applied by judges. Thus, Hart's two-level model of law, consisting of primary rules of obligation and secondary rules of alteration, adjudication and recognition, must be extended to a three-level model, where the *primary* rules of obligation, the *secondary* rules of change and adjudication, and a *third-level* rule of recognition each have their place. But how is the rule of recognition itself identified? Will a fourth-level rule of recognition be required for the task, itself to be identified by a fifth-level rule of recognition, and so on *ad infinitum*? The question will be considered at length below in chapter 8.

The content of the rule of recognition is, roughly, to the following effect: "valid (or not valid), given the system's criteria of validity".[40] Hart's own standard example of the rule of recognition is the *Queen rule*, i.e. what the

[36] Ibid., 16–17.

[37] Wittgenstein's idea of family resemblance and the pragmatics-laden credo of the Oxford school of ordinary language should also be kept in mind. Cf. Hart, above at n. 8, 234, note to p. 15.

[38] See M.D. Bayles, *Hart's Legal Philosophy: An Examination* (Kluwer, 1992), 12, 13–15, 74–7. Cf. Hart, above at n. 8, 208 ff., where the author would seem to apply a cluster or paradigm approach to the definition of international law. Hart writes that the "book is offered as an elucidation of the *concept* of law, rather than definition of 'law' which might naturally be expected to provide a rule or rules for the use of these expressions" (emphasis in original).

[39] Ibid., 97.

[40] Ibid., 107.

Queen in Parliament enacts is (valid) law.[41] In a modern, diversified legal system, the rule of recognition is far more complex. As Hart points out, it comprises a reference to various sources of law, like constitutional provisions, statutory enactments and judicial precedents.[42] Moreover, while there may be several operative rules of recognition in the various fields of law, there can only be one ultimate and supreme rule of recognition in a legal system.[43]

Hart uses the analogy of the scoring rule of a game in order to elucidate the rule of legal recognition, but the illustration may prove to confuse the issue, rather than properly to clarify it:[44]

> "for when courts reach a particular conclusion on the footing that a particular rule has been correctly identified as law, what they say has a special authoritative status conferred on it by other rules. In this respect, as in many others, the rule of recognition of a legal system is like the scoring rule of a game. In the course of the game the general rule defining the activities which constitute scoring (runs, goals, &c.) is seldom formulated; instead it is used by officials and players in identifying the particular phases which count towards winning."

Anticipating the line of argumentation that will follow, the issue could be reformulated so that an *operative* use of a given rule, or set of rules, on the surface-structure level of law need not be accompanied by a more profound, deeper-structure level *theoretical* understanding of the ideological and conceptual prerequisites involved in judicial adjudication, on the part of judges and the legal profession generally.

However, the scoring rule of, e.g., football is evidently not a rule of recognition to be used by the umpire and the players alike as an infallible criterion of valid rule identification. Instead, it is one of the constitutive rules of the game which lay down the objective to be attained and the permitted "moves" in the game. A rule of recognition for football, in turn, would consist of the ideological and/or operative criteria for the identification of valid rules which the umpire is likely to apply in the course of the game. In football, the identification of valid rules of the game usually causes no great difficulties. However, if football, chess or cricket were played on several, slightly different and mutually incompatible sets of rules, a frequent recourse to some rule of recognition, providing for the criteria of valid rulebook identification, would indeed be needed.

4. OBJECT OF INQUIRY: PRECEDENTS AND PRECEDENT-FOLLOWING

Wróblewski's insights into the judicial application of law were confined mainly to the statutory norms of continental civil law. Any references to the more

[41] M.D. Bayles, *Hart's Legal Philosophy: An Examination* (Kluwer, 1992), 99, 104, 108, 113, 117.

[42] Ibid., 98. *Travaux préparatoires* are not mentioned by Hart, since they are not acknowledged as permissible legal source material in England.

[43] Ibid., 102–4.

[44] Ibid., 98–9 (emphasis in original).

openly precedent-based common law systems were said to be there only "to draw attention to analogies, parallels and differences in a macro-comparativistic way".[45] Since individual judicial decisions—and thereby precedents—were expressly excluded from his field of study, Wróblewski's three ideologies of judicial decision-making effectively evade the impact of precedents on a subsequent judge's legal discretion.[46] But what would be the corresponding *ideologies of precedent-based judicial decision-making* if Wróblewski's frame of analysis were extended to cover judge-made law and, thereby, precedents?

Ross outlined his theory of a judge's normative ideology from the point of view of statute-oriented civil law tradition, or the Danish legal system to be more precise, without ruling out the impact of precedents on a judge's discretion in the manner Wróblewski did above. However, he did not single out precedent-based law for a more detailed study, either. Thus, what would be the contents of a judge's *precedent ideology*,[47] or the normative ideology of a judge *vis-à-vis* the identification and interpretation of precedents, if Ross' theoretical frame of analysis were given such a specific reading?

Hart, as a representative of the Oxford philosophy of ordinary language in the field of law and jurisprudence, was deeply embedded in the precedent-based common law tradition when he outlined the rule of recognition for the English legal system, and for any modern legal system where a variety of legal source material is acknowledged. The *Queen rule*, or "what the Queen in Parliament enacts is (valid) law", may be taken as an operative rule of recognition for the identification of statutory law. However, the identification of the *ratio decidendi* of a case is touched upon only in passing by Hart, as part of the wider source doctrinal frame covered by the prevalent rule of recognition. Therefore, what would be the exact content of the *rule of precedent-recognition*, or the criteria for the identification (and subsequent reading) of the *ratio* of a case, if Hart's rule of recognition were imported to the specific context of precedent-following?

Below, the analytical frame of a judge's *view from the bench*, as analysed in more general terms by Wróblewski, Ross and Hart (i.e. Wróblewski's three ideologies of judicial decision-making, Ross' account of a judge normative ideology, and Hart's rule of recognition) will be given a specific interpretation in the context of precedent-identification and precedent-following: what are the operative and ideological criteria for the identification and interpretation of the

[45] Wróblewski, above at n. 1, 3. In Wróblewski's essay, "The Concept and Function of Precedent in Statute-Law Systems", attention is drawn to the role of precedents within the civilian context. However, there the approach is significantly different from that adopted in the present discussion, where Wróblewski's major contribution, *The Judicial Application of Law*, has instead been chosen as one frame of reference.

[46] "The legal system is constituted by sufficiently general and abstract rules, but does not include individual law applying decisions and *inter alia* judicial decisions. What is needed is a comparison of the normative basis of decision and its content, but for this elementary comparison singling out two 'kinds' of law is not necessary. It is also not necessary to study the role of precedents in the justification of judicial decisions": Wróblewski, above at n. 1, 296.

[47] I am much obliged to Neil MacCormick for suggesting the concise term *precedent ideology*.

binding element (*ratio decidendi*) of a case, as distinguished from its argumentative context (*obiter dicta*)? Neglected by the said three masters of analytical jurisprudence, a theory of precedents, as grounded on the basic *ratio/dicta* distinction and framed by the formal doctrine of *stare decisis*, would seem to require some conceptual tools of its own, modifying the general frame of analysis provided above by Wróblewski, Ross, and Hart.

In light of Hart's perceptive reflections on the issue, precedents would appear to be an evasive subject matter of jurisprudential analysis. When reflecting upon the open texture of language and law, Hart acutely discerned three persistent dilemmas which affect the operative functioning of the doctrine of *stare decisis* in the English system of law, without yet elaborating the issue any further:[48]

> "*First*, there is no single method of determining the rule for which a given authoritative precedent is an authority. Notwithstanding this, in the vast majority of decided cases there is very little doubt. The head-note is usually correct enough. *Secondly*, there is no authoritative or uniquely correct formulation of any rule to be extracted from cases. On the other hand, there is often very general agreement, when the bearing of a precedent on a later case is in issue, that a given formulation is adequate. *Thirdly*, whatever authoritative status a rule extracted from precedent may have, it is compatible with the exercise by the courts that are bound by it of the following two types of creative or legislative activity. On the one hand courts deciding a later case may reach an opposite decision to that in a precedent by narrowing the rule extracted from the precedent, and admitting some exception to it not before considered, or, if considered, left open. This process of 'distinguishing' the earlier case involves finding some legally relevant difference between it and the present case, and the class of such differences can never be exhaustively determined. On the other hand, in following an earlier precedent the courts may discard a restriction found in the rule as formulated from the earlier case, on the ground that it is not required by any rule established by statute or earlier precedent. To do this is to widen the rule. Notwithstanding these two forms of legislative activity, left open by the binding force of precedent, the result of the English system of precedent has been to produce, by its use, a body of rules of which a vast number, of both major and minor importance, are as determinate as any statutory rule."

Hart's three dilemmas of the (English) doctrine of *stare decisis* thus concern the weakly articulated methodology used by the judges in identifying the *ratio* of a case, the frequent lack of an exact formulation of the *ratio* to be extracted from a case, and the relatively loosely defined techniques of modifying or departing from a precedent.

One could plausibly argue that such theoretical perplexities are caused by the inherent properties of precedent-following. Only rarely do the *rationes decidendi* of a line of cases await a subsequent judge "neatly labelled" as such,[49] or clearly marked off from their argumentative context (*obiter dicta*) in the previous court decisions. In stark contrast to precedents, norms of statutory origin

[48] Hart, above at n. 8, 131–2.
[49] Cf. ibid., 123.

are institutionally cut off from the axiological and/or teleological background reasons for the act of legislation, as the *travaux préparatoires* or other drafting material are documented on different terms and are endowed with significantly weaker normative force than the outcome of legislation, if such argumentative relevance is acknowledged at all.[50] In addition, the operative distinguishing of the ruling and the justificatory reasons of a court decision, or its *dispositif* and *motif*,[51] usually causes no great difficulties for law-enforcement officials.

When it comes down to the identification of the *ratio* of a case under the constraints derived from the formal doctrine of *stare decisis*, things may be far more complicated. The particular ruling which was tailor-made to the facts of the previous case may not be held as equal to the true *ratio decidendi* of that case, when judged in light of the facts of a new case to be ruled upon. Instead, the initially neat division into the ruling and reasoning elements of a previous decision may have to be levelled off, and recourse be taken to the normative and/or factual reasoning premises behind such a ruling, when the true *ratio* of a case is to be identified later on. The theoretical dilemmas of precedent-following would, however, appear generally to affect legal scholars only. Practitioners of law, e.g. judges and other officials engaged in operative adjudication, seem to cope with normative information derived from precedents far more satisfactorily, at least as concerns the English judges of Hart's reasoning.

To anticipate the line of argument that will follow, one could say that a less than fully self-reflected notion of the *ratio decidendi* of a case, and of the formal constraints of precedent-following (*stare decisis*), might well suffice on the *operative* surface-structure level of law, if the doctrine and tradition on *how to read precedents* is strong and detailed enough among the judiciary and the legal profession generally. Supported by the strictly practical know-how of precedent-following which stems from legal tradition, judges may blindly adhere to the patterns of legal argumentation once taken into use, no matter how inadequate such a conception of precedents and precedent-following might turn out to be if subjected to closer scrutiny. Yet, even at the presence of a relatively rich tradition among the judiciary on how to read precedents, an insight into the *deeper-structure* level premises of law and legal adjudication may still bring about profound changes in the practice of precedent-following, by virtue of the increased level of professional self-understanding among judges and other lawyers. In civil law systems, specifically, there is often no thoroughly reflected conception of the inherent potentials and limitations of precedents even among judges of the highest courts. Yet, a common law judge might not prove to be any better equipped

[50] In the United Kingdom, the argument drawn from the *travaux préparatoires* is in principle prohibited, and the same is also the case for the "Brandeis Brief" type of material. See Z. Bankowski and D.N. MacCormick, "Statutory Interpretation in the United Kingdom", in D.N. MacCormick and R.S. Summers (eds), *Interpreting Statutes: A Comparative Study* (Dartmouth, 1991), 380–2.

[51] On the French terms "*motif*" and "*dispositif*", see M. Troper and C. Grzegorczyk, "Precedent in France", in D.N. MacCormick and R.S. Summers (eds), *Interpreting Precedents: A Comparative Study* (Ashgate/Dartmouth, 1997), 107.

in terms of such professional self-reflection, despite being vastly more experienced in the more practical side of the issue.

5. OBJECT OF INQUIRY REDEFINED: THEORETICAL AND PHILOSOPHICAL PREMISES OF THE *RATIO* OF A CASE, AS DERIVED FROM THE MULTI-LEVEL STRUCTURE OF LAW

I will argue that the inherent dilemmas of precedent-following, as acutely discerned by Hart above, are to a great extent induced by a less than fully self-reflected and well-articulated conception of the *jurisprudential* and *philosophical* premises of precedent-following "beneath" the operative surface-structure level of law, on the part of judges and other lawyers engaged in precedent-identification and precedent-following. Therefore, the discussion will be extended to the deep-structure level preconditions of the *ratio* of a case, or the conceptual analytics of *precedent-norm formation*, where the three ideologies of judicial decision-making (Wróblewski), a judge's normative ideology (Ross), and the judges' rule of recognition (Hart) will be read in the specific context of precedent-following. However, the sum total of such ideological factors affecting a judge's formulation of the *ratio* of a case is only one set of the deeper-structure premises of law. Therefore, in Part B of this book, "A Theory of the Multi-Level Structure of Law", the discussion will be extended to the *discourse-theoretical frame* of law and the *infrastructure* level preconditions of legal norm constitution and judicial signification under precedent-following.

To put it concisely, an extensive inquiry will be made into the specific *jurisprudential* and *philosophical* preconditions of precedent-norm formation on the four levels of analysis discerned. An adequate answer will be sought to the following four questions:

(1) What are the *operative* premises of the *ratio* of a case as it is manifested on the linguistic-positivist surface-structure level of judicial adjudication?
(2) What are the *ideological* premises of precedent-norm formation, or the feasible contents of a judge's precedent ideology (Ross), the rule of precedent-recognition (Hart), or the various ideologies of precedent-based judicial decision-making (Wróblewski)?
(3) What are the *discourse-theoretical* or *conceptual* prerequisites of legal argumentation "beneath" the level of legal ideology, or the axiomatic postulates of law according to analytical positivism, and what are the discourse-theoretical consequences derived therefrom?
(4) What are the ultimate or final *infrastructure* level prerequisites of legal norm constitution and judicial signification under precedent-following still "beneath" the discourse-theoretical frame of law?

The operative premises of the identification and subsequent reading of the *ratio* of a case, as distinguished from its argumentative context or *dicta*, at the surface-structure level of law are glossed by practice-oriented *legal dogmatics*. The ideological premises of the *ratio* of a case and the discourse-theoretical or conceptual preconditions of rational legal argumentation at the deep-structure level of law are analysed by *jurisprudence*, i.e. *legal theory*. Finally, the quest for the "final" or "ultimate" premises of law, language and reason at the infrastructure level of law is reflected upon by *legal philosophy*.

The main point of the present discussion is to shed light on the jurisprudential and philosophical preconditions of precedent-norm formation which are frequently taken for granted—and therefore left unstated—by judges, advocates, and other lawyers engaged in precedent-based judicial adjudication, and even by legal scholars. Since the operative side of the issue proved to be far less problematic in the preliminary Hart-based analysis above, I will focus on the down-reaching edifice of law which consists of the ideological, discourse-theoretical, and infrastructure level preconditions of precedent-norm *constitution* (and *disintegration*), or the production of the formal *ratio/dicta* distinction in a case, and *judicial signification* in precedent-following, or the *proliferation* (and *dissolution*) of a norm's meaning-content for the novel case at hand. Although the focus will be on the formative premises of the *ratio* of a case, in chapter 7 and chapter 8 the frame of analysis will be extended to comprise legal norms in general, since the discourse-theoretical frame of law, plus the grounding/effacing infrastructure level preconditions of legal norm constitution, are shared by all legal norms, irrespective of their mode of origin in either legislation or jurisdiction.

The analytical conception of law, as put forth by Wróblewski, Ross and Hart, provided the inspiration for Part A of this treatise, "How to Do Things with Precedents", where the contents of a judge's *intellectual toolbox vis-à-vis* precedents will be presented, and an adequate answer will be sought to Hart's three dilemmas of precedent-identification and precedent-following (or precedent-evading). Tuori's theory of law provided the initial source of inspiration for Part B of this treatise, "A Theory of the Multi-Level Structure of Law", where the down-reaching edifice of the surface-structure, deep-structure, and infrastructure level prerequisites of the *ratio* of a case, and of law in general, will be outlined in detail. Finally, the decisive influence of the non-conventional French philosopher Derrida can be seen in the discussion of the "final" or "ultimate" premises of law, as effected/effaced in the infrastructure level phenomena of law.[52]

6. LEGAL SYSTEMIC FRAME: PRECEDENTS IN THE CIVIL LAW AND COMMON LAW CONTEXT

Actual court practice as conceived of and reflected upon by the judges and other legal professionals is a given reference for any systematic outline of a judge's

[52] The infrastructures of law, as effected/effaced on the deep-structure and surface-structure levels of law, will be tackled in detail in chs 8 and 9, where the truly equivocal status of legal norm constitution/disintegration and the proliferation/dissolution of meaning within law will be discussed at length.

ideological stance towards precedent-identification and precedent-following, no matter how detached from actual court practice the method or methods of arriving at such ideological premises may initially have been. The theory of precedent-ideology put forth in Part A of the book may be read as a set of legal theoretical reconstructions which link together two distinct elements, i.e. precedents as analysed in legal theoretical literature and precedents as materialised in judges' professional self-understanding and actual court practice.

The research group *Bielefelder Kreis* has thus far published two legal-comparative studies on the use of statutory law and precedents, respectively, in the legal argumentation practice of the highest courts selected for the analysis.[53] As there already exists a fairly reliable account of the role and function of precedents in the eleven legal systems included in *Interpreting Precedents: A Comparative Study*,[54] the legal comparative aspect of the issue will, for the most part, be excluded from the scope of the present discussion. Yet, some illustrative examples will be given of the precedent ideology adopted in the six legal systems selected for the purpose in chapter 5 below. The idea is to test the validity of the modelling approach, and to provide a direct link to the results attained by the *Bielefelder Kreis* in its comparative study on precedents. The legal systems chosen for the relatively modest legal comparative part of the present study are: United States (State of New York), United Kingdom, France, Italy, Federal Republic of Germany and Finland.

The inclusion of the United States and the United Kingdom in the legal comparative part of the study is self-evident, due to the prominent role of precedents in both. France, Italy, and the Federal Republic of Germany have been selected because they fairly well represent the different approaches to precedent-following in the major legal systems of the continent.[55] The Finnish experience with precedents,[56] in turn, neatly exemplifies one of the key findings of the study of precedent ideology, i.e. the theoretical perplexities which are bound to emerge, if some particular precedent ideology is at least semi-officially professed by the judiciary, without being adequately supported by an insight into the potentials and, to an even greater degree, the inherent shortcomings and restrictions of the ideology in question. Some critical comments on the relative merits, weaknesses and defects of the major precedent ideologies will also be given below.

[53] MacCormick and Summers, above at n. 50; and MacCormick and Summers, above at n. 51. I had the privilege of acting as the secretary for the *Bielefelder Kreis* in its two meetings in Florence and Bologna in 1994, and in Tampere in 1996.

[54] These were: Federal Republic of Germany, Finland, France, Italy, Norway, Poland, Spain, Sweden, United Kingdom, and United States (State of New York), plus the legal system of the European Community. Nine countries were included in the book *Interpreting Statutes: A Comparative Study*, above at n. 50.

[55] Inclusion of the decisions of the International Court of Justice and the Court of Justice of the European Communities in the study was initially considered. They were, however omitted from the analysis because the focus of the present study is on questions of jurisprudence and legal philosophy, and not on those of full-scale legal comparison.

[56] The Finnish legal system is, of course, the one I was initiated into in the course of my legal education.

The present analysis will be based on the jurisdiction of the courts of general jurisdiction only, omitting the constitutional, administrative and other courts.[57] There is one exception thereto, however. In chapter 5, the German Federal Constitutional Court will be included as an illustrative example of the "law in action" in the context of precedents, due to the Court's key position in the German system of adjudication and the quite openly professed self-reflection on precedents by its justices. Institutional and constitutional issues will be omitted from analysis.[58] The present research interest being on the normative or legal side of the issue, the questions of legal fact-finding, burden of proof, or evaluation of evidence will not be considered, except in the context of the various precedent ideologies. To put it concisely, the main goal of the present discussion is to work out an extensive *legal theoretical (jurisprudential)* and *philosophical* frame for the analysis of precedent-identification and precedent-following, viewed predominantly from the point of view of a civil law judge. Yet, since the feasible methods of precedent-identification, precedent-following and precedent-evading are, self-evidently, more developed and refined within precedent-based common law tradition, in contrast to the more statute-oriented civil law systems, arguments will, to a great extent, be drawn from the former when analysing the constituents of a judge's precedent ideology.

7. THEORETICAL FRAME OF REFERENCE: FROM ANALYTICAL POSITIVISM TO A POST-ANALYTICAL PHILOSOPHY OF LAW

Analytical positivism is the theoretical frame of reference of the present discussion in a two-fold sense. Part A of this book is based on a rather straightforward adoption of the methodological tools that have been introduced and put into fruitful use by the said school of law; Part B, and especially the two chapters on the infrastructures of law (chapters 8 and 9), will eventually evolve into a critical unfolding of the final or ultimate premises of law, and thereby also of the analytical frame.

The term "Analytical Positivism", as used in the present context, is intended to be a shorthand expression for a set or cluster of philosophical and jurisprudential tenets, as exemplified by the scientific contributions of, e.g. Austin, Kelsen, Hart, Wróblewski, Ross, MacCormick, Alexy, Peczenik, Aarnio and, to a somewhat lesser extent, Summers, whose writings bear the decisive impact of American legal pragmatism, too. There need not be any straight historical

[57] In the Federal Republic of Germany, for instance, there are six distinct courts of last instance, with respect to: (1) general jurisdiction, hearing civil and criminal law cases; (2) administrative jurisdiction; (3) jurisdiction in labour law cases; (4) jurisdiction in social law cases; (5) fiscal jurisdiction; and (6) constitutional jurisdiction. R. Alexy and R. Dreier, "Precedent in the Federal Republic of Germany", in MacCormick and Summers, above at n. 51, 17–18.

[58] The impact of the institutional factors in precedent-based judicial adjudication is analysed in M. Taruffo, "Institutional Factors Influencing Precedents", in MacCormick and Summers, above at n. 51, 437–60.

connection between the various representatives of analytical positivism, as Ross pointed out with respect to Kelsen's *Pure Theory of Law* and Austin's *The Province of Jurisprudence Determined*.[59]

For instance, the following individual contributions to the field of jurisprudence can be classified under analytical positivism as the term is defined here: J. Austin, *The Province of Jurisprudence Determined*;[60] W.N. Hohfeld, *Fundamental Legal Conceptions as Applied in Judicial Reasoning*;[61] H. Kelsen, *Pure Theory of Law*[62] and *General Theory of Law and State*;[63] H.L.A. Hart, *The Concept of Law*;[64] J. Wróblewski, *The Judicial Application of Law*;[65] A. Ross, *Om ret og retfærdighed*;[66] N. MacCormick, *Legal Reasoning and Legal Theory*;[67] A. Peczenik, *The Basis of Legal Justification*[68] and *On Law and Reason*;[69] R. Alexy, *A Theory of Legal Argumentation*;[70] A. Aarnio, *The Rational as Reasonable*[71] and *Reason and Authority*;[72] and R.S. Summers, *Essays on the Nature of Law and Legal Reasoning*.[73] Self-evidently, the two books published by the *Bielefelder Kreis*, i.e. *Interpreting Statutes: A Comparative Study*[74] and *Interpreting Precedents: A Comparative Study*,[75] may be added to the list, along with several articles from the authors mentioned. As can be seen in the above list of publications, the rationality conditions of legal argumentation have been at the core of research of those scholars identified with analytical positivism. As is quite natural, the present research interest will be on the modern versions of analytical legal positivism, in the image of Kelsen's, Ross', Hart's and Wróblewski's theories of law, and not on the historical roots of the intellectual movement in Austin's or Hohfeld's writings.

The term "legal positivism" is employed here in the *jurisprudential* sense, with reference to the definition of law in terms of its formal source of origin and the effected separation of valid law from the realm of universal morals, thus contesting the contrary conception that is upheld by natural law theory. "The existence of law is one thing; its merit or demerit is another. Whether it be or be not is one enquiry; whether it be or be not conformable to an assumed standard,

[59] Ross, above at n. 22, 2. Cf. W. Friedmann, *Legal Theory* (Stevens & Sons, London, 5th ed. 1967), 275 ff.

[60] Cambridge University Press, 1995.

[61] Yale University Press, 1964.

[62] Above at n. 4.

[63] Harvard University Press, 1949.

[64] Above at n. 8.

[65] Above at n. 1.

[66] Above at n. 23.

[67] Oxford University Press, 1978.

[68] Infortryck AB, 1983.

[69] Kluwer, 1989.

[70] Clarendon Press, Oxford, 1989.

[71] D. Reidel Publishing Co., 1987.

[72] Ashgate/Dartmouth, 1997.

[73] Duncker & Humblot, Berlin, 1992.

[74] Above at n. 50.

[75] Above at n. 51.

is a different enquiry. A law, which actually exists, is a law, though we happen to dislike it", as Austin pointed out in the celebrated passage of *The Province of Jurisprudence Determined.*[76] Similarly, Hart defended the separation of law from morals with force and rigour.[77] Law, according to the basic tenets of legal positivism, is positive law (*jus positivum*), as duly enacted by the legislator or issued by the courts, and not a collection of rules which might, or perhaps even ought to, find correspondence with the standards of ideal morals. In addition, legal positivism claims to occupy an entirely neutral position with respect to various political ideologies. Kelsen even boasted of the entirely formal, ideologically open and value-free character of his *Pure Theory of Law*, boldly claiming in its defence that it could yield equally well to the service of totally opposing legal and political ideologies.[78]

Notably, no reference is made here to the concept of positivism as the term is employed in the theory of science, i.e. logical positivism of the *Wiener Kreis*.[79]

Legal positivism has often been treated as a cluster concept which may comprise various features, while none of them is held to be decisive, conclusive or definitive as such.[80] Hart, for one, lists the Austinian criterion that laws are commands of human beings or, to be more exact, coercive orders issued by the sovereign and backed by the threat of force, which contention Hart deliberately rejected in *The Concept of Law*. Moreover, the analysis of the meaning of legal concepts is regarded as an important branch of the study of law, as distinguished from a historical, sociological or any other kind of approach to the legal phenomena. In terms of the present classification, the latter element would find its proper place under the notion of analyticity, and not that of positivism.[81]

[76] Austin, *The Province of Jurisprudence Determined*, above at n. 60, 157. The text continues with a vehement critique of Sir William Blackstone whose notion of common law notably entailed elements of natural law.

[77] H.L.A. Hart, "Positivism and the Separation of Law and Morals", in *Essays in Jurisprudence and Philosophy* (Clarendon Press, Oxford, 1983).

[78] H. Kelsen, *Reine Rechtslehre* (Verlag Franz Deuticke, Wien, 1960), V; Kelsen, *Reine Rechtslehre* (1934), 24.

[79] Cf. H. Kelsen, "*Was ist Juristischer Positivismus?*", in H. Klecatscky, R. Marcic and H. Schambeck (eds), *Die Wiener Rechtstheoretische Schule. Schriften von Hans Kelsen, Adolf Merkl, Alfred Verdross* (Europa Verlag, Wien, 1968), 941 ff.

[80] On the definition of legal positivism as a cluster of different definitional features, see Hart, above at n. 8, 253, note to p. 181; and M. Jori, "Introduction", in M. Jori (ed.), *Legal Positivism* (Dartmouth, 1992), XI–XL. Cf. M. Troper's entry on "Positivism" in A.-J. Arnaud (ed.), *Dictionnaire encyclopédique de théorie et de sociologie du droit* (LGDJ, Paris, 1993), 461–3. The entry comprises legal positivism only, despite the more general title adopted in it.

[81] In all, the following five criteria are given by Hart, above at n. 8, 253, note to p. 181: (1) laws are commands of human beings; (2) there is no necessary connection between law and morals; (3) the analysis or study of meanings of legal concepts is an important study to be distinguished from historical inquiries, social inquiries and the critical appraisal of law in terms of morals, social aims, functions and so on; (4) a legal system is a "closed logical system" in which correct decisions can be deduced from predetermined legal rules by logical means alone; and (5) moral judgments cannot be established, as statements of fact can, by rational argument, evidence, or proof (i.e. non-cognitivism in ethics). Austin is said to have held the views expressed in (1), (2) and (3), but not those in (4) or (5); while Kelsen held the views expressed in (2), (3) and (5), but not those in (1) or (4). Hart himself would seem to be committed to points (2), (3) and (5), but not to points (1) and (4), since he rejected

Bobbio, in turn, has identified legal positivism with reference to the following three criteria: (1) a neutral, scientific approach to law; (2) a set of theories depicting the law as a product of the modern state, amounting to a set of positive rules of human origin; and (3) an ideology of law which gives value to positive law as such.[82]

Analyticity, in turn, refers to a set of methods or, rather, a style of argumentation adopted by the "intellectual heirs of Russell, Moore, and Wittgenstein", as the standard description in a philosophy dictionary puts it.[83] Analytical philosophy has obtained some sober insights into the nature and function of language from the Oxford philosophy of ordinary language, known for its austere attitude towards all kind of metaphysical speculation. In broad terms, the analytical approach may be described by its respect for (rational) argument and clarity, along with the emphasis laid on linguistic analysis, seen as free from any effort towards metaphysical synthesis. However, since analytical positivism needs ultimately to ground its assertions concerning law on something, that "something" will be subjected to a closer scrutiny at the end of this investigation, necessitating a decisive change in the frame of analysis adopted.

It may well be that analytical positivism, if defined with the full-fledged rigour that is proclaimed in the methodological chapters of Kelsen's *Pure Theory of Law*, is an intellectual position which cannot be sustained in a fully consistent manner. At least, there are deviations from and modification to the initial positivist ideal in the writings of most, if not all, of the authors identified with the said approach to the law. Kelsen, as is well known, made a decisive concession to the idea of empirical facticity when he imposed the requirement of "by and large" effectiveness upon the *Grundnorm* and the system of valid legal norms enacted under its (presumed) authority. Hart imported a set of elements from natural law theory into his positivist theory of law in terms of the *minimum content of natural law*.[84] MacCormick's idea of the *underpinning reasons of law* and Peczenik's moral and/or political *background reasons of law* signify a plain deviation from the positivist frame, strictly defined.

Therefore, the notion of analytical positivism ought to be taken in the sense of a theoretical (re)construction or Weberian pure type in the present context, i.e. an intellectual stance which is abstracted from the relevant legal theoretical and philosophical literature. However, the present conception of analytical positivism is not a mere lifeless "strawman" of jurisprudential thinking, or the outcome of a legal scholar's presumably innocent imagination, with no reference outside of the realm of legal theory so carefully purified. On the contrary,

both the Austinian "command theory of law" and the idea that a legal system could be formally closed, or unaffected by the open textured character of language.

[82] Bobbio is commented in Jori, above at n. 80, XII.

[83] Audi (ed.), *The Cambridge Dictionary of Philosophy* (Cambridge University Press, 1995), 22. On analytical philosophy in general, see also the entry in T. Honderich (ed.), *The Oxford Companion to Philosophy* (Oxford University Press, 1995), 28–30.

[84] Hart, above at n. 8, 189–95.

the impact of the positivist and analytical tenets can clearly be seen in the legal theoretical contributions of the authors mentioned, even if in a slightly modified form.

In all, the book might be said to proceed from Wróblewski, Ross and Hart to Derrida, or from analytical positivism to a *post-analytical philosophy of law*, where the "final" or "ultimate" premises of law, and of the positivist-analytical frame, are critically unfolded and, eventually, subjected to radical questioning. The analytical approach is not without exceptions in Part A of this book, since Dworkin's theory of legal principles, as elaborated in chapter 2, is a far cry from such analyticity pure and simple. Yet, even Dworkin is eventually read through an analytical frame, i.e. the categories of legal formality as outlined by Summers.

To put it concisely: Part A of this treatise (chapters 1–5), will focus on the constitutive elements and theoretical implications of a judge's precedent ideology. First, the theoretical and methodological frame of analysis will be presented concisely (chapter 1). The concept of a legal norm will be outlined in light of the recent, Dworkin-inspired legal rule/principle discourse, leading to a novel definition of the concept of a legal rule and legal principle, which will then be adjusted to the specific context of precedent-following (chapter 2). A novel theory of a judge's precedent ideology will be set out in terms of the six main categories or "pure types", and the relative merits and shortcomings of each of the key approaches to precedents will be considered briefly (chapter 3). Some of the ideological fragments entailed in the different types of precedent-ideology will be briefly contrasted with each other (chapter 4). Finally, the validity of the modelling approach will be tested in light of the precedent ideology adopted in the six legal systems chosen for the purpose, and some comments will be made as to the law in action in precedent-following (chapter 5).

In Part B of this treatise (chapters 6–10), the down-reaching edifice of the ideological, discourse-theoretical and infrastructure level prerequisites of precedent-identification and precedent-following will be unfolded. First, a general presentation of the multi-level conception of law will be given, followed by a formal definition of the rule of precedent-recognition and an outline for a specific, Fuller-inspired rule of law ideology for precedents (chapter 6). The discourse-theoretical frame of law will be presented in terms of the postulated axioms of legal validity and legal rationality under the theoretical premises of analytical positivism, thus giving effect to the felicity conditions of adjudication in terms of the conceptual, mental and institutional criteria involved (chapter 7). Finally, the infrastructure level prelogical and preconceptual prerequisites of law will be considered under the two headings of legal norm constitution (chapter 8) and judicial signification under precedent-following (chapter 9). The concluding chapter (chapter 10) will sum up concisely some of the key findings of this treatise.

8. AUXILIARY FRAME OF REFERENCE: DERRIDA, THE CRITICAL LEGAL STUDIES AND DECONSTRUCTION

"Deconstruction is not a method and cannot be transformed into one."[85]

Apart from rejecting the grounding axioms of analytical positivism, this treatise will decline to accept the specific reading of Derrida and the philosophy of deconstruction which has been professed within the loose-edged American *Critical Legal Studies* (CLS) movement. Deconstruction as initially suggested by Derrida, and not as adopted within the CLS movement, might therefore be taken as the auxiliary frame of reference for the present inquiry into the constitutive (and disintegrating) preconditions of law. The deconstructive undertone will gain more ground towards the end of the treatise, where the infrastructures of law, and of Western philosophy in general, will be considered at length.

The (mostly) leftist lawyers, intellectuals and legal scholars identified with the CLS movement (i.e. *Crits*) do not make up a tightly knit school of law of their own, drawn together by a shared constructive project in legal analysis, some uniform ideology of law, or a conception of legal methodology to be employed. That, of course, is equally true of their intellectual predecessors, the Legal Realists of the 1920s and 1930s.[86] Rather, the only creed held in common by the various representatives of the CLS movement is their highly critical stance towards the mainstream conception of law. Building partly on the intellectual legacy of the Legal Realists, and partly on a less-than-systematic reception of the various philosophical schools of the continent, the CLS movement has gathered a loose collection of critical approaches under its coverage. Diffuse ideas drawn from Marxism, phenomenology, semiotics, feminism, and structuralism, to name only a few continental schools of philosophy or other fields of research, have been woven together with the basic tenets of legal realism, the latter sometimes taken to extremes.[87] Here, only one particular strand of the CLS movement will be examined in more detail, i.e. the concept of legal methodology that has been adopted within it.

Within the circles of literary and legal studies in the United States, deconstruction has been welcome as a novel method of textual analysis and textual criticism, laden with the seductive promise of unveiling the hidden implications of any literary, philosophical or legal text before the eyes of an attentive reader. Such a *method of deconstruction* denotes sharpened awareness of the concep-

[85] J. Derrida, "Letter to a Japanese Friend", in D. Wood and R. Bernasconi (eds), *Derrida and Différance* (Northwestern University Press, 1988), 3.

[86] See, e.g., Fuller, "American Legal Realism", in R.S. Summers, *American Legal Theory* (Dartmouth, 1992), 430, n. 6.

[87] See Abel's and Kennedy's insightful comments on the Critical Legal Studies movement in Arnaud (ed.), *Dictionnaire encyclopédique de théorie et de sociologie du droit*, above at n. 80, 133–9 (entry on "*Critique 2—Critical Legal Studies*"), and the bibliographical notes on the movement in ibid., 133–4, esp. 135–7.

tual dichotomies operative in the text, and of the ideological bias that is brought into effect by privileging one or the other element within such dichotomies. Typically such a "deconstruction" of some legal doctrine or argument takes the form of reversing or inverting the internal priority order within the conceptual pairs involved, with the outcome of consistently privileging the "weaker", the suppressed, the exceptional, the subordinated, or the peripheral element of each dichotomy, at the cost of the "stronger", the normal, the central, or the standard element which, however, is taken to structure the phenomenon under scrutiny according to the mainstream conception of law (or literature).[88]

Balkin has analysed law in terms of *nested oppositions*, or dichotomies which involve a "relation of dependence, similarity, or containment between the opposed concepts".[89] Deconstruction, according to Balkin, is a tool of analysis or an analytical tool, by means of which the inherent hierarchies of thought and language are revealed and made ineffective.[90] Dalton, in turn, has discerned three inherent conceptual dichotomies within the prevalent contract law doctrine (i.e. public/private, objective/subjective, and form/substance) where one element is constantly favoured at the cost of the other.[91] By means of such dichotomies, she argues, the underlying problems of power and knowledge are displaced and not tackled with integrity.[92]

However, the CLS conception of deconstruction need not sustain a firm belief in the emancipatory effects brought into existence by reversing the binary dichotomies of the text. A profound setting-out of balance or even shattering of the grounds of law, with no promise of doctrinal redemption or reconciliation in sight, might well do for the purpose. In Koskenniemi's strongly CLS-inspired *From Apology to Utopia: The Structure of International Legal Argument*, the structure of international legal argumentation is proven to be inherently volatile, facing the constant threat of collapsing into either the utopian-moral or the apologist-political discourse, with no autonomous space left in-between for a legally qualified discourse formation.[93] Koskenniemi writes, "the kind of

[88] See J.M. Balkin, "Deconstruction", in D. Patterson (ed.), *A Companion to Philosophy of Law and Legal Theory* (Blackwell Publishers, Oxford, 1996), 367–73, esp. 367–8; cf. Balkin, "Tradition, Betrayal, and the Politics of Deconstruction", in S.J. Brison and W. Sinnott-Armstrong (eds), *Contemporary Perspectives in Constitutional Interpretation* (Westview Press, Oxford, 1993), 190–206, and Brison's and Sinnott-Armstrong's introductory notes in ibid., 189.

[89] Balkin, "Nested Oppositions" (1989) 99 *Yale Law Journal* 1669, 1671; Balkin, "Deconstruction", above at n. 88, 369.

[90] Balkin, "Deconstructive Practice and Legal Theory" (1987) 96 *Yale Law Journal* 743, 765 ("deconstruction operates by a momentary reversal of privileging") and 786 ("tool of analysis").

[91] To be more precise: contract law "describes itself" as more private than public, interpretation deals with objective rather than subjective understanding of the contractual terms, and consideration deals more with form than substance: Dalton, "An Essay in the Deconstruction of Contract Doctrine" (1985) 94 *Yale Law Journal* 997, 1000–3. The notion of "'deconstructive' textual strategies" is clarified in ibid., 1007–9, where an explicit allusion to Derrida is made.

[92] Dalton ibid., 1000–1.

[93] See M. Koskenniemi, *From Apology to Utopia: The Structure of International Legal Argument* (Lakimiesliiton Kustannus, Helsinki, 1989). On Koskenniemi's self-reflection on the methodological use of deconstruction, see ibid., XVII–XXIV, esp. n. 1 on pp. XVII–XVIII, where "deconstruction" is affiliated with structuralist linguistics in France, and where "deconstructive readings of legal

deconstruction operated in the foregoing Chapters [of the book] may be taken to imply that ultimately all discourse will disperse into an unending play of conceptual oppositions in which there is ultimately no basis to prefer conflicting ideas vis-à-vis each other".[94] Despite its—in my opinion—misplaced methodological reading of deconstruction, the outcomes of Koskenniemi's study, as put forth in the critical or "deconstructive" part of that inquiry where the inherently unstable or volatile character of (international) law is presented, bear a closer affinity to the present inquiry than the CLS-oriented research on the average. However, his attempt at "saving the phenomena" at the very end of the study, where the new credo of being "normative in the small" is introduced,[95] is less than entirely convincing and will not be adopted here.

Finally, even the blunt, although even less accurate term *trashing* has been employed in the CLS movement under the heading of "deconstruction", with reference to the disclosure of the "fundamentally incoherent" or "self-contradictory, ideologically biased, or indeterminate" character of legal doctrines or arguments.[96]

Rejecting the CLS reception of Derrida and deconstruction, I will argue that any forthrightly instrumentalist reading of deconstruction counts as a misconception or mispresentation of what Derrida himself, and some of his more attentive or more "orthodox-minded" readers on the continent, have been doing when engaged in deconstruction. Gasché, for one, has expressly argued against such a (mis)reading of Derrida in his *The Tain of the Mirror*.[97] Although Gasché deals mainly with the circles of literary criticism in the United States, his criticism may also be extended to apply to the CLS movement. However, even Gasché fails to keep the two issues of deconstruction and methodology distinct enough, since he argues that the Derridean infrastructures may be taken as instances of what he calls a "deconstructive methodology".[98] If the theoretical implications of the identity-evading infrastructures of Western metaphysics—as *effected/effaced* in self-effacing self-referentiality of the "ultimate" edges, grounds, criteria, or premises of the Western philosophical tradition or any specific discourse formation within its closed sphere, or the endless movement of *deferral/distancing* in the production/dissemination of sense in linguistic sig-

texts" is identified with reference to the CLS movement, as exemplified by Dalton and Balkin. Cf. also ibid., n. 6 on p. XX, where reference is made to Balkin's reading of Derrida and the CLS conception of law.

94 Ibid., 479.

95 Ibid., 496–7.

96 Balkin, "Deconstruction", above at n. 88, 370; Balkin, "Deconstructive Practice and Legal Theory", above at n. 90, 743–4.

97 R. Gasché, *The Tain of the Mirror: Derrida and the Philosophy of Reflection* (Harvard University Press, 1986), 2–3.

98 Ibid., 121–76. Cf. G.V. Spivak, "Translator's Preface", in J. Derrida, *Of Grammatology* (The Johns Hopkins University, 1976), LXXII, where allusion is made to the Derrida-inspired "method of deconstruction" which has been employed within the circles of literary criticism. As Spivak rightly points out, such a notion of a "critical method", and the conclusions derived by means of it, implies the (misplaced) ultimate reconciliation or locking up of the binary oppositions found operative in the text.

nification, to name but two examples of such infrastructures—are fully acknowledged, there cannot be any repeatable "method of deconstruction", either. Therefore, Gasché's otherwise insightful reading of Derrida has not been adopted in a wholesale manner in the present treatise.

Derrida is by no means entirely innocent of such a widely-spread misconception of deconstruction, however. In an interview in 1971, he described the "general strategy of deconstruction" ("*stratégie générale de la déconstruction*") with reference to the double move of, first, reversing the hierarchically ordered oppositions in the conceptual pairs operative in the text and, secondly, inventing a novel "concept" with a cancelling effect on the original conceptual order.[99] If deconstruction is taken in such an instrumental, technical or methodological sense, then at least the effected erasure and the *Aufhebung* of the initial binary dichotomy, as brought into existence by the second move in "deconstruction", ought to be taken into account as well. A mere "trashing" of law, i.e. the unveiling of the self-divergent, ideologically biased or inherently indeterminate character of law, or the violent act of reducing law into politics or morals, is evidently not what is meant by such a cancelling/uplifting effect of deconstruction, laden with distinctively Hegelian overtones.

In his subsequent writings on the issue, Derrida has explicitly denied any instrumentalist, methodology-oriented conception of deconstruction: "Deconstruction is not a method and cannot be transformed into one".[100] Rejecting the notion of a critique-enhancing method of textual analysis that would be blessed with the promise of setting the reader free from the strictures forced upon him by the binary dichotomies operative in the text and their ideological implications, Derrida has underscored the more "philosophical" dimensions of deconstruction and its intimate contact with the inherently aporetic structures of Western metaphysics, writing (*écriture*) and linguistic signification.

Elements of self-deconstruction can be traced in, for instance, Rousseau's self-contradictory rejection of writing in favour of speech in his (written) philosophical and autobiographical texts, as reflected upon in the "quasi-concepts" of *supplément*, *archi-écriture* and *trace* in Derrida's *On Grammatology* and other texts dating from the same period, with allusion to the suppressed, although indispensable element of a philosophical stance (*supplément*) and the erased element of alterity entailed in a sign whose exact meaning-content is never "there" or fully present, since it is deferred/differed and determined by what lies outside of it in a system of signs (*archi-écriture*, *trace*). Equally, elements of self-deconstruction can be seen in *pharmakon* as Plato's equivocal

[99] J. Derrida, *Positions: Entretiens avec Henri Ronse, Julia Kristeva, Jean-Louis Houdebine, Guy Scarpetta* (Editions de Minuit, Paris, 1972), 56–61.

[100] Derrida, above at n. 85, 3; J. Derrida, "*Lettre à un ami japonais*", in *Psyché: Inventions de l'autre* (Éditions Galilée, Paris, 1987), 390: "*La déconstruction n'est pas une méthode et ne peut être transformée en méthode*". Cf. "Deconstruction as such is reducable to neither a method nor an analysis (the reduction to simple elements); it goes beyond critical decision itself": Derrida, *Points . . . Interviews, 1974–1994* (Stanford University Press, California, 1995), 83.

term for writing, with reference to both remedy and poison, or the inside and the outside (or neither of them) in "Plato's Pharmakon"; *l'hymen* with its equivocal reference to both virginity and consummation, or identity and difference (or neither of them) in "The Double Session", and so on.[101] As concerns the quasi-concept of *gramme*, Derrida writes that it is "neither a signifier nor a signified, neither a sign nor a thing, neither a presence nor an absence, neither a position nor a negation, etc."[102]

Derrida has also pointed out that the disintegrating forces of deconstruction will take place and have their decomposing effect on the processes of signification quite irrespective of whether there is anyone to "turn the switch on", i.e. without having to presuppose the active interference of an attentive reader *vis-à-vis* the text *quod erat deconstruendum* (QED): "What is the law of this self-deconstruction, this "auto-deconstruction"? Deconstruction is not a method or some tool that you apply to something from the outside. Deconstruction is something which happens and which happens inside; there is a deconstruction at work within Plato's work, for instance".[103] Occasionally, Derrida has underscored the unique character of each individual "event" of deconstruction, likening it to a singular idiom or signature,[104] whereby the idea of turning deconstruction into an easily applicable method of textual analysis and textual criticism is, of course, rejected. This might be called Derrida's *turn to singularity*, which has found expression in a different context in, for instance, the private allusions entailed in his *Glas*.

The outcomes of deconstruction, as effected/effaced by Derrida's attentive close-reading of certain philosophical and/or literary texts, have taken the shape of an open-ended sheaf of identity-evading neologisms, neographisms or quasi-concepts, like *marge*, *trace*, *supplément*, *khōra*, *l'hymen*, *gramme*, *parergon*, *l'entame*, *pharmakon*, *archi-écriture*, *différance*, etc.[105] Each time the inherently volatile, self-distancing and self-effacing outcomes of deconstruction are impatiently ascribed some conceptual identity, the very idea of transcending the given limits of language and Western philosophy collapses, as the infrastructures are drawn within the realm of Western metaphysics whose grounding/cancelling conditions of possibility (and impossibility) Derrida is self-defeatingly trying to describe. Then, a novel search needs to be initiated for the "final" premises of judgment, with an equally novel effort to escape the formal closure of Western metaphysics. Far from being a convenient method of textual and/or

[101] Derrida, above at n. 99, 58–9; J. Derrida, *On Grammatology* (The Johns Hopkins University Press, London, 1976); and G. Spivak's insightful comments in the "Translator's Preface" to that book; Derrida, above at n. 85.

[102] Derrida, above at n. 99, 59.

[103] J. Derrida and J.D. Caputo, *Deconstruction in a Nutshell: A Conversation with Jacques Derrida* (Fordham University Press, New York, 1997), 9.

[104] Derrida, "*Lettre à un ami japonais*", above at n. 85, 391.

[105] On Derrida's self-reflection on the open-ended list of such infrastructures, see his "*Lettre à un ami japonais*", ibid., 392.

philosophical analysis, deconstruction thus concerns the predicaments encountered at the very "ultimate" edges of Western philosophy.

Two Derridean infrastructures will be reflected upon in more detail in the present treatise, i.e. radical *undecidability* and *différance*. The structures or radical undecidability or equivocality are aligned with the unresolved character of the "ultimate" criteria behind the categories of Western ontology, successfully defying both the alternatives of double exclusion (*neither/nor*) and all-encompassing inclusion (*both/and*). Like Plato's *khōra*, which effectively transcends the basic categories of Plato's otherwise dualist ontology and remains endlessly oscillating between the two categories of sensible/intelligible, visible/invisible, form/substance, destructible/immutable, *logos/mythos*, etc., the predicament of radical undecidability denotes the self-evading or self-differentiating character of the "ultimate" grounds of judgment within Western metaphysics.[106] In the context of law, such radical undecidability will have the effect of incessantly dislocating and relocating the ontological, methodological and epistemological status of the "ultimate" criteria of legal validity and legal rationality, as caught unresolved between the two categories of norm/fact, validity/existence, *Sein/Sollen*, reason/non-reason, *logos/mythos*, etc.

Différance, in turn, denotes the endless differentiation of a sign's meaning-content in terms of the fugitive dissemination, proliferation, dissolution or dispersement of meaning, giving effect to an incessant play of synchronic-spatial distancing and diachronic-temporal delay—or deferral/distancing—in the production (and disintegration) of a sign's meaning-content. There is no predetermined reference ground, fixed end point of argumentation, solid argumentative bedrock, firm foundation for judgment, or transcendental signified by means of which the sense (presumably) carried by a sign might, once and for all, be settled and locked up. Instead, the production of meaning for a sign is in a constant state of flux, determined by what lies outside of it in a system of signs in a synchronic and diachronic sense. The source of inspiration for both types of infrastructures is, of course, derived from Derrida's philosophy of deconstruction.

Deconstruction is not a method, at least not in the conventional sense of the term. A "method of deconstruction", if such a highly volatile phenomenon could be said to exist, is no more than a *disposable tool* or a *self-effacing instrument* of textual and philosophical disintegration which is itself wiped out of existence in close-reading a philosophical, legal or other text.[107] Yet, relaxing for a moment the allusion to the quasi-transcendental condition of possibility (and impossibility) of judgment entailed in the Derridean infrastructures, a deconstructive reading of a text might provisionally be operationalised by means of the following open-ended list of "manoeuvres" or "tricks" available:

[106] J. Derrida, *On the Name* (Stanford University Press, California, 1995), 89–127. Cf. Plato, *Timaeus*, in *The Dialogues of Plato* (Clarendon Press, Oxford, 4th ed. 1953), § 49a (p. 735), § 52a–c (pp. 738–9).

[107] On the self-effacing character of infrastructures, see J. Derrida, *Dissemination* (The Athlone Press, London, 1993), 157; Gasché, *The Tain of the Mirror*, above at n. 97, 150.

(1) an insight into the endlessly sense-dislocating and sense-differentiating forces of fugitive dissemination, incessant proliferation, and constant dispersement of meaning of a sign; rather than having a firm belief in semantic determinacy, linguistic "transparency", or the existence of a somehow privileged angle of approach to reading a text;
(2) unfolding of the truly aporetic, inherently equivocal or radically undecidable structures and processes of linguistic signification; rather than safeguarding a naive belief in linguistic clarity, precision, and the semantics of the "plain cases and settled meanings" (Hart);
(3) a search for neglected margins, latent presuppositions and disruptive lapses of attentive reason in the text; rather than adhering to some sober insights into the standard uses of language in various discursive contexts or "language-games", as outlined by Wittgenstein and the Oxford philosophy of ordinary language;
(4) awareness of the pitfalls of semantic open-endedness and linguistic porosity, with the text breaking free from the vain pretensions held by the author—or by the reader, for that matter—of having gained an absolute control over the forces of meaning-production; rather than violent enforcement of semantic closure, all-encompassing textual coherence (Dworkin), or overstrained uniformity in the meaning structures of the text;
(5) unveiling of meaningful silences, suppressed intentions, and sudden shifts or deviations of meaning in a text; rather than having blind loyality and respect for the author's manifest intentions;
(6) sensitivity to argumentative loop(hole)s, inherent self-contradictions and inescapable patterns of self-referentiality, plus the levelling-off of any sharp-edged confines between the constative and the performative mode of language (J.L. Austin); rather than having blind faith in a picture-like relation between language and the order of things in the (external) world, as claimed by Wittgenstein in his *Tractatus*;[108] and
(7) having an alert eye on the tiniest crevices, cracks and fractures on the surface-structure and the deep-structure levels of the text; rather than having naive belief in the benevolence and sovereign might of the author of a text within the domain of linguistic signification.

Bearing in mind the openly self-deceptive element entailed in any violent conceptualisation forced upon the "ultimate" grounds of knowledge and judgment within Western philosophical tradition, such a straightforward praxeology might be called—somewhat degradingly—a "method of deconstruction", in stark contrast to the "philosophy of deconstruction" where an allusion to the self-evading infrastructures of Western metaphysics is made.[109] However, even

[108] L. Wittgenstein, *Tractatus Logico-Philosophicus* (Routledge & Kegan Paul, 1986).

[109] Such an operationalised illustration of deconstructive reading is, of course, itself quite defenceless against the self-disintegrating forces operative in the binary structures involved, the expressed intentions of the present author, the constative/performative status of the list in terms of

then the "strategies" of close-reading need to be chosen for the individual text at hand only, without provoking the method-enhancing claim that deconstruction could be transformed into a universal tool of textual analysis, textual criticism and, eventually, emancipation from the strictures imposed upon the reader by the binary oppositions that are operative in the text.[110] Thus, the present reading of Derrida and deconstruction denotes a self-conscious deviation from the current reception of his ideas within the CLS movement, where it has been taken at face value as a convenient method of reversing, upsetting or simply trashing the binary dichotomies entailed in the text.

A method of textual analysis—or a method of any kind, for that matter—implies the *repeatability* of the (reading) procedure employed. A "method" that could be utilised only once would not count as a method, but as an event, occasion or some process that took place. A perfectly idiosyncratic "method of deconstruction", if the term is used in a slightly Pickwickian sense here, would be formed in the image of a flow of private language, as in Joyce's *Finnegans Wake*, or in nonsense poetry such as the *Jabberwocky* and the other nonsensical—but not necessarily senseless—nursery rhymes that can be found in Lewis Carroll's two books on Alice. Alternatively, such an idiosyncratic "method" of reading needs to be effaced and wiped out in the very act or event of "applying" it, i.e. on the occasion of close-reading a legal, philosophical, or other kind of text. The latter option has been adopted in chapters 8 and 9 of this treatise, where the *relentless quest* for the "ultimate" premises of law, as *effected/effaced* by the infrastructures of Western metaphysics, satisfies the requirement of radical non-repeatability and the idea of sustaining "the unlimited right to ask any question, to suspect all dogmatism, to analyze every presupposition, even those of the ethics or the politics of responsibility".[111]

9. QUESTIONS ON METHOD: FROM ANALYTICAL MODEL CONSTRUCTION TO A RADICAL QUESTIONING OF THE ULTIMATE PREMISES OF LAW ("... UP AGAINST THE LIMITS OF LANGUAGE")

In the first part of this treatise, precedents are analysed with the plain intention of *analytical model construction*. By means of the various models or pure types of precedent ideology, I do not claim to have anything like a privileged access to a judge's state of mind at the moment of his formulating the *ratio* of a prior case, to be then applied to the facts of the novel case at hand. The objective is far more modest, dictated by an insight into the inherent nature of the field of inquiry

the Austinian speech act theory, the (suspicious) distinction established between the "method" and the "philosophy" of deconstruction, etc.

[110] In any case, that is how deconstruction is defined in a standard dictionary: "Deconstruction (n.): a method of critical analysis of philosophical and literary language": *The Concise Oxford Dictionary*, 350.

[111] Derrida, above at n. 106, 28.

concerned. In the study of precedents, there is no room for the empirically verifiable truths of a positivist theory of science, nor to the self-evident conceptual truths of Cartesian rationalism. There is no brute empirical evidence available from the court rulings, except in the trivial sense of certain bodily movements of the men and women "dressed in robe", and their "ways of spilling ink" in the actual judicial decisions. Instead, all the relevant information of court rulings and the reasons displayed in their support is given in a linguistic form, necessitating a self-consciously interpretative, text-sensitive approach to the law. Therefore, a theoretical mid-ground needs to be found somewhere in-between observation-oriented crude empiricism and inner-directed Cartesian contemplation. In the first part of this treatise, the notions of *ideal types* or *rational reconstructions* will be employed, the former as introduced by Weber and the latter as utilised by, for instance, the research group *Bielefelder Kreis*.[112]

Weber made fruitful use of the pure type (*rein Typus*) or ideal type (*Idealtypus*) approach to the analysis of society in his masterwork *Wirtschaft und Gesellschaft*. The question of method in social science is touched upon in passing at the beginning of that work, where explicit reference is made to some of the representatives of the *Geisteswissenschaften*, or the human sciences,[113] and at more length in the essay "*Die 'Objektivität' sozialwissenschaftlicher und sozialpolitischer Erkenntnis*".[114] There, Weber states that an ideal type is not an average concept, nor a scientific hypothesis, nor still a description of social reality as such. Rather, it is an abstraction of reality, a conceptual and methodological device that is based on concrete historical data but constructed with conceptual purity and usefulness in scientific explanation in mind.[115] Because of their "utopian" character, Weber's ideal types, such as the different forms of legal rationality discerned by him, do not exist in a conceptually purified form in society. If correctly constructed, such ideal types will provide a scholar with a well-formed conceptual scheme by means of which to then analyse the variety of social phenomena.

The research group *Bielefelder Kreis* has described its methodological "tools" in the following way:[116]

112 The term "cultural-linguistic reconstructions" might also be mentioned, in the sense utilised by G.H. von Wright. See Aarnio, *Laintulkinnan teoria* (WSOY, Juva, 1989), 189.

113 M. Weber, *Wirtschaft und Gesellschaft* (JCB Mohr, Tübingen, 1972), 1–11; M. Weber, *Gesammelte Schriften zur Wissenschaftslehre*, 541–62.

114 M. Weber, *Gesammelte Aufsätze zur Wissenschaftslehre* (JCB Mohr, Tübingen, 1988), 146–214, esp. 190 ff. That collection of essays is focused on the method of the human sciences (*Kulturwissenschaften*) and the hermeneutical approach in sociology (*verstehende Soziologie*).

115 M. Weber, "*Die 'Objektivität' sozialwissenschaftlicher und sozialpolitischer Erkenntnis*", in Weber, above at n. 114, 190–1.

116 D.N. MacCormick and R.S. Summers, *Interpreting Statutes: A Comparative Study* (Dartmouth, 1991), 19 (emphasis in original). On the methodology of rational reconstruction, see ibid., 18–24. On a similar methodological approach in the second research report of the *Bielefelder Kreis*, see D.N. MacCormick and R.S. Summers (eds), *Interpreting Precedents: A Comparative Study* (Ashgate/Dartmouth, 1997), 7, 10–11.

> "By 'rational reconstruction' we mean the activity of explaining fragmentary and potentially conflicting data by reference to theoretical objects in the light of which the data are seen as relatively coherent, because presented as parts of a complex, well-ordered whole. In a wide sense, this can apply to the methods of the natural as well as the human sciences, but in the case of cultural objects, such as law, the object presented as a coherent whole is so presented on the assumption of some degree of internal rationality in the relevant human activity. Specifically, in the present case, the rational reconstruction of interpretational justification involves *presenting it as consisting in structured types of arguments which all belong within a coherent mode of justificatory reasoning.*"

Like Weber's notion of ideal types, the method of rational reconstruction as adopted by the *Bielefelder Kreis* is a compound of descriptive and normative elements.[117] The aim is to give an accurate description of the subject matter of study, but the very idea of presenting a "relatively coherent", "well-ordered" or "structured" account of the phenomena being studied, based on the assumption of "some degree of internal rationality" to be found in them, denotes an obvious deviation from the ideals of pure descriptivity.

The method of *analytical model construction* adopted in the first part of the present study is closely related to the Weberian ideal types and the idea of rational reconstruction of legal or social phenomena. In all three approaches mentioned, the level of abstraction or normativity in study is intentionally raised, so as to gain an insight into the "deeper", underlying identity of the phenomena under scrutiny. The price for such a methodological move is paid in a loss of descriptive accuracy with respect to the internal diversity and contingent features of the object of inquiry. The models of precedent ideology are, by definition, abstractions, subject to the laws of a scholar's well-ordered universe, and the fragmentary, contingent and divergent features of actual legal adjudication cannot possibly be captured thereby.

The sum total of the various types of precedent ideology is intended to be an all-encompassing, internally coherent scheme of legal analysis in the context of precedents. I will unfold the contents of a judge's *intellectual toolbox vis-à-vis* precedent-identification and precedent-following at the level of legal ideology, in order to give an adequate account of the methods of distinguishing the binding element (*ratio decidendi*) of a case from its argumentative context (*obiter dicta*), and of the ideological consequences to be drawn therefrom. In light of the comparative material collected and analysed by the *Bielefelder Kreis*, such precedent ideologies would seem to find a reasonably adequate match with the "law in action" of precedent-following, as will be argued in detail in chapter 5, below.

In the latter part of this treatise, "A Theory of the Multi-Level Structure of Law", the extensive frame consisting of the operative, ideological, discourse-theoretical or conceptual, and finally, infrastructure level prelogical and

[117] On the mutual role of the descriptive and normative elements in rational reconstruction, cf. MacCormick and Summers, *Interpreting Statutes*, ibid., 21–2.

preconceptual premises of law will be unfolded in detail. While the analytical approach is still prevalent in chapters 6 and 7, where the ideological and conceptual deep-structure level prerequisites of law are analysed, such analyticity will gradually be discarded towards the end of this treatise. However, the frame of the four paradigms of judicial signification under precedent-following, to be outlined in chapter 9, entails an element of scientific reconstruction, but the "final" premises of such discourse formations will prove to defy any efforts of an overtly rationalistic kind.

Derrida's philosophical self-reflection might serve as a self-proclaimed methodological credo for chapters 8 and 9, where the relentless quest for the final premises of law will be launched in terms of the *infrastructures* of law:[118]

> "The only attitude (the only politics—judicial, medical, pedagogical and so forth) I would *absolutely* condemn is one which, directly or indirectly, cuts off the possibility of an essentially interminable questioning, that is, an effective and thus transforming questioning."

In the analysis of the legal infrastructures, analytical model construction will recede, allowing room for a *critical unfolding* or *radical questioning* of the "final" premises of legal validity and legal rationality, extending far beyond the commonsensical confines self-imposed by the analytical and positivist frame—radical in the sense of being concerned with the quest for the "ultimate" or "final" conditions of possibility (and impossibility) of the resulting positivity of the legal phenomena, and radical also in the sense of endlessly deferring, reframing, relocating or redefining the *ontological*, *epistemological* and *methodological* status of the deep-structure level phenomena of law.

In refusing to give up the relentless, unyielding quest for the ultimate premises of law even when "the justifications have been exhausted, the bedrock has been reached, and the spade is turned",[119] such radical questioning by necessity transcends and transgresses the methodological constraints of the analytical frame, as the criteria of legal validity and legal rationality are pushed beyond their conventional limits and, finally, are self-referentially folded back to apply to the said "ultimate" criteria themselves. The term *post-analytical philosophy of law* may therefore be adopted with reference to the unfolding of the infrastructures of law in chapters 8 and 9, the prefix "post" of course taken here in the logico-conceptual, and not in the temporal or chronological, sense.

[118] Derrida, *Points . . . Interviews, 1974–1994*, above at n. 100, 239 (emphasis in original). By "effective and thus transforming questioning" Derrida refers to "a thoughtful reflection on the axioms of this problematic and on all those discourses that inform it": ibid., 239–40. Cf. Derrida's reflection in *On the Name*, above n. 106, 28: "the unlimited right to ask any question, to suspect all dogmatism, to analyze every presupposition, even those of the ethics or the politics of responsibility".

[119] Wittgenstein, *Philosophische Untersuchungen—Philosophical Investigations* (Basil Blackwell, Oxford, 1967), § 217 (p. 85/85[e]): "*Habe ich die Begründungen erschöpft, so bin ich nun auf dem harten Felsen angelangt, und mein Spaten biegt sich zurück. Ich bin dann geneigt, zu sagen: 'So handle ich eben'*".

In the present treatise, Derrida is read as a radically non-conventional philosopher who puts forth the decisively *post*-metaphysical or, rather, *pre*-metaphysical question of the *meta* of Western metaphysics since Plato and Aristotle, obstinately "running up against the limits of language" and ignoring the bumps that might then emerge in the forehead of reason,[120] in an openly self-defeating effort of "saying the unsayable" or trying to account for the fugitive conditions of possibility and impossibility of Western philosophy itself. The term "self-defeating" is adopted since eventually such an enterprise is bound to transcend the solipsistic confines of a scholar's intuitive insight or the strict idiosyncracy and contextuality of an ostensive reference to what lies there "beyond", and is forced to yield to the constraints of ordinary linguistic conceptuality, if the philosophical pitfalls of a purely idiosyncratic, speaker-specific private language are to be evaded. Therefore, Derrida might also be characterised as a disillusioned *quasi-transcendental*[121] philosopher who seeks to identify the radically equivocal *grounding* conditions of possibility and, at the same time, the *effacing* conditions of impossibility of the Western philosophical tradition, by displaying the deeply felt necessity and, with equal right, the absolute impossibility of finding some predetermined reference ground, solid argumentative bedrock, end point of justification, or transcendental signified for the conceptual "order of things" within Western *épistémè*.

Due to their prelogical and preconceptual status as the radically equivocal condition of possibility and impossibility of Western metaphysics, there is no legitimate way to apprehend the infrastructures themselves by the conceptual categories of inevitably metaphysics-impregnated language. In the present analysis, any "definition" given of the infrastructures of law, language and reason ought to be read in the highly tentative, metaphorical and volatile sense of the philosopher's ladder at the end of Wittgenstein's *Tractatus*: once you have climbed up on it, you must throw away the (conceptual) device utilised.[122] Therefore, the infrastructures might be said to be *self-effacing* or *self-consuming* as to their ontological status,[123] operative for each particular occasion of "reality-construction" and/or "sense-making" only, and fleeing endlessly ahead of any attempt at being conceptualised or drawn within the closed sphere of Western metaphysics.

For the Wittgenstein of *Philosophische Untersuchungen*, the legitimate domain of philosophy was outlined in terms of an attentive, though detached description of the actual uses of language in the various discursive contexts or

[120] Ibid., § 119, p. 48/48e: "*Die Ergebnisse der Philosophie sind die Entdeckung irgend eines schlichten Unsinns und Beulen, die sich der Verstand beim Anrennen an die Grenze der Sprache geholt hat. Sie, die Beulen, lassen uns den Wert jener Entdeckung erkennen*".

[121] See J.D. Caputo, "On Not Circumventing the Quasi-Transcendental: The Case of Rorty and Derrida", in G.B. Madison (ed.), *Working through Derrida* (Northwestern University Press, Illinois, 1993), 157–8, where reference is made to Derrida's *Glas* and Gasché's reading of it.

[122] Wittgenstein, above at n. 108, § 6.54 (p. 188/9).

[123] On the self-effacing nature of infrastructures, see Derrida, above at n. 107, 157: ". . . constantly disappearing as they go along. They [i.e. the infrastructures operative in Plato's Pharmakon] cannot, in classical affirmation, be affirmed without being negated". Cf. Gasché, above at n. 97, 150.

"language games". Philosophy was denounced unqualified for providing any deeper foundation for such linguistic and social practices,[124] while its task was merely to "bring words back from their metaphysical to their everyday use".[125] The present inquiry into the infrastructures of law denotes an obvious deviation from such a modest end as designated for philosophy by Wittgenstein and the Oxford philosophy of ordinary language. To twist a Wittgensteinian metaphor, the aim of the present discussion is not, at least not insofar as the quest for the "final" premises of law is concerned, "to shew the fly the way out of the fly-bottle",[126] as Wittgenstein defined the proper task of philosophy in *Philosophische Untersuchungen*. The idea is rather "to break through the fly-bottle (*Fliegenglas*) and see what is there behind", so as to reach beyond the limits of ordinary language and the effected "order of things" in the (external) world, down right into the prelogical and preconceptual preconditions of Western metaphysics itself.

The role of the infrastructures of Western philosophy might be exemplified by twisting slightly another well-known Wittgensteinian argument with which the Austrian philosopher both begins and ends *Tractatus Logico-Philosophicus*: *Wovon man nicht sprechen kann, darüber muss man schreiben—Whereof one cannot speak, thereupon must writing be inscribed.*[127] The possibility of writing, in the sense of the *locus* wherein linguistic signification takes place and unfolds in time, is ultimately conditional on the preconceptual and prelogical infrastructures of Western metaphysics which, by force of their self-evading non-identity, are decisively beyond the reach of linguistic conceptualisation.

10. OBJECTIONS AND REFUTATIONS

Q.1: "But thereby you take the method of 'relentless questioning' as the given, unquestionable premise of your own philosophical investigation, as the solid bedrock that is beyond the reach of criticism, radical or other. As Wittgenstein rightly noted: 'If you tried to doubt everything, you would not get as far as doubting anything. The game of doubting itself presupposes certainty.'[128] And: 'A doubt without an end is not even a doubt.'[129] Your (language) game of doubt, or of radical questioning, ultimately rests on the certainty of the method employed."

[124] "Philosophy may in no way interfere with the actual use of language; it can in the end only describe it.—For it cannot give it any foundation either. It leaves everything as it is": Wittgenstein, above at n. 119, § 124 (p. 49/49[e]).

[125] Ibid., § 116 (p. 48/48[e]).

[126] Ibid., § 309 (p. 103/103[e]): "*Was is dein Ziel in der Philosophie?—Der Fliege den Ausweg aus dem Fliegenglas zeigen*".

[127] Or: *Wovon man nicht sprechen kann, darüber muss man Schreiben gründen.*—Cf. "*Wovon man nicht sprechen kann, darüber muss man schweigen*" ("Whereof one cannot speak, thereof one must be silent"). Wittgenstein, above at n. 108, § 7 (p. 188/189). Cf. ibid., Vorwort (Preface), 26.

[128] Wittgenstein, *Über Gewissheit—On Certainty* (Harper & Row, New York, 1972), § 115 (p. 18/18[e]).

[129] Ibid., § 625 (p. 83/83[e]).

Apparently, but the seeming certainty is on the surface only, since not even the grounding axioms of such a relentless quest for the "final" premises of law can effectively resist "the unlimited right to ask any question, to suspect all dogmatism, to analyze every presupposition, even those of the ethics or the politics of responsibility",[130] if Derrida's methodological self-reflection is read in a fully consistent and, therefore, ultimately self-referential—and self-effacing—manner. In the last resort, the "method" of radical questioning is no more than a "disposable tool" or a self-effacing instrument of textual analysis that is itself wiped out of existence once the self-referential quest for its own grounding premises is voiced. Besides, the self-evading, self-distancing and inherently volatile character of the final outcomes of philosophical analysis, in the sense of the infrastructures of law, language and metaphysics thereby discovered, will make the approach highly resistant to any claims of philosophical foundationalism or essentialism.

Q.2: "But: 'in order to draw a limit to thinking we should have to be able to think both sides of this limit (we should therefore have to be able to think what cannot be thought). The limit can, therefore, only be drawn in language and what lies on the other side of the limit will be simply nonsense' ".[131]

Not quite. You are absolutely right in pointing out that the limits of language can be expressed only "from within", by the conceptual tools provided by ordinary language itself, if the inherent precepts of Western discourse rationality and common intelligibility are to be observed. However, the Wittgensteinian (and Kantian) credo of "reason delimiting itself", or the former's belief in the neatly converging confines of language and the world in *Tractatus*,[132] cannot possibly provide an account of the prelogical and preconceptual infrastructures of reality-constitution and sense-making "beneath" the positivist manifestations of reason and language.

Apart from being occupied by the utterly nonsensical elements of mute silence, helpless stammering or the meaningless babble of a philosopher's private language, the realm of the "beyond" of the conceptual order of things in the (external) world lodge the infrastructural level preconditions of Western metaphysics which make up the fragmented, prelogical and preconceptual preforms of what might be called a *metaphysics preceding metaphysics*—*prelogical* since they defy and transcend the laws of ordinary two-valued logic, being "both/and" and "neither/nor" at the same time, and *preconceptual* since they cannot be apprehended by the conceptual categories of language without erasing and cancelling their infrastructure level status as the "ultimate" conditions of possibility (and impossibility) of human knowledge and judgment. It is only

[130] Derrida, above at n. 106, 28.

[131] Wittgenstein, above at n. 108, 26–7.

[132] "*Die Grenzen meiner Sprache bedeuten die Grenzen meiner Welt*" ("The limits of my language mean the limits of my world"): Wittgenstein, above at n. 108, § 5.6 (p. 148/149).

on the condition that the "existence"[133] of the "identity-evading" infrastructures of Western metaphysics (i.e. the Derridean quasi-concepts like *marge*, *trace*, *supplément*, *khōra*, *l'hymen*, *gramme*, *archi-écriture*, *différance*, etc., pushed "beyond" the outer edge of two-valued logic and ordinary conceptuality into the realm of the prelogical and the preconceptual) is silently presupposed in the reality-constituting and sense-making discourse formations on the order of things in the (external) world that the Western philosophical tradition has been able to produce "order from noise", sense-laden textuality from a disorderly piling up of signs, or a well-structured logico-conceptual universe from a mere inarticulate chaos of shifting meanings and transient phenomena.

Q.3: "The *infrastructures* of law are said to be the 'condition of possibility' of legal validity and legal rationality. Are they then not the ultimate, deepest foundation of law?"

Yes, and no. As will be argued at length below, legal validity and legal rationality are premised on the effective functioning of the preconceptual, radically equivocal infrastructures of law which create and sustain—and, with equal force—efface and level off the conceptual dichotomies of norm/fact, *Sein/Sollen*, validity/existence, reason/non-reason, *logos/mythos*, and so on, thereby establishing and, at the same time, revoking the logico-conceptual space for rational legal argumentation. Which of the two functions of the two-fold, Janus-faced infrastructures of law is privileged over the other, i.e. the *grounding*, constituting condition of *possibility* or the *effacing*, cancelling condition of *impossibility* of legal phenomena, is in the last resort a matter of intellectual choice and preference. Still, the profoundly indecisive, volatile or unresolvable character of the "ultimate" edges of law ought to be kept in mind.

By force of their radically equivocal, grounding/cancelling and sense-constituting/sense-dislocating function "behind", "before", or "beyond" the resulting positivity of Western philosophy and its manifestations in specific discourse formations, the infrastructures of knowledge and judgment cannot themselves be apprehended by the conceptual categories of metaphysics-impregnated language, since they are the "ultimate" preconditions of such a conceptual order of things in the (external) world in the first place, with reference to Foucault's terminology in his *Les Mots et les choses*.[134] The self-evading "essence" of the infrastructures is, exactly, to be without any constant metaphysical identity or conceptual core, except in the Pickwickian sense of "non-identity" or "identityless identity", consisting of the twin preconceptual movement of endlessly self-effacing self-referentiality in legal norm constitution/disintegration and the fugitive double-play of deferral/distancing in the production/dissolution of

[133] Since the infrastructures lack any fixed metaphysical identity or linguistic-conceptual core, but their evasive "quasi-existence" can only be intuitively grasped or ostensively pointed at, the assertion of their existence is, of course, quite misplaced; and therefore the quotes in "existence".

[134] M. Foucault, *Les Mots et les choses: Une Archéologie des Sciences Humaines* (Éditions Gallimard, Paris, 1966).

meaning for the norm thus constituted. Therefore, the infrastructures of Western metaphysics might be said to have a *quasi-transcendental*—and not genuinely transcendental—ontological status, since there is no solid ground for judgment to be found at the "ultimate" edges of Western metaphysics or at the very core of linguistic and legal signification.

Besides, the prefix *infra* in infrastructures is no more than a spatial metaphor, derived from Derrida's (and Gasche's)[135] conceptual usage. In fact, the prefix *intra* might be used for the purpose as well, since the infrastructures function from within the deep-structure level phenomena of law, language and reason. The prefix *infra*, however, better captures the idea of the "almost nothing of the unpresentable"[136] that is entailed in *différance*. Therefore, the term *infrastructures* will be retained in the following reflections on law and legal discourse.

Q.4: "But why such a complicated model, comprising a judge's ideological stance towards precedents and the specific rule of law criteria for precedent-following, the axiomatic postulates of legal validity and legal rationality plus the institutional and mental felicity conditions of judicial adjudication, along with the oddities of the "ultimate" or "final" premises of legal norm constitution and judicial signification, in the sense of the infrastructures of law? Will not a frank and straightforward *reversal-of-the-binary-oppositions* that is cherished within the CLS movement bring about the very same end result, trashing the formalism that is entailed in the mainstream conception of law while giving social interests, power and ideology the credit they deserve, without so much ado about any precedent ideologies, the felicity conditions of judicial adjudication, the infrastructures of law, or any other suspicious metaphysical entities that are so carelessly imported into the realm of law?"

Definitely not, since the aim is not to "trash" or get rid of the prevalent analytical and positivist conception of law, but to display the deeply felt *necessity* and, at the same time, the absolute *impossibility* of grounding the self-declared validity and rationality claims of law, and the production of fixed meaning content within legal discourse, ultimately on "something", as reflected in the impatient quest for a fixed reference ground, end point of justification, solid argumentative bedrock (Wittgenstein), firm foundation of judgment, or transcendental signified for the law in the theoretical efforts of analytical positivism. In a word, not the trashing of law but a persistent, non-compromising quest for the "ultimate" premises of law within and, eventually, beyond the self-imposed constraints of the positivist and analytical frame.

Q.5: "You speak about 'radical, relentless questioning' and 'critical unfolding' of the final premises of law. Why not *deconstruction* then?"

The effects of such radical questioning are materialised in the self-effacing self-referentiality, or radical *undecidability*, of the "final" grounds, edges, criteria,

[135] See the references to the entry on "infrastructure" in the index to Gasché, above at n. 97, 345.
[136] Derrida, *Points . . . Interviews, 1974–1994*, above at n. 100, 83.

or premises of legal norm constitution, and in the fugitive double-play of spacing/temporisation or deferral/distancing, i.e. *différance*, in judicial signification under precedent-following. If you wish to call it *deconstruction*—well, I have no objection.

Rejecting the "deconstruction as method" outcry of the CLS movement as not finding adequate support in Derrida's own reflections on the issue, and equally declining to accept the vain search for a final reference ground or solid argumentative bedrock for the law under analytical positivism, the right allegory for reading the law would be long-distance *skating on thin ice* in the late springtime. There may be cracks and fractures on and below the visible surface of the ice, weakening its internal structure and inviting even further splits. Equally, legal discourse may be affected by the latent cracks, cleavages and discontinuities of an ontological, epistemological or methodological kind beneath the resulting positivity of law. The surface-structure level manifestations of law, despite their seemingly solid and reified character, are ultimately framed and structured by the self-dislocating infrastructures of "reality-constitution" and "sense-making" within the Western *épistémè*. In consequence, what is needed is a careful, attentive close-reading of the legal and/or philosophical text in question.

When reading the law, as when skating on the precariously thin ice of a great forest lake or sea in the late springtime, you need to listen cautiously to the *song of the ice* underneath the skates, telling of the inherent strength and composition of the ice/text,[137] while all the time keeping an alert eye on the tiniest cracks and fractures on and below the visible surface of the ice/text which might induce it to break into pieces under pressure. If violently turned into a tool, method or instrument, the philosophy of deconstruction is like the long metal-pointed *ice-pike* by which you may try the strength of the ice before and around you, or—once the ice has broken—the pair of needle-sharp *ice-prods* which you are expected to always carry along with you on the ice, worn around your neck where they are easily accessible in a state of emergency, and with the help of which you may then drag yourself out of the ice-cold water.[138]

To extend the skating metaphor, a sceptic-minded *Crit* might point out that "it's all water, anyhow, and sooner or later it will break", since law is nothing but "frozen politics",[139] or an inherently fragile and volatile social phenomenon that is likely to melt down into a mixture of interests, power and ideology at the slightest touch of a pragmatism-inspired, reductionist critique.[140] The *Legal*

[137] The thinner the ice, the higher the tone—thus signalling danger for the skater.

[138] An *ice-pike* is a relatively heavy steel-pointed stick, used for testing the strength of the ice. The original design of the device is said to have resembled the Mediaeval weapon called a "pike". Nowadays lighter skiing-sticks are sometimes used for the purpose. A pair of *ice-prods* is a simple but effective life-saving device, i.e. a pair of sharp steel points with either wooden or plastic handles attached to the two ends of a rope. They are used for climbing back onto the ice out of the water. I owe the skating terminology to Christopher Wilson in Stockholm, as found in his useful five-page *Swedish–English Skating Dictionary* on the WorldWideWeb.

[139] R.M. Unger, *The Critical Legal Studies Movement* (Harvard University Press, 1983), 92, 108.

[140] Cf. R.M. Unger, *False Necessity: Anti-Necessitarian Social Theory in the Service of Radical Democracy* (Cambridge University press, 1987), 1: "*False Necessity* . . . carries to extremes the

Positivists, because of their love for the solid ground and "argumentative bedrock" of their own choice and definition,[141] might quickly put forward the ardent request that no-one enter into such hazard in the first place, or defy the given confines of law, language and reason as drawn by Wittgenstein and the Oxford school of analytical philosophy. The dauntless skater, in turn, while boldly overlooking the well-intentioned warnings of the Positivists and the sarcastic comments voiced by the *Crits*, may then fully enjoy the silent beauty of the vast ice-covered lake, broken only by the shifting tone of the "song of the ice" under the skates and the sudden sounds of ice cracking or refreezing around him every now and then. Later on, when safely back on the solid ground, he may try to share his daring skating/reading experience, and the rare insights thereby gained into the inherently volatile character of the law/text/reality, with the disbelieving or even hostile spectators waiting on the shore.

thesis that everything in society is politics, mere politics, and then draws out of this seemingly negativistic and paradoxical idea a detailed understanding of social life".

[141] Cf. Wittgenstein, above at n. 119, § 217 (p. 85/85[e]).

2

The Concept of a Legal Norm: Legal Rules and Principles

1. THE IDEA OF STRONG AND WEAK LEGAL IMPUTATION

According to Kelsen, the natural sciences like physics, chemistry or astronomy investigate *causal* relations, or causal laws, which are thought to prevail in the world of natural phenomena, in the sense of tying together some natural causes and their consequences. A causal relation is of the type: "if p, then q" or "p → q", where "p" and "q" refer to two states of affairs in the world of facts. Legal science, on the other hand, does not dwell on questions of natural causality. Rather, it seeks to give an account of the normative relations, or relations of *imputation*, that have been established between a set of legal facts and legal consequences by the norm-creating act of the legislator or a court of justice. In *Pure Theory of Law*, Kelsen argues that a valid legal norm may always be presented in the form of a hypothetical judgment or statement to the following effect: "if p, then *S*q" or "p → *S*q", where "p" and "q" refer to two distinct states of affairs in the world of facts and *S* (= *Sollen*) stands for the *deontic operator*, or the *ought* element, in the normative relation brought into effect.[1] Thus, certain elements derived from a Neo-Kantian philosophy can be detected in Kelsen's conception of the different fields of human inquiry and the resulting methodology of the science of law.

The impact of the deontic operator *S* draws legal and other kinds of norms apart from the laws of natural causality. Legal norms are further distinguished from the precepts of universal morals or, say, those of transcendental religion by force of their formal source of origin in legislation or jurisdiction. The validity of a legal norm is always derived from another norm which, moreover, is endowed with a relatively higher status in the *Stufenbau*, or the norm pyramid, by which the internal structure of a legal order is depicted in Merkl's and

[1] To be accurate, Hans Kelsen made the distinction between legal norms and "rules of law (in a descriptive sense)" in *Pure Theory of Law* (Peter Smith, 1989), 71–5. The latter term is slightly misleading, however, as Kelsen sought to draw a distinction between *prescriptive* norms (*Rechtsnormen*), as issued by the competent norm-giver in the sense of either the legislator or a court of justice, and *descriptive* statements or hypothetical judgments (*Rechtssätze*) concerning the former, as produced by legal science. In such a terminology, "if p, then *S*q" is a descriptive statement or hypothetical judgment which gives information of the respective legal norm. Cf. H. Kelsen, *General Theory of Law and State* (Harvard University Press, 1949), 45–7; H. Kelsen, *Reine Rechtslehre. Mit einem Anhang: Das Problem der Gerechtigkeit* (Verlag Franz Deuticke, Wien, 1960), 73–7.

Kelsen's theories of law. Thus, administrative decrees derive their validity from equally valid and hierarchically higher norms of statutory origin, and statutes derive their binding force from the norms of the valid constitution. In the process of delegated norm-giving and legal adjudication, the initially rather abstractly formulated statutory norms become gradually concretised. If Kelsen's theoretical stance is accepted, as it is here, there can be no qualitative difference, but only a difference in degree, in-between the two types of legal norms, i.e. those of legislative origin and those of judicial origin.[2]

In light of Kelsen's theory of law, the recent Dworkin-inspired legal rule/principle debate may be read as concerning the exact definition of the deontic operator *S* in Kelsen's conception of a legal norm. In legal rules, the deontic operator *S* signifies an ordinary or *strong relation of imputation*: "if *p*, then it *ought to* be that *q*". There, the deontic operator *S* lays down a self-sufficient, conclusive or unconditional normative *ought* in the relation between a set of legal facts and legal consequences: if certain legal facts are present in a case, then the legal consequences prescribed in the norm *ought to* be enforced by the judge.

In the case of legal principles, in turn, the deontic operator *S* signifies no more than a deficient or *weak relation of imputation*: "if *p*, then it *ought to* be that *q*, unless there are strong enough countervailing reasons present with reference to which *q* may be outweighed in the case at hand", or "if *p*, then it *ought to* be that more-or-less *q*, depending on the relative impact of other countervailing reasons in the case at hand". Now, the deontic operator *S* lays down no more than a weak, deficient or open-ended normative *ought* in the relation between a set of legal facts and legal consequences: if certain facts are present, then the prescribed legal consequences ought to be enforced by the judge, although subject to being modified by an open-ended allusion to such axiological and/or teleological background reasons of law as are endowed with a *sense of appropriateness*,[3] enjoy *institutional support* in society,[4] or find an adequate match with the *soundest conception of political morality* in society,[5] in Ronald Dworkin's terminology. The exact content of such a qualifying factor in legal imputation depends on the particular conception of legal principles adopted. In the present analysis, Dworkin's conception of legal principles will be employed, with the exclusion of other feasible definitions of formally defective legal norms.

The novel term "weak imputation" and the concept of a legal principle with its open-ended allusion to the modifying elements of either axiological and/or teleological kind naturally do not find a place in Kelsen's *Pure Theory of Law*,

[2] H. Kelsen, *Pure Theory of Law* (Max Knight, Gloucester, 1989), 233 ff. On p. 233 he states: "The legal order is a system of general and individual norms connected in such a way that the creation of each norm is determined by another and ultimately by the basic norm". Wróblewski, on the other hand, excludes individual judicial decisions from his definition of a legal system: J. Wróblewski, *The Judicial Application of Law* (Kluwer, London, 1992), 296.

[3] R. Dworkin, *Taking Rights Seriously* (Harvard University Press, 1978), 40.

[4] Ibid., 40, 68.

[5] Ibid., 67–8, 90, 126; R. Dworkin, *Law's Empire* (Contana Masterguides, London, 1986), 239, 255, 262–3.

where the stern methodological request of "purifying" law from all non-formal elements is put forth. Instead, in the present context, the two concepts of a strong or *ordinary* and a weak or *deficient* imputation will be adopted, with reference to the conclusive or non-conclusive normative relation established between a set of facts and consequences in legal rules and legal principles (or policies), respectively.

2. DWORKIN'S CHALLENGE TO LEGAL POSITIVISM

According to legal positivism, a legal system is a collection of formally valid legal rules, as authoritatively laid down by the legislator and/or the courts of justice. In Kelsen's *Pure Theory of Law*, the existence of non-formal, open-ended legal principles was ruled out by force of the very definition of a legal norm, while the reason for a norm's validity was found in its formal source of origin and relative place in the *Stufenbau* structure of a legal system. Austin's "command theory of law" was severely criticised in Hart's *The Concept of Law*, on the ground that the notion of generally binding legal rules was missing in his predecessor's theory of law. However, the notion of a legal rule was taken in the traditional sense even in Hart's theory of law. As we know, Hart's landmark book was to become the main target of Dworkin's criticism of legal positivism. In "The Model of Rules, I", Dworkin argued that in the hard cases of legal adjudication where legal rules cannot provide for any conclusive criteria of judicial decision-making, judges frequently have resort to "standards that do not function as rules, but operate differently as principles, policies, and other sorts of standards".[6] Dworkin made an express reference to two court decisions, *Riggs* v. *Palmer*[7] and *Henningsen* v. *Bloomfield Motors Inc.*,[8] where such standards proved to have decisive influence on the outcome of adjudication.[9]

In Dworkin's analysis, the legal rule/principle distinction is based on a *qualitative* or "logical" difference, and not a merely quantitative difference, between the two types of norms.[10] Legal rules, and only rules, may be endowed with the attribute of legal-systemic validity or conclusive binding force. If applicable to the facts of a case, a legal rule is said to determine, necessitate or dictate the outcome of judicial deliberation in an all-or-nothing fashion. There may be exceptions to a rule but, in theory at least, all the exceptions could be individually

[6] Dworkin, above at n. 3, 22.

[7] 115 N.Y. 506, 22 N.E. 188 (1899).

[8] 32 N.J. 358, 161 A. 2d 69 (1960).

[9] Since the present focus is on precedent-following under the premises acknowledged by analytical positivism, the German discussion on legal principles will not be entered into. Cf. for instance, J. Esser, *Grundsatz und Norm in der richterlichen Fortbildung des Privatrechts* (JCB Mohr, Tübingen, 1956).

[10] Ibid., 22–8, 71–80. The terms *strong* and *weak demarcation thesis* could also be employed, with reference to either qualitative or quantitative difference between the two norm types. See A. Aarnio, *Reason and Authority: A Treatise on the Dynamic Paradigm of Legal Dogmatics* (Ashgate/Dartmouth, 1997), 174–6.

specified and enumerated. Legal principles, in turn, follow a different kind of "logic". All the exceptions to a legal principle cannot, not even in theory, be comprehensively enumerated. As Dworkin points out, there exists a legal principle in common law, to the effect that *no man may profit from his own wrong*, but quite often people do in fact profit—and perfectly legally—from their own legal wrongdoing.[11]

Secondly, it makes sense to ask how important or weighty a certain legal principle is. Legal principles, in other words, have a *dimension of weight* or *importance*, a property which legal rules do not have, and the binding force they exert on a judge's discretion is significantly weaker than that of legal rules. A legal principle no more than states "a reason that argues in one direction, but does not necessitate a particular decision".[12] Legal principles are applicable, not in an *either/or* fashion as rules are, but *more-or-less*, since the binary logic of legal rules is replaced by graded *fuzzy logic*. Fuzzy logic makes room for the indefinite number of mid-values between the two binary poles of "true" and "untrue", or the binary values of 1 and 0. Legal principles are soft-edged or "porous" in character, in stark contrast to legal rules which apply to the facts of a case as lifted "straight-out-of-the-box".

Thirdly, if two legal rules conflict, either of them will have to lose its status as a formally valid, binding rule in the legal system concerned. If two principles clash or, to be more exact, are found mutually incompatible, in the sense that they incline the outcome of a case in opposite or otherwise irreconcilable directions, a judge must *weigh and balance* the relative weight of each principle involved. The specific legal principle that is deemed less important for the case at hand will then have less bearing, or no bearing at all, on the final outcome of the case, but it will not lose its significance as a potential criterion of decision-making in future cases. In Dworkin's words:[13]

> "Only rules dictate results, come what may. When a contrary result has been reached, the rule has to be abandoned or changed. Principles do not work that way; they incline a decision one way, though not conclusively, and they survive intact when they do not prevail."

If a legal rule and a legal principle clash, Dworkin argues that such a normative conflict must be resolved by raising the level of abstraction so as to concern two distinct (sets of) principles, the one as already identified and the other as specified with reference to the particular background principle or principles which ground and lend support to the contested rule. The judge will need to evaluate the relative weight of each of the two (sets of) legal principles, when deliberating on whether or not to maintain the challenged rule. Dworkin tends to see

[11] Dworkin, above at n. 3, 25.

[12] Ibid., 26. Similarly, on the very same page: "All that is meant, when we say that a particular principle is a principle of our law, is that the principle is one which officials must take into account, if it is relevant, as a consideration inclining in one direction or another".

[13] Ibid., 35.

legal rules as *shorthand notes* which exemplify and instantiate the underlying net of legal principles, although in a somewhat fragmentary and compromising manner.[14]

Fourthly, legal rules are recognised as valid because of their formal source of origin or "pedigree", as Dworkin puts it. A statute is identified as valid law if it has been enacted in accordance with the formal enactment procedure laid down in the currently valid constitution. The exact content of the statute is, in principle at least, irrelevant as to its normative binding force, if the basic postulates of legal positivism are acknowledged. In contrast, no such test of formal pedigree, or any other functional equivalent to Hart's rule of recognition, can possibly be adopted in the identification of legal principles.[15] The degree of *institutional support* that a legal principle is capable of drawing from the documented legal tradition in society is yet an indication of its relevance in judicial decision-making. The requirement of institutional support may comprise prior court decisions, statutory arrangements, *travaux préparatoires*, and the like "archives" of political morality in society.[16] Dworkin is, however, quick to point out that the idea of such institutional support cannot be taken as a convenient rule of recognition for the identification of legal principles:[17]

> "The test of institutional support provides no mechanical or historical or morally neutral basis for establishing one theory of law as the soundest. Indeed, it does not allow even a single lawyer to distinguish a set of legal principles from his broader moral or political principles."

The relevance of legal principles in legal decision-making is not derived from their formal source of origin, but from a certain "sense of appropriateness" that is accorded to them among the legal profession and the public at large,[18] or their match with the soundest theory of political morality in the legal community concerned.[19]

Finally, and in perfect match with Dworkin's firm denial of the existence of a formal rule of recognition for principles, the notion of legal *validity* cannot be extended to comprise legal principles without inducing serious theoretical difficulties. Dworkin does not address the issue directly, but writes—for some reason in parentheses only—as follows:[20]

> "(It seems odd to speak of a principle as being valid at all, perhaps because validity is an all-or-nothing concept, appropriate for rules, but inconsistent with a principle's dimension of weight.)"

14 Ibid., 77–8.

15 Dworkin explicitly rejects the idea that Hart's rule of recognition might be used for the identification of legal principles in ibid., 44 and 71–2.

16 The term "archives" is not, however, used by Dworkin.

17 Dworkin, above at n. 3, 68. Cf. also 40.

18 Ibid., 40.

19 Ibid., 126.

20 Ibid., 41.

In light of Dworkin's conception of law, a legal principle cannot be endowed with the property of formal legal validity, but its existence and relevance in judicial decision-making is dependent on its substantive content and the degree of institutional support it is able to draw from the documented "archives" of legal, moral and political tradition in society. Thereby, the formal validity conception applicable for legal rules is rejected with respect to legal principles.

Hart, for one, has challenged Dworkin's conception of law, contesting the claimed qualitative difference between legal rules and legal principles.[21] According to Hart, legal principles are broad, general or non-specific in scope, to the effect that several legal rules might exemplify or instantiate a single legal principle. Secondly, principles are considered socially desirable from some angle of approach, since they make reference to a "purpose, goal, entitlement or value", and thus contribute to the justification of legal rules.[22] Thirdly, Hart criticises Dworkin's account of legal rules and principles in legal decision-making procedure on account of Dworkin's own theory.[23] As Hart correctly points out, Dworkin's claim of the essentially non-conclusive character of legal principles does not hold water even in Dworkin's own theory of law. In his classic example, *Riggs* v. *Palmer*,[24] a legal principle to the effect that *no man may profit from his own wrong* was allowed to displace a perfectly valid statutory rule which made no exception as to the right of inheritance of a grandson who had murdered his grandfather or, in more general terms, as to the right of a would-be beneficiary of a will who has been found guilty of murdering the testator of the will. In a conflict situation between a legal rule and a legal principle, the argumentative move preferred by Dworkin was to redefine the normative conflict so as to take place between the two (sets of) principles involved. The relative weight of the two (sets of) principles constructed for the case will then determine whether the judge ought to uphold or, alternatively, overrule the legal rule in that case.[25] Self-evidently, any strict or qualitative distinction between legal rules and legal principles is thereby effectively levelled off.

An alternative account of legal principles has been presented by Alexy. Like Dworkin, and unlike Hart, Alexy sees the difference between legal rules and legal principles as a truly qualititative distinction, and not one of degree only.[26]

[21] Hart's Postscript to the second edition of *The Concept of Law* (Clarendon Press, Oxford, 1994), 259–63.

[22] Ibid., 260.

[23] Ibid., 260–2; Cf. Dworkin, above at n. 3, 24 ff.

[24] 115 N.Y. 506, 22 N.E. 188 (1899), as cited in Dworkin, *Taking Rights Seriously*, above at n. 3, 23, n. 2.

[25] "The court must be understood as deciding that the set of principles calling for the overruling of the established rule, including the principle of justice just mentioned, are as a group of greater weight under the circumstances than the set of principles, including the principle of stare decisis, that call for maintaining the rule as before. The court weighs two sets of principles in deciding whether to maintain the rule . . .": ibid., 78.

[26] "*Das bedeutet, dass die Unterscheidung zwischen Regeln und Prinzipien eine qualitative Unterscheidung und keine Unterscheidung dem Grade nach ist. Jede Norm ist entweder eine Regel oder ein Prinzip*": R. Alexy, *Theorie der Grundrechte* (Nomos Verlagsgesellschaft, Baden-Baden, 1985), 77.

He defines legal principles as *Optimierungsgebote*,[27] i.e. "optimization precepts" or "norms which require that a certain state of affairs be realized to the highest degree possible relative to legal and factual possibilities"[28] in the case at hand. Alexy's conception of legal principles is based on Dworkin's conception of law, but the element of weight or importance is given a novel interpretation, in the sense of an optimisation precept. Yet, the Dworkinian conception of legal principles will be taken as the basis for further elaboration below, due to its theoretical fecundity and wider reception in jurisprudential literature.

3. SUMMERS ON THE CATEGORIES OF LEGAL FORMALITY

Below, I will set out a redefinition of legal rules and legal principles, based on Dworkin's above analysis and the conceptual framework which has been introduced by Summers in his analysis of legal formality. The concept of legal formality[29] has been elaborated by Summers in various contexts. In the legal comparative monograph *Form and Substance in Anglo-American Law*, co-authored by Summers and Atiyah, the following classification was introduced: (1) authoritative formality, (2) content formality, (3) interpretive formality, and (4) mandatory formality.[30] In each category, the degree of legal formality may be either high or low. The phenomena included in the analysis of legal formality comprise, for instance, rules, judgments and verdicts.[31]

Authoritative formality is divided into two subcategories: *validity formality* and *rank formality*. Legal validity refers to a legal instrument's quality of being recognised as having normative, binding force in a given legal system. Some legal criteria are entirely source-oriented, having a high degree of authoritative formality; while others are more content-oriented or substantive in kind, having no more than a low degree of authoritative formality. Rank formality, in turn, may be taken as a reference to Merkl's and Kelsen's idea of the pyramid-like *Stufenbau* structure of a legal system, where valid norms are arranged according

[27] Ibid., 75 ff.

[28] "Optimization precept" is Alexy's own translation, used in his "Individual Rights and Collective Goods", in C. Nino (ed.), *Rights* (Dartmouth, 1992), 166.

[29] On legal formalism, see M. Jori's and A.-J. Arnaud's entry on "*Formalisme juridique*", in Arnaud (ed.), *Dictionnaire encyclopédique de théorie et de sociologie du droit* (LGDJ, Paris, 1993), 268–70, and the bibliographical notes included therein. See also F. Schauer, "Formalism" (1988) 97 *Yale Law Journal* 509–48. H.L.A. Hart's ideas of legal formality are found in *The Concept of Law*, above at n. 21, 121–50, under the heading 'Formalism and Rule-Scepticism'.

[30] P.S. Atiyah and R.S. Summers, *Form and Substance in Anglo-American Law: A Comparative Study of Legal Reasoning, Legal Theory and Legal Institutions* (Clarendon Press, Oxford, 1987), 11–21. Similarly, in R.S. Summers (1986), "Form and Substance in Legal Reasoning", in R.S. Summers, *Essays on the Nature of Law and Legal Reasoning* (Duncker & Humblot, 1992) (144–53.

[31] Atiyah and Summers, above at n. 30, 10–11; Summers, above at n. 30, 143–4. The list also includes procedural laws; matters of status; arbitrary norms as to time, place, or quantity; and rules crystallising right or duties out of many variables. The exemplary typology given by Atiyah and Summers can easily be reduced to concern phenomena that are peculiar to legislation and jurisdiction.

to their formal source of origin. The valid constitution, statutes, administrative regulations, bye-laws, etc., are thought to make up an internally coherent whole in this respect, with the hypothetical *Grundnorm* at the apex of the norm pyramid as the ultimate reason for the validity of the legal system as a whole.[32]

Content formality, according to Summers (and Atiyah), is determined by two different criteria: the degree of (technical) arbitrariness or fiat in shaping the content of a legal norm, as contrasted to the role of content-bound or substantive reasons, and the relative over-inclusiveness or under-inclusiveness of a legal norm *vis-à-vis* its stated objectives.[33] A statute which prohibits "driving without due care" exemplifies a low level of content formality, whereas one which prohibits driving more than, say, 55 mph exemplifies a high level of content formality. Yet, the impact of fiat in shaping the content of a legal norm is slightly problematic in the present context. Accepting the basic postulates of legal positivism, the validity of a legal norm is—in principle, at least—quite independent from its substantive content and, as a consequence thereof, all legal norms are essentially arbitrary in content under such premises. The other element of content formality, i.e. the possible over-inclusiveness or under-inclusiveness of a legal instrument in relation to its objectives, would seem to have more relevance for legal regulation under the analytical and positivist premises acknowledged. In the present context, however, such content formality will not be further elaborated.

Interpretive formality (or interpretative formality) refers to the role of "literal" meaning in legal interpretation.[34] If a court's reading of a legal norm or some other source material is confined to the literal meaning of the words and phrases used in it, a high degree of interpretive formality is involved. If, on the other hand, a court may disregard the literal meaning of a statute or a court decision and instead have recourse to the underlying purposes and rationale "beneath" such linguistic expressions, or even to some substantive reasons which cannot be traced back to the enactment or the judicial decision concerned, a low degree of interpretive formality is involved.[35]

Finally, the category of *mandatory formality* denotes the *overriding force* of a legal argument, or its capability of ruling substantive reasons out of the realm of legal discretion or, at the least, of diminishing their relative significance in

[32] Atiyah and Summers, above at n. 30, 12–13; Summers, above at n. 30, 144–5. No explicit reference is, however, made to Kelsen by the two authors, who merely state the priority order of the various kinds of legal sources.

[33] Atiyah and Summers, above at n. 30, 13–14; Summers, above at n. 30, 145–7.

[34] The notion of a "literal" meaning is highly problematic, however. Fish, for example, has convincingly argued that there is no context-free "literal meaning" of a text, but all meaning is by necessity context-bound. See Fish, *Doing What Comes Naturally: Change, Rhetoric, and the Practice of Theory in Literary and Legal Studies* (Duke University Press, 1989), 126–7, 294–6, 329. What is commonly called "literal meaning" is no less context-free than a common sense conception that the world "out there" could be free of all theory-laden or "metaphysical" elements of reality-constitution. Cf. also the discussion in chapter 9 below.

[35] Atiyah and Summers, above at n. 30, 14–16; Summers, above at n. 30, 147–8.

legal deliberation.[36] If a legal argument cannot be overridden by some countervailing arguments of an axiological and/or teleological kind, a high degree of mandatory formality is entailed; whereas a low degree of mandatory formality is, of course, the case in the reverse situation. Summers and Atiyah make the further distinction between *prima facie* mandatory formality, prevalent in legislation, and (*all things considered*) mandatory formality which is prevalent in law-application.

The theory of legal formality has been further elaborated by Summers in a series of theme-related articles.[37] In "Statutes and Contracts as Founts of Formal Reasoning", for instance, the following classification was adopted: (1) *constitutive* formality: either source-oriented or substantive standard of legal validity; (2) *expressional* formality: linguistic precision of a statute, contract or other legal instrument; (3) *close-ended* formality: completeness of a legal instrument at the point of inception; (4) *interpretative* formality: a judge's adherence to the exact wording of a statute or other legal instrument, and (5) *mandatory* formality: degree of unmodifiability of the law in judicial adjudication.[38] However, no final version of Summers' theory of legal formality is so far in sight.

4. LEGAL PRINCIPLES REDEFINED AS NORMS WITH LOW LEGAL FORMALITY

Although Summers' categories of legal formality and Dworkin's theory of legal rules and principles would seem to have few things in common, both are, in fact, dealing with the very same topics, even if by means of different conceptual tools. I will put forth an argument to the effect that Summers' categories of legal formality, as slightly modified for the present context, neatly overlap with Dworkin's legal rules/principles dichotomy, and vice versa. Thus, Summers' categories of legal formality may be taken to characterise different facets of Dworkin's conception of legal rules and principles, while Dworkin's theory of law may be read as a concise, relatively non-analytical "shorthand expression" of the various categories of legal formality discerned by Summers (and Atiyah). In all, legal rules and principles (or policies) may be defined with reference to the level of legal formality involved in such types of norms.

While it may well be true that legal principles are often expressed in a non-technical and relatively imprecise linguistic form, expressional formality will not be dealt with in the present analysis. Two Summers' categories of legal

[36] Atiyah and Summers, above at n. 30, 16; Summers, above at n. 30, 148.

[37] See, e.g., the following articles by R.S. Summers: "Theory, Formality and Practical Legal Criticism", "Statutes and Contracts as Founts of Formal Reasoning", both in R.S. Summers, *Essays on the Nature of Law and Legal Reasoning* (Duncker & Humblot, 1992), "The Formal Character of Law" (1992) 51 *Cambridge Law Journal* 242, "Der Formale Charakter des Rechts II" (1994) 80 ARSP 66, "The Formal Character of Law III" (1994) 25 *Rechtstheorie* 125, and "The Juristic Study of Law's Formal Character" (1995) 8 *Ratio Juris* 237.

[38] Summers, "Statutes and Contracts as Founts of Formal Reasoning", above at n. 37, 179–90.

formality, i.e. *constitutive* formality and *mandatory* formality, will be adopted as such. The notions of close-ended formality and rank formality will be gathered under the concise heading of *systemic* formality. *Methodological* formality will be used, instead of interpretive or interpretative formality.[39] Furthermore, one additional item will be added to the present classification, i.e. *structural* formality, or the internal, "logical" structure of a legal norm as outlined in terms of the either binary or graded code entailed.

In all, we thus have the following five criteria of legal formality:

(1) *constitutive formality*: validity ground of a legal norm;
(2) *systemic formality*: systemic coherence in a set of legal norms;
(3) *mandatory formality*: binding force of a legal norm, or its resistance against subsequent modifications in judicial adjudication;
(4) *structural formality*: binary/graded code entailed in the internal structure of a legal norm;
(5) *methodological formality*: the method or methods of reading the law in judicial adjudication.

Below, the functional equivalents of each of the Summers-inspired categories of legal formality will be briefly outlined with respect to Dworkin's rule/principle distinction.

(1) Constitutive formality

Constitutive formality, or validity formality, is defined as the formal, source-bound or substantive, content-oriented reason for the validity of a legal norm. Legal rules are recognised as valid by force of their formal source of origin, or "pedigree" as Dworkin chose to put it. Legal principles, in turn, do not satisfy such formal criteria of legal validity. Instead, Dworkin speaks of a certain *sense of appropriateness* that is accorded to them, *institutional support* which they are able to draw from the documented legal tradition, or their match with the *soundest political theory* in the legal community. In addition, Dworkin very explicitly turned down the possibility that the criterion of institutional support could be taken as a simple and mechanical test for distinguishing legal principles from the principles of morals or politics.[40] According to Dworkin, there can be no formal criterion for the identification of legal principles. In all, legal rules are subject to the binary code of an *on/off* or *either/or* validity conception, while the dimension of weight or importance, or the *more-or-less* property of legal principles, denotes their falling short of such formal validity criteria. In Summers' terms, legal rules entail a high level of constitutive or validity formality, while legal principles rank low under such premises.

[39] The term *argumentative formality* might also be used.
[40] Dworkin, above at n. 3, 40, 68, 71.

(2) Systemic formality

The notion of *systemic formality* is defined by the degree of internal coherence within a set of legal norms. A system of legal rules cannot tolerate the existence of conflicting rules, according to Dworkin's analysis. In a norm conflict between two legal rules, either one of them must be declared invalid, so as to settle the aporetic situation. A "system" of legal principles, on the other hand, may well comprise a set of mutually incompatible or irreconcilable principles, and their relevance will then be determined by *weighing and balancing* the relative weight of each in the context of the new case. The principle (or principles) which is judged contextually weaker than that followed in the decision will not lose its potential bearing on subsequent cases. Legal principles, as Dworkin put it, "survive intact when they do not prevail".[41] In consequence, valid legal rules may be arranged into the form of a closed, internally coherent system of law, shaped in the image of Merkl's and Kelsen's *Stufenbau*. Legal principles, on the other hand, or at least the kind of principles defended by Dworkin in "The Model of Rules, I–II" in *Taking Rights Seriously*, fulfil the criteria of no more than an open-ended, "free-floating" system of *pro et contra* arguments, inclining the outcome of judicial decision-making in one direction or another. In Summers' terms, a system of legal rules entails a high degree of systemic formality, while a set of legal principles ranks low under such criteria.

However, Dworkin is not entirely consistent with regard to the systemic character of principles. As will be argued at length below, in chapter 3 at 7.1, the level of systematicity would seem to increase in his later, more "mature" writings on the issue. Here, however, Dworkin's earlier, non-systemic account of legal principles will be adhered to. His more system-bound conception of a *seamless web of reasons* in law, as put forth under the doctrine of *law as integrity*, will be considered in detail in chapter 3 at 7.2.

(3) Mandatory formality

Mandatory formality is defined as the *overriding* or *binding force* of a formally valid legal argument, i.e. its capacity to exclude any non-formal, substantive arguments in judicial decision-making or, at the least, to weaken the impact of such arguments in judicial discretion. The issue could be rephrased as an argument's resistance against any subsequent, content-based modifications made to it. If Dworkin's conception of law is adopted, legal rules—by force of their very definition—put forth a much stronger request for norm-compliance, as compared with the essentially weaker level of binding or overriding force that is attached to legal principles. Dworkin argued that a legal rule, if applicable to a case, is able to dictate, determine or necessitate a particular outcome. A legal

[41] Ibid., 35.

principle, in turn, can do no more than provide a judge with "a reason that argues in one direction", and a principle is said to "incline a decision one way, though not conclusively".[42] In Summers' terminology, legal rules entail a high level of mandatory formality, while legal principles rank low under such premises.

However, there is a plain contradiction in Dworkin's line of reasoning. His argument to the effect that a normative conflict between a valid legal rule and a (not formally valid but in that context relevant) legal principle is resolved by lifting the level of argumentation to concern the two competing (sets of) principles involved—one as already present in the case and the other as latently operative behind the valid rule that was challenged[43]—is equal to an argumentative move where the degree of mandatory formality of the legal rule is deliberately cut down and room is given for the less formal criteria of judicial decision-making. As Hart rightly noted, the claimed qualitative distinction between legal rules and legal principles is thereby effectively levelled off.[44] If a valid legal rule may be defeated by some legal principle,[45] then legal rules evidently cannot "dictate" or "determine" the outcome of the case, and Dworkin's contention of the essentially stronger mandatory force of legal rules is also defeated. In fact, that is exactly what happened in Dworkin's own master case, *Riggs* v. *Palmer*, where a formally valid legal rule was let to be defeated by a countervailing legal principle.[46]

(4) Structural formality

Summers' close-ended formality concerns the open-textured character of a legal norm. It covers the conceptual extension from "hard-and-fast" legal rules, with no exceptions at all or with all the exceptions duly specified beforehand, to those cases where a broad area of loose, unspecified discretion has been granted to the courts of justice. Dworkin, on the other hand, argues that, in theory at least, all the exceptions to a legal rule could be enumerated, while in the case of legal principles that is not possible, not even in theory.[47] Legal rules and principles are claimed to be different as to their internal or "logical" structure.[48] Legal rules are applicable in an all-or-nothing fashion, while legal principles do no more than incline a decision in one direction or another. The issue can be reframed in terms of the either *binary* or *graded* code entailed in the internal structure of a legal rule and legal principle (or policy), respectively.

[42] Dworkin, above at n. 3, 24–6, 35.

[43] Ibid., 77–8.

[44] Hart, above at n. 21, 262.

[45] "The court weighs two sets of principles in deciding whether to maintain the rule": Dworkin, above at n. 3, 78.

[46] Hart, above at n. 21, 262.

[47] Dworkin, above at n. 3, 24–6.

[48] Ibid., 24: "The difference between legal principles and legal rules is a logical distinction". Cf. ibid., 71–2.

Moreover, a norm with a binary internal structure may be called a weak, *defeasible* legal rule, if exceptions may be made to it, and a fully *conclusive* rule, if no exceptions are permitted. A norm with a graded internal structure may be called an *outweighable* legal principle (or policy), if some content-bound countervailing reasons may displace it in a law-applying situation, and a *highly persuasive* legal standard, if no such departure from the legal principle (or policy) is permitted. Here, the concise term *structural formality* will be used with reference to such inherent or "logical" characteristics of a legal norm—the latter term as, perhaps somewhat misleadingly, employed by Dworkin.

(5) Methodological formality

Methodological or argumentative formality is defined as the degree of formality involved in either interpreting or weighing a legal norm in judicial adjudication. It is, in other words, equivalent to the method or methods of reading the valid law. The range of feasible alternatives extends from a strictly literalist reading of a legal rule to such cases where the underlying rationale of law or some substantive reasons of either an axiological or teleological kind may exert a decisive impact on a judge's legal discretion. In Dworkin's theory of law, as put forth in "The Model of Rules, I–II", the interpretation of legal rules is bypassed as a relatively uninteresting and non-problematic area of judicial adjudication, since it is *per definitionem* aligned with the routine cases of law-application. Dworkin's argument to the effect that rules dictate or determine a particular outcome in a legal dispute would seem to imply that the application of legal rules will not cause noteworthy theoretical problems for judges.

Legal principles, in turn, come into play in the context of hard cases, where no legal rules as lifted "straight-out-of-the-box", may provide a satisfactory outcome for the new case. The "interpretation" of legal principles, once duly identified by reference to the loose-edged criteria of a sense of appropriateness and institutional support, should instead be described as the process of *weighing and balancing* the relative importance of each principle for the case at hand.

In sum: deontic formality

Above, legal rules were defined with reference to Kelsen's idea of legal *imputation*, or a legally qualified normative relation which is thought to exist between a set of legal facts and legal consequences. A legal norm is of the general form: *if p, then Sq*, where *S* denotes the normative, *deontic* operator (= *Sollen*). Due to their status and function as criteria of legal decision-making which fall short of satisfying the criteria of formal legal validity (*constitutive* formality; do not make up an internally coherent system of non-conflicting norms, but only a free-floating system of *pro et contra* arguments (*systemic* formality); are non-conclusive and do no more than incline a decision in one direction or another, subject to being outweighed in the case at hand if there are strong enough countervailing reasons present (*mandatory* formality); are graded as to their internal, "logical" structure (*structural* formality); and cannot be interpreted in the sense of elucidating the semantics of the concepts involved, but rather are weighed and balanced against each other (*methodological* formality), legal principles and/or policies fall short of establishing a strong, standard, ordinary, self-sufficient, or unconditional relation of imputation between a given set of legal facts and legal consequences, as specified by the legislator or the courts of justice. Legal principles (and policies), in other words, are able to establish no more than a *weak* or deficient *relation of imputation* between a given set of legal facts and legal consequences, subject to be modified by some countervailing arguments of either an axiological or teleological kind.

The attribute of establishing no more than weak imputation is the conceptual price to be paid for the close connection which legal principles have retained with the axiological and/or teleological pre-legal background premises of law, since the two tenets of formal conclusiveness and axiological and/or teleological open-endedness cannot possibly be attained at the same time. The term *deontic formality* may therefore be adopted, with coverage of all the categories of legal formality discerned above. Legal principles ranked relatively low under such formality premises, as compared to the relatively high level of legal formality entailed in legal rules. The strong/weak relation of imputation effected in legal rules and principles, respectively, is the norm-logical consequence of such formal characteristics of the two types of legal norms. The exact meaning of the deontic operator *S* in Kelsen's definition of a legal norm, "if p, then *S*q", should be read accordingly.

5. RULES, PRINCIPLES, AND BACKGROUND REASONS OF LAW

As will be argued at length in chapter 7 below, legal discourse is conceptually framed by the specific validity and rationality conditions of law, if the grounding postulates of analytical positivism are accepted. The axiological and/or teleological background reasons of law, on the other hand, frame and structure two kinds of *pre-legal* or *extra-legal* discourse formations, i.e. discourse on value-laden morality and discourse on interest-laden politics. Legal principles and policies are, metaphorically speaking, located on the "conceptual edge" which divides practical discourse into the two realms of legal discourse and pre-legal or extra-legal discourse. Legal principles and policies are, in other words, an intermediate link between formally valid legal rules and non-formal background reasons of law, conveying arguments from the realm of social expediency and social justice or fairness into the formal edifice of law, and vice versa.

As was argued above, legal rules are able to satisfy the deontic criterion of establishing a *strong*, *standard*, *conclusive*, *unconditional* or *self-sufficient* relation of legal imputation; whereas legal principles (and legal policies) establish no more than a *weak*, *deficient*, *conditional* or *open-ended* relation of legal imputation. The axiological and/or teleological background reasons of law do not satisfy any criteria of legal formality, thus falling short of grounding a relation of normative imputation in the first place. Instead, openly value-bound or goal-oriented arguments, as are derived from moral and/or political discourse, are given effect under such premises. Legal principles and policies might be called *proto-norms*, since they have retained a close contact with the value-bound or goal-oriented background reasons of law, while in the case of legal rules such a connection has been decisively cut off. The prefix *proto* in proto-norms refers to the fact that legal principles and policies are a "pre-form" of conclusive, self-sufficient legal rules, laden with an inherent potential to be transformed into full-fledged legal rules, endowed with the properties of formal conclusiveness and strong imputation, once all the categories of legal formality have been satisfied. Alternatively, if the requirement of having gained an adequate degree of institutional support in the archives of political morality in society proves to wither in time, the formerly relevant legal principles and/or policies may then fall (back) into the category of entirely non-formal, extra-legal background reasons of law only.

In Dworkin's analysis of law, legal principles are associated with values and citizens' individual rights *vis-à-vis* the state and other citizens, while legal policies concern collective goals and issues of social expediency. Moreover, a rights-grounding argument based on legal principles is often deemed to have far more argumentative weight than an argument based on some collective policy.[49] The term "proto-norm" has the decisive advantage of being entirely neutral *vis-à-vis* the value/goal dimension and the ideological consequences drawn therefrom. MacCormick has contested the plausibility of Dworkin's legal principles/policies division and the essentially stronger argumentative weight attached to rights-grounding legal principles. He has argued that social values and social goals may be defined in a mutually interchangeable manner, so that legal principles and policies are "not distinct and mutually opposed, but irretrievably interlocking", and "to articulate the desirability of some general policy-goal is to state a principle" and "to state a principle is to frame a possible policy-goal".[50] The present notion of "proto-norms", and the theoretical implications of such linguistic usage, is in line with MacCormick's intellectual stance. If, on the other hand, such a priority order between legal principles and policies is to be maintained, Dworkin's conceptual usage may instead be opted for.

[49] Dworkin, above at n. 3, 82–4, 90 ff., 274; Alexy, above at n. 28.

[50] N. MacCormick, *Legal Reasoning and Legal Theory* (Oxford University Press, 1978), 259–64, and esp. 263–4. In perfect match with the postulates of the Oxford school of ordinary language, MacCormick even makes a reference to the *Shorter Oxford English Dictionary* when he challenges Dworkin's notion of "policy": see ibid., 262.

Since the different categories of legal formality are conceptually independent from each others, there are (at least) four or five ways in which a legal norm may "fail" to gain the status of a full-fledged legal rule. A legal instrument which falls short of the formal characteristics of a legal rule in one or several respects is neither a fully conclusive legal rule, in the strict Dworkinian sense of the term, nor a genuine legal principle or policy, in the sense defined above. Such *hybrid legal instruments*, which borrow elements from both legal rules and legal principles and/or policies, are situated on the "no-man's-land" which extends between the realm of fully formal legal rules and the no more than weakly formal criteria of judicial decision-making, i.e. legal principles/policies.

In reality, the conceptual territory between legal rules and legal principles is occupied by a variety of less than entirely formal legal instruments, such as: flexible legal standards in the image of the *bonus pater familias* criterion of Roman law; resource norms where a decision-maker is endowed with wide powers of legal discretion, constrained only by the limited set of resources granted to its disposal; policy norms where the goals to be pursued are well predetermined, while the means of reaching them are left open, to be specified only subsequently; legal guidelines of various types and with divergent formal characteristics; and legal rules whose formal facets have been cut down in some other way. Frequently, a recourse to such formally defective instruments of legal regulation is a matter of deliberate legislative policy, in the sense of a means to evade the *Montesquieu'ean dream*, or perhaps rather a nightmare, of an entirely passive judiciary, deprived of any powers of genuine legal discretion.

Dworkin has spoken somewhat loosely of "principles, policies, and other sorts of standards" which do not function as legal rules proper in legal decision-making.[51] Above, the formal definition of legal rules and legal principles (and policies) was given in terms of the differing degree of legal formality involved in the two types of norms. That tentative definition may now be supplemented by taking legal norms with a mixed level of legal formality into account. A *highly persuasive legal standard* is an imperfect or deficient legal norm which ranks high as to its constitutive and mandatory formality, but low as to its systemic, structural, and methodological formality. A *weak, defeasible rule*, in turn, is an imperfect or deficient legal norm which ranks high as to its structural and methodological formality, but low as to its constitutive, systemic and mandatory formality.

The different pure types of legal norm, together with the differing degree of legal formality involved, can be presented in the form of Figure 1.

Finally, a concise definition of legal rules, legal principles and policies (i.e. "proto-norms"), and background reasons of law may be given, with reference to the theory of law as expounded by Dworkin and Summers. A legal instrument which *ranks low* in all of the five categories of legal formality discerned, i.e. (1) constitutive formality, (2) systemic formality, (3) mandatory formality, (4)

[51] Dworkin, above at n. 3, 22.

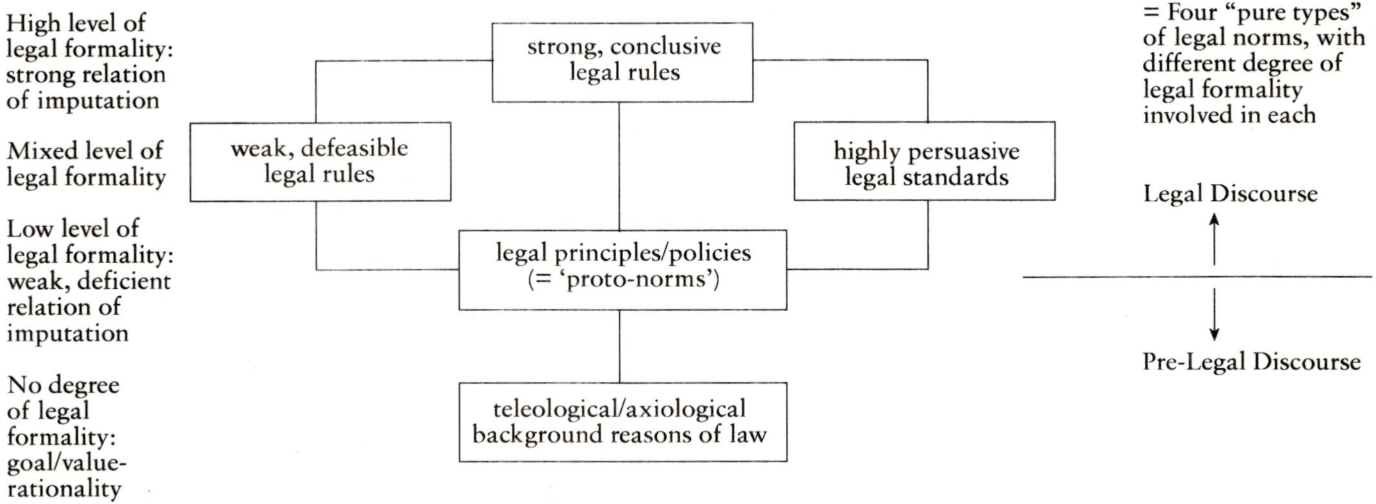

Figure 1: Four "pure types" of legal norms, background reasons of law, degree of legal formality involved, and the confines of the legal and pre-legal discourse formations

structural formality, and (5) methodological formality, is a *legal principle* or *legal policy*. The further subdivision into legal principles and legal policies may be brought into effect by reference to the axiological or teleological premises entailed in the two types of proto-norms concerned. Legal principles and policies, due to their low degree of legal formality and the resulting open-endedness *vis-à-vis* substantive arguments, function as an intermediate link between fully formal legal rules and entirely non-formal arguments of social expediency and social justice or fairness which constitute the pre-legal background reasons of law. Dworkin's "systemic deviation", or the highly system-bound conception of legal principles that is put forth in his later writings on the issue, could be read in the sense of legal principles which rank high as to the systemic criteria involved and low as to all the other criteria of legal formality.

A legal instrument which *ranks high* under all of the five categories of legal formality discerned is a fully conclusive *legal rule*, in the Dworkinian sense of the term. A legal instrument with a *mixed* profile of such formal characteristics, ranking high in some and low in other categories of legal formality, is an imperfect or deficient legal norm, i.e. a *highly persuasive legal standard* or a *weak, defeasible legal rule*, or something in-between. Finally, the axiological and/or teleological background reasons of law, with no degree of legal formality involved, belong in the realm of value-laden or goal-oriented *background reasons of law*, endowed with a formally pre-legal or extra-legal status. The distinction between legal principles and axiological and/or teleological background reasons of law is drawn on the basis of their institutional support, sense of appropriateness, or match with the soundest political theory in society. Legal principles, as was argued above, are situated "on the edge" of the legal and pre-legal discourse formations, conveying axiological and/or teleological arguments from the realm of pre-legal discourse into the formal edifice of law. The status of legal principles and legal policies can be traced back to the documented *archives of political morality* in society, as captured in the idea of institutional support, and legal rules are often said to represent a compromise between conflicting legal principles. No traces of such institutional support can be discovered in society in relation to the axiological and/or teleological background reasons of law.

6. LEGAL RULES AND LEGAL PRINCIPLES/POLICIES IN THE CONTEXT OF PRECEDENTS

In the context of precedents, the requirement of high *systemic* formality must be relaxed, due to the essentially case-bound and non-systemic character of precedent-based judicial adjudication, with the one exception of the Dworkinian "law as integrity" approach to precedent-following. Thus, a set of *rationes decidendi* extracted from a line of prior court decisions will make up a loose, casuistic set of legal norms, unless there are some expressly acknowledged systemic constraints to the counter-effect present in the legal system concerned. A judicial norm which satisfies all the other criteria of legal formality discerned, but which falls short of satisfying the requirement of such systemic formality, will be counted as a formal legal rule in the present classification. It is only on the somewhat non-standard premises of the Dworkin-inspired underlying reasons model, analysed in detail below, that the systemic element of law is given a predominant role in precedent-following.

The two concepts of a legal rule and a legal principle (or policy) must be modified in some other respects as well, in the context of precedent-identification and precedent-following. The relative impact of the two courts involved must be taken into account in precedent-norm formation, along with the two divergent points of reference for the the construction of the *ratio* of a case, i.e. the authoritative rule and the justificatory reasons of a court decision. In consequence, a precedent-based legal rule may be distinguished from a legal principle or policy by means of the following criteria:

(1) *Constitutive formality*:
    (a) *point of reference*: rule versus reasons of a case;
    (b) *source of origin*: formal "pedigree" versus institutional support, with reference to the role of the prior court and the subsequent court in identifying the *ratio* of a case;
(2) *structural formality*: binary versus graded code entailed in the internal structure of the *ratio* of a case;
(3) *mandatory formality*: binding force of the *ratio* of a case; and
(4) *methodological formality*: semantics-aligned interpretation versus weighing and balancing of the legal norm in question.

The category of constitutive formality is divided into two subcategories: point of reference and source of origin of the *ratio* of a case. *Point of reference* comprises the allocation of binding force within a prior court decision. If the *ratio* of a case is defined with reference to the legal rule laid down in the previous case, a relatively higher level of formality is involved. If, on the other hand, the *ratio* of a case is defined with reference to a set of justificatory reasons, as given in support of the prior court ruling, a relatively lower level of such formality is present. The *source of origin* of the *ratio* of a case is determined by which of the two courts, the first or the subsequent court, is endowed with discretionary powers on the definition of the *ratio* of a case. If the *ratio* of a case is identified with reference to its formal source of origin in the first court's decision, a relatively higher level of such formality is involved. If, on the other hand, the *ratio* of a case is identified by having recourse to the no more than loosely defined criteria of a "sense of appropriateness" or the degree of "institutional support" which it may draw from the documented archives in society, the subsequent court will have a key position in precedent-identification, and a lower level of such legal formality will be present.

A precedent-norm is formal as to its *internal structure*, if it follows the binary code of an *on/off*, *all-or-nothing*, or *either/or* type, and if, moreover, it may be defeated by some subsequent exceptions made to the original norm. A precedent-norm is less formal in relation to its internal structure, if it follows the "logic" of a graded code with a *more-or-less* type of reasoning, and if, moreover, it may be outweighed by some substantive reasons to the counter-effect. The term "logical structure" of a norm may also be used, with reference to Dworkin's conceptual usage. A binary norm is, in other words, more formally structured than a graded, open-ended norm. *Mandatory* formality is defined as the mandatory binding force of the *ratio* of a case, in the sense of resistance against subsequent modifications made to it. Finally, *methodological* formality is defined in terms of *how to read a precedent*, in the sense of either a semantics-aligned interpretation of a legal rule or the weighing and balancing of a legal principle (or principles) concerned.

Adding the impact of the five main categories of precedent ideology from judicial reference to judicial revaluation, plus the categories of general judicial ideology where no doctrine of *stare decisis* is acknowledged, the following combinations are set out in Figure 2.[52]

A precedent-norm which ranks high in all the categories of legal formality discerned—i.e. point of reference, source of origin, mandatory force, internal structure and method of argumentation—is a fully conclusive *legal rule*, in the Dworkian sense of the term. It establishes a standard, conclusive, unconditional, self-sufficient or *strong relation of imputation* between a set of legal facts and legal consequences, as specified in the prior court case. A precedent-norm which ranks low in all the categories of legal formality discerned is a non-conclusive, outweighable *legal principle* or *legal policy*. Such "proto-norms" are able to establish no more than a deficient, conditional, open-ended or *weak relation of imputation* between a set of legal facts and legal consequences, subject to be modified by the intervening criteria of social expediency and/or social justice in the subsequent cases. The broken vertical line which extends between legal principles/policies and the pre-legal axiological and/or teleological background reasons of law denotes the less-than-clear-cut, soft transition from the formally legal frame of judicial adjudication to that of a non-formal or extra-legal one, i.e. from the realm of legal discourse proper to that of a pre-legal or extra-legal discourse formation, and vice versa.

Legal principles and policies are situated on the conceptual edge which separates legal and pre-legal discourse formations from each other or, to put it

[52] The Dworkin-inspired underlying reasons model, with its systemic emphasis, is notably missing in the diagram. It would be placed between the two categories of a highly persuasive legal standard of the "ruling by reasons" ideology, and an outweighable legal standard of the "revalued reasons" ideology, sharing all the characteristics of the two pure types of precedent ideology mentioned except for the degree of normative binding force of the *ratio* of a case which would be somewhere between strongly binding or mandatory and weakly binding or no more than persuasive. In addition, the effected degree of systematicity in such a set of precedents would be high under the normative idea of "the best constructive interpretation of past legal decisions".

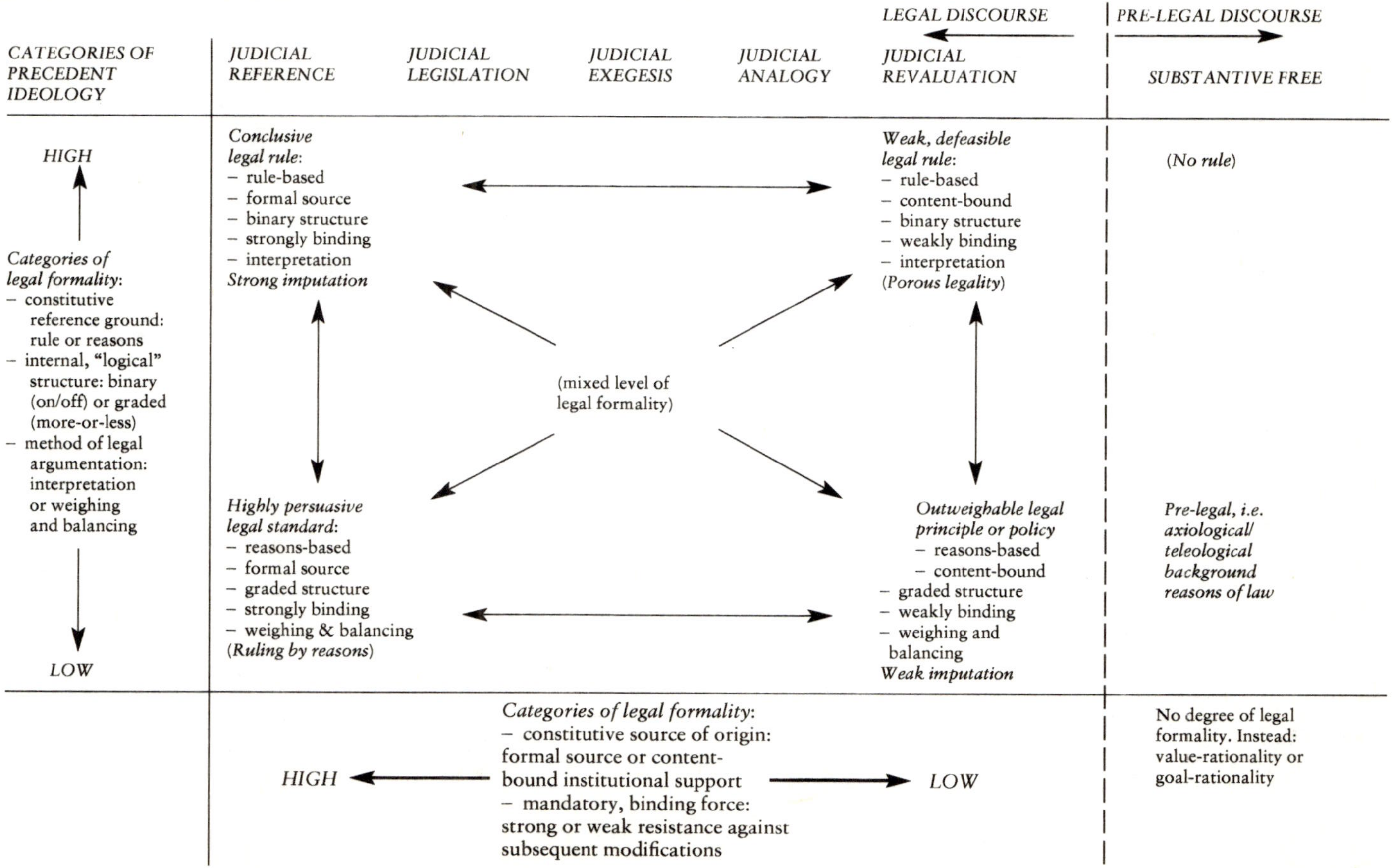

Figure 2: Deontic mode of the *ratio* of a case, in the sense of the degree of different kinds of legal formality entailed, under the five main categories of precedent ideology and the two categories of general judicial ideology

differently, connects the two discourse formations to each other. Once some open-ended, either value-based or goal-oriented argument based on considerations of social expediency or social justice has duly entered the documented archives of political morality in society, it may be called a legal principle or a legal policy, having a low (but still some) degree of legal formality. The idea of a less-than-sharp-edged border drawn between legal principles (or policies) and the pre-legal background reasons of law is further supported by Dworkin's argument to the effect that there can be no formal or straightforward technical criterion for the identification of a legal principle (or policy), nor any fixed level of institutional support the attainment of which would automatically accord some argument the status of a legal principle (or policy).[53]

A norm which ranks high in relation to its point of reference and internal structure, but low in relation to its formal source of origin and degree of binding force—i.e. a weakly binding precedent-norm which is binary in its internal structure and is constituted by reference to the original rule element of the prior case, while its exact meaning content is left to the discretion of the subsequent court—is a *weak, defeasible legal rule*. The catchwords "soft-edged legalism", "porous legality" or "legal porosity", the last two notions as introduced by de Sousa Santos,[54] might also be adopted with reference thereto. Finally, a norm which ranks low in relation to its point of reference and its internal structure, but high in relation to its formal source of origin and degree of binding force—i.e. a strongly binding precedent-norm which is graded in its internal structure, is constituted by reference to the justificatory reasons of the prior case, and whose exact meaning content is authoritatively laid down by the first court—is a *highly persuasive legal standard*. The term "ruling by reasons" ideology might also be used.

Once *methodological* formality is added to Figure 2, both conclusive legal rules and weak, defeasible legal rules may be said to exemplify a high degree of such formality, as the canon of semantics-oriented legal interpretation is employed in reading the *ratio* of a case. Highly persuasive legal standards and weak, outweighable legal principles or policies, on the other hand, exemplify low methodological formality, since the less formal procedure of weighing and balancing is to be employed when utilising such legal instruments in argumentation.

Under a strictly drawn definition of the *ratio* of a case, only the *reference model* and the *quasi-legislative model* of precedent ideology would be classified as entirely formal *vis-à-vis* all the formality criteria discerned, giving effect to a fully conclusive legal rule. The *revalued reasons model*, on the other hand,

[53] Dworkin, above at n. 3, 40: "Yet we could not devise any formula for testing how much and what kind of institutional support is necessary to make a principle a legal principle, still less to fix its weight at a particular order of magnitude".

[54] Cf.: "We live in a time of porous legality or of legal porosity, of multiple networks of legal orders forcing us to constant transitions and trespassings": B. de Sousa Santos' own theoretical frame is that of interlegality and legal pluralism in "Law: A Map of Misreading. Towards a Postmodern Conception of Law" (1987) 14 *Journal of Law and Society* 279, 298.

would count as an example of low legal formality with respect to all the five categories of legal formality discerned, giving effect to an outweighable legal principle or policy. All the other pure types of precedent ideology are laden with a mixed level of legal formality, occupying the "no-man's-land" which extends between a highly persuasive legal standard under the *binding reasons model* and a defeasible legal rule under the *reinterpreted rule model*. Dworkin's "systemic deviation", with a highly system-bound conception of legal principles, would find its place in the category of the *underlying reasons model*. Finally, the approaches based on judicial consequentialism, recourse taken to rightness reasons in adjudication, and the free-evolving judicial hunch or intuition of the judge do not admit of any degree of legal formality. Therefore, they find their proper place within pre-legal or extra-legal discourse, rather than formally framed legal discourse. All the precedent ideologies mentioned, plus a few others, will be analysed in detail in the next chapter.

3

A Theory of Precedent Ideology

1. TERMINOLOGICAL DEFINITIONS

From an analytical point of view, a precedent comprises two elements: the *ratio decidendi* and the *obiter dicta* of a case. *Ratio decidendi* is equal with the binding element of a previous decision *vis-à-vis* the subsequent court's legal discretion, extending the normative impact of the earlier case beyond the *res judicata* or the facts originally ruled upon by the first court. *Obiter dicta*, by contrast, is the argumentative context of the *ratio decidendi*. The criteria of distinguishing the *ratio* from the *dicta* in a case, and the degree of normative binding force ascribed to the *ratio*, is the core and essence of the doctrine of *stare decisis*.[1] Cross (and Harris) give the standard textbook definition of *stare decisis* as follows:[2]

> "When it is said that a court is bound to follow a case, or bound by the decision, what is meant is that the judge is under an obligation to apply a particular *ratio decidendi* to the facts before him in the absence of a reasonable legal distinction between those facts and the facts to which it was applied in the previous case."

The resulting binding force of a precedent is brought into effect by the mutual co-effort of the two or more courts involved, i.e. the *prior court* or courts and the *subsequent court*.[3] There will be at least two cases involved, the previous case, or a set of such cases, and the subsequent case with its new facts to be ruled upon. A relation of precedent-following may be said to prevail between the two courts and the two cases, respectively, if the formal and material preconditions of the doctrine of *stare decisis* are duly satisfied. In the present treatise, the key terms *precedent* and *precedent-norm* will be employed in the legal-technical and functional sense, as distinct from the specifically common law doctrine of *stare decisis*. In other words, the present notion of a *precedent-norm*, and the sheaf of concepts related thereto, are the functional equivalent to the common law notion of *ratio decidendi*, while less laden with the specific doctrinal commitments and theoretical preconditions of a common law orientation which are likely to be accompanied by any discourse on "why cases have *rationes* and what these are".[4]

[1] The full phrase is: *stare decisis et quieta non movere*. See the entry on "stare decisis" in B.A. Garner, *A Dictionary of Modern Legal Usage* (Oxford University Press, 2nd ed. 1995), 827.

[2] R. Cross and J.W. Harris, *Precedent in English Law* (Clarendon Press, Oxford, 4th ed. 1991), 98.

[3] The term "deciding court" will not be used here, as it may lead to misunderstandings.

[4] See N. MacCormick, "Why Cases Have Rationes and What These Are", in L. Goldstein (ed.), *Precedent in Law* (Oxford University Press, 1991).

Any prior court decision which has or, at least, may have a normative, binding effect on a subsequent court's legal discretion is taken as a precedent in the civil law context. Frequently, decisions rendered by the higher national court or courts of justice in a given legal system are endowed with binding force or normative value well beyond the particular facts initially ruled upon, but the scope of such legal authority need not be restricted only to the higher national courts. Alexy's definition of a precedent, though originally set out with the German legal system in mind, comprises the present usage of the term "precedent":[5]

> "Precedent" (Präjudiz) is usually taken to mean any prior decision possibly relevant to a present case to be decided. The notion presupposes some kind of bindingness, but its use in legal discourse does not imply anything definitive about the nature or the strength of that bindingness. Also it is not necessary that the deciding court expressly adopt or formulate a decision to guide future decision making in order to talk about it as a precedent. Being relevant for any future decision is sufficient."

The normative effect of the *ratio* of a case upon subsequent adjudication may vary from strictly binding or mandatory force to no more than persuasive or weakly binding effect. In civil law systems, precedents with persuasive normative impact are, of course, the main rule, and strictly binding, mandatory precedents are a somewhat rare exception thereto.

In light of the various types of precedent ideology outlined below, a precedent-norm may take its shape from among a wide range of different legal instruments, extending from *conclusive legal rules* through the mid-category of *highly persuasive legal standards* and *weak, defeasible legal rules*, to the domain of *outweighable legal principles* or *policies*. In the substantive and entirely free models of judicial ideology, the term "judicial norm" should be used instead, due to the absence of the doctrine of *stare decisis* and precedent-following under such premises of adjudication.[6] Unless otherwise stated, the angle of approach will be the subsequent court's point of view *vis-à-vis* a previous case or line of cases.

A judicial decision may be said to entail a legal norm, as concretised or "tailor-made" for the particular facts brought before the judge. An alternative account of a judicial decision, to the effect that a court decision is no more than a declaration or restatement of a more general legal rule, usually of a statutory origin, has been rejected here. The present conception of a judicial decision, and of the legal norm entailed in the former, is in line with Kelsen's intellectual stance to the issue: "That "judgment" is, instead, a norm—an *individual* norm,

[5] R. Alexy and R. Dreier, "Precedent in the Federal Republic of Germany", in D.N. MacCormick and R.S. Summers (eds), *Interpreting Statutes: A Comparative Study* (Dartmouth, 1991), 23. Aarnio's definition of precedent for the Finnish legal system is given in roughly similar terms: A. Aarnio, "On the Predictability of Judicial Decisions", in M. Hyvärinen and K. Pietilä (eds), *The Institutes We Live By* (University of Tampere, 1997), 207. Cf. Aarnio, "Precedent in Finland", in D.N. MacCormick and R.S. Summers (eds), *Interpreting Precedents: A Comparative Study* (Ashgate/Dartmouth, 1997), 80.

[6] The term "judge-made law" will not be used, even though a precedent-norm is, of course, an example of such court-made law.

limited in its validity to a concrete case, as distinguished from a general norm, called a 'law'".[7] A precedent-based *rule* may be distinguished from a reasons-bound legal *principle*, *policy* or *standard*. If the scope of a rule is limited to the particular facts of a case only, one could also speak of a concrete, context-bound *ruling* or *holding*,[8] in contrast to a more general rule.

Chapter 3 and chapters 4 and 5 below may be read as a systematic effort to outline the contents a judge's "ideological toolbox" *vis-à-vis* the identification and interpretation of the *ratio* of a case, as distinguished from its argumentative context or *dicta*.[9] Since there is no widely used phrase for a judge's normative ideology *vis-à-vis* precedent-following in common English usage, the terms *precedent ideology* (Ross), *rule of precedent-recognition* (Hart), and the *models of precedent-based judicial decision-making* (Wróblewski) will be used below, with reference to the theoretical constituents of the *ratio* of a case at the level of legal ideology. Unless otherwise stated, the term "ideology" is meant to confer a technical, non-political sense below, with allusion to the conceptual usage of Ross and the school of analytical positivism in general, ruling out the overtly political overtone attached to the term by the American Critical Legal Studies movement.

2. THE MODELS OF PRECEDENT IDEOLOGY

2.1 Fragments of a judge's precedent ideology

By means of the six main categories and no less than 13 models or pure types of precedent ideology I will present the judge's feasible professional stances towards precedent-following. The said models of precedent ideology are supplemented by three models of general jurisdiction where no doctrine of *stare*

[7] H. Kelsen, *Pure Theory of Law* (Max Knight, Gloucester, 1989), 19 (emphasis in original). The reason for the inverted commas in "judgment" (in German: *Urteil*) is related to the fact that Kelsen sought to distinguish a legal judgment from a logical judgment. Cf. H. Kelsen, *Reine Rechtslehre. Mit einem Anhang: Das Problem der Gerechtigkeit* (Verlag Franz Deuticke, Wien, 1960), 20.

[8] Cf. R.S. Summers, "Precedent in the United States (New York State)", in D.N. MacCormick and R.S. Summers (eds), *Interpreting Precedents: A Comparative Study* (Ashgate/Dartmouth, 1997), 380: "The holding of a case is not only different from the rationale (or justification), but is also distinct from any general rule or principle derivable from the holding. Whereas a holding is a specific resolution of a specific issue, a rule or principle is a generalization which may be derived from the holding. The process of derivation may yield a rule or principle of varying degrees of breadth".

[9] Corresponding efforts of classifying various models, types or ideologies of precedent-following have been suggested by, e.g., Eisenberg and Alexander. Eisenberg has made the distinction between the minimalist, the result-centered, and the announcement approaches to precedents, in M.A. Eisenberg, *The Nature of the Common Law* (Harvard University Press, 1988), 52–6. Alexander, in turn, has distinguished the natural model, the rule model and the result model of precedential constraint. See L. Alexander, "Constrained by Precedent", in M. Arnheim (ed.), *Common Law* (Dartmouth, 1996), 5 ff.; L. Alexander, "Precedent", in D. Patterson (ed.), *A Companion to Philosophy of Law and Legal Theory* (Blackwell Publishers, 1996), 505–9. Since they both retain at a somewhat lower level of analytical precision, Eisenberg's and Alexander's models of precedent-following will not be taken as a basis for further elaboration here.

decisis is acknowledged. The models of precedent ideology may be characterised by the following *ideological fragments* involved:

(1) Operative precedent-norm conception

Operative precedent-norm conception refers to the analytical division drawn between the normative/binding element (*ratio decidendi*) of a case and its non-binding argumentative context (*obiter dicta*) at the operative, surface-structure level of law. However, the operative precedent-norm conception is no more than the *tip of the iceberg*, or the visible end result of the down-reaching edifice of precedent-norm formation which consists of the ideological and discourse-theoretical deep-structure level premises of law and, in the last resort, the infra-structure level premises of law. Frequently, such deep-structure premises of law and legal adjudication are not expressly articulated by judges and other lawyers engaged in legal decision-making, since they are often inclined to take the prevalent patterns of adjudication as more or less given, as conveyed to them by unbroken legal tradition.

(2) Point of reference: rule, facts and consequences, or reasons

The legal *rule* which was authoritatively laid down in a previous court decision is a self-evident point of reference for the construction of the *ratio* of a case, no matter whether given in relatively abstract or concrete terms.

A combination of the *proven facts* and *normative consequences* of the prior case is an alternative way to identify the *ratio* of a case. What Oliphant wrote in 1927 might be taken as a battle-cry for the *facts and consequences* approach to judicial reasoning. Oliphant carefully rules out the impact of the reasons element of a precedent:[10]

> "Not the judges' opinions, but which way they decide cases will be the dominant subject matter of any truly scientific study of law. This is the field for scholarly work worthy of best talents because the work to be done is not the study of vague and shifting rationalizations but the study of such tough things as the accumulated wisdom of men taught by immediate experience in contemporary life—the battered experiences of judges among brutal facts. The response of their intuition of experience to the stimulus of human situations is the subject-matter having that constancy and objectivity necessary for truly scientific study."

Similarly, Bingham wrote, in 1912:[11]

> "Concrete sequences of facts and their legal consequences are the external phenomena for investigation and prediction. . . . Rules and principles . . . are only mental tools

[10] H. Oliphant, "A Return to Stare Decisis: Stare Decisis—Continued", in R.S. Summers (ed.), *American Legal Theory* (Dartmouth, 1992), 150.

[11] J.W. Bingham, "What Is the Law?", in Summers, ibid., 11. Also: "There is nothing authoritative in the existence of a rule or a principle. Courts produce concrete legal consequences": ibid., 22. Cf. Fuller's comments on Bingham in L. Fuller, "American Legal Realism", in Summers, ibid., 429, n. 3.

which are used to classify, carry, and communicate economically the accumulated knowledge of the law similarly to the use of generalizations and definitions in other sciences."

According to Legal Realists like Oliphant, Bingham, and Cook,[12] the facts of a case and the legal consequences authoritatively attached to them should have far more significance than any express norm formulation or *ex post facto* rationalisations expressive of the prior court's original intentions. The idea of having the courts formulate generally binding rules is also rejected.[13] The model of judicial realism professed by the Realists is equal to the credo that the *law in action* is far more important than the *law in books*,[14] or the law that can be found in judicial opinions.

The facts and consequences approach to precedent-following has the decisive advantage, or perhaps rather a disadvantage, of being prima facie indeterminate as to the deontic mode of the *ratio* of the case concerned. The exact qualification of the deontic operator is left "free-floating", to be determined only later by the judge, or judges, of the subsequent court. Since the enforcement of a proven facts—normative consequences relation in a case is merely another way of saying that there exists a normative relation, or a relation of imputation, to the effect described, such a type of precedent ideology might also be called an *indirect rule model* or *indirect reasons model*. The exact qualification of the *ratio* of a case on the legal rule/principle dimension depends on whether the binary code of legal rules or the graded code of legal principles is given priority in the subsequent court's reading of the prior case.

Thirdly, the set of justificatory *reasons* put forth by the prior court in support of the legal outcome then rendered might serve as a point of reference for the *ratio* of a case. In such a situation, the prior decision gives effect to a highly persuasive legal standard or an outweighable legal principle (or policy). Also, the point of reference of a precedent-norm (*ratio decidendi*) might be attached to a system of underlying reasons beneath the expressly given reasons of the prior case or line of cases.

(3) Deontic mode

The deontic mode of the *ratio* of a case is determined by the exact qualification of the deontic operator *S* in Kelsen's account of a legal norm: *if p, then Sq*. The

[12] "In making our observations we shall, however, find it necessary to focus our attention upon what courts have *done*, rather than upon the description they have given of the reasons for their action. Whatever generalizations we reach will therefore purport to be nothing more than an attempt to describe in as simple a way as possible the concrete judidial phenomena observed, and their 'validity' will be measured by their effectiveness in accomplishing that purpose": W.W. Cook, "The Logical and Legal Bases of the Conflict of Laws", in Summers, ibid., 460.

[13] "The business of judges is to dispose of litigation, not to formulate rules, that is, not to state accurate generalizations of the result of their decisions or accurate forecasts of future decisions": Frank, *Law and the Modern Mind* (Peter Smith, 1970), 299.

[14] The phrase was coined by R. Pound in "Law in Books and Law in Action" (1910) 44 *American Law Review* 12.

feasible alternatives extend between the two end poles of full-fledged legal formality, in the sense of a conclusive legal rule (reference model, quasi-legislative model of precedent-following), and a low level of such legal formality, in the sense of an outweighable legal principle or policy (revalued reasons model, underlying reasons model of precedent-following). The mid-range between the two end poles is occupied by an array of more or less formal legal instruments. A weak, defeasible legal rule is brought into effect under the reinterpreted rule model, while a strongly persuasive legal standard is outlined in terms of the ruling by reasons ideology of precedent-following.[15]

(4) Precedent-norm individuation

Some prominent legal authors have expressly rejected the idea that non-general rules might be called legal rules in the proper sense of the term. Thus, John Austin sought to distinguish "laws or rules" from "occasional or particular commands" in *The Province of Jurisprudence Determined.*[16] The obligation to act or to forbear something is determined by reference to either a general class of acts or forbearances, as laid down in the "laws or rules", or by reference to a specific or individual act or forbearance, as laid down in "occasional or particular commands", according to Austin.[17] Judicial decisions were given as an example of "occasional or particular" commands by the author himself.[18]

Wróblewski ruled individual judicial decisions out of his definition of a legal system in explicit terms: "The legal system is constituted by sufficiently general and abstract rules, but does not include individual law applying decisions and *inter alia* judicial decisions".[19] A few lines later he argues against the notion of judge-made law in the civilian context, to the effect that it is not necessary to investigate the role of precedents in the justification of judicial decisions in a system of statutory law. Yet, Wróblewski's conception of a legal system needlessly cuts down the argumentative potentials of a civilian judge or legal scholar, as the impact of precedents is thereby excluded. Since also civilian judges take prior court decisions into account in judicial decision-making, such an overtly rigorous definition of the legal system cannot be grounded on the concept of law as it is enforced in the courts of justice. The role and function of precedents in judicial adjudication is, of course, the very subject matter of the present treatise.

[15] On the two ideal cases of an "excess of rule legality" and an "excess of reason legality", see R.S. Summers, "Working Conceptions of the Law", in R.S. Summers, *Essays on the Nature of Law and Legal Reasoning* (Duncker & Humblot, Berlin, 1992), 108–12.

[16] Cambridge University Press, 1995.

[17] "Commands are of two species. Some are *laws* or *rules*. The others have not acquired an appropriate name, nor does language afford an expression which will mark them briefly and precisely. I must, therefore, note them as well as I can by the ambiguous and inexpressive name of '*occasional* or *particular* commands' ": J. Austin, ibid., 25.

[18] Ibid., 27.

[19] J. Wróblewski, *The Judicial Application of Law* (Kluwer, 1992), 296.

However, I prefer to follow Kelsen's conception of law, to the effect that norms of statutory origin and norms of judicial origin differ only in their relative degree of abstractness or concreteness.[20] In the gradual unfolding of delegated norm-giving and case-to-case adjudication, the initially relatively abstract and context-free statutory norms become concretised, so as to better match up with individul cases to be ruled upon by the courts. In consequence, I see no reason why not to call norms of judicial origin, or precedent-based norms in specific, legal norms proper. Depending on the type of precedent ideology concerned, however, the degree of norm-individuation of the *ratio* of a case will vary to a great extent. Precedent-norm individuation can, in other words, be outlined with reference to the degree of contextuality or the abstractness/concreteness of the *ratio* of a case. At one end of the continuum, there is a sky-soaring abstract norm, sharply cut off from the contingent features of the original case and endowed with a wide field of fact-coverage. At the other end of the continuum, there is a down-to-earth concrete or contextualised norm, tightly bound up with the contingent facts of the original case and endowed with a narrow coverage of actual or merely hypothetical cases.

(5) Argumentative closure

Argumentative closure, or the relative close/open-endedness of a set of precedents, refers to the type of arguments acknowledged as having relevance in legal reasoning. A system of precedents which gives exclusive effect to formally valid arguments may be called close-ended. Open-endedness, on the other hand, refers to a system of law and legal argumentation where the argumentative impact of non-formal, extra-legal reasons of either axiological or teleological kind is officially recognised in law-application.

(6) Static systemic structure: degree of systematicity in a set of precedents

The static systemic structure of a set of precedents refers to the fulfillment or non-fulfillment of certain systemic criteria in it at a given moment of time. The angle of approach to precedent-following is thus synchronic, not diachronic. If a set of precedents comes up to the standards of internal coherence, consistency, non-redundancy and non-contradiction, a high degree of systematicity is involved; in the reverse situation, loose casuistics is instead prevalent.

(7) Dynamic systemic structure: binding force of the ratio of a case

The dynamic, systemic structure of a line of precedents is defined by its level of internal ridigity or flexibility, or the area of free discretion left to the subsequent

[20] Kelsen, *Reine Rechtslehre. Mit einem Anhang: Das Problem der Gerechtigkeit*, above at n. 7, 242–5.

court in precedent-following. The issue can also be outlined in terms of the binding force of the *ratio* of a case, or the subsequent court's obligation to adhere to the *ratio* of a case as originally laid down by the prior court. Such dynamic features in a line of precedents concern the law's inherent responsiveness to the external demands for flexibility, thus being aligned with the diachronic, and not synchronic, dimension of law. In common linguistic usage, the rigidity of law is often taken to endorse some negative connotations, being equivalent with the legal system's "stiffness", when set against the requirements of social change. Yet, from an analytical point of view, the degree of flexiblility may be taken as a purely technical and value-free notion, as outlined in terms of the predictability or even transparency of future court decisions. A high level of systemic flexibility will bring about elasticity in law, but the cost of creating such responsiveness in a legal system is paid for in terms of legal uncertainty.

(8) Source/effect of the ratio *of a case*

The *source* of the *ratio* of a case is determined by whether the prior court or the subsequent court has decisive control over the allocation of binding force within a precedent, in the sense of the exact definition of the *ratio decidendi* of that case. There are, of course, three alternatives available: the prior court may have all such discretion; the subsequent, constrained court may have wide discretion as to the definition of the *ratio* of a case; or the normative effect of a case may be produced by a more or less balanced co-effort of the two courts. If the subsequent court has total discretion, the formal doctrine of *stare decisis* is of course not recognised in that legal system.

From a slightly different angle of approach, the issue may be rephrased as the relative strength of a precedent's constraining *effect* on subsequent adjudication. A *ratio decidendi* with a fully *prospective* binding force is expressly laid down by the prior court, with a clear intention of directing the future course of adjudication. In the case of a *retroactive* binding force of a precedent, in turn, the argumentative weight and significance of the *ratio* is determined only afterwards by the subsequent court or courts.[21] The normative impact of a case may, of course, be somewhere between these two extremes, in the sense of having some intended prospectivity which may then be modified by the subsequent court's conception of what will count as the true *ratio* of a case, or line of cases.

[21] In the Finnish discussion on precedents, Jääskinen has introduced the distinction of *prospective* and *retrospective* precedential relation between two court cases. A prospective precedential relation is defined with reference to the rule-making competence of the prior court, while a retrospective precedential relation is defined with reference to the reconstruction of the *ratio* of a case by the subsequent court. Jääskinen argues that the prospective precedential relation has been adopted in Finland, while in common law only a retrospective precedential relation is recognised: N. Jääskinen, "Ennakkopäätösten merkityksestä yleisen lain alalla", in U. Kangas and K. Tuori (eds), *Liber Amicorum Carolo Makkonen Deditus* (Yliopistopaino, Helsinki, 1986), 36–56, esp. 37–9.

(9) Method of argumentation

The method of argumentation refers to the legitimate techniques of argumentation adopted in a legal system when reading a precedent. Feasible alternatives extend from strict literalism to unconstrained semantic freeplay or sheer methodological anarchism, with the mid-categories of logico-deductive inference, judicial exegesis, realignment of the *ratio* of a case by analogy/distinguishing, systemic construction of underlying reasons from a line of precedents, judicial revaluation in more or less radical or moderate terms, and openly axiological or teleological argumentation.

The international research group *Bielefelder Kreis* has analysed the structure of the highest court decisions in terms of whether the style of argumentation is: (a) deductive or discursive; (b) legalistic or substantive; and (c) magisterial or argumentative.[22] In the present treatise, the question of a deductive/discursive and legalistic/substantive style of argumentation is tackled using the method of argumentation adopted in a precedent ideology, while the issue of a magisterial/argumentative style in legal reasoning will not be considered. Clearly, the level of formal magisteriality decreases, and the level of non-formal argumentativeness increases, as one proceeds from the models of judicial reference and judicial legislation towards judicial analogy and judicial revaluation of the merits of the prior case.

(10) Techniques of departure from a precedent

The feasible techniques of departing from a (binding) precedent include distinguishing, overruling, defeating and outweighing the precedent.

Distinguishing denotes the disregard of a precedent with reference to some legally relevant dissimilarity in the factual (or legal) basis of the two cases.[23] The analogical models of precedent-following, specifically, are aligned with the legally relevant similarities and dissimilarities of the two cases. If the legally relevant dissimilarities are judged to have more importance, a judge may legitimately distinguish the two cases; while in the reverse situation, the original ruling would have to be extended analogically to cover also the facts of the subsequent case.

Overruling means the formal invalidation of a precedent, when no reasonable ground for distinguishing the two cases can be produced. The subsequent judge may also simply prefer to expressly overrule the prior decision, since it is outdated by force of subsequent changes in society, or because the ruling is deemed to be "less than perfect" from the very beginning.

[22] MacCormick and Summers, above at n. 8, 552. Cf. D.N. MacCormick and R.S. Summers, *Interpreting Statutes: A Comparative Study* (Dartmouth, 1991), 496–501, esp. the summary table on p. 501.

[23] On the relation between distinguishing and overruling, see C.K. Allen, *Law in the Making* (Oxford University Press, 7th ed. 1964), 297.

Defeasibility is intertwined with the concept of a legal rule. Defeating a precedent is equal to making an exception to a formally binding precedent rule, whereby its meaning-content is somehow modified or revised. *Outweighability*, on the other hand, is affiliated with the concept of a legal principle or legal standard, in the sense defined in chapter 2 of this book. If a legal principle (or standard, or policy) is overridden by some stronger countervailing principle or principles in the new case, it is said to be outweighed by them.[24] Other techniques of evading the binding force of a precedent could be named as well. *Sub silencio* overruling, for instance, would denote an act of overruling a precedent without stating the fact of doing so in open terms.

Unlike overruling, defeating or outweighing a precedent, the act of *distinguishing* two cases leaves the *ratio* of the prior case intact, since it is deemed merely "not in point" or material in the subsequent case, due to some factual dissimilarity. Therefore, in the strict sense of the term, distinguishing would not qualify as a departure from a precedent. In the other three techniques of departing from a precedent, however, the precedent is declared invalid (overruled), an exception is made to it (defeated), or the legal principle/policy derived from the reasons of the prior case is outweighed by some countervailing reasons present in the later case (outweighed). In all those situations, the content of the original *ratio* of a case is thus modified.

(11) Criteria of justice

The leading criterion or criteria of justice refers to the conception of justice pursued under the ideology of precedent-following. The basic choice is made between formal, abstracting and content-indifferent legal predictability, on the one hand, and content-bound, substantive, individualising and case-bound correctness, on the other. Formal predictability corresponds to the uniformity of judicial adjudication, giving priority to the "transparency" and foreseeability of future litigation at the cost of the any content-bound considerations in subsequent cases. Substantive correctness, in turn, underscores the individual facets of a particular case, in disregard of any formal criteria which might lend support to the values of judicial predictability and uniformity. Other values may also be introduced, e.g. the idea of systemic match or coherence with a line of prior decisions, but the two process values mentioned, i.e. formal predictability and substantive correctness, are the two most pertinent values in this context.

(12) Theoretical background rationale

The theoretical background rationale of a *ratio* of a case refers to the overarching normative background ideology behind the model of precedent ideology in

[24] The notions of *defeating* and *outweighing* a precedent are derived from MacCormick and Summers, above at n. 8, 554–5, where the common questionnaire of the study is presented with respect to the binding force of a precedent. The category of precedents "not formally binding but having force" is further divided into two subcategories: "defeasible force", which should be applied unless exceptions come into play, and "outweighable force", which should be applied unless countervailing reasons apply.

question, as given in terms of legal positivism, legal realism, legal historicism, or natural law theory.

Thus, we have the following ideological fragments of a judge's precedent ideology:

A. *Definitional features*:
   (1) operative precedent-norm conception
   (2) point of reference
   (3) deontic mode
   (4) precedent-norm individuation
B. *Systemic features*:
   (5) argumentative closure
   (6) static systemic structure: degree of systematicity in a set of precedents
   (7) dynamic systemic structure: binding force of the *ratio* of a case
C. *Pragmatic features*:
   (8) source/effect of a the *ratio* of a case
   (9) method of argumentation
   (10) techniques of departure from a precedent
D. *Justificatory features*:
   (11) criteria of justice
   (12) theoretical background rationale

Points (1)–(4) are *definitional* determinants of the *ratio* of a case, as either laid down by the prior court or as later (re)constructed by the subsequent court. Point (1), or the operative precedent-norm conception, is a shorthand description of the manifestly given, surface-structure level notion of the *ratio* of a case, as framed by the latent, deep-structure level premises of law. Point (2) refers to the allocation of binding force between the two elements within a prior case, i.e. the authoritative norm and the justificatory reasons for the decision. Point (3) refers to the qualification of a precedent-norm's deontic operator *S* on the Dworkinian rule/principle dimension, giving effect to either strong or weak imputation in the facts–consequences relation. Point (4) deals with the individuation of the *ratio* of a case, as given in terms of its relatively abstract or relatively concrete character.

Points (5)–(7) are *systemic* notions, dealing with a line or set of precedents and the systemic characteristics involved. Argumentative closure refers to the inclusion or exclusion of non-formal, axiological and/or teleological arguments in precedent-based judicial argumentation. Static systemic structure refers to the degree of systematicity or casuistics entailed in a system of precedents at a given point of time. Dynamic systemic structure refers to the binding force of the *ratio* of a case and the resulting degree of rigidity or flexibility in a set of precedents.

Points (8)–(10) are *pragmatic* notions concerning the use of precedents in adjudication. Point (8), or the source/effect of the *ratio* of a case, refers to the allocation of norm-defining power between the two courts involved, plus the temporal "directionality" of a precedent-norm's normative effect. Point (9), or the method of argumentation adopted in reading the *ratio* of a case, is somewhat difficult to classify: it is located at the intersection of judicial semantics and judicial pragmatics, combining elements of both. Point (10) refers to the various techniques of departure from a precedent.

Points (11) and (12) are *justificatory* notions. Point (11), or the leading criteria of justice, bears closest affinity to the source/effect of the *ratio* of a case, as either the prospective or retroactive "mode of operation" of the *ratio* partly overlaps with the criteria of justice adopted in the legal system concerned. The theoretical background rationale of the precedent-norm, and of the model of precedent ideology at large, provides for the normative frame of reference in light of which the outcome of legal argumentation may be evaluated.

2.2 General outline of the models of precedent-ideology and their relation to Wróblewski's ideologies of judicial decision-making

The models of precedent ideology may be divided into six main categories, as supplemented by the two categories of general judicial ideology where the doctrine of *stare decisis* is not acknowledged. Below, the models are presented in an order of declining binding force of the *ratio* of a case, extending from full semantic predetermination of the judicial reference ideology to full-fledged semantic freeplay of the judicial hunch model. In all, the individual models or pure types of precedent ideology, plus the two models of general judicial ideology, may be presented concisely as follows:

A. *Precedent ideologies*:
- (1) judicial reference:
  - (a) reference model
- (2) judicial legislation:
  - (b) quasi-legislative model
  - (c) binding reasons model
- (3) judicial exegesis:
  - (d) reconstructed rule model
  - (e) material facts model
  - (f) material reasons model
- (4) judicial analogy:
  - (g) model rule approach
  - (h) paradigm case model
  - (i) model reasons approach
- (5) systemic construction of underlying reasons from a prior case (or a line of cases):
  - (j) underlying reasons model
- (6) judicial revaluation:
  - (k) reinterpreted rule model
  - (l) requalified facts model
  - (m) revalued reasons model

B. *General judicial ideologies*:
  (7) substantive approach:
    (n) consequentialist model
    (o) rightness reasons model
  (8) semantic freeplay:
    (p) judicial hunch model

The general outline of the models of precedent ideology may be taken as a precedent-aligned functional parallel to Wróblewski's classification of the three ideologies of judicial decision-making, as outlined above in chapter 1. The two extreme alternatives at (a) and (p)—the absolutely bound reference model and the entirely free judicial hunch model—self-evidently correspond to Wróblewski's categories of *bound* and *free* ideologies of judicial decision-making respectively.

The qualification of the positivist models ((b) and (c)) of judicial legislation in the present classification is problematic in Wróblewski's terms, since he outlined the idea of bound judicial decision-making with reference to the criteria of systemic consistency, completeness and legal codification.[25] As was argued above, such systemic criteria cannot be sustained in the case-bound context of precedents. Unlike the legislator, no court of justice can possibly have access to a preframed, all-encompassing scheme of social regulation, unless the non-standard premises of the Dworkinian underlying reasons ideology of precedent-following are consistently upheld by the judiciary. Despite the low level of such systemic features, the positivist models of precedent ideology may be regarded as a parallel to Wróblewski's ideology of bound judicial decision-making.

The substantive models of judicial ideology ((n) and (o)) are also difficult to classify in Wróblewski's terms of analysis. His category of free judicial decision-making consists of, quite literally, "free" ideologies of adjudication, in the image of the German *Freirechtslehre* or Gény's original idea of *libre recherche scientifique*. Under the substantive ideology of adjudication, on the other hand, the subsequent judge is not left entirely free of constraint, but his discretion is bound by the some pre-legal or extra-legal reasons of either teleological or axiological kind. Thus, the substantive models of judicial ideology satisfy the rationality criteria, but not the legality criteria, in Wróblewski's three-fold classification where "legal and rational" judicial decision-making occupies the mid-ground between the bound and the free alternatives.

All the other categories of precedent ideology, as gathered under the headings of exegetical, analogical, systemic and discretionary approaches ((d)–(m)), instantiate Wróblewski's mid-category of *legal and rational* judicial decision-making in the context of precedents.

[25] Wróblewski, above at n. 19, 278. As mentioned above, Wróblewski confines his analysis of the three ideologies of judicial decision-making to the context of statutory law only, ruling the impact of "judge-made law", and thereby precedents, out of his study.

The domain of precedent-following may be described by the concise terms of *judicial reference*, *judicial legislation*, *judicial exegesis*, *judicial analogy*, *systemic construction of the underlying reasons of law*, and more or less radical *judicial revaluation*. The substantive and free models of judicial adjudication, where no doctrine of *stare decisis* is acknowledged, have been included in the classification for systemic-didactic reasons, i.e. for the purpose of providing a direct link to the concept of a legal norm outlined above in chapter 2 at p. 54ff. The said models of adjudication give effect to the pre-legal or extra-legal background reasons of law, dwelling outside the sphere of formally valid legal arguments. Since devoid of any formal characteristics by force of its very definition, a "rule-based substantive approach" to judicial adjudication would be a plain case of *contradictio in adjecto*.—The discussion below will be on the level of the six main categories of precedent ideology, even though some individual models of precedent ideology will be given a more detailed consideration.

3. THE REALM OF PREDETERMINED MEANINGS: JUDICIAL REFERENCE

The *reference model* of precedent ideology is outlined in terms of total argumentative closure and semantic predetermination of the meaning-content of the *ratio* of a case, supported by an absolute ban on any later modifications made to it on the part of the subsequent court. The subsequent court is, in other words, deprived of any genuine legal discretion as to the formal constitution and exact meaning-content of the *ratio* of a previous case. If there is any doubt about the correct reading of the *ratio* in light of the facts of the novel case, the subsequent court is under a strict obligation to refrain from applying the contested norm until some predetermined legislative or judicial organ has rendered an authoritative ruling on its correct interpretation.

Under the reference ideology of precedent-following, the subsequent judge is no more than "the mouth which reads (aloud) the letter of the law", rephrasing Montesquieu's well-known ideology of an entirely passive judge, deprived of any powers of genuine legal discretion. From the subsequent court's point of view, the theoretical background ideology of the reference ideology stems from Montesquieu's doctrine of the separation of powers in society. The highly activist role of the prior court is, however, in plain contradiction to Montesquieu's original idea of withholding all legislative, norm-giving power exclusively to Parliament, while under the reference model (and other positivist models) of precedent ideology, the idea of judicial legislation is openly acknowledged.

Historically, the roots of such a judicial reference technique can be seen in, for example, the German seventeenth-century practice of *Aktenversendung*, where the record of a difficult, contested case was dispatched to a nearby law faculty so as to obtain a "collective and binding decision" on the case from the professors of law. As Dawson points out in his landmark treatise on the birth of judge-made law in Europe, such law professors were not appointed members of the court; their role was limited only to the giving of an authoritative statement on the content of law in force. They had no say on the course of the ongoing judicial proceedings, and the law faculty consulted in the case may even have been under the formal jurisdiction of a totally different territorial ruler in the seventeenth-century Germany which was divided into numerous small principalities.[26]

Today, the judicial reference technique has been adopted in, for example, the Federal Republic of Germany,[27] Spain[28] and Italy[29] in the domain of constitutional jurisdiction. When the constitutionality of some legal enactment is challenged, the contested case is referred to the constitutional court and the proceedings in the "ordinary" court are suspended until the former has rendered an authoritative ruling on the issue.[30]

Another example of reference-based judicial ideology can be found in the legal system of the European Communities, i.e. Article 177 of the EC Treaty, and the corresponding articles in the ECSC Treaty (Article 41) and the Euratom Treaty (Article 150). Under Article 177 EC, the European Court of Justice (ECJ) is endowed with jurisdiction to render a *preliminary ruling* on a reference made by a national court of any of the Member States if the contested case deals with, e.g., the interpretation of the EC Treaty, or the validity or interpretation of acts issued by the institutions of the Community.[31] A national court in a Member State is entitled to make such a reference for a preliminary ruling, if the case brought before it deals with the correct interpretation of EC law. Notwithstanding the implications of the doctrine of *acte clair*, which has been recognised to some extent by the ECJ itself, a reference for a preliminary ruling is obligatory for a national court of last instance if there is any doubt as to the correct reading of EC law.

Under the reference ideology of precedent-following, the *ratio* of a prior case is authoritatively laid down by the prior court itself. Deontically, such a norm is fully formal under all the feasible categories of legal formality that might be discerned. Due to the absolute ban on subsequent legal interpretation or discretion on the part of the later court, the reference ideology of precedent-following is entirely closed in relation to the types of argument admitted. Its systemic

[26] J.P. Dawson, *The Oracles of the Law* (Greenwood Press, 1978), 200–5, esp. 201.

[27] R. Alexy and R. Dreier, "Statutory Interpretation in the Federal Republic of Germany", in MacCormick and Summers, above at n. 22, 74, 108; cf. also 110–14 and 115–16.

[28] A. Ruiz Miguel and F. Laporta, "Precedent in Spain", in MacCormick and Summers, above at n. 8, 261, 262–3, 289.

[29] M. La Torre, E. Pattaro and M. Taruffo, "Statutory Interpretation in Italy", in MacCormick and Summers, above at n. 22, 213–14, 248.

[30] Due to the intellectual legacy of the French Revolution, the prevalent doctrine in France still holds fast to the idea that the law-making power or interpretive role of the courts is very limited. See, e.g., M. Troper, C. Grzegorczyk and J.L. Gardies, "Statutory Interpretation in France", in MacCormick and Summers, above at n. 22, 203–4.

[31] When evaluating the validity of an act by a Community institution, the ECJ has a role analogical to a constitutional court.

structure is, by necessity, casuistic and extremely rigid. The source of a precedent-norm is, by definition, the prior court, and the *ratio* of a case is intended to be laden with a fully prospective effect on later adjudication. The method of argumentation under such premises is given in terms of absolute judicial self-restraint on the part of the subsequent court and the doctrine of *référé juridictionnel*, under which the subsequent court is required to refrain from all legal discretion and, instead, refer the contested issue back to the prior court for an authoritative ruling. Thus, there cannot possibly be any legitimate techniques of modifying or departing from a valid precedent under such premises. The only criterion of justice acknowledged is the formal predictability of future court decisions, with no substantive elements involved. The theoretical background rationale is anchored in the idea of absolute judicial passivism, or *Montesquieu'ean orthodoxy*, on the part of the subsequent court, and judicial activism with truly legislative ambitions, on the part of the prior court.

Notwithstanding the reception of some of its elements in the constitutional jurisdiction of, for example, the Federal Republic of Germany, Spain and Italy, and in the preliminary rulings procedure of the legal system of the European Communities, a full-scale adoption of the reference ideology of precedent-following would gravely undermine the proper functioning of judicial adjudication. The "privileged" court, given the task of providing authoritative rulings on the interpretation of precedents, would soon become overloaded with the flood of contested, hard cases of judicial litigation, resulting in a backlog of cases and serious delay in judicial adjudication.[32] The role of the subsequent court, in turn, would be reduced to a mere passive reading or reciting of the letter of the law, as envisioned by Montesquieu.

4. A LAWGIVER, DRESSED IN ROBE: JUDICIAL LEGISLATION

Under the *quasi-legislative model* of precedent ideology, the prior court is conceived of as a small-scale, interstitial legislator, with similar, although in many respects more limited, norm-issuing power as Parliament. Unlike Parliament, no court is endowed with norm-creation power out of its own initiative or motion, but its norm-issuing competence is restricted to the context of some actual legal dispute brought before the court. One could also argue that such judicial norm-creation power is no more than a by-product of the court's more basic dispute-solving function. On the other hand, the highest national court of justice may

[32] Of course, a major delay in legal adjudication need not be induced by the adoption of the reference ideology, as is amply testified by the backlog of pending cases in the French *Cour de Cassation* and the Italian *Corte di Cassazione*. On judicial delay and the reform proposals made in the context of European Law, see the discussion in H.G. Schermers *et al.*, *Article 177 EEC: Experiences and Problems* (TMC Asser Instituut, Holland, 1987); and M. Andenas, *Article 177 References to the European Courts—Policy and Practice* (Butterworths, 1994), and especially H. Rasmussen's comments on the docket control mechanism suggested for the ECJ in "Docket Control Mechanism, the EC Court and the Preliminary References Procedure", in Andenas, ibid.

have been granted wide discretion as to the selection of cases to be ruled upon by it, depending on the particular system of *certiorari* or docket control adopted in the legal system concerned. In addition, the role of the highest court may—at least partially—be detached from the initial dispute-solving function, granting it more freedom in framing the *ratio* of a case in openly quasi-legislative terms.

Under judicial quasi-legislation, the *ratio* of a case is provided in a canonical and final formulation by the prior court. The yardstick of legal validity is a simple test of formal source of origin, or "pedigree" in Dworkin's terminology: only such legal rules which have been issued by the prior court with an express intention of laying down a precedent are to be treated as such by the later courts. The quasi-legislative precedent ideology simulates the legislator proper in that the precedent rule is effectively raised above the contingent features of the particular case ruled upon and is framed in relatively abstract and context-free terms. The method of argumentation available for the subsequent court is, in principle at least, restricted to the use of deductive reasoning in the unveiling of the logical and legal-systemic consequences of a precedent once laid down. The *ratio* of a prior case will serve as the general clause of a logico-deductive syllogism, thus providing the sole normative premise for the subsequent court's act of logical deduction. Any value-bound considerations relating to axiological fairness or the expediency of social consequences attained by the court ruling are, in principle at least, ruled out. The source of the *ratio* of a case resides exclusively with the prior court, while the *ratio* is taken to have a fully prospective normative effect on future legal adjudication.

Since no court may possibly have an equally all-encompassing view of society as the legislator proper is often presumed to have, the gradual piling-up of such quasi-legislative rules is bound to lead to a system of relatively loose casuistics. The actual burden of the court's case-load and the resources available for legal research also affect the degree of systematicity that may be attained. It seems that both extreme alternatives, i.e. an uncontrollable overload of cases as well as the scarcity of "raw material" for judicial decision-making, may prove to be dysfunctional from the point of view of legal systematicity and the efficient functioning of the system of precedents in more general terms. A vast overload of cases, as in the Italian *Corte de Cassazione*, will make it extremely difficult for judges to master the totality of cases, and inconsistent and even contradictory court decisions are likely to emerge from such a flood of cases. The Italian *Corte de Cassazione*, with its some 400 judges, renders approximately 12,000 civil cases and 35,000 criminal law decisions per annum.[33] As is self-evident, no judicial system can withstand such a profusion of new cases each year and still plausibly hold fast to the illusion of laying down abstract, quasi-legislative norms with a genuine guiding effect on the course of future jurisdiction.

[33] M. Taruffo and M. La Torre, "Precedent in Italy", in MacCormick and Summers, above at n. 8, 144.

A shortage of cases, as may be the situation of the present case-load of the Finnish Supreme Court, will make it (almost) equally difficult to produce a well-functioning system of precedents, as the vast field of divergent social phenomena and fact-constellations will have to be governed by no more than a handful of cases. That may lead to legal gaps and the corresponding need for over-extended analogical interpretation of the few precedents in fact available to judges and other lawyers. The case-load of the Finnish Supreme Court is approximately 200 cases or less per annum, with reference to cases where a leave of appeal has been granted by the Court itself.[34]

A system of quasi-legislative precedent rules is by necessity rather rigid, since only the prior court is formally qualified to modify or expressly overrule a precedent once laid down. Argumentatively, such a system of law is closed, ruling out the impact of non-legal arguments. The binding force of precedent is relatively strong, although subject to the constraints derived from the prevalent source doctrine of the legal system in question. The inherent rigidity of a system of quasi-legislative precedents may even have the negative side-effect of "freezing" the future course of adjudication, since there exist no effective or legitimate means of departing from a precedent by the subsequent courts. The presumably common judicial practice of utilising previous court decisions as a lingustic model for subsequent decisions may also prove to be misleading.

In the judicial practice of the Finnish Supreme Court, the criterion to the effect that "the accused must have realised that . . . the death of the victim was a highly expectable outcome of his deed" has been adopted since the late 1970s when defining the lowest degree of the *mens rea* requirement in intentional homicide, as distinguished from the requirement of *culpa* in the less-severely punishable crime of death caused by gross negligence. In the famous murder case KKO 1988: 73, the Finnish Supreme Court made use of such *dolus eventualis* construction when evaluating the *mens rea* requirement: "[the accused] A *must have realised* that, by forcefully strangling the 10-year old B by neck with two strings, *the death [of the victim] would be a highly expectable outcome of his deed*".[35] In that case, adult man had forcefully strangled a ten-year-old boy to death. The reported facts of the case indicated a clear case of *dolus determinatus* on behalf of the accused, or a firm intention to deprive the boy of his life, while the legal reasoning of the Supreme Court gives the impression that the drawing of the thin border between *dolus* and *culpa*, or intentional homicide and death caused by gross negligence, was at issue.

Under judicial quasi-legislation, the leading criterion of justice is the formal predictability of future court decisions, ruling out the impact of substantive, case-bound correctness on the course of adjudication. As the validity of a precedent is defined in terms of its formal source of origin, in the sense of being equal

[34] Aarnio, above at n. 5, 70. As will be argued at length below, the precedent ideology semi-officially proclaimed by the justices of the Finnish Supreme Court in the mid-1980s was more or less equal to the theoretical postulates of the quasi-legislative model of precedent ideology.

[35] Translation and emphasis by author.

with the prior court's own infallible announcement of what will count as the genuine *ratio* of that case, the theoretical rationale of the quasi-legislative model is firmly anchored in legal positivism.

Taken strictly in their historical meaning, however, some versions of classical legal positivism may not satisfy the present criteria imposed upon the concept of a legal norm. Austin, for instance, expelled "occasional or particular" judicial decisions from the field of legal norms proper in his positivist "command theory of law", as Hart labelled his predecessor's conception of law. Still, the quasi-legislative rules of the present theory would pass the Austinian litmus test of legal norms, due to their highly abstract and context-free character. For Kelsen, quasi-legislative precedent ideology would count as a gross misrepresentation of the formal norm hierarchy (*Stufenbau*), as envisioned by Kelsen and Merkl, since the prior court is placed in the role of the legislator proper, i.e. the source of general legal norms. In Hart's more moderate version of legal positivism, the emergence of such quasi-legislative norms would not cause theoretical difficulties, on the condition that the judges' operative rule of recognition is duly extended to cover the impact of such norms in judicial adjudication.

The *binding reasons* ideology of precedent-following is a reasons-bound variant of such judicial legislation, seeking to give effect to the doctrine of *ruling by judicial reasons*. The manifest reasons of the previous case are, in other words, taken as the point of reference wherefrom the *ratio decidendi* of the case is to be constructed, thereby giving birth to a *highly persuasive legal standard* in terms of the legal rule/principle dichotomy elucidated above. The degree of legal formality of the *ratio* of a case is, accordingly, high insofar as its source of origin and mandatory force are concerned, and low in relation to its point of reference, method of argumentation and internal or "logical" structure. Because of the decreased level of legal formality, such a reasons-oriented approach is better suited to give effect to the value-bound or goal-oriented elements of judicial adjudication, if compared to the rule-based, quasi-legislative model. Except for the deontic mode of the *ratio* of a case, the binding reasons ideology thus follows the characteristics of the quasi-legislative (rule) model as already described. According to Alexy, there are certain elements in the style of reasoning and professional self-understanding of the German Federal Constitutional Court (*Bundesverfassungsgericht*) which bear obvious affinity to the "ruling by reasons" ideology. Such issues will be considered in more detail below in chapter 5.

Unlike statutory legislation, quasi-legislative judicial adjudication is always tied up with the contingent features of the individual legal disputes brought before the court, limiting the court's legislative powers to issues of small-scale or interstitial legislation only. No judge, no matter how whole-heartedly he is committed to the ideals of judicial legislation, can have access to an equal set of resources of fact-collection and fact-evaluation which the Parliament has at its disposal, in the form of the *travaux préparatoires* and other drafting material produced by legislative committees. The social statistics contained in a *Brandeis*

Brief or similar documents are a functional equivalent to the *travaux préparatoires* in judicial adjudication, but are, of course, more restricted both in scope and scholarly depth.

One could argue that the positivist models of precedent ideology, and the rule-bound quasi-legislative model in particular, unhappily reproduce some of the inherent weaknesses of ordinary statutory legislation, because of the rigidity of the resulting system of precedents. Such a conception of precedents will fail to attain the properties of high judicial flexibility and fast social responsiveness which are often associated with a well-functioning system of adjudication. In addition, the power to initiate a ruling on some specific legal issue lies solely at the discretion of the litigants of a particular legal dispute, while no court can issue a precedent out of its own motion or initiative. Wachtler, the former Chief Justice of the New York Court of Appeals, has summarised the risks involved in the practice of too extensively "legislating from the bench" as follows:[36]

> "It is the legislature and not the judiciary that is possessed of resources by which to understand general circumstances, and it is that body which is designed to make law in the abstract. Thus judicial lawmaking outside of the context of a concrete dispute not only risks erroneous determinations, it is nothing more than simple arrogation of legislative power, without the safeguards that allow a legislature to make law in the abstract."

If the prior court ignores the semantic confines of the facts of the case at hand, and instead chooses to lay down a highly abstract legal rule in line with its own legislative aspirations, the end result may be the "freezing" of all subsequent jurisdiction. What is even more fatal to the proper functioning of a legal system is that there will be no incentive for judges, and the legal profession generally, to learn to master the specific techniques of genuinely case-bound reasoning, if the prior court's rulings are thought to be shaped in the image of statutory rules. Under such premises, there will be no essential difference between the rules of statutory origin and the rules of judicial origin, nor between the methods of legal argumentation involved in reading both.

5. IN SEARCH OF THE PRIOR COURT'S ORIGINAL INTENTIONS: JUDICIAL EXEGESIS

Under judicial exegesis, the *ratio* of a case is not necessarily equal with the express norm formulation issued by the prior court, as under judicial legislation. Instead, the *ratio* needs to be constructed, or rather *reconstructed*, from the normative and/or factual premises of the prior court's reasoning which led to the effected outcome in that case. Thereby, the "rulelikeness", or the formal features

[36] Wachtler, "Judicial Lawmaking", 21, quoted also in R.S. Summers, "Precedent in the United States (New York State)", in MacCormick and Summers, above at n. 8, 386. The text is continued with a reference to O.W. Holmes's famous dictum, to the effect that "the life of the common law has not been logic but experience". When a court renders a decision based on hypothetical facts, such a guideline is not duly followed, Wachtler concludes.

of the *ratio* of a case, decreases as the focus of analysis is shifted from the original would-be precedent-norm, as expressly laid down by the prior court, to the normative and/or factual premises of the reasoning structure employed by that court.

The exegetical model may be divided into two subcategories, with reference to whether the *normative* or *factual* premises of the prior court's reasoning are deemed to be decisive. Cross, voicing the standard conception of the *ratio decidendi* of a case in the United Kingdom, and MacCormick, building on the theoretical foundation laid down by Cross, are two examples of such judicial exegesis in which the normative, rule-bound premises of judicial adjudication are taken to be relevant in the subsequent reconstruction of the *ratio* of a case. Goodhart, on the other hand, puts the emphasis on the role of the material facts of the prior case. What is common to all variants of judicial exegesis is the essentially backward-looking, reconstructive mode of reasoning adopted by the subsequent court in the identification and interpretation of the *ratio* of a case.

5.1 Reconstructing the *ratio* from the normative premises of a prior decision

Under the *reconstructed rule model* of precedent-following, the *ratio* of a case is to be reconstructed by the subsequent court from the necessary or sufficient reasoning premises which led to the final outcome in that case. Whether some would-be rule formulation has, in fact, been put forth by the prior court is not decisive as to the allocation of binding force within that decision. According to Cross (and Harris), the *ratio decidendi* of a case can be defined as follows:[37]

> "The *ratio decidendi* of a case is any rule of law expressly or impliedly treated by the judge as a necessary step in reaching his conclusion, having regard to the line of reasoning adopted by him, or a necessary part of his direction to the jury."

In a footnote, Cross and Harris point out that a case may have several *rationes decidendi*, instead of just one *ratio*. Moreover, they make the concession that, "strictly speaking", MacCormick is right in stating that reference should be made to a "ruling of a point of law", instead of a "rule of law", in the definition of the *ratio* of a case. Still, Cross and Harris prefer to use the two terms, "rule" and "ruling of law", interchangeably in their standard textbook on the English law of precedent.[38]

Cross and Harris underscore the necessary inferential relation which is thought to exist between the rule-bound reasoning premises and the final outcome of a prior case. In Simpson's alternative definition of the *ratio* of a case, the relation between the legal rule and the outcome of a case is described as a sufficient, rather than necessary, relation.[39] In both accounts, however, the *ratio*

[37] Cross and Harris, above at n. 2, 72.

[38] Ibid., 72.

[39] A.W.B. Simpson, "The *Ratio Decidendi* of a Case and the Doctrine of Binding Precedent", in A.G. Guest (ed.), *Oxford Essays in Jurisprudence* (Oxford University Press, 1961), 148–75.

is extracted from a case by means of backward-proceeding reasoning, based on the idea of retracing the prior court's original intentions from the normative premises of that decision. Moreover, in both Cross' (and Harris') and Simpson's theories of precedent, the relation between the *ratio* and the final outcome of the case is outlined in *logico-inferential*—and not openly justificatory or evaluative—terms. Thus, the precedent rule is to be reconstructed from the expressly given or merely implicit reasoning premises of the prior case, judged as either necessary (Cross and Harris) or sufficient (Simpson) for the outcome then reached.

MacCormick has defined the *ratio decidendi* of a case as follows:[40]

> "A *ratio decidendi* is a ruling expressly or impliedly given by a judge which is sufficient to settle a point of law put in issue by the parties' arguments in a case, being a point on which a ruling was necessary to his justification (or one of his alternative justifications) of the decisions in the case."

MacCormick's definition of *ratio decidendi* is a modification of Cross' (and Harris') standard definition. Yet, he would seem to define the *ratio* of a case in relatively more context-bound terms than his predecessors, in the sense of underscoring the context-bound character of the ruling of a case, and also in the sense that his reading of the *ratio* of a case stays in closer contact with the justificatory reasons given for the prior decision.[41] As a "crossover ideology" which seeks to combine both the authoritative ruling and the justificatory reasons given in support of that decision, MacCormick's account of the *ratio decidendi* of a case avoids the theoretical pitfall of laying undue emphasis on the logico-inferential side of the issue, in neglect of the reasons for the decision. Thereby, his definition of the *ratio* is drawn closer to the reasons-based reading of judicial exegesis, i.e. the model reasons approach in the present classification.

Under the reconstructed rule approach to precedent-following, the point of reference of the *ratio* of a case is equal to the rule-bound reasoning premises of that case. Such a conception of a precedent is endowed with at least some degree of intended prospectivity. However, the idea of subjecting a prior case to an essentially reconstructive reading brings with it an element of retroactivity, no matter how accurate or authentic the outcome of such judicial reconstruction is claimed to be. In consequence, the formal characteristics of the precedent rule are somewhat less developed under judicial exegesis than under the ideology of judicial legislation. Yet, as was argued above, in MacCormick's reading of the *ratio* of a case, the point of reference of the binding element of a precedent may be seen as a combination of the rule-bound and the reasons-based elements.

A system of judicial exegesis in precedent-following is argumentatively closed and, in that sense, based on weakly legal positivist premises, since the impact of moral and/or political arguments with no formal legal backing is ruled out. Such a set of precedents is by necessity rather casuistic, as the course of precedent-

[40] N. MacCormick, above at n. 4, 170.
[41] Ibid., 170–1.

following is thought to proceed on a case-to-case basis without any pre-defined systemic frame. The binding force of a precedent is relatively strong but still weaker than in the ideology of judicial legislation, since the necessary element of judicial reconstruction brings with it legal flexibility. Self-evidently, the method of argumentation employed by the subsequent court is an instance of backward-proceeding, reconstructive logic, in search of the original rule-bound premises of the prior decision. The notion of the *logic of abduction* could also be adopted, as introduced by Peirce, who described the inference pattern of hypothesis, or *inference to the best explanation*, by means of it.[42] In his later writings, however, the logic of abduction was extended to embody the logic of discovery in general, i.e. "all the norms which guide us in formulating new hypotheses and deciding which of them to take seriously".[43] Here the notion of abductive reasoning is, of course, detached from its original meaning in the sense of the production of novel scientific hypotheses, so as to deal with the reasoning premises of precedent-based judicial argumentation.

The leading criterion of justice is given in terms of formal predictability of the future course of legal adjudication, although in a somewhat weaker sense than in the models based on forthright judicial legislation, since the idea of a reconstructive reading of prior case law brings with it elements of context-bound, substantive correctness to such judicial exegesis. The theoretical rationale of the approach is found in the texts on classical and modern common law, as expounded by e.g. Cross and Harris, Simpson, and MacCormick. The exegetical approach to precedents may also be classified as a weaker version of judicial positivism—weaker because of the less formal characteristics involved, when compared with the ideology of judicial legislation.

5.2 Facts treated as material by the prior court

> "The crucial question is: 'What facts are we talking about?' The same set of facts may look entirely different to two different persons. The judge founds his conclusions upon a group of facts selected by him as material, from among a larger mass of facts, some of which may seem significant to a layman, but which, to a lawyer, are irrelevant. The judge, therefore, reaches a conclusion upon the facts *as he sees them*. It is on these facts that he bases his judgment, and not on any others. It follows that our task in analyzing a case is not to state the facts and the conclusion, but to state the material facts as seen by the judge and his conclusion based on them. *It is by his choice of the material facts that the judge creates law*."[44]

Under the *material facts* approach to precedent-following, the subsequent court is thought to reconstruct the precedent rule from the facts of the prior case,

[42] On abduction and abductive reasoning, see, e.g., the entry on the former by T. Baldwin, in T. Honderich (ed.), *The Oxford Companion to Philosophy* (Oxford University Press, 1995), 1.

[43] Ibid., 1.

[44] A.L. Goodhart, "Determining the *Ratio Decidendi* of A Case", in A.L. Goodhart, *Essays in Jurisprudence and the Common Law* (Cambridge University Press, 1931), 10 (emphasis in original).

treated as material for the outcome originally reached. This ideology could also be called the *Goodhartian approach*, since it was originally suggested by Goodhart.[45] His emphasis on the material facts of a case and the legal consequences attached to them, may be read as giving effect to a deontically indeterminate relation of facts and consequences which is to be qualified as either a (formal) legal rule or a (less-formal) legal principle only subsequently.

In the concluding section of his essay "Determining the *Ratio Decidendi* of a Case", Goodhart outlines some meta-level criteria for the identification of the *ratio decidendi* of a case. He states that the *ratio* is not to be found in the reasons given in support of a decision, nor in the rule laid down in that decision, nor necessarily in the combination of the facts and the final outcome of a case.[46] Thus, neither the express rule formulation, nor the express reasons of a case, are held to be decisive in the allocation of binding force within a case. Thereby, the positivist models of judicial legislation are decisively ruled out in Goodhart's theory of law. Instead, the *ratio decidendi* of a case is to be found "by taking account (a) of the facts treated by the [prior] judge as material, and (b) his decision as based on them".[47] Goodhart's set of methodological rules for distinguishing the *ratio* out of the *dicta* of a case include criteria of the following kind: all facts related to person, time, place, kind and amount are immaterial unless otherwise stated; all facts stated to be material are to be taken as such; all facts either expressly stated or impliedly treated as immaterial are to be taken as such; if the prior court's opinion does not make the distinction between material and immaterial facts, all the facts are to be taken as material; and any conclusions based on hypotheticals are merely a *dictum*.[48]

Any express precedent rule or formulation of reasons may—no more than—provide further support for the inclusion or exclusion of certain factual elements from the sphere of material facts of that case. The starting point of analysis is, again, the intentions originally held by the prior court, as now judged in light of the material facts and consequences of that case. As to its other definitional characteristics, the Goodhartian approach follows the model of judicial exegesis as exemplified by Cross', Simpson's and MacCormick's line of argumentation above, except that the point of reference of the *ratio* of a case is attached to the *facts treated as material* by the prior court.

Stone has criticised Goodhart's definition of the *ratio* of a case on the ground that there exists an indefinite variety of ways of (re)constructing the material facts of a case, on different levels of abstraction. All such (re)constructions embrace the facts of the prior case adequately, but the outcome they provide for the subsequent case may vary to a great extent, depending on the particular

[45] Goodhart, ibid.; A.L. Goodhart, "The *Ratio Decidendi* of a Case" (1959) 22 *Modern Law Review* 117. The term "intended results model" may also be used, since it is the normative consequences as originally intended by the prior court which are taken into account here.

[46] Goodhart, above at n. 44, 25.

[47] Ibid., 25.

[48] Ibid., 25–6.

reading of the fact-constellation in the subsequent case. In the famous "snail in the ginger ale bottle" case, *Donoghue* v. *Stevenson*, the material facts of the case might be taken to comprise, for example, the following elements:[49]

> "(a) *Facts as to the Agent of Harm*. Dead snails, *or* any snails, *or* any noxious physical foreign body, *or* any noxious foreign element, physical or not, *or* any noxious element.
>
> (b) *Facts as to Vehicle of Harm*. An opaque bottle of ginger beer, *or* an opaque bottle of beverage, *or* any bottle of beverage, *or* any container of commodities for human consumption, *or* any container of any chattels for human use, *or* any chattel whatsoever, *or* any thing (including land or buildings).
>
> (c) *Facts as to Defendant's Identity*. A manufacturer of goods nationally distributed through dispersed dealers, *or* any manufacturer, *or* any person working on the object for reward, *or* any person working on the object, *or* anyone dealing with the object.
>
> . . .
>
> (f) *Facts as to Plaintiff's Identity*. A Scots widow, *or* a Scotsman, *or* a woman, *or* any adult, *or* any human being, *or* any legal person."

Even though some of Stone's examples above of material fact-(re)construction may be rejected as plainly inconsistent with the normative premises of any system of law in force, and thus inconceivable from a legal point of view, he is certainly correct in pointing out that there is no logical or semantic obstacle to the construction of the material facts of a case in an indefinite variety of ways.[50] That is so because there is (nor can there be, taken the theoretical premises of Goodhart's backward-looking theory of judicial exegesis) no unique, authoritatively binding formulation of the material facts of a prior case, and because of the resulting need for judicial reconstruction by the subsequent court.[51] Stone's "indeterminacy argument" may, of course, be extended to cover all conceivable variants of judicial exegesis to the extent that a backward-looking method of judicial argumentation is adopted in all of them. Thus, Stone's critique of Goodhart's material facts approach to precedent-following may be read as lending support to either the overtly positivist approach of judicial legislation, where the *ratio* of a case is expressly laid down by the prior court, or to the more case-bound models of judicial analogy, systemic construction of underlying reasons from a line of prior cases, or even more or less radical judicial revalution.

The *material reasons* model of precedent-following may still be discerned within the scope of judicial exegesis. Under such premises, the justificatory premises or material reasons of a case are taken as the point of reference for any subsequent reconstructions of the *ratio* of that case. The *ratio* is conceived of as a legal standard, instead of a more formally framed legal rule. Such a conception

[49] J. Stone, "The *Ratio* of the *Ratio Decidendi*" (1959), 22 *Modern Law Review* 597, 603.

[50] Naturally, Stone's argument may also be extended to apply to the facts of the subsequent case, since there is an indefinite variety of ways in which to describe its fact-constellation on various levels of generality or abstractness.

[51] Cf. Llewellyn's comments on "confining the case to its particular facts", in C. Llewellyn, *The Bramble Bush: On Our Law and Its Study* (Oceana Publications Inc., New York, 1991), 72–3.

of the *ratio* is endowed with some degree of the Dworkinian "dimension of weight", having retained affinity with the axiological and/or teleological background reasons of law despite the other kinds of formal elements involved. In all other aspects, the material reason ideology follows the rule-based counterpart of judicial exegesis. MacCormick's strong emphasis placed on the reasoning context of the *ratio* of a case might be read in light of the material reasons approach, on the condition that the prior case is taken to give effect to a legal standard and not to a legal rule in the technical sense of the term.

The exegetical models signify a decisive shift of focus from the expressly given precedent-norm formulation, as authoritatively and canonically laid down by the prior court under the premises of judicial legislation, to the legal intentions presumably held by the prior court at the time of deciding the case. The task left for the subsequent court is then to retrace or reconstruct the authentic meaning of the case from the normative and/or factual background premises of the prior court's reasoning.

As the reconstructive element gains more ground in precedent-norm formation, the very "rulelikeness" of the *ratio* of a case, in the sense of the formal characteristics entailed in it, also begin to fade. Although guided by the striving for judicial authenticity, the later court by necessity enjoys a certain degree of judicial discretion in resorting to such a backward-proceeding mode of legal reasoning. Thereby, the flexibility and malleability of a system of precedents also increases, as compared to the precedent ideology of judicial legislation. The normative and factual premises of the prior decision must, of course, be expressed in sufficient detail and precision by the prior court, since without access to such reasoning premises no judicial exegesis would be possible in the first place. Moreover, the idea of a reconstructive reading of a case requires that a set of precedent-specific reading skills and techniques of argumentation be adequately mastered by the judges and other lawyers involved in precedent-based judicial adjudication. If the proper techniques of *how to do things with precedents* are not mastered by the members of the legal profession, the resulting system of precedents and precedent-following may be turned into a system of judicial quasi-legislation where the more familiar logic of deductive reasoning will be adopted even in the context of precedent-following.

However, one may legitimately ask why the prior court's historically authentic—and possibly outdated—intentions ought to be held in such high esteem after all, at the cost of the more dynamic models of reading a precedent. Holmes' shrewd comment, to the effect that if the only reason for holding a certain legal rule valid is the fact that "so it was laid down in the time of Henry IV",[52] certainly has some cutting edge *vis-à-vis* the ideology of judicial exegesis.

[52] O. W. Holmes, "The Path of the Law" (1897) 10 Harv LR 457, 469.

6. AN INTERPLAY OF SIMILARITY AND DISSIMILARITY IN PRECEDENT-FOLLOWING: REASONING BY ANALOGY AND DISTINGUISHING

Under the quasi-legislative ideology of precedent-following, the *ratio* of a case is authoritatively and canonically laid down by the prior court itself, in its role of a small-scale, interstitial legislator. From the subsequent court's point of view, there is no essential difference in reasoning based on statutory norms and reasoning based on precedents, since both yield equally to the logico-deductive mode of argumentation. Under judicial exegesis, on the other hand, the original intentions of the prior court are held to be decisive in the subsequent reconstruction of the *ratio* of a case. The role of the subsequent court is to retrace and reconstruct, as authentically as possible, those historical intentions from the normative and/or factual reasoning premises of the prior court's decision. Under the *analogical* approach to precedent-following, to be considered below, the prior court decision is taken as a model or paradigm to be followed analogically in subsequent cases. The *ratio* of a case is detached from the original intentions of the prior court, and also from any quasi-legislative pretensions held by it. Instead, the less rigid rules of analogy-based reasoning are employed.

If the specific ruling of a prior case is taken as a model rule to be either followed analogically or cut down by distinguishing in subsequent adjudication, the ideological stance may be labelled the *model rule approach* to precedent-following. If the binding force of the prior case is, instead, attached to a deontically indeterminate relation of the proven facts and legal consequences in the prior case, taken as a paradigm or exemplary decision to be followed, the term *paradigm case model* may be adopted. The third variant of such a precedent ideology may be called the *model reasons approach*, where the set of reasons—and not the judicial rule—given in support of the prior case is taken as a model to be followed. There, the *ratio* of a case is taken as a graded legal principle or policy, endowed with an inherent dimension of weight or importance, and not as a formally valid legal rule. Due to the less than fully developed formal characteristics of the *ratio* of a case under such analogy-oriented premises, the "rule-likeness" of the *ratio*, in the sense of the formal characteristics entailed in it, also fades, and the conceptual distance between the rule-based and reasons-based variants of the approach tends also to decrease.

An apt illustration of judicial adjudication based on the interplay of analogy and distinguishing is given in Levi's classic study *An Introduction to Legal Reasoning*.[53] There, Levi gives a vivid account of the step-by-step unfolding of

[53] E.H. Levi, *An Introduction to Legal Reasoning* (Chicago University Press, 1994), 1. C.S. Smith describes Levi as a forerunner of the systems-theoretical approach to law in his insightful article, "The Redundancy of Reasoning", in Z. Bankowski, I. White and U. Hahn (eds), *Informatics and the Foundations of Legal Reasoning* (Kluwer, 1995), 191–204. The terms "reasoning by example" and "reasoning from case to case" are used by Levi, but not "model rule approach", "paradigm case model" or "model reasons approach" which have been adopted here.

the doctrine of *articles found inherently dangerous* in the development of American common law of the nineteenth and early twentieth centuries. The rule was utilised in analysing "the potential liability of a seller of an article which causes injury to a [third] person who did not buy the article from the seller".[54] By 1912, the following articles had been classified as inherently dangerous: a loaded gun, possibly a defective gun, mislabeled poison, defective hair wash, scaffolds, a defective coffee urn, and a defective aerated bottle. The category of articles *not* inherently dangerous included a defective carriage, a bursting lamp, a defective balance wheel for a circular saw, a defective boiler, and a defective soldering lamp.[55]

The catalogue of "inherently dangerous articles" seemed well settled in 1915, when the federal Circuit Court of Appeals for the Second Circuit rephrased the content of the rule in *Cadillac* v. *Johnson*:[56]

> "One who manufactures articles inherently dangerous, e.g. poisons, dynamite, gunpowder, torpedoes, bottles of water under gas pressure, is liable in tort to third parties which they injure, unless he has exercised reasonable care with reference to the articles manufactured. . . . On the other hand, one who manufactures articles dangerous only if defectively made, or installed, e.g. tables, chairs, pictures or mirrors hung on the walls, carriages, automobiles, and so on is not liable to third parties for injuries caused by them, except in cases of willful injury or fraud."

However, the same court was—quite unexpectedly—to reverse that rule in still another appeal in the case *Johnson* v. *Cadillac*, to the effect that:[57]

> "We cannot believe the liability of a manufacturer of an automobile has any analogy to the liability of a manufacturer of 'tables, chairs, pictures or mirrors hung on the walls.' The analogy is rather that of a manufacturer of unwholesome food or of a poisonous drug."

The collapse of the rule of articles found inherently dangerous had, in fact, taken place in 1916, when the New York Court of Appeal ruled in *MacPherson* v. *Buick* that the former exception, i.e. liability for negligence where the article is probably dangerous, had now become the new main rule, thereby reversing the original rule of no liability of a manufacturer or supplier to a remote vendee of such articles.[58] Levi also makes reference to the evolvement of the parallel English case-law tradition, beginning with the "snail in the ginger ale bottle" case, *Donoghue* v. *Stevenson*, in 1932. That case was to be the legal ground upon which the liability of a manufacturer of a defective article was later founded.[59]

[54] Levi, ibid., 10 ff. The category of "inherently dangerous" articles was finally acknowledged by the court in *Langmed* v. *Holliday* in 1851: ibid., 13.

[55] Ibid., 18–19.

[56] Ibid., 19–20.

[57] Ibid., 24, quoting *Johnson* v. *Cadillac* (1919).

[58] Ibid., 24–5.

[59] Ibid., 25–6. The case was touched upon above in chapter 3 at 5.2 in the context of the material facts model of precedent ideology.

The outcomes of such initially strictly case-bound reasoning, as framed in terms of analogy and distinguishing, would seem to have the intrinsic tendency to become raised to the level of more abstract and general rules, once the "critical mass" of such case-law material has been collected, on the condition that the court decisions in question do in fact seem to follow some internal pattern, line or "logic". In Levi's example of the articles found inherently dangerous, this would denote the construction of a specific rationale for a given set of cases by means of which a new legal rule with wider semantic coverage may tentatively be laid down. The validity of such an abstracted rule is, however, based on the highly volatile premise that the pattern of legal adjudication will not break down in the next case to be ruled upon by the court. The gross atypicality of any new case to be considered, or a sudden change in the court's own reading of the line of prior cases, may have the outcome of striking down the abstracted rule, opening up the semantic confines of case-law adjudication once again.

In Levi's account, the valid law based on individual court decisions is a *moving classification system*, where the very classification changes while being accomplished.[60] The exact semantic boundaries of a judge-made legal rule or concept, like the articles found inherently dangerous in Levi's example, cannot possibly be drawn until all the relevant court decisions have been gathered. Any premature effort at a formulation of an abstracted rule, based on a line of such court cases, is bound to fail, since each classification may collapse at the emergence of a new case to be considered by the court. That, in fact, is exactly what took place in *MacPherson* v. *Buick* in 1916. Since case-law adjudication is a "going concern", without any natural end point in the course of time when the judicial conclusions based on the case-law material collected might finally be made, all efforts towards defining the exact boundaries of the *ratio* of a case, or raising the level of abstraction involved in individual court rulings, can only be tentative or provisional in kind. There is no solid, fixed end point of semantic reference under the premises acknowledged.

Levi's account of the common law jurisdiction as a moving classification system may be taken as a precise description of *how to read precedents* under the analogy-based approach to precedent-following. The crucial question before a judge who is placed under such premises of legal adjudication is: taken that a loaded gun, mislabeled poison, defective hair wash, scaffolds, a defective coffee urn, and a defective aerated bottle have been classified as articles which are inherently dangerous, while a defective carriage, bursting lamp, defective balance wheel for a circular saw and defective boiler have been classified as articles which are not inherently dangerous, how should a defective soldering lamp, or some other article, be then classified? There are two options or strategies open to a judge: either the original ruling is *analogically extended* to cover the facts

[60] Ibid., 3–4; Smith, above at n. 53, 196–7. Cf. L. Wittgenstein, *Philosophische Untersuchungen—Philosophical Investigations* (Basil Blackwood, Oxford, 1967), § 83 (p. 39/39[e]): "And is there not also the case where we play and—make up the rules as we go along? And there is even one where we alter them—as we go along."

of the new case or, alternatively, the coverage of the model rule, the paradigm case or the set of model reasons is *cut down by distinguishing* the two cases on the ground of some legally relevant, fact-based dissimilarity. Although the semantic frame of adjudication is initially set by the prior court's ruling, the incessant interplay of the two techniques of analogy and distinguishing denotes a continuous realignment of the *ratio* of a case and of the conceptual distinctions derived from it. Since the criteria of analogy or distinguishing must be interpreted by the subsequent court, it will have a decisive say on the correct reading of the precedent-norm's meaning-content.[61]

The use of analogy and distinguishing are the two sides of a same coin: resort to analogy signifies a disregard of any fact-based dissimilarities between the two cases which, in contrast, would have gained relevance, if the technique of distinguishing had instead been adopted by the court.[62] Due to the highly context-bound character of the individual court rulings and the use of the two alternative techniques of analogy and distinguishing, the binding force of the *ratio* of a case is now remarkably weaker than under the ideologies of judicial legislation or judicial exegesis. The feasible techniques of departing from a valid precedent include overruling, especially at a later stage, when an effort has been made to cast a set of case-bound rulings into the form of an abstract rule. Defeating or outweighing a precedent are of less use under such premises, since the technique of distinguishing the two cases may be easily moulded to have a corresponding effect on subsequent adjudication.

As to its systemic structure, the analogical approach to precedents resembles "a chaos with a full index", as the common saying puts it.[63] There will be a realm of loose casuistics, expressive of none or only few facets of legal systematicity proper. Such a set of precedents is argumentatively closed, since it is

[61] As Levi put it: "Where case law is considered, there is a conscious realignment of cases; the problem is not the intention of the prior judge": Levi, above at n. 53, 30. On legal reasoning by analogy, see also Z. Bankowski, "Analogical Reasoning and Legal Institutions" in Bankowski, White and Hahn, above at n. 53.

[62] In statutory interpretation, the analogical approach to precedent-following would seem to have its functional equivalent in Ekelöf's idea of *teleological construction of statutes*. According to Ekelöf, the legislator's intended solutions to the ordinary or typical cases should be taken as a point of reference for special or extraordinary cases which *per definitionem* cannot adequately be foreseen by the legislator. Such hard cases should then be resolved by analogically extending the standard solutions provided by the legislator for typical or ordinary cases. Ekelöf refers to Heck's two semantic categories of the *Begriffskern* and *Begriffshof* of a concept, with approximate correspondence to Hart's later judicial semantics of the *core of settled meaning* and the *penumbra of doubt*, or the easy and hard cases of judicial adjudication, respectively. In his later writings, however, Ekelöf partly gave up of his original stance, advocating instead the preferability of a "reductive" inference, or the exclusion of the facts of the later case from the coverage of the original statutory norm, rather than having resort to wide-ranging analogical reasoning. Thereby, the critical edge entailed in Ekelöf's original theory of interpretation is, of course, effectively levelled off. See P.O. Ekelöf and R. Boman, *Rättegång. Första häftet* (Nordstedts Förlag, 1990), 69–86, esp. 82–3.

[63] "The old fashioned English lawyer's idea of a satisfactory body of law was a chaos with a full index": Holmes' review of Holland's *Essays* made the witty remark famous: O.W. Holmes, "Book Review" (1870) 5 *American Law Review* 114, as cited by T.D. Eisele, "'Our Real Need': Not Explanation, But Education", in D.M. Patterson (ed.), *Wittgenstein and Legal Theory* (Westview Press, San Francisco, 1992) 50, n. 29.

based on arguments of a formally legal, and not openly moral or political, kind. The degree of systemic malleability is high, due to the judicial dynamics brought into effect by the method of reasoning adopted, i.e. the interplay or mutual switching of the two feasible techniques of analogy and distinguishing. The cost of such social responsiveness is then paid in terms of decreased judicial predictability and foreseeability, when compared with the ideologies of judicial legislation and judicial exegesis. The leading criterion of justice is a relatively well-balanced mixture of formal predictability and substantive, case-bound correctness.

The analogical approach to precedent-following would seem to be well equipped to meet with the requirements of genuine case-to-case reasoning. It successfully evades the pitfalls of small-scale judicial legislation, i.e. the constant threat of "freezing" the inherent responsiveness and flexibility of case-law into a rigid collection of canonised rules, valid only because they were once authoritatively laid down (possibly at the time of Henry IV, as Holmes J. might have added). In addition, in relation to the categories of backward-proceeding judicial exegesis and future-oriented judicial revaluation, the analogical approach would seem to rank reasonably well, in not paying overdue respect to the prior court's original and possibly outdated intentions, while not ignoring such intentions altogether. Under the analogy-aligned premises, a prior case provides no more and no less than a *model rule*, a *paradigm case*, or a set of *model reasons* for the subsequent court, to be either analogically extended to cover also the facts of the new case, or cut down by distinguishing the two cases on the ground of some factual dissimilarity. On the other hand, the obvious shortcomings of the substantive and entirely free approaches to adjudication (to be considered below) are also avoided. Thus, reasoning based on analogy/distinguishing would seem to offer a fairly well balanced, "Aristotelian" compromise between the two extreme options of being either too bound or too unconstrained *vis-à-vis* the *ratio* of a prior case. There is room for both legal continuity and dynamic change under the premises acknowledged.

One could still plausibly argue that the proper task and function of the courts is to resolve the concrete legal disputes brought before them, while it is for Parliament to provide judges and the legal community with abstract legal rules. Any ardent, quasi-legislative pretensions held by the courts is a likely "road to (legal) serfdom", if judges and lawyers do not master the precedent-specific techniques of legal reasoning. With such reading skills, the resulting free-floating interplay of analogy and distinguishing, where the *ratio* of a case is defined in terms of a model rule, a paradigm case, or a set of model reasons to be followed in subsequent adjudication, would provide a well-functioning theoretical frame for precedent-identification and precedent-following.

7. SYSTEMIC CONSTRUCTION OF UNDERLYING REASONS FROM A PRIOR COURT DECISION OR LINE OF DECISIONS

7.1 Evolvement of legal systematicity in Dworkin's theory of law

Even though the idea of systemic-constructive elements of law, operative beneath the positivist, surface-structure level manifestations of law, has always had a key position in Dworkin's conception of law, it seems that his commitment to the very idea of such legal systematicity has significantly increased in time, if we extend the scope of analysis from the essays, "The Model of Rules, I–II" (1967/72) to "Hard Cases" (1975), "Law as Interpretation" (1982) and, finally, to the monograph *Law's Empire* (1986). The decisive change, it seems, took place between the articles "The Model of Rules, I–II" and "Hard Cases".

In his widely influential "The Model of Rules, I",[64] Dworkin argued that legal principles are endowed with no more than weak argumentative force, since they only incline a decision in one direction or the other, without having the conclusive capacity to determine, "dictate", or "necessitate" the outcome of the case.[65] In "The Model of Rules, II", he did not alter his conception of law in this respect. In "Hard Cases",[66] Dworkin introduced the fictitious super-judge Hercules J., to illustrate the legal-systemic constraints imposed upon the judge in hard cases of adjudication, where there is no conclusive legal rule available which would determine the outcome of the case. Hercules J. is described as *a lawyer of superhuman skill, learning, patience, and acumen.*[67] Therefore, he is able to weigh correctly the "gravitational force"[68] of each individual legal principle which may have some bearing on the issue, and render the legal judgment accordingly:[69]

> "The law may not be a seamless web; but the plaintiff is entitled to ask Hercules to treat it as if it were. . . . He [i.e. Hercules, J.] must construct a scheme of abstract and concrete principles that provides a coherent justification for all common law precedents and, so far as these are to be justified on principle, constitutional and statutory provisions as well."

[64] R. Dworkin, *Taking Rights Seriously* (Harvard University Press, 1978) 14–45. "The Model of Rules, II" contains Dworkin's answer to the criticism attracted by part I of the essay.

[65] As was argued above, Dworkin is not entirely consistent in his account of legal principles. As Hart pointed out, in *Riggs* v. *Palmer* 22 N.E. 188 (1889), the legal principle to the effect that "no one shall be permitted to profit by his own fraud, or to take advantage of his own wrong, or to found any claim upon his own iniquity, or to acquire property by his own crime" was found conclusive enough to determine the final outcome of the case, despite the presence of a perfectly valid legal rule to the contrary effect in that case.

[66] R. Dworkin, "Hard Cases" (1975), reprinted in Dworkin, above at n. 64, 81–130.

[67] Dworkin, above at n. 64, 105. The "true" Hercules of ancient mythology is, of course, better known for his great physical strength, rather than intellectual faculties, but that does not seem to trouble Dworkin.

[68] Ibid., 112–15.

[69] Ibid., 116–17.

The idea of constructing a "seamless web" of law, in the sense of providing a coherent justification for all common law precedents, plainly endorses a decisively more systemic conception of law, when compared with Dworkin's earlier articles, "The Model of Rules, I–II". In "Law as Interpretation" (1982) and *Law's Empire* (1986), Dworkin introduced the *chain novel* metaphor, likening a judge to the author of a chain novel, engaged in writing a novel *seriatim*. The key idea of the *best constructive interpretation of the community's legal practice*[70] was also initiated. Thus, the more "mature" Dworkin of "Hard Cases", "Law as Interpretation" and *Law's Empire* of the mid-1970s and 1980s, would seem to attach far more weight to the systemic elements of law than the "early" Dworkin of the 1960s and early 1970s.

In consequence, Dworkin's later systemic emphasis on legal principles should be kept separate from the general definition of legal principles (and policies) put forth in chapter 2 of this book, based on a close cross-reading of Dworkin's "The Model of Rules, I" and Summers' categories of legal formality. There, legal principles were defined as legal norms which rank relatively low in terms of Summers' categories of constitutive, mandatory, structural and methodological formality, apart from being no more than weakly systemic in character. In the present context of the *underlying reasons* approach to precedent-following, the more systemic notion of law and legal principles will yet be adopted.

7.2 "[T]he best constructive interpretation of past legal decisions"

In 1889 a New York court set out the following line of argumentation in support of its ruling:[71]

> "What could be more unreasonable than to suppose that it was the legislative intention in the general laws passed for the orderly, peaceable, and just devolution of property that they should have operation in favor of one who murdered his ancestor that he might speedily come into the possession of his estate? Such an intention is inconceivable. We need not, therefore, be much troubled by the general language contained in the laws. Besides, all laws as well as all contracts may be controlled in their operation and effect by general, fundamental maxims of the common law. *No one shall be permitted to profit by his own fraud, or to take advantage of his own wrong, or to found any claim upon his own iniquity, or to acquire property by his own crime.*"

[70] R. Dworkin, *Law's Empire* (Fontana Masterguides, 1986) 225 ff. See Fish's witty comments on Dworkin's theory of law in the essays "Working on the Chain Gang: Interpretation in Law and Literature", "Wrong Again", and "Still Wrong After All These Years", reprinted in S. Fish, *Doing What Comes Naturally: Change, Rhetoric, and the Practice of Theory in Literary and Legal Studies* (Duke University Press, 1989), 87–102, 103–19 and 356–71.

[71] *Riggs* v. *Palmer*, 22 N.E. 188 (1889), New York Court of Appeals (emphasis added). The case was, in fact, a majority decision, with Gray J. dissenting. See Dworkin, above at n. 64, 23.

New Jersey court reasoned in the following manner in 1960, in a case concerning an automobile manufacturer's liability for a defect in an article manufactured by it:[72]

> "In assessing its significance [i.e. the significance of an express warranty seeking to limit the manufacturer's liability to replacement of defective parts] we must keep in mind the general principle that, in the absence of fraud, one who does not choose to read a contract before signing it cannot later relieve himself of its burdens. . . . And in applying that principle, the basic tenet of freedom of competent parties to contract is a factor of importance. But in the framework of modern commercial life and business practices, such rules cannot be applied on a strict, doctrinal basis. The conflicting interest of the buyer and seller must be evaluated realistically and justly, giving due weight to the social policy evinced by the Uniform Sales Act, the progressive decisions of the courts engaged in administering it, the mass production methods of manufacture and distribution to the public, and the bargaining position occupied by the ordinary consumer in such an economy. The history of the law shows that legal doctrines, as first expounded, often prove to be inadequate under the impact of later experience. In such a case, the need for justice has stimulated the necessary qualifications or adjustments. . . . Freedom of contract is not such an immutable doctrine as to admit of no qualification in the area in which we are concerned."

The two famous court cases are, of course, *Riggs* v. *Palmer* and *Henningsen* v. *Bloomfield Motors, Inc.* Although they were originally introduced and analysed in Dworkin's "The Model of Rules, I", where a less-than-fully systemic notion of legal principles was prevalent, the theoretical consequences drawn from them may still be transferred to his "more mature" theory of law where a more systemic idea of law is acknowledged.

In those cases, the court's reasoning may be read in light of the positivist *ruling by reasons* ideology, on the condition that the criteria laid down by the court—to the effect that "no one shall be permitted to profit by his own fraud, or to take advantage of his own wrong, or to found any claim upon his own iniquity, or to acquire property by his own crime" (*Riggs* v. *Palmer*), and the specific qualifications or modifications made to the doctrine of the freedom of contract in *Henningsen* v. *Bloomfield Motors, Inc.*—are taken as highly persuasive legal standards, resulting from the court's conscious efforts towards future-oriented judicial legislation. Alternatively, the cases may be read in light of the *underlying reasons model*, if no such quasi-legislative pretensions are deemed to have been held by the prior court and, moreover, if the line of cases is approached with an eye on the "deeper-level" legal rationale involved. The latter option will be followed here, since it is in better match with Dworkin's own reading of the two court decisions.

In *Riggs* v. *Palmer*, the legal basis of the judgment was derived from the "general, fundamental maxims of the common law". The resort taken to such legal principles signified an open deviation from a semantically clear statutory provi-

[72] *Hennigsen* v. *Bloomfield Motors, Inc.*, 161 A., 2nd 69 (1960), Supreme Court of New Jersey. See Dworkin, above at n. 64, 24.

sion where no exception was made with respect to such beneficiaries who have wilfully murdered the testator of the will. *Henningsen* v. *Bloomfield Motors, Inc.* equally denotes a deviation from the express wording of the contract originally made between the two parties. The outcome of that case was based on a set of relatively soft-edged legal standards, such as the "social policy evinced by the Uniform Sales Act, the progressive decisions of the courts engaged in administering it, the mass production methods of manufacture and distribution to the public, and the bargaining position occupied by the ordinary consumer in such an economy".

In the underlying reasons approach to precedent-following, the *ratio decidendi* of a case or line of cases is not defined with reference to the expressly given ruling or reasons element of a prior case, as in judicial legislation; nor with reference to the normative and/or factual premises structure of the prior decision, as in judicial exegesis; nor still with reference to a constant, "free-floating" interplay of analogy and distinguishing, as in the analogy-aligned approach to precedents. Instead, the underlying, system-bound reasons for the prior case, prevalent "beneath" any manifest precedent-norm and/or reasons formulation, are taken to be decisive in the allocation of binding force in that decision. The idea of deep-structure level argumentative coherence is essential for Dworkin's notion of precedent-identification, or rather precedent-construction, and precedent-following. With direct allusion to Dworkin's theory of law, the term *law as integrity* could also be adopted:[73]

> "Law as integrity asks judges to assume, so far as this is possible, that the law is structured by a coherent set of principles about justice and fairness and procedural due process, and it asks them to enforce these in the fresh cases that come before them, so that each person's situation is fair and just according to the same standards. . . . Judges who accept the interpretive ideal of integrity decide hard cases by trying to find, in some coherent set of principles about people's rights and duties, the *best constructive interpretation of the political structure and legal doctrine of their community*."

Similar formulations of the law as integrity doctrine are found scattered all over Dworkin's book, e.g. "the best constructive interpretation of the community's legal practice"[74] or "the best constructive interpretation of past legal decisions".[75] As mentioned, Dworkin employs the chain novel metaphor to illustrate the role of the judge in case-law adjudication.[76] The resulting conception of law is as if Levi's idea of the gradual unfolding of case-law were now cast into a legal systemic mould, held together by the constraints of legal coherence, the notion of "law as integrity" and the adequacy of institutional support enjoyed by the legal principles concerned. It may also be the case that Dworkin's theory has retained some elements of the traditional common law conception of law.

[73] Dworkin, above at n. 70, 243, 255 (emphasis added).

[74] Ibid., 225.

[75] Ibid., 262.

[76] Ibid., 228 ff.; R. Dworkin, "Law as Interpretation", in A. Aarnio and D.N. MacCormick (eds), *Legal Reasoning, Vol. II* (Dartmouth, 1992), 255–78.

At least Lord Mansfield's doctrine of judicial consistency would seem to match fairly well with Dworkin's idea of law: "Precedents serve to illustrate principles . . . The reason and spirit of cases make law, not the letter of particular precedents. . . . But the law does not consist in particular cases, but in general principles, which run through the cases and govern the decision of them".[77] Other examples of a similar kind could presumably also be pointed out.

The leading idea of the precedent ideology now under consideration is to unfold the latent, underlying reasons of past adjudication, as are prevalent beneath the manifest norm/reasons formulation of the prior case or line of cases. Therefore, the *ratio decidendi* of a case is to be constructed by the judge's "Herculean" insight into the deeper rationale of past judicial decisions, resulting in a system-bound legal principle, or a set of principles, where both legal and moral and/or political arguments are closely intertwined. In stark contrast to the other ideologies of precedent-following discerned in the present discussion, the underlying reasons model aims at satisfying the criteria of high argumentative coherence. Other systemic criteria, such as consistency, non-contradiction and non-redundancy, could also be added. Coherence refers to the alignment of the outcome of the case with the sum total of normative premises which have bearing on the issue. Consistency denotes the requirement of continuity and predictability in judicial decision-making. The requirement of non-contradiction rules out any court decisions which are inconsistent with the present one. Finally, the less-than-fully conclusive criterion of non-redundancy in adjudication entails the idea of reducing unnecessary repetition or systemic overlap within a line of precedents.

As the *ratio* of a case must be constructed from the latent signification structure beneath the manifest norm/reasons formulation of a prior case, there is, by necessity, a certain amount of discretionary leeway left to the subsequent court. The prior court is thought to lay down the basic legal frame for subsequent adjudication, and by means of constructive legal interpretation the subsequent court may then unveil the true *ratio* of the case or line of cases. Thereby, a touch of retroactivity is brought into the precedent ideology concerned. In this aspect, the underlying reasons model resembles the analogical approach to precedents, where the prospective and retroactive elements of precedent-following are held in balance. The binding force exerted by a prior case under such Dworkinian premises may vary within the relatively loose-edged borders set by judicial exegesis and open-ended judicial revalution *vis-à-vis* the *ratio* of a case. A departure from a precedent is relatively easily attained simply by modifying the frame of interpretation so that the outcome of adjudication will find better match with the facts of the novel case. The leading criterion of justice acknowledged is a combination of case-bound substantive correctness and formal predictability, as derived from the essentially systemic-constructive frame of adjudication. Self-evidently, the theoretical rationale of the approach stems

[77] Lord Mansfield is quoted in Allen, above at n. 23, 216–17.

from Dworkin's idea of *law as integrity*, combining elements drawn from tradition-oriented legal historicism, formal legal positivism and substantive natural law theory into a tightly-knit whole.

The pitfalls of judicial legislation, with its inherent rigidity and freezing effect on jurisdiction, are avoided in the systemic construction of underlying reasons from a line of precedents, provided that judges display openness and honesty in argumentation and, moreover, do not use the constructive elements of legal interpretation as a *Trojan horse* for the importation of a personal ideological bias into the formal edifice of law. Clearly, the main defects of the approach concern the lack of any effective means of controlling how judges actually construct the underlying rationale of law from a line of prior legal decisions. How can we know whether judges really provide us with the *best constructive interpretation of past legal decisions*? A full-scale adoption of the ideology would require a firm—and, perhaps, more than slightly naive—trust in the reading skills and professional ethics of the judiciary, when viewed from the point of view of the legal community.

There exists, in other words, a constant threat of turning the *Rechtsstaat*, or a state governed by the rule of law, into a *Richterstaat*, where judges have the status of, not the princes of the "law's empire", as Dworkin himself would have it,[78] but the unconstrained sovereign ruler of a Hobbesian nightmare, or a mere tyrant, dressed in robe. The only counterweight to the judges' legal discretion under such premises of adjudication would be an adequately self-reflected and well-developed doctrine, tradition and theory of precedent against which any actual court rulings could then be evaluated. However, the critical edge of legal science could easily be reduced to the role of mere witty scholarly criticism, issued *ex post facto* and endowed with no effective means of truly changing or affecting the course of future jurisdiction. If, on the other hand, judges could indeed be entrusted with the constructive powers to make the Dworkinian dream come true—a dream had by "the noblest dreamer of them all", as Hart put it in high Shakespearean style[79]—it would provide a solid ground for precedent-based judicial adjudication, where the conflicting demands for consistency and dynamic change would be held in balance under the *law as integrity*. The exigencies of judicial reality may, however, still prove to be a far cry from such noble dreams, spun out of a legal philosopher's social imagery.

[78] Dworkin, above at n. 70, 407: "The courts are the capitals of law's empire, and judges are its princes, but not its seers and prophets".

[79] H.L.A. Hart, "American Jurisprudence through English Eyes: The Nightmare and the Noble Dream", in *Essays in Jurisprudence and Philosophy* (Clarendon Press, 1983), 137.

8. REJUDGING A PRIOR COURT DECISION: JUDICIAL REVALUATION

Frank, one of the leading figures of the American Legal Realist movement,[80] reflected on the various definitions of the *ratio* of a case as follows:[81]

> "'It is,' says Allen, a defender of the doctrine of '*stare decisis*' (i.e. standing by the precedents), 'it is for the court, of whatever degree, which is called upon to consider the precedent, to determine what the *true* ratio decidendi was.' The 'authoritative' part of a former decision, on this theory, is not the rule announced by the judge in the former case, nor what that judge thought was the principle back of the rule he was applying. What 'binds' the judge in any later case is what that judge determines was the 'true' principle or 'juridical motive' involved in the prior decision. *The earlier case means only what the judge in the later case says it means.* Any case is an 'authoritative' precedent only for a judge who, as a result of his own reflection, decides that it is authoritative."

Frank, in effect, restates three different operative definitions of the *ratio* of a case. The first candidate, "the rule announced by the judge in the former case", may be read in light of judicial legislation. The second, "what that judge thought was the principle back of the rule he was applying", may be read as a reformulation of judicial exegesis or of systemic construction of underlying reasons from a line of prior decisions, depending on the degree of systematicity involved. The definition of the *ratio* of a case, finally approved of by Frank, viz. "the earlier case means only what the judge in the later case says it means", may be read as giving effect to more or less radical *judicial revaluation* of the *ratio* of the prior case.

The idea of judicial revaluation follows the methodological credo of the legal realists and their highly sceptical stance towards anything like the doctrine of formal *stare decisis*. By importing some basic tenets of the realists into the doctrine of precedents, the focus of analysis is switched from a reverently backward-looking frame of judicial legislation or judicial exegesis, and also from the

[80] As Frank rightly points out, the term "legal realism" is less than entirely accurate as to its sense or reference. The only aspect held in common by the various scholars identified with the Legal Realist movement is no doubt their critical stance towards the (then) prevailing conception of law, without sharing any common credo as to its preferred alternatives. Frank himself suggested the two terms "constructive skeptics" and "experimentalists" in *Law and the Modern Mind*, above at n. 13, IX ff., but the proposal never gained wider acceptance among legal scholars. "Pragmatic instrumentalism" is Summers' suggestion for the three phenomena of philosophical pragmatism, sociological jurisprudence (à la Holmes and Pound), and certain tenets of American Legal Realism proper since the 1920s. See R.S. Summers, *Instrumentalism and American Legal Theory* (Cornell University Press, 1982), 36–7. On the relation between Legal Realism and empiricism, see, generally J.H. Schlegel, *American Legal Realism and Empirical Social Science* (University of North Carolina Press, 1995).

[81] Frank, above at n. 13, 160, n. 1 (emphasis in original), where Frank comments upon Allen's analysis of *ratio decidendi*. Allen himself concluded that the *ratio* of a case is in a constant state of flux, in *Law in the Making*, above at n. 23, 260. Cf. Llewellyn, above at n. 51, 53: "For one of the vital elements of our doctrine of precedent is this: that any later court can always reexamine a prior case".

gradual realignment of the *ratio* of a case under the Levian or Dworkinian premises of case-law adjudication, to an openly future-oriented rejudgment of the merits of prior decisions. Technically, the point of reference of the *ratio* of a case may again be attached to one of the three alternatives of the authoritative rule, the deontically indeterminate relation of proven facts and normative consequences, or the reasons given in support of the prior case, as then expressed in terms of the *reinterpreted rule* model, *requalified facts* model, and *revalued reasons* model of precedent ideology, respectively.

Speaking of legal rules in the Dworkinian sense of the term, i.e. as fully conclusive and self-sufficient criteria of judicial decision-making which would then "dictate" or "necessitate" a certain outcome in that case, is, however, highly misleading in the present context. Here, the rule originally laid down by the prior court is no more than a pre-form or an empty shell of a legal norm, subject to be thoroughly modified or recast into a totally new shape, once the facts of the new case have been given due consideration. The terms "weak, defeasible legal rule" and "soft-edged, porous legality" were used above, with reference to the low level of legal formality involved in such defective or imperfect rules.[82]

In consequence, a prior case is given only such weight and significance in legal adjudication that the subsequent court regards as justified in the context of a new case. Such an openly discretion-based approach to precedent-following, in other words, takes the decisive step towards full-fledged retroactivity in judicial adjudication and legal argumentation.[83] While the subsequent court nominally pays respect to the legal frame of analysis, its wide powers of judicial discretion will allow some *de facto* policy-orientation or value-ladenness to enter the process of judicial decision-making. If such an open-ended conception of the *ratio* of a case is shown to enjoy an adequate degree of documented institutional support in society and is, moreover, endowed with a certain sense of appropriateness as to its content, it may be called a legal principle or policy, in the sense defined above in chapter 2. Due to the open-ended character of such legal principles or policies, a high degree of flexibility, malleability and responsiveness to demands for social change will follow, along with effected loose casuistics and unpredictability in case-law adjudication. The leading criterion of justice is naturally the substantive, case-bound correctness of the individual legal decision, at the cost of any formal considerations related to legal predictability. Self-evidently, the theoretical background rationale of the approach stems from legal realism.

[82] In consequence, the conceptual space that extends between the rule-based, the facts and consequences-oriented, and the reasons-based definition of the *ratio* of a case tends to narrow down or collapse altogether under the theoretical premises of judicial revaluation ideology.

[83] Cf. Llewellyn's comments on the essentially retroactive character of precedent-based law, in Llewellyn, above at n. 51, 87: "Now the essential differences between statutes and the law of case decisions are these. A judge makes his rule in and around a specific case, and looking backward. The case shapes the rule; the judge's feet are firmly on the particular instance; his rule is commonly good sense, and very narrow. . . . Knowing that the effect of their ruling will be retroactive, and unable to foresee how many men's calculations a new ruling may upset, the judges move very carefully into new ground".

There is one major difficulty in trying to illustrate such a discretion-proliferating approach to precedents with the texts of the Legal Realists. Holmes, for example, described his new legal prediction theory with reference to the fictitious *bad man*, only interested in predicting "what the Massachusetts or London courts will do in fact",[84] i.e. in trying to foresee the court's likely response to his (evil) action. The young Llewellyn, in turn, voiced a similar methodological credo: "*What these officials do about disputes is, to my mind, the law itself*... And *rules*, in all of this, are important to you so far as they help you see or predict what judges will do or so far as they help you get judges to do something. That is their importance, except as pretty playthings".[85] In the postscript added to a later edition of *The Bramble Bush*, Llewellyn tried to level off the critical edge of those words, claiming that his *dictum* should be read as "a very partial statement of the whole truth".[86] However, at least Llewellyn's earlier stance plainly lends support to the "deeds, not words" ideology widely supported by the Legal Realists.

Legal prediction theory, as exemplied by Holmes' bad man theory of law or Llewellyn's "what officials do about disputes" definition of law, endorses an essentially *external* point of view to the law. Legal phenomena are looked upon from the point of view of a social scientist or a disengaged external observer of the court's rulings. The aim is to detect some observable facts whereupon predictions of "what the courts will do in fact" might then be grounded. A judge who is presiding over court proceedings, on the other hand, has an *internal* point of view of the law, seeking to find some normative criteria which lend support to the outcome of judicial decision-making.[87] The prediction theory of law, voiced from the external point of view, must be converted into the internal point of view of a judge in order to find it a proper place in the present discussion.

The practical importance of judicial revaluation, as defined with reference to the wide powers of discretion granted to the subsequent judge, would not seem to be great, nor openly professed outside of the sphere of American legal realism. The fundamental disadvantage endorsed by such an ideology of precedent-following is, clearly, the low level of judicial control and legal predictability that is made possible thereby. In a trivial sense, Llewellyn, Frank and Allen are, of course, right in pointing out that the decision on the exact semantic boundaries of the *ratio* of a case eventually lies at the discretion of the subsequent court, if the impact of judicial reference and judicial legislation, strictly defined, is ruled out. If the affirmation or denial of the binding force of the *ratio* lies solely at the hands of the subsequent court, there can be no doctrine of formal *stare decisis*,

[84] Holmes, above at n. 10, 460–1. On Holmes' shrewd comment on the task of legal science, with reference to "the scattered prophecies of the past upon the cases in which the axe will fall", see ibid., 457.

[85] Llewellyn, above at n. 51, 3, 5 (emphasis in original).

[86] Ibid., IX–XI.

[87] On the dichotomy of an internal/external point of view to the law, see, e.g. H.L.A. Hart, *The Concept of Law* (Clarendon Press, Oxford, 1961), 99 and Ross, *On Law and Justice* (University of California Press, 1958), 11–18.

either. Such a model of precedent ideology, with no more than a loosely spun frame of constraints imposed upon the judge's discretion, would closely resemble Hart's idea of the *game of scorer's discretion*.[88] In consequence, the end result might turn out to be a genuine *Richterstaat*, or a state governed by judges, displacing the ideal of a *Rechtsstaat*, or a state governed by the rule of law.

9. AXIOLOGICAL AND TELEOLOGICAL BACKGROUND REASONS OF LAW: JUDICIAL CONSEQUENTIALISM AND RIGHTNESS REASONS IN JUDICIAL DECISION-MAKING

Judicial consequentialism and *rightness reasons* model in adjudication, where the judge is constrained only by the axiological or teleological background reasons of law, plus the *judicial hunch* model, where the judge's unconstrained "hunch", intuition or semantic freeplay is allowed to decide the case, function as a set of counter-ideologies to the categories of precedent-ideology discerned above. Although no doctrine of formal *stare decisis* is recognised in the substantive and entirely free approaches to adjudication, their inclusion in the present classification is justified by systemic-didactic reasons, since they provide a straight link to the concept of a legal norm outlined above in chapter 2 at p. 41

Under judicial revaluation, the binding force of the prior case is no more than weak, but the frame of analysis is still—at least nominally—legal. Under the substantive approaches to adjudication, the judge discards the initial legal frame and enters the domain of social expediency and goal-rationality of a means/end analysis, if the premises of judicial consequentialism are adopted. Alternatively, arguments derived from social justice, fairness, equitableness and value-rationality are held to be decisive, if the background premises of the rightness reasons approach to adjudication are instead opted for. The two kinds of substantive models of adjudication are distinguished from the principle/policy-grounding premises of judicial rejudgment by the lack of adequate institutional support for the goal-reasons or the value-reasons profferred. As was argued above with reference to MacCormick's theory of law, legal principles and legal policies may be defined interchangeably, whereby the neat division of arguments into value-reasons and goal-reasons is effectively levelled off. For didactic reasons, that dichotomy will be upheld below.

Cook wrote as follows:[89]

> "The logical situation confronting a judge in a new case being what it is, it is obvious that he must legislate, whether he will or not. By this is meant that since he is free so far as compelling logical reasons are concerned to choose which way to decide the case, his choice will turn out upon analysis to be based upon considerations of social or economical policy. An intelligent choice can be made only by estimating as far as that is possible the consequences of a decision one way or the other. To do this,

[88] Hart, ibid., 138–42.

[89] W.W. Cook, "Scientific Method and the Law" (1927) XIII *American Bar Association* 308 (emphasis added).

however, the judge will need to know two things: (1) *what social consequences or results are to be aimed at*; and (2) *how a decision one way or other will affect the attainment of those results*. This knowledge he will as a rule not have; to acquire it he will need to call upon the other social sciences, such as economics."

Cook's reflection on law may be taken as a battle-cry for a *consequentialist, teleological* or *finalistic* approach to judicial adjudication,[90] where the constraints of a formally legal frame of analysis are relaxed, and decisive importance is instead given to some preferable social goals. Self-evidently, the doctrine of *stare decisis* cannot conceivably be upheld under such premises, any more than under the axiological premises of the rightness reasons approach to adjudication. The resulting frame of a judge's decision-making is defined in terms of an instrumentalist, finalistic, teleological or pragmatic conception of the socio-legal outcomes to be attained through case-law jurisdiction. Such a system of law-enforcement is, of course, highly dynamic, easily malleable and responsive to the changing conditions in society. The prevalent conception of justice is given in terms of case-bound correctness, as judged in light of goal-rationality and social expediency. The theoretical rationale of the approach is derived from the ideas presented by Legal Realists.

The *rightness reasons* approach to judicial decision-making gives decisive priority to the value-bound, axiological considerations of social justice, social fairness and equitableness in social matters. Like judicial consequentialism, the rightness reasons approach casts off any remnants of the formally legal frame of adjudication and the doctrine of *stare decisis*. The argumentative weight of a prior case is acknowledged on the one condition that the content of the decision is deemed to be morally correct. As Thomas Aquinas put it: *Lex injusta non est lex*[91] (unjust laws are not (valid) law). Unjust laws are not to be observed by citizens, nor given recognition in the courts of justice; instead a system of political morality or natural justice is to be enforced. The exclusive criterion of justice is the correctness or moral merits of the prior court decision. The theoretical rationale of the approach is of course anchored in natural law theory, whether in the sense of the law of reason of the enlightenment era or some more modern variant of such legal thinking.

[90] MacCormick strongly emphasises the role of the consequentialist argument in *Legal Reasoning and Legal Theory* (Oxford University Press, 1978), 106, 108–19, 129–51. In the Finnish discussion Klami has laid a strong emphasis on the finalistic or teleological aspects of legal decision-making: see H.T. Klami, *Anti-Legalism: Five Essays in the Finalistic Theory of Law* (Turun yliopiston julkaisuja, 1980); H.T. Klami, *Finalistinen oikeusteoria* (Turun yliopiston yksityisoikeuden laitoksen julkaisuja, 1980); H.T. Klami, *Ihmisen säännöt: Tutkimus oikeuden olemuksesta, synnystä ja toiminnasta* (Turun yliopiston julkaisuja, 1983), 217 ff., where he argues that teleological considerations are the final arguments of legal justification. Cf. A. Peczenik, *The Basis of Legal Justification* (Infotryck AB, 1983) 34, where the author makes a reference to the notions of consequentialist reasoning, goal-reasoning and teleological reasoning.

[91] Cf.: "*non lex sed legis corruptio*", i.e. "not law but a corruption of law", and: "*magis sunt violentiae quam leges*", i.e. "more outrages than laws", as St. Thomas Aquinas characterised laws which fall short of such content-bound criteria. Quoted in J. Finnis, *Natural Law and Natural Rights* (Oxford University Press, 1980), 363.

10. THE JUDGMENT INTUITIVE: "BY FEELING AND NOT BY JUDGMENT"

Finally, the *judicial hunch* ideology claims to do without any restrictions on a judge's discretion. The key element of judicial decision-making is the impact of the judge's free intuition or "hunch". In perfect match with the sceptic credo of Legal Realists, the manifest reasons given in support of a judicial decision need not be more than a mere façade or camouflage, raised only *ex post facto* with the intention of concealing the arbitrariness entailed in judicial decision-making. The judge, far from being a perfectly impartial arbiter who would devote equal attention to the merits and defects of the arguments presented by the litigants during court proceedings, may, in fact, have reached the verdict simply by tossing a coin or by giving effect to his own ideological preferences.

The idea of a judge's intuition or hunch in judicial decision-making was introduced by Hutcheson in his essay "The Judgment Intuitive: The Function of the 'Hunch' in Judicial Decision" in 1929. Hutcheson wrote with reference to Radin's earlier text *The Theory of Judicial Decision*, as follows:[92]

> "Now what is he saying except that the judge really decides by feeling and not by judgment; by 'hunching' and not by ratiocination, and that the ratiocination appears only in the opinion?"

Drawing on Hutcheson's judicial hunch argument, Frank points out in *Law and the Modern Mind* that the *hunch-producers* of a judge may include such factors as the political, economic and moral prejudices of that judge.[93] A few lines later he adds that the:[94]

> "peculiar traits, disposition, biases and habits of the particular judge will, then, often determine what he decides to be the law. . . . To know the judge's hunch-producers which make the law we must know thoroughly that complicated congeries we loosely call the judge's personality."

And, as early as 1881, Holmes had, in effect, argued that the common prejudices held by the judges and citizens have had a far greater influence on the content of legal rules than any patterns of formal syllogistic reasoning.[95]

The judicial hunch model of adjudication, being based on the judge's mental faculties of hunch or intuition, is entirely open-ended as to the social and political environment of law. It sees no difference in the mutual role of formally legal

[92] J.C. Hutcheson, "The Judgment Intuitive: The Function of the 'Hunch' in Judicial Decision" (1929) 14 *Cornell Law Quarterly* 274, 285.

[93] Frank, above at n. 13, 113.

[94] Ibid., 119–20.

[95] "The life of the law has not been logic: it has been experience. The felt necessities of the time, the prevalent moral and political theories, intuitions of public policy, avowed or unconscious, even the prejudices which judges share with their fellow-men, have had a good deal more to do than the syllogism in determining the rules by which men should be governed": O.W. Holmes, "The Common Law", in *The Essential Holmes: Selections from the Letters, Speeches, Judicial Opinions, and Other Writings of Oliver Wendell Holmes, Jr.* (The University of Chicago Press, 1992), 237.

and other kinds of arguments, or "hunch-producers", in judicial decision-making, thereby levelling off the confines between the formally legal and the non-legal premises of adjudication. Such a resort to the judge's free-floating intuition is bound to lead to legal casuistics pure and simple, by force of the elements of retroactivity involved. Prediction of the future course of adjudication can be based only on an insight into the specific hunch-producers of a particular judge's free intuition, as Frank argued. Finally, the method of argumentation adopted is based on the meta-rule of *anything goes*, i.e. sheer methodological disorder or anarchism, as suggested by Feyerabend. Clearly, a full-scale or even small-scale adoption of such a model of adjudication would bring about a total collapse of judicial adjudication as we know it in any Western type of legal system, due to the lack of any constraints on a judge's free discretion. What was said of Hart's idea of the *game of scorer's discretion*[96] in the context of judicial revaluation holds at least equally true for the present intuition-based model of adjudication. Under the judicial hunch conception of adjudication, the judge is free to rule upon the facts of the new case, acting out of truly Solomonic motives or, alternatively, mere personal prejudice and whim. Yet, there can be no effective guarantee that some noble, Solomonic motives would in fact be pursued by the judiciary under such free-floating premises of judicial decision-making.

[96] Hart, above at n. 87, 138–42.

4

Confrontations

1. OPERATIVE PRECEDENT-NORM CONCEPTION

Below, some of the individual fragments or facets of the feasible precedent ideologies available to a judge will be compared, starting with the operative precedent-norm conception endorsed in each ideology. In judicial reference and judicial legislation, the *ratio decidendi* of a case is relatively easy to distinguish from its argumentative context or *obiter dicta*, since the *ratio* is given in a canonical and authorised formulation by the prior court itself. In judicial exegesis, the *ratio* of a case is later reconstructed from the normative and/or factual premises of the prior decision, with the aim of retracing the original intentions of the prior court. In judicial analogy, the operative definition of the *ratio* is based on the constant interplay of analogy and distinguishing in the gradual case-to-case realignment of the *ratio vis-à-vis* the facts of each novel case. In the Dworkin-inspired underlying reasons model of precedent-following, the *ratio* of a case is produced by having recourse to the "deeper", underlying, system-bound reasons "beneath" a prior decision or line of decisions. In judicial revaluation, the *ratio* of a case is thoroughly reinterpreted or reconsidered by the subsequent court in light of the facts of the novel case.

To put it concisely, the operative precedent-norm conception in the various types of precedent ideology, and the corresponding conception of the judicial norm to be applied by the subsequent court in the two types of general judicial ideology where no doctrine of *stare decisis* is acknowledged, can be presented as follows:

Precedent ideology	*Operative precedent-norm conception*
(1) *Judicial reference*:	—the *ratio* of a case as expressly formulated and authoritatively interpreted by the prior court;
(2) *Judicial legislation*:	—the *ratio* of a case as expressly formulated by the prior court;
(3) *Judicial exegesis*:	—the *ratio* of a case as later reconstructed from the normative and/or factual reasoning premises of the decision;
(4) *Judicial analogy*:	—the *ratio* of a case as analogically extended to cover also the facts of the subsequent case, or as cut down in scope by distinguishing the two cases on some factual ground;

(5) *Systemic construction*: —the *ratio* of a case as later constructed from the underlying reasons of the prior decision or line of decisions, thereby giving effect to Dworkin's idea of the *best constructive interpretation of past legal decisions*;

(6) *Judicial revaluation*: —the *ratio* of a case as more or less radically revaluated or reinterpreted by the subsequent court.

2. DEONTIC MODE: DEGREE OF LEGAL FORMALITY INVOLVED

The degree of legal formality entailed in the *ratio* of a case is high in the absolutely bound reference model and the strongly binding quasi-legislative model of precedent ideology, giving effect to a fully *conclusive legal rule*. The degree of legal formality is low in the revalued reasons ideology, giving effect to an *outweighable legal principle* or *legal policy*. Between these two end poles of high and low legal formality, there extends the mid-domain of a mixed level of legal formality, giving effect to a *weak, defeasible legal rule* in the reinterpreted rule ideology, and a *highly persuasive legal standard* in the binding reasons ideology. In the substantive and entirely free ideologies of judicial adjudication, there is no degree of legal formality acknowledged, while the openly value-rational or goal-rational premises of adjudication are held to be decisive. Figure 2 in chapter 2 above (on page 61) represents the deontic mode of the *ratio* of a case, or the degree of legal formality involved in the *ratio* of a case, in a concise manner.

3. SYSTEMIC STATICS OF PRECEDENT-FOLLOWING: DEGREE OF SYSTEMATICITY IN A SET OF PRECEDENTS

All the models of precedent ideology presented, except for the underlying reasons model, are essentially casuistic as to their static systemic structure. The reasons thereto vary from the contingencies of piecemeal judicial legislation and judicial exegesis or the inherent limits of case-to-case reasoning to the prominent role played by socio-legal consequences in precedent-based legal adjudication. In the absence of any specific legal systemic constraints to the contrary effect, the end result of case-law adjudication is bound to be rather casuistic in kind. Only the underlying reasons model strives towards the construction of a *seamless web of reasons* in law, in the sense of attaining a high level of legal systematicity.

4. SYSTEMIC DYNAMICS OF PRECEDENT-FOLLOWING

4.1 Systemic dynamics, I: legal source doctrine and other factors which exert influence on the binding force of the *ratio* of a case

The ideological context of precedent-following provided by the *legal source doctrine* is a legal systemic modifier which sets the higher and lower limits of the binding force that the *ratio* of a case may legitimately have in a legal system. The constraining effect of the prevalent source doctrine on the subsequent court's legal discretion may be called the *transcategorical* argument[1] or context of precedent-following, since it transcends or precedes the various categories of precedent ideology. By force of the prevalent legal source doctrine—or, in other words, the transcategorical context of precedent-identification and precedent-following—the binding force accorded to a precedent may vary to a great extent in various legal systems, despite the fact that a formally similar conception of precedent ideology may have been adopted in each.

The following four-level classification was utilised by the *Bielefelder Kreis vis-à-vis* the binding force of a precedent:

"(1) *Formal bindingness*: a judgment not respecting a precedent's bindingness is not lawful and so is subject to reversal on appeal. Distinguish:
   (a) formal bindingness not subject to overruling: (i) strictly binding—must be applied in every case, (ii) defeasibly binding—must be applied in every case unless exceptions apply (exceptions may be defined or not);
   (b) formal bindingness (with or without exceptions) that is subject to overruling or modification.

(2) *Not formally binding but having force*: a judgment not respecting a precedent's force, though lawful, is subject to criticism on this ground, and may be subject to reversal on this ground. Distinguish:
   (a) defeasible force—should be applied unless exceptions come into play (exceptions may or may not be well defined);
   (b) outweighable force—should be applied unless countervailing reasons apply.

(3) *Not formally binding and not having force (as defined in (2)) but providing further support*: a judgment lacking this is still lawful and may still be justified, but not as well justified as it would be if the precedent were invoked, for example, to show that the decision being reached harmonises with the precedent.

(4) *Mere illustrativeness of other value.*"[2]

[1] On another type of transcategorical argument, see D.N. MacCormick and R.S. Summers, "Interpretation and Justification", in D.N. MacCormick and R.S. Summers (eds), *Interpreting Statutes: A Comparative Study* (Dartmouth, 1991), 515, 522–5, where such an argument was employed with reference to legislative intention, in the sense of providing the final ground of statutory interpretation.

[2] D.N. MacCormick and R.S. Summers, *Interpreting Precedents: A Comparative Study* (Ashgate/Dartmouth, 1997), 554–5. The fourth category of "mere illustrativeness or other value" does not seem indispensable, and it might well be included in the third category of "not formally binding and not having force but providing further support". See also Peczenik's remarks in "The Binding Force of Precedent", in ibid., 461–517, esp. 463–4, where the classification is further explicated.

In some common law courts and in the German Federal Constitutional Court, the binding force of a precedent belongs to the category of strictly binding or mandatory force.[3] In most civil law systems, however, the legitimate binding force of a precedent is restricted to the category of mere persuasiveness only, placed under the third category of "not formally binding but having force" in the classification used by the *Bielefelder Kreis*.

Apart from the source doctrinal frame of adjudication, there are at least four other kinds of external determinants which have bearing on the binding force of a precedent (see Figure 3).

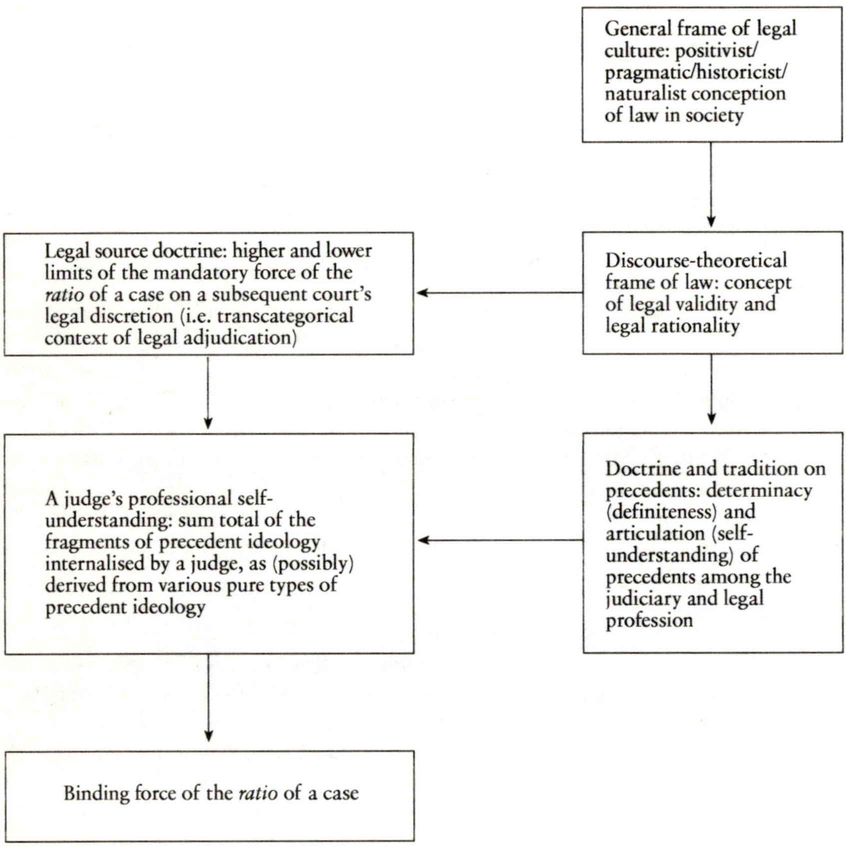

Figure 3: Legal systemic constraints on the binding force of a precedent

[3] With respect to the German Federal Constitutional Court, see R. Alexy and R. Dreier, "Precedent in the Federal Republic of Germany", in MacCormick and Summers, above at n. 2, 26–7. The status of the rulings of the Spanish Constitutional Court is slightly contested in this respect. See A. Ruiz Miguel and F. Laporta, "Precedent in Spain", in MacCormick and Summers, above at n. 2, 272.

The binding force of the *ratio* of a case on the subsequent court's legal discretion is determined, first, by the judge's understanding of *how to read precedents*, i.e. his professional self-understanding of the *precedent ideology*. The sum total of a judge's precedent-ideology is itself framed by two factors. First, the prevalent *legal source doctrine* sets the higher and lower limits of a precedent's legitimate binding force in the legal system concerned, providing for the transcategorical context of the *ratio* of a case, as was argued above. Moreover, the existence of a constant trend or continuous and permanent practice of the courts in precedent-following may strengthen the binding force of a line of precedents.[4] Secondly, the determinacy and articulation of the *doctrine and tradition on precedents* is equal to the judges' and other lawyers' professional understanding of the role and function of precedents in judicial adjudication.

If the prevailing doctrine and tradition on precedents is no more than weakly articulated among the judiciary and the legal profession, there will be no proper insight gained into the potentials and, even more so, inherent limitations of precedent-based reasoning. In consequence, the conception of the *ratio* of a case, and the binding force it may legitimately have on a subsequent court's discretion, will be relatively loosely drawn, leaving room for divergent, mutually inconsistent conceptions of how to read and utilise precedents in judicial adjudication. If, on the other hand, the doctrine and tradition on precedents is articulated in an adequate manner, based on a self-reflected idea of the identification and reading of the *ratio* of a case among the judiciary, the doctrinal constraints on the use of precedents are relatively sharp-edged, lending support to a more-or-less uniform conception of precedent-following in society. The judicial experience drawn from Finland, Italy and France exemplifies a situation where the doctrine and tradition on precedents is only weakly articulated. In the United Kingdom, in contrast, there is a relatively well-developed and well-articulated doctrine and tradition on precedents, as illustrated in the multi-faceted discourse on "why cases have *rationes* and what these are". In the United States (State of New York), the degree of articulation may be compared to the other common law system included in the *Bielefelder Kreis* study, i.e. the United Kingdom. However, the American system of adjudication is far more difficult to classify due to its vast internal divergence and highly pragmatics-laden undertone.

The *discourse-theoretical frame* of law, as reflected and concretised in the legal source doctrine, and the degree of precision and articulation of the doctrine and tradition on precedents among the judiciary, lay down the axiomatic postulates of legal validity and legal rationality in a legal system. Finally, the discourse-theoretical frame of law is itself framed by the frame of *legal culture* and the

[4] On "*jurisprudence constante*" in France, see M. Troper and C. Grzegorczyk, "Precedent in France", in MacCormick and Summers, above at n. 2, 128, 130 *in fine*; on "*giurisprudenza costante*" or "*giurisprudenza consolidata*" in Italy, see M. Taruffo and M. La Torre, "Precedent in Italy", in MacCormick and Summers, above at n. 2, 160–1, 172–4; and on "*ständige Rechtsprechung*" in the German system of adjudication, see Alexy and Dreier, above at n. 3, 50–1.

specific conception of law entailed therein. The very concept of law may, accordingly, be defined in terms of the basic categories of, e.g., legal positivism, legal realism, legal historicism, or natural law theory.

4.2 Systemic dynamics, II: degree of binding force of the *ratio* of a case

In judicial reference ideology, the binding force of the *ratio* of a case is absolute, depriving the subsequent court of any powers of discretion as to its meaning-content. In the judicial hunch model of adjudication, on the other hand, no binding force whatever is attached to the prior case, leaving the subsequent court with unlimited free discretion. The conceptual space between these two extreme ideologies is occupied by the six ideologies of legal and rational judicial decision-making, using Wróblewski's terminology, even though the exact classification of judicial legislation and the substantive approach to adjudication proved to be somewhat conventional in that respect, as was argued in chapter 3 at 2.2 above. In judicial legislation, the *ratio* of a case is given in a final form by the prior court, but the act of interpretation, in the sense of drawing the logical consequences out of the *ratio* of the case, is entrusted to the subsequent court and is not withheld at the norm-issuing authority. Thus, there may be a narrow field of free discretion left to be specified by the later court. In the substantive models of adjudication, on the other hand, the binding force of the *ratio* of a case is non-existent, since the outcome of the subsequent case is to be determined by recourse to some extra-legal, non-formalised criteria of either axiological or teleological kind.

Realignment of the *ratio* on a strict case-to-case basis, reflecting the constant interplay of judicial analogy and distinguishing, gives effect to a "balanced" level of the binding force of the precedent. In other words, the *ratio* of a case is regarded as a model rule, a paradigm case, or a set of model reasons to be followed analogically in subsequent legal adjudication. However, the later evaluation of the existence of a legally relevant similarity or dissimilarity in the facts of the two cases has the effect of weakening the binding force of the *ratio*, if compared with the ideologies of judicial legislation or judicial exegesis. In judicial reality, however, the degree of such binding force may vary to a considerable extent, depending on the transcategorical context of precedent-following adopted in the legal system in question. The characterisation of the underlying reasons approach to precedents is not entirely unproblematic in this respect. The binding force of a prior case or line of cases is weak, but there are still systemic constraints which exert a relatively strong impact on the subsequent court's discretion. The Dworkin-inspired approach might be likened to the ideology of judicial analogy as far as the binding force of the *ratio* of a case is concerned. In the "law in action", however, the degree of such binding effect may vary greatly, in accordance with the particular conception of legal systematicity and legal coherence adopted by the judiciary.

The idea of retracing the prior court's original intentions from the normative and/or factual premises of a case in judicial exegesis has the effect of increasing the binding force of the *ratio*, while the reconstructive elements involved in such precedent-following will make the binding force of the *ratio* fall below the level sustained in the ideology of judicial legislation. In the prececent ideology based on a more-or-less radical revaluation of the prior decision, on the other hand, the subsequent court notably enjoys wide legal discretion, as the *ratio* is always subject to be reconsidered in light of the facts of the new case. The binding force of the *ratio* of a case is, accordingly, weak.

5. METHOD OF ARGUMENTATION ADOPTED IN A PRECEDENT IDEOLOGY

The method of argumentation adopted in a precedent ideology is intertwined with the conception of legal semantics. Full semantic *predetermination* is effected under judicial reference ideology, while semantic *freeplay* is effected under judicial hunch ideology. Semantic *overdetermination* is effected under judicial legislation ideology, while semantic *underdetermination* is effected under judicial revaluation ideology. The ideologies of judicial exegesis and judicial analogy may be placed in-between semantic overdetermination and semantic underdetermination, since the specific meaning-content attached to the *ratio* of a case is defined by the mutual co-effort of the two courts involved. Systemic construction of the *ratio* of a case from the underlying reasons of a prior case or line of cases is semantically conditioned by the "deeper" rationale or latent signification structure beneath the manifest precedent-norm and/or reasons formulation. Moreover, a predominantly *past-oriented* conception of legal interpretation is adopted in the ideologies based on judicial reference, judicial legislation and judicial exegesis, while a predominantly *future-oriented* conception of legal interpretation is adopted in judicial revaluation ideology. The Levian analogical and the Dworkinian systemic approaches to precedent-following are placed between the past-oriented and the future-oriented alternatives in this respect.[5]

As to the method of argumentation adopted, the reference ideology adheres to a "literalist" reading of the *ratio* of a case, assigning all legal discretion to the prior court. In judicial legislation, the subsequent court is thought merely to unfold the logical consequences of the abstractly formulated *ratio* of a case, as laid down in express terms by the prior court. Under such theoretical premises, all legal argumentation more or less follows the pattern of statutory interpretation, where the abstract legal norm of either statutory or precedential origin functions as the general clause of the logical syllogism. In judicial exegesis, the key idea of legal argumentation is to retrace the authentic meaning-content of

[5] On Dworkin's own account of the time dimension in the law as integrity approach, see R. Dworkin, *Law's Empire* (Fontana Masterguides, 1986), 225.

the *ratio* of a case, in the sense of the original intentions of the prior court. In judicial analogy, the method of legal reasoning is based on the constant interplay of fact-based analogy and distinguishing where the *ratio* of a case is left "free-floating", to be extended analogically to cover the facts of the new case or, alternatively, cut down by distinguishing the two cases on factual grounds. In the underlying reasons model of precedent-following, the method of legal argumentation is based on *the best constructive interpretation of past legal decisions*,[6] in the sense of a systemic-constructive reading of prior case-law as constrained by the criteria of legal coherence. The ideology of judicial revaluation gives effect to a dynamic, future-oriented and highly malleable notion of legal argumentation, where the relative merits and shortcomings of the prior decision are thoroughly revalued in light of the facts of the new case.

In the substantive models of judicial adjudication, the method of argumentation is finalistic, teleological and goal-oriented, if the theoretical premises of judicial consequentialism are adopted, or axiological and value-bound, if the theoretical premises of the rightness reasons approach to adjudication are instead opted for. In the approach based on a judge's intuitive hunch, the "method" of argumentation, if the term is used in a somewhat Pickwickian sense here, is based on sheer methodological anarchism as envisioned by Paul Feyerabend, now adjusted to the reading of precedents.

The array of methods of reading the *ratio* of a case covers the conceptual extension from Montesquieu-inspired strict literalism (*judicial reference*), deductive reasoning (*judicial legislation*), backward-proceeding reasoning from the outcome of a prior case to the normative and/or factual premises entailed in it (*judicial exegesis*), a constant interplay of analogy and distinguishing on the basis of factual similarity and dissimilarity in the two or more cases involved (*jucicial analogy*), and systemic-constructive reading of the line of prior cases in light of the "deeper" rationale involved (*underlying reasons model*) to a dynamic re-reading of the merits of the prior case in light of the novel case at hand (*judicial revaluation*).

6. TECHNIQUES OF DEPARTURE FROM A PRECEDENT

The legitimate *techniques of departure* from a valid precedent tend to become more relaxed as the binding force of the *ratio* of a case decreases. Express *overruling* of the *ratio* is acknowledged under all the precedent ideologies, except the ideologies of judicial reference and (partly) judicial legislation. In judicial legislation, the act of overruling a precedent is allowed only to the prior court which initially laid down the *ratio* of the case. In judicial revaluation, on the other hand, express overruling of a precedent is the routine course of action, unless some other technique of evading the binding effect of a prior decision is opted for.

[6] Dworkin, ibid., 262.

Defeasibility,[7] i.e. the act of defeating a valid precedent rule by making an exception to it, is acknowledged in all approaches to precedent-following where the *ratio* of a case is defined as a legal rule, rather than a legal principle, and where the binding force of a precedent is less than absolutely or strictly binding. In other words, the ideologies of judicial reference and judicial legislation are ruled out in this respect. *Outweighability*, i.e. the act of disregarding a legal principle (or legal policy) because of the argumentative impact of some strong enough countervailing reasons, is restricted to those models of precedent ideology where the *ratio* of a case is defined as a legal principle, rather than a legal rule, and where the binding force of a precedent is less than absolutely or strictly binding. Thus, the two ideologies of judicial reference and judicial legislation are excluded from such considerations. In the judicial hunch ideology and the two substantive models of axiological and teleological kind there is, of course, no need for any specific techniques of departure from a prior decision, since no effect of *stare decisis* is acknowledged in them in the first place.

7. THEORETICAL RATIONALE OF A PRECEDENT IDEOLOGY

The six categories of precedent ideology and the three models of judicial ideology may be collected under the auspices of four or six groups as to their theoretical background rationale: (1) *judicial positivism*, (2) *legal realism* or *pragmatic instrumentalism*, (3) *historical school of law* or *legal historicism*, and (4) *natural law theory*. As a fifth category, (5) *free law movement* might be discerned, with reference to the judicial hunch ideology, unless it is classified as an extreme case of legal realism. In a similar manner, a sixth term, (6) *Montesquieu'ean orthodoxy*, might be used for the judicial reference ideology, when viewed from the subsequent court's (and not the prior court's) point of view, unless it is classified as an extreme case of judicial positivism.

The "organic" development of case-law in England and in the United States may be read in light of the specific doctrine of law professed by the historical school of law. Thus, the notion of case-law as a *moving classification system*, as Levi described the gradual unfolding of judge-made law in the United States and England in the sense of a constant interplay of fact-based analogy and distinguishing, would match the evolvement of legal ideas under the *historicist* frame of analysis.

The Dworkin-inspired underlying reasons model of precedent ideology is somewhat selective as to its theoretical background rationale. The idea of "the best constructive interpretation of past legal decisions" and the requirement of "institutional support" extended to legal principles notably evade any positivist standards of law-identification, whether of Hartian or any other origin. Instead,

7 On the notion of defeasibility in argumentation, see N. MacCormick, "Defeasibility in Law and Logic", in Z. Bankowski, I. White and U. Hahn (eds), *Informatics and the Foundations of Legal Reasoning* (Kluwer, 1995), 99; and G. Sartor, "Defeasibility in Legal Reasoning", in ibid. 119.

such a historically and culturally laden conception of law ought to be read in light of the basic ideas of the historical school of law. However, certain tenets of legal positivism and natural law theory can be detected in the Dworkinian *law as integrity* doctrine. The frame of adjudication is said to be determined by the line of past political and legal decisions, and not (it is hoped) the timeless and utopian visions of a judge's social imagery. Such tenets no doubt signify the impact of at least weakly positivist elements in Dworkin's conception of law. The resulting historicist and positivist frame of analysis is, however, modified by the essentially systemic elements of legal argumentation. The idea of constructing and enforcing a *seamless web of underlying reasons* of law, laden with a certain *sense of appropriateness* or having roots in the *soundest political theory* in society, can be taken as allusions to natural law theory. In all, the Dworkinian theory of law might be described as a historicist account of the constitutive premises of legal adjudication, as further modified by certain tenets drawn from a weakly positivist and a moderately natural law oriented conception of law, respectively.

The ideological variants of judicial legislation and judicial exegesis instantiate different forms of *judicial positivism* where the *ratio* of a case is defined by reference to the formal norm-giving power of the prior court. In the stronger version of judicial positivism, the *ratio* of a case is given in an express norm-formulation by the prior court; while in the weaker version of positivism, the *ratio* of a case must be reconstructed from the normative and/or factual premises of the prior decision. Judicial positivism is, of course, a subcategory of legal positivism, as exemplified by the various writings of Austin, Kelsen, and Hart, among others. The judicial reference model may be taken as an extreme instance of the positivist ideology of adjudication. When seen from the subsequent court's point of view, it might also be labelled as an example of a *Montesquieu'ean orthodoxy*.

The influence of *pragmatic instrumentalism* or *American legal realism* extends from the ideology of judicial revaluation through openly goal-oriented judicial consequentialism to the semantic freeplay or free-floating intuition of the judicial hunch model of adjudication. The scholars identified with the realist movement crossed the thin line between the nominally legal frame of reference of judicial revaluation ideology and the openly extra-legal frame of judicial consequentialism, rightness reasons in adjudication, and judicial hunch ideology, without any major difficulties. Thus, Oliphant and Llewellyn, classified as "robust predictivists" by Summers, argued that the premises for predicting the outcome of future adjudication might include—apart from legal rules—anything that might have an impact on a judge's discretion, e.g.: the past examples of judicial behaviour; the ideas induced by the "raw" facts of the case; plus the personality, ideologies, social background and personal values of the judge himself.[8] The judicial hunch model could be classified as an extreme case of such

[8] R.S. Summers, *Instrumentalism and American Legal Theory* (Cornell University Press, 1982), 118, 143–4.

pragmatic instrumentalism, or as an instance of the *Free Law Movement*, with reference to the ideas professed by Geny, Ehrlich and Kantorowicz, among others. In the rightness reasons approach to legal adjudication, the outcome of judicial decision-making is, of course, determined by the judge's conception of social justice and social fairness, grounded on the essentially non-positivist premises of natural law theory.

5

Theory and Practice of Precedent-Following

Below, some illustrative examples will be given of the precedent ideology adopted in the highest courts of justice of the six legal systems chosen for the purpose. I do not intend to enter too deeply into the domain of such legal comparison, since that task has already been accomplished by, for example, the international research group *Bielefelder Kreis*. The aim of the comparison is far more modest, i.e. to prove the theoretical fecundity of the modelling approach and the relevance of the outcomes thereby reached for the law in action in precedent-following. The legal systems selected for the comparison are as follows: United States (State of New York), United Kingdom, France, Italy, Federal Republic of Germany, and Finland. The source material will be drawn mainly from *Interpreting Precedents: A Comparative Study*, i.e. the study on precedents conducted by the *Bielefelder Kreis*. The precedent ideology acknowledged by the Finnish Supreme Court of Justice will be analysed in more detail, since it neatly illustrates the perplexities induced by a less-than-fully self-reflected conception of precedent-identification and precedent-following on the part of judges. I will also argue that the leading scholarly stance towards precedents in Finland cannot find adequate support in the normative premises found in the prevalent legal source doctrine, other legal literature and the current professional understanding of the justices of the Supreme Court.

1. JUDICIAL EXEGESIS WITH FORMALLY DEFINED *RATIO DECIDENDI* (UNITED KINGDOM)

Due to its basic common law orientation, precedents have a key role in judicial adjudication and legal argumentation in the United Kingdom. Precedents are commonly used as important legal source material. Moreover, their strongly binding, mandatory effect on subsequent adjudication is acknowledged on the condition that the prior decision was given by a hierarchically higher, or the highest, court in the country. If that is not the case, the prior decision may still be endowed with persuasive binding force.[1] Judges in the United Kingdom do

[1] Z. Bankowski, D.N. MacCormick and G. Marshall, "Precedent in the United Kingdom", in D.N. MacCormick and R.S. Summers, *Interpreting Precedents: A Comparative Study* (Ashgate/Dartmouth, 1997), 325–7.

not often seek to lay down some explicit *ratio decidendi* of a case. There is always an elaborate set of reasons given in support of the outcome reached, providing the subsequent court with plenty of normative material to draw upon. The fact-description of a prior court decision is, in other words, usually rich and detailed enough to enable the subsequent court to "read the decision backwards", i.e. from the outcome reached in the prior case to the normative and factual premises of that decision.[2] The subsequent court may thus reconstruct the prior court's reasoning from the normative and factual premises set out in the decision. Sometimes the prior court may be concerned about "what sort of precedent the decision might make for future cases", as in *MacLellan* v. *MacLellan*,[3] the case concerning artificial insemination by a donor.

If the fact-description of a prior case is outlined in highly abstract and laconic terms, as in the French or Italian system of legal adjudication,[4] subsequent courts will have no access to the proven facts of the prior case, and the legal qualification given to those facts by the prior court will be the only point of reference for all subsequent reasoning based on that decision. In constrast, a relatively detailed fact-description, as provided by the English courts, will provide subsequent judges with sufficient information to use the specific techniques of judicial exegesis or reasoning by analogy/distinguishing, provided the argumentative skills of *how to read precedents* are adequately mastered by judges and other members of the legal profession.[5]

Despite the formalistic overtone of the system of precedents in the United Kingdom, the discursive rather than openly deductive mode of reasoning prevails. Very occasionally, the syllogistic form is said to occur.[6] The formal characteristics of precedent-following in the legal system of the United Kingdom, in stark contrast to the far more flexible and pragmatic system of precedents in the United States, may be partly explained by the assurance of legislative intervention by Parliament if the outcome of jurisdiction proves to be unsatisfactory.[7] The authors cite Lord Reid in *R.* v. *Knuller (Publishing, Printing and Promotions Ltd.)* [1973] A.C. 753, in favour of a formal doctrine of *stare decisis*: ". . . however wrong or anomalous the decision may be, it must stand and apply to future cases unless or until it is altered by parliament". In recent years, such a strict adherence to judicial formalism has declined, the authors conclude. The Practice Statement in 1966 has had a similar effect on adjudication, loosening the doctrine of formal *stare decisis* and authorising the House of Lords, "while treating former decisions of this House as normally binding, to depart

[2] Ibid., 322.

[3] Ibid., 323, 325.

[4] M. Troper and C. Grzegorczyk, "Precedent in France", in MacCormick and Summers, above at n. 1, 107; M. Taruffo and M. La Torre, "Precedent in Italy", in ibid., 146–51.

[5] In the United Kingdom (and the United States) this should cause no difficulties, due to the centuries-old tradition of "how to read precedents". See Bankowski, MacCormick and Marshall, above at n. 1, 324.

[6] Ibid., 319–20.

[7] Ibid., 348.

from a previous decision when it appears right to do so".[8] There is no clear-cut division between rules, principles, and values or policies in judicial decisions, although legal rules are said to come first.[9]

A remarkable portion of legal literature is dedicated to the question of how to distinguish the normatively binding *ratio decidendi* from *obiter dicta*, or the argumentative context of the *ratio*, in a case. The various definitions of the *ratio* of a case, as put forth by for instance Cross (and Harris), Simpson, Goodhart and MacCormick, is an indication of the existence of a strong doctrine and tradition of precedents in the United Kingdom.[10] Cross' and MacCormick's definitions of the *ratio* of a case were classified under the rule-based variant of judicial exegesis above, while Goodhart chose to place the emphasis on the material facts of a prior case. Thus, the system of precedents in the United Kingdom would seem to bear closest affinity to the ideology of *judicial exegesis*, with occasional elements drawn from the ideology of *judicial legislation* on such occasions where the prior court consciously intends to put forth a rule to be followed in future legal adjudication.

2. A FLEXIBLE SYSTEM OF SUBSTANTIVE RULES UNDER LEGAL PRAGMATISM (UNITED STATES/STATE OF NEW YORK)

Because of the inevitable diversity of the vast case-law material produced each year in the various courts of the 50 American states and in the federal system of jurisdiction, the American experience of precedents and precedent-following cannot be reduced to a single catchword or one particular type of precedent ideology without inducing serious flaw and distortion of the source material. In the broadest terms, however, the system of precedents in the United States, like the American legal culture in general, might be described as being significantly less formal than the system of adjudication in the United Kingdom.[11]

Atiyah and Summers have discerned seven key differences in the use of precedents in the two common law systems.[12] First, American judges have a more extensive power to disregard a valid precedent than English judges. A departure

[8] R. Cross and J.W. Harris, *Precedent in English Law* (Clarendon Press, Oxford, 4th ed. 1991), 104–8. The Practice Statement is cited in ibid., 104.

[9] "Rules come first, but these are bedded in grounds of principle and, when appropriate, substantive elements of value or policy. Again the discursive nature of the opinions and often their length (though one might say that in general they are extended rather than elaborate) makes it difficult to separate out rules, principles, and policies": Bankowski, MacCormick and Marshall, above at n. 1, 319.

[10] Ibid., 337–8.

[11] See P.S. Atiyah and R.S. Summers, *Form and Substance in Anglo-American Law: A Comparative Study of Legal Reasoning, Legal Theory, and Legal Institutions* (Clarendon Press, Oxford, 1987), esp. 118–33, where the doctrine of *stare decisis* is considered in the two legal systems.

[12] The list of distinguishing features between the American judge and his English colleague in the context of precedent-following is given in ibid.,120–7.

from a valid precedent may occur on substantive grounds, on the basis of institutional reasons such as the absence of a clear *ratio decidendi* in a "plurality opinion" of a court, or in a situaton where anticipatory overruling may legitimately be used. Second, American judges have relatively more power in openly overruling a precedent. Third, American judges are more likely to evade the binding effect of a formally valid precedent by, for example, excessive distinguishing, i.e. confining the *ratio* of a case to the particular facts of that case, or by simply ignoring a precedent.

Fourth, the operative definition of the *ratio decidendi* is more formal in the United Kingdom, while in the United States the holding of a case is conceived of in more substantive terms, in the sense of the reasons or rationale for the decision made. As Llewellyn wrote, "the rule follows where its reason leads; where the reason stops, there stops the rule."[13] Atiyah and Summers even put forth the argument that the conception of a legal rule is different in the two legal systems: a substantive or reasons-oriented notion of a rule is prevalent in the United States, while a more formal conception is acknowledged in the United Kingdom.[14] Fifth, English judges are more likely to take recourse to "synthesizing" a line of precedents into a concise *ratio*, or an abstracted rule, while their American colleagues are less likely to aim at such a synthesis. Sixth, the binding force or weight of a precedent is generally lower in the American legal system, in comparison with its English counterpart. Finally, English judges are more prone to follow precedents which are endowed with no more than persuasive binding force than American judges.

Atiyah and Summers described the general features of precedent-following in relatively broad terms, as part of their insight into the similar and differentiating features of the two common law systems. The research group *Bielefelder Kreis*, on the other hand, focused its inquiry on the use of precedents only in its legal comparative study, and the results are therefore given in more specific terms. Yet, because of the vast volume of relevant case-law material available in the United States, Summers concentrated only on the judicial practice of the New York Court of Appeals.

The role of precedents in the United States (State of New York) varies in the different branches of law. If there is no statutory law on the issue, as is the situation in contract law, tort law and property law in New York, precedents are said to have decisive importance in legal decision-making.[15] In general, precedents are frequently cited and discussed in court opinions, and may also be used

[13] K. Llewellyn, *The Bramble Bush: On Our Law and Its Study* (Oceana Publications, New York, 1991), 189; quoted also in Atiyah and Summers, above at n. 11, 88.

[14] Atiyah and Summers, ibid., 88–93. With regard to the rule conception, the determination of the *ratio decidendi* of a case and the authoritative or binding force of precedents, Summers (and Atiyah) draw on arguments initially put forth by the American Realists, such as Pound, Llewellyn, and Radin. See ibid., 88, nn. 56, 57, 125, n. 37, and 126, nn. 44, 46. Thereby, the originally critical impact of the three 'pragmatic instrumentalists' is turned into part of the mainstream legal doctrine.

[15] R.S. Summers, "Precedent in the United States (New York State)", in MacCormick and Summers, above at n. 1, 365.

as supportive arguments in the context of statutory interpretation. The style of reasoning of the New York Court of Appeals is openly argumentative, rather than deductive, although the existence of one right answer to a legal dispute is often said to be presumed.[16]

What draws the system of precedents in the United States most strikingly apart from the system of law in the United Kingdom is the importance given to substantive reasons of principle or policy, on side with the formal, legalistic or precedent-based arguments, especially in "cases of first impression" but also in other situations where the rule extracted from a precedent is found to be inadequate.[17] An American judge is not likely to stay passive and wait for the legislator to settle the issue, since a recourse to the "fundamental principles of [American] jurisprudence", in the sense of comprising the formal and non-formal criteria of decision-making, is always open to him. In effect, such a direct reference to social values and goals, raised on a level which is equal to, or only slightly below, the formal criteria of legality and the doctrine of formal *stare decisis* denotes a clear concession made to the *substantive* approach in judicial adjudication.

The (subsequent) court is said to have a duty to "re-examine the precedents and bring them in line with current social realities", and to adjust the laws from time to time.[18] Such a practice of "adapting and altering" a precedent, with an eye on the needs of the new context of adjudication, is in perfect accord with *judicial revaluation* of the relative merits of the prior case. Apart from the pragmatic and instrumentalist credo of the Legal Realists which was analysed above, the words of Justice Frankfurter lend support to such a judicial realignment of cases: "*stare decisis* is a principle of policy and not a mechanical formula of adherence to the latest decision, however recent and questionable".[19]

The standard role of precedents, however, as argued by Levi in *An Introduction to Legal Reasoning*, is to provide legally relevant arguments for the subsequent court in case-by-case reasoning, where the two argumentative strategies of analogy and distinguishing are always available for a judge.[20] A

[16] Ibid., 361. Yet, the adoption of the syllogistic model of reasoning has been frequently associated with the one right answer in continental Europe, while the openly argumentative, *pro et contra* type of justification is thought to endorse a more relaxed position in this respect.

[17] Ibid., 361, 366–8. At 361 Summers notes: "the style [of reasoning of the New York Court of Appeals] is often as substantive as it is legalistic. That is, the court will often give substantive reasons of policy or principle, as well as cite binding precedent".

[18] Ibid., 374.

[19] Quoted in ibid., 375. The citation was included in *People* v. *Bing*, 76 N.Y. 2nd 338 (1990), where the court also stated: "Precedents remain precedents, however, not because they are established but because they serve the underlying 'nature and object of the law itself', reason and the power to advance justice. . . . Although a court should be slow to overrule its precedents, there is little reason to avoid doing so when persuaded by the 'lessons of experience and the force of better reasoning' ".

[20] E.H. Levi, *An Introduction to Legal Reasoning* (Chicago University Press, 1994). Cf.: "In particular, the court will frequently refer to one or more precedents relied on by counsel in support of their respective arguments and will state whether or not the precedents are being followed or whether they are distinguishable from the case under consideration. Closely intertwined with the

leading case, in particular, may exert normative influence far beyond the semantic confines of the original ruling.[21] The said conception of precedents matches perfectly with the *analogical* approach to precedent-following.

The idea of extracting a holding from a prior case where it was left more or less implicit by the prior court[22] would seem to bear some obvious affinity to the reconstructive, backward-proceeding mode of reasoning, or "inference to the best explanation", held to be prevalent under *judicial exegesis*. However, the idea of a reconstructive reading of a prior case is much weaker in the United States than in the more formally framed system of precedent-following in the United Kingdom. Finally, some elements of openly future-oriented *judicial legislation* may be seen in those cases where the prior court lays down some general rule to be followed by subsequent courts. Such an approach is usually applicable in those cases where there are no statutory provisions available, and, as such, the courts need to compensate for the legislator's passivity.[23]

Thus, the system of precedents in the United States (State of New York) cannot be classified under any one particular type of precedent ideology. Instead, it entails elements drawn from the substantive, revaluative, analogical and, to some extent, even exegetical and legislative approaches to precedents. In addition, even within one particular court of justice, such as the New York Court of Appeals analysed by Summers, there may be totally opposing ideologies of precedent-following prevalent among the judges. Summers points out that for many judges, precedents offer no more than a set of substantive reasons which are then to be weighed against other policies or principles available. For some judges, on the other hand, the binding force of a precedent is almost equal to the much stronger conception of the *ratio* of a case adhered to in the United Kingdom, with the implication that precedents ought to be followed, except in the "most compelling circumstances".[24]

However, the decisive impact of *legal pragmatism* may be taken as the predominant or most typical feature of the American experience on precedents, signifying a clear deviation from the positivist-exegetical frame of adjudication and the adherence to a formal conception of *stare decisis* in the United Kingdom. The American response to precedents is, accordingly, captured by the *analogical* approach to precedent-following, as modified by a pragmatic recourse to the ideas of *judicial revaluation* and the *substantive* reasons behind the initial ruling of a case, with an occasional recourse to the more formal tenets of *judicial exegesis* or *judicial legislation*.

court's discussion on precedent will be the court's rationales or reasons for its ruling": Summers, above at n. 15, 360. See also ibid., 387–88, where illustrative examples of the use of analogy and distinguishing are given.

[21] Summers, ibid., 389–90.

[22] Ibid., 384.

[23] Ibid., 378–9, 383–4. "Sometimes the court will *explicitly state* the holding on an issue quite broadly": ibid., 383 (emphasis in original).

[24] Ibid., 379–83.

3. DIVERGENCE OF OFFICIAL ACTION AND PROFESSIONAL SELF-UNDERSTANDING OF THE JUDICIARY (FRANCE)

The system of precedents is France is characterised by a curious divergence of the officially expounded ideology of adjudication and the judges' own professional self-understanding of their role in judicial adjudication. According to the official ideology, the courts are not allowed to profess their power to create precedents openly, and the creation of new rules in adjudication is presented, or rather disguised, as an act of interpreting pre-existing statutory norms.[25] Precedents are very rarely cited in express judicial argumentation; but they are frequently used as a highly relevant, or even the most important, legal source by judges.[26] Needless to say, precedents lack any kind of formal binding force on the subsequent court's discretion, and a reference to a prior case, if given as an exclusive ground for a judicial decision, would render the decision "not motivated and illegal", under Article 455 of the French Code of Civil Procedure.[27]

Although their true impact on adjudication is concealed by the outward legal argumentation displayed to the litigants in a case and the public at large, precedents are frequently utilised in actual court practice in France, and there even exists a weak, *de facto* obligation to follow the decisions of hierarchically higher courts. Thus, the *de jure* prohibition on the use of precedents is accompanied by a perfectly contradictory *de facto* obligation to follow precedents which have been laid down by the higher courts.[28]

The French style of judicial reasoning has been described as deductive, legalistic and magisterial,[29] due to the intellectual legacy of the French Revolution and the great volume of cases in the highest courts in France.[30] A decision is a combination of the *motif* and the *dispositif*, or the reasons for the decision and the operative ruling on the facts of the case, respectively. The main part of the *motif* is a statement of the general rule applied to the case, and it is often no more than a mere (re)formulation or restatement of a statutory provision.[31] In line with the terse and laconic style of judicial reasoning, the facts of a precedent are never expressly discussed by the subsequent court, although they are, of

[25] Troper and Grzegorczyk, above at n. 4, 115. Cf. ibid., 126, 117: "The general principle at the basis of the French legal system, derived from the French interpretation of the separation of powers, is that statutes are the only source of law". French judges are expected to exercise, not judicial power proper, but a "judicial function" only: ibid., 107.

[26] Ibid., 112–13.

[27] Ibid., 115: "There is no formal bindingness of previous judicial decisions in France. One might even argue that there is an opposite rule: that it is forbidden to follow a precedent only because it is a precedent".

[28] Ibid., 118.

[29] Ibid., 107–8.

[30] In 1993, 25,000 cases were decided by the *Cour de Cassation*, while 33,000 were still pending: ibid., 105.

[31] Ibid., 107. The authors also list *mentions*, *visas* and *formule exécutoire*; or general information about the decision such as the names of the parties to the case, a list of the documents examined by the court, and the official enforcement order of the decision, respectively.

course, taken into account by it when the relevant similarity or dissimilarity of the two cases is being judged.[32]

The prohibition on making a direct reference to precedents in legal argumentation is avoided by using statutory law as the expressly given point of reference of judicial reasoning, or by using the normative content of a prior decision as such, without mentioning its source of origin in a prior court decision. At most, an allusion might be made to the *jurisprudence constante*, i.e. a constant trend in the case-law or a "continuous and permanent practice" of the courts.[33] Such an unspecified reference to a constant trend in case-law adjudication might be read as an expression of customary law which has gained recognition in the courts of justice. The binding force of a prior decision is attached, not to the decision as originally formulated by the prior court, but to the rule, principle or rationale it exemplifies.[34] In consequence, precedents function only to illustrate "deeper" legal principles, or they may be a reason for legal analogy in the French system of adjudication, where no distinction is made between the mere illustrativeness of a case and the use of legal analogy in reasoning based on precedents.[35]

The divergence of official court ideology and the judges' unfeigned professional understanding of their role in jurisdiction, or the gap between "saying" and "doing" in adjudication,[36] makes it difficult to place the French system of precedents in the present classification of precedent ideologies. As far as judicial pragmatics or the "law in action" behind outward legal argumentation is concerned, the French system of precedents would seem to have some affinity with the reasons-based *analogical* approach, i.e. the model reasons approach to precedent-following, since the point of reference of the *ratio* of a case is not the precedent rule as such, but the more general principle or rationale behind it. However, the laconic and highly formal style of argumentation is an indication of the formally acknowledged impact of *statutory positivism* even on precedent-based legal argumentation, which is thus prevalent on the level of the "law in books". Due to the lack of an openly disclosed legal argumentation *vis-à-vis* precedents in the French legal system, the exact classification of the precedent ideology internalised by French judges must, in the last resort, remain open or unclassifiable.

4. A FLOOD OF DISCORDANT PRECEDENTS UNDER MUTUALLY INCONSISTENT THEORETICAL PREMISES (ITALY)

The system of precedents in Italy is truly fascinating, endowed with some features derived from a "Borgesian" imagery, rather than from the requirements of

32 Ibid., 126, 127–8.
33 Ibid., 128, 130 *in fine*.
34 Ibid., 127, 128.
35 Ibid., 130.
36 Ibid., 137–8.

formal legal effectiveness. As in France, the highest Italian court of general jurisdiction, the *Corte di Cassazione*, has no power to select cases upon which it will then have an obligation to rule. The annual case-load is therefore enormous, with approximately 12,000 civil cases and 35,000 criminal cases being decided by approximately 400 judges in the *Corte di Cassazione* each year.[37]

The distinctive feature of the Italian system of precedents is the role given to the *Ufficio del Massimario* and the *massima* (plural: *massime*) which it extracts from the decisions given by the *Corte di Cassazione*. The *Ufficio del Massimario* is a specific institution annexed to the *Corte di Cassazione*, consisting of judges alike. However, the judges who were initially involved in making the court decision will not have a say on the exact formulation of the *massima* or *massime* which the *Ufficio del Massimario* will then extract or extrapolate from the court decision. A *massima* is a short and concise statement, usually of no more than five to ten lines, concerning the legal rule or principle of a court decision. A *massima* is detached from the original facts of the case, usually having reference only to the legal issue or issues of the case. In extremely rare cases, there may be a very short note of the facts of the case. *Pro and contra* arguments are not reproduced in the *massima*, but there may be a short reference to a justificatory argument in favour of some legal position included in the *massima*.[38]

Thus, the *massima* is frequently the only part of a ruling given by the *Corte di Cassazione* which is openly published. Since there is no access to the authentic line of reasoning, nor to the actual facts of the case concerned, the *massima* (or *massime*) will often be the only source of information on prior court decisions available to the subsequent court. Some of the highest court decisions are published at length in the Italian law journals, the extent of the report varying from the coverage of the decision in whole to a selection of legal arguments given in its support.[39] With respect to an extensively reported decision, the *ratio* of the case may subsequently be (re)constructed from the combination of the *massima*, the final outcome of the case, and the line of reasoning leading to that outcome, supplying the later courts and the legal profession with significantly more material to rely on. Similar to the legal rule stated briefly in the *motif* of a judgment of the French *Cour de Cassation*, the *massima* is frequently no more than a restatement of a statutory rule, and it may even be more general in scope than its statutory counterpart.[40]

The *massima* need not be equal to the true *ratio decidendi* of the case. Although it deals exclusively with the legal side of the issue, a *massima* may also contain elements of the *obiter dicta*, in addition to the *ratio decidendi*, of the case.[41] Therefore, it is left for the subsequent court to draw the distinction

[37] Taruffo and La Torre, above at n. 4, 144. The figures date from Taruffo's and La Torre's report from 1997.

[38] Ibid., 148–9, 150.

[39] Ibid., 168.

[40] Ibid., 183.

[41] Ibid., 148–9, 167–8, 171, 176, 183.

between the *ratio* and *dicta* elements in a case, usually with no other information at hand than a collection of short-worded and concise *massime*, cut off from their factual setting in the original legal dispute. Occasionally, there may be access to the whole set of premises of the court's reasoning, if the decision has been reported at length in an Italian law journal. As in the French legal system, the style of reasoning adopted by the *Corte di Cassazione* is structured in a series of logical deductions, proceeding from a set of premises to the "necessary" conclusions contained in the ruling of the case. The style of argumentation is, as in France, legalistic and magisterial, and not discursive or openly argumentative.[42]

Although precedents are said to be "by far the most important justificatory material" used by the Italian courts,[43] an individual precedent, or line of precedents, is endowed with no more than a *de facto* or persuasive binding force. Due to the enormous volume of precedents produced each year in Italy, the decisions given by the *Corte di Cassazione* may be conveniently collected into "lines", "chains" or "strings" of precedents.[44] Subsequent judicial adjudication and precedent-based legal argumentation may then be based on such collections of cases, instead of having recourse directly to the individual decisions. If there is a consistent line of jurisdiction, in the sense of a *giurisprudenza costante* or *giurisprudenza consolidata*, the binding force of a precedent-based argument is at its greatest in case-law adjudication.[45] The situation is similar to the French judicial system in this respect.

In actual court practice, however, the argumentative impact of an individual precedent or line of precedents is impaired by the frequent emergence of normative conflicts and other systemic defects induced by the vast overproduction of precedents. The existence of discordant, conflicting and mutually irreconcilable precedents is even said to be a common phenomenon in the Italian system of law.[46] Often, mutually inconsistent *massime* are given in support of a subsequent decision,[47] and different lines of precedents may provide support for all the conceivable outcomes in a legal dispute.[48] Nor is the *Corte di Cassazione* itself entirely free from such inconsistencies. In a study covering only five years and only such civil law judgments which were published in the twelve legal journals chosen for the study, the *Corte di Cassazione* was found to have contradicted its own rulings no less than 864 times.[49] In consequence, the binding force of a precedent, or even line of precedents, is very low, with the subsequent courts left either to choose freely between conflicting cases or to disregard them altogether.[50]

42 Taruffo and La Torre, above at n. 4, 146–8.
43 Ibid., 153.
44 Ibid., 173.
45 Ibid., 160–1, 172–4.
46 Ibid., 173.
47 Ibid., 170.
48 Ibid., 181.
49 Ibid., 165. On conflicts within the Italian system of precedents, see ibid., 164–5 and 181.
50 ". . . Italian courts exercise broad discretion in deciding to follow or not to follow a precedent": ibid., 156.

The argumentative skills needed for mastering such a "chaotic and complex case law"[51] are—understandably—generally absent among lawyers. Since there is frequently no access to the facts of a precedent, judicial reasoning is focused on the collections of highly abstract, context-free *massime* extracted from court decisions. Thus, the necessary prerequisites for fact-based distinguishing are usually missing, as are the preconditions for a well-functioning system of openly departing from a precedent.[52] The emphasis laid on the *massime* has also affected the legal argumentative skills of the legal profession: deductive reasoning, moulded in the image of more familiar statutory reasoning, is said to be fostered at the cost of the analogical and inductive modes of legal reasoning which, however, would be better suited for the task of reading precedents.[53] In light of the shortcomings detected in the current Italian system of precedents, Taruffo and La Torre argue, *de sententia ferenda*, for a substantial reduction of the caseload of the *Corte di Cassazione*, for the abolition of the *massime*, and for the introduction of an effective system of reporting the true *ratio decidendi* of a case, together with its relevant facts.[54]

The Italian system of precedents is thus a mixture of two kinds of conflicting and mutually inconsistent theoretical positions: one *positivist* and the other *pragmatic*. On the one hand, there is a self-proclaimed intention of the judges of the *Corte di Cassazione*—or rather those judges who constitute the *Ufficio del Massimario*—to guide the future course of adjudication by means of the abstractly formulated *massime*, sharply cut off from the factual context of the prior case and shaped in the image of statutory rules proper. Insofar as the point of view of the prior court is concerned, the Italian system of precedents would seem to bear the decisive impact of the *positivist* approach to precedent. Because of the key role ascribed to the *massime* in precedent-based judicial adjudication, one could point out several affinities to the *quasi-legislative* model of precedent-ideology, though the *ratio* of a case need not always be held as equal with the *massima* extracted from the case.

On the other hand, by force of the unbroken flood of decisions issued by the *Corte di Cassazione* each year, the normative guidance of future adjudication by means of such *massime* falls short of the positivist ideal professed. "Lines", "chains" or "strings" of mutually discordant, "zigzagging" or openly conflicting precedents get piled up, leaving judges with no effective means of mastering or harmonising the potentially inconsistent normative information derived therefrom. From the point of view of the subsequent courts, the Italian legal system exemplifies a *pragmatic* approach to precedents, as outlined in terms of *judicial*

[51] Ibid., 171.

[52] "Italian courts did not develop any practice of 'distinguishing' a precedent as a special legal technique. If they do not intend to refer to a precedent, they either ignore it or abruptly say that they do not agree with the precedent in question, and that they consider it a piece of wrong statutory interpretation": ibid., 176. Cf. 178: "in the Italian system, even in the trial courts of general jurisdiction, precedents are frequently abandoned or set aside or overruled, both implicitly and explicitly".

[53] Ibid., 182–3.

[54] Ibid., 187.

revaluation and the wide range of judicial discretion entailed therein. There are some hints thereto even in the professional understanding of the judges of the *Corte di Cassazione*, as Taruffo and La Torre report in their summary of the issue. The judges' own reflection, to the effect of "deciding correctly (justly) the individual case", rather than trying to establish a coherent system of precedents,[55] speaks clearly in favour thereof. A corresponding shift seems also to have occurred recently in the prospectivity/retroactivity of decisions given by the *Corte di Cassazione*: the court is said to have been looking backward in time more often in its rulings. Thereby, the idea of guiding future legal adjudication by means of abstractly formulated *rationes decidendi* is, of course, silently dropped.[56]

5. A FREE-FLOATING SYSTEM OF OUTWEIGHABLE AND FORMALLY BINDING REASONS (FEDERAL REPUBLIC OF GERMANY)

The legal system of the Federal Republic of Germany is strongly statute-oriented, in that the binding force of a precedent is thought to be derived from a valid norm of either statutory or customary origin. If there is no statutory provision on a contested issue, recourse is taken to the "general grounding principles", or the most basic normative premises, of the German legal system.[57] The concept of a precedent is defined broadly, in the sense of any prior court decision or decisions which may have bearing on a later case,[58] while decisive emphasis is still laid on the justificatory reasons given in support of the prior decision. Precedents are frequently cited by the higher courts, and they are usually followed by the lower courts. However, if a court deviates from a precedent, it will usually identify the prior decision in question and openly set out its reasons for departing from it.[59]

The structure of the higher court decisions is a mixture of elements of deductive and discursive, legalistic and substantive, plus magisterial and argumentative kind. The basic undertone of legal argumentation is deductive, legalistic and magisterial, while the degree of formality tends to decrease as the disputed issue becomes more complicated and takes on the quality of a contested, hard case of adjudication, and vice versa.[60] In the jurisdiction of the Federal Constitutional Court (*Bundesverfassungsgericht*), a thoroughly discursive and argumentative style of reasoning has been proclaimed by the judges themselves:[61]

[55] Taruffo and La Torre, above at n. 4, 184.
[56] Ibid., 184, 186.
[57] The German term is *allgemeine Rechtsgrundlagen*. See R. Alexy and R. Dreier, "Precedent in the Federal Republic of Germany", in MacCormick and Summers, above at n. 1, 33–4.
[58] Ibid., 23.
[59] Ibid., 27, 31.
[60] Ibid., 21.
[61] Ibid., 22.

"The interpretation especially of constitutional law has the character of a discourse in which even by methodologically perfect work no absolutely right answers, indisputable by experts, are presented, but reasons and counter reasons are, and a decision is finally expected to be brought about by the better reason."

The German courts—other than the Federal Constitutional Court—do not generally identify the exact *ratio decidendi* of a case, while reference is instead made to the case in more loosely defined terms. The Federal Constitutional Court, on the other hand, has frequently ruled that the "supporting reasons" (*tragende Gründe*) of a decision are the element which is endowed with binding force *vis-à-vis* subsequent adjudication. Therefore, such reasons are the real point of reference for the *ratio* of a case in the German system of precedents.[62] Occasionally, the Federal Constitutional Court has even declared that the whole of its reasoning in a case is to be treated as the true *ratio decidendi* of that decision.[63]

The decisions of the Federal Constitutional Court are usually published at length, and an extensive selection of the most important decisions of the other federal courts is also published in the official series. The decisions of the higher courts are frequently compiled in non-official digests, and legal journals may choose to pay attention to some individual decisions which are deemed to have some common interest.[64] Unlike, for example, the Italian system of law, there is thus relatively easy access to the information contained in court decisions given by the Federal Republic of Germany. The whole line of reasoning of a precedent may be used as source material in subsequent adjudication, detached from—or even irrespective of—the original intentions of the prior court on the exact meaning-content of the *ratio* of a case.[65] As in France and Italy, a consistent line of precedents (*ständige Rechtsprechung*) tends to have more argumentative weight than an individual precedent.[66]

The decisions given by the Federal Constitutional Court are considered formally or strictly binding on other courts. The rulings given by the other courts, including the Federal Court of Justice (*Bundesgerichtshof*), do not have mandatory or strictly binding force, but may still exert considerable argumentative, persuasive or *de facto* influence on the subsequent courts' legal discretion.[67] In the German system of precedents, the binding force of a case is, to a great extent, determined by the quality and appositeness of reasons given in its support, plus the "authority and competence" of the prior court, as stated in express terms by

[62] The role of justificatory reasons in the German system of precedents is described as follows: "The soundness of the supporting arguments in the opinion is of greatest importance for subsequent decisions. According to the opinion of the Federal Constitutional Court already quoted, the soundness of the supporting arguments is the main reason for following a precedent": ibid., 35.

[63] Ibid., 48.

[64] Ibid., 22.

[65] Ibid., 49.

[66] Ibid., 50–1.

[67] Ibid., 26–31.

the Federal Constitutional Court.[68] Thus, the existence of a better set of reasons for a decision would justify a deviation from a precedent, according to the stance of the Federal Constitutional Court. The Federal Court of Justice, however, has taken a different stance on the issue. In its opinion, the presence of "clearly outweighing" or "absolutely compelling reasons" is needed to justify a deviation from an otherwise pertinent precedent, thus placing more emphasis on the requirements of legal certainty and uniformity in judicial adjudication.[69]

Alexy and Dreier describe the German system of precedents, the rulings of the Federal Constitutional Court notwithstanding, as endowed with "outweighable force".[70] In their reading of the issue, the argumentative impact of a precedent may be concisely stated in the form of the following meta-rule: "whoever wishes to depart from a precedent carries the burden of argument." In the professional understanding on precedents of the judges of both the Federal Constitutional Court and the Federal Court of Justice, decisive emphasis is laid on contextual evaluation, or rather *re*valuation, of the reasons given in support of a precedent, and not on some formally defined criteria of *stare decisis* as in the United Kingdom. Since there are, moreover, no specific guarantees of attaining systemic coherence in the German system of adjudication, the term "free-floating" model of precedent-based reasons would seem justified.

The technique of distinguishing a prior case on factual grounds does not appear to be very sophisticated in the German legal system,[71] as is quite common place in the continental civil law systems of Europe. Since precedents are not held to be formally binding, with the one exception of decisions of the Federal Constitutional Court, there is, in fact, no need or incentive, first, to discern the normative *ratio* from the *dicta* of a case, and secondly, to find some legally relevant distinction between the two cases or evade the normative effect of the precedent by some other technically correct means. However, the overruling of a precedent is frequently performed in explicit terms in the German system of law. Even the anticipatory overruling of a precedent by a lower court may occasionally occur.[72]

The classification of the German system of precedents in light of the various precedent ideologies is somewhat problematic, due to the strongly statute-oriented legal tradition and professional self-understanding of the German judiciary. Outside of the field of constitutional jurisdiction, the impact of a precedent is based on the argumentative weight of its supportive reasons, rather than the formal authority of the court. A subsequent judge will face the burden of argumentation, if he departs from a precedent in some later case. Since the justificatory reasons for a precedent may effectively be put aside, if there are

[68] The term "*überzeugungskraft ihrer Gründe*", or the "convincing power of the reasons [presented]", was used by the court: ibid., 29.

[69] Ibid., 30. Cf. ibid., 37–8.

[70] Ibid., 30.

[71] See, in general, ibid., 54–9.

[72] Ibid., 58.

strong enough countervailing reasons present in the new case at hand, the *revalued reasons approach* to precedent-following might be used in describing the German system of precedents, in areas other than constitutional jurisdiction. Depending on the degree of binding force attached to such legal reasons, there may also be some affinity to the *model reasons approach* to precedent-following.

The legal argumentation of the Federal Constitutional Court is even more discursive and reasons-oriented with regard to its internal structure, since it has openly acknowledged the need to weigh and balance legal principles, interests or values in adjudication. Endowed with strong, mandatory binding force, the decisions rendered by the Federal Constitutional Court may be thought to instantiate the *ruling by reasons* ideology *vis-à-vis* precedent-following. The Constitutional Court, in other words, aims at guiding the future course of adjudication by the manifest reasons given in support of its rulings. There may even be some elements drawn from the Dworkin-inspired *underlying reasons model* of precedent-following, if the professional self-understanding of judges and the degree of systemic coherence involved in case-law are read in light of such a "seamless web" of reasons beneath the resulting positivity of law.

6. JUDICIAL POSITIVISM UNDER A PERPLEXED RELATION OF A CASE'S HEADNOTE AND THE WHOLE OF JUDICIAL REASONING (FINLAND)

6.1 A preliminary outline of the precedent ideology adopted by the Finnish Supreme Court of Justice

In 1980, the criteria for leave of appeal to the Supreme Court of Justice in Finland were tightened, and the court's status as a precedent-issuing court was significantly raised.[73] Now, the decision whether a leave of appeal to the Supreme Court is to be granted is made on the basis of the following criteria:[74]

> "A leave of appeal [to the Supreme Court] may be granted only if, having regard to law application in other similar cases or because of the consistency of judicial adjudication, it is important to have the case decided by the Supreme Court; or if there is some specific reason thereto because of a procedural or some other fault committed in the judicial proceedings, being in itself a reason to declare the decision void and null; or if there is some other weighty reason to grant a leave of appeal."

The criteria may be classified as (1) *precedential* argument, (2) argument based on *annullability* of a decision, and (3) argument based on *some other weighty reason*.[75] In the present context, the first type of argument is, of course, the most

[73] The Act of Judicial Procedure, 30 Chapter, L. 79/104.

[74] The Act of Judicial Procedure 30:3[1] (translation from Finnish by the author).

[75] M. Miettinen, "*Prejudikaattidispenssistä valituslupaan*", in *Korkein Oikeus 60 vuotta* (Valtion painatuskeskus, Helsinki, 1979), 147–55. Aarnio makes use of the four categories of *precedential argument*, *uniformity argument*, *rescission argument*, and the argument that the case is of

important, while the other two other grounds of appeal relate to non-precedential reasons of either procedural or *ad hoc* kind.

The precedent ideology adopted by the Supreme Court of Justice in Finland, as analysed by Aarnio in his contribution to the standard reference work in this field, *Interpreting Precedents: A Comparative Study*,[76] would seem to be a combination of elements drawn from the field of *judicial legislation* and *judicial exegesis*, or to be more exact, a mixture of the quasi-legislative model and the reconstructed rule model of precedent ideology. Accordingly, the *ratio* of a case is either expressly laid down by the court in the headnote of a case, or it may have to be reconstructed from the combination of the headnote and the entire justificatory reasoning given in support of the decision. The emphasis laid on the headnote clearly refers to the impact of judicial legislation, while the idea of reconstructing the *ratio* of a case from its headnote and the whole of judicial reasoning denotes the influence of rule-bound judicial exegesis.[77] If expressly given in the headnote, the *ratio* of a case is formulated in relatively abstract and context-free terms. If, on the other hand, recourse needs to be taken to the supporting reasons of that decision, the *ratio* will be more concrete and context-bound in character.

The traditionally rather formal, syllogistic and terse style of reasoning of the court has been modified by a shift towards a more discursive approach to legal argumentation in the 1980s and 1990s.[78] The *ratio* of a case, as laid down by the Supreme Court itself in the headnote, is claimed to be endowed with binding effect on subsequent adjudication, as then possibly modified by elements drawn from judicial exegesis. The *transcategorical context* of precedent-following, i.e. the prevalent legal source doctrine in Finland, reduces the binding force of the *ratio* of a case to the category of *not formally binding, but having force*, in the sense of having no more than a persuasive effect on subsequent jurisdiction. There is one exception, however. According to Article 16 of the Internal Rules of Procedure of the Supreme Court, the Supreme Court is itself under an obligation to adhere to its own case-law, to the effect that a deviation from its prior line of rulings must be referred to and decided by a plenary session or enlargened panel of the court.

The impact of the legalistic and statute-oriented undertone of the Finnish legal system can be clearly seen in the headnote-oriented conception of precedents, which offers no real incentives or motivation for lawyers to cultivate the skills of genuine case-by-case reasoning. Therefore, the techiques of precedent-based argumentation are less than fully developed among the Finnish judiciary and legal profession generally. The same is true of the techniques of distin-

special importance for the party, in A. Aarnio, "Precedent in Finland", in MacCormick and Summers, above at n. 1, 70.

[76] Aarnio, ibid., 65–101.

[77] Ibid., 92. Cf. ibid., 78–9, 80. The two characterisations of judicial legislation and judicial exegesis are based on my reading of the source material contained in *Interpreting Precedents: A Comparative Study*, and are not adopted by Aarnio in his contribution, "Precedent in Finland".

[78] Ibid., 72–3.

guishing or otherwise departing from a precedent. The theoretical rationale of the Finnish system of precedent-following self-evidently stems from the doctrine of statutory-oriented legal positivism. The binding force of the decisions rendered by the Supreme Court, and especially the role of the headnote of a case, was intensely debated among the Finnish legal profession in the mid-1980s. The debate was to a great extent induced by the justices' reflection on certain tenets of the precedent ideology in fact acknowledged by the court. Such intellectual strife cooled down by the turn of the decade, but some remnants of a headnote-oriented doctrine of precedent-identification and precedent-following can still be found in current Finnish legal literature.

6.2 The doctrine of judicial headnotes, defined as equal with the *ratio decidendi* of a case

Unlike the Italian *massime*, which are extracted from a court case by a specific institute established for that purpose, i.e. the *Ufficio del Massimario*, the headnote[79] of a decision rendered by the Supreme Court of Finland is formulated by the same justices who made the judicial decision in the first place. The practice of issuing such headnotes is based on the court's Internal Rules of Procedure.[80] According to the Internal Handbook used by the court's personnel, "the headnote comprises an abstract of the legal issue [which was given attention by the court] and, if needed, further information of the case and the grounds for the decision made".[81]

The *quasi-legislative* precedent ideology has a special position in Finland, since Olavi Heinonen, then one of the justices and later the Chief Justice of the Supreme Court,[82] openly professed the court's adherence to such a conception of precedent-identification in the mid-1980s.[83] The exact terminology of the present treatise was not, of course, used by Justice Heinonen, but the emphasis laid on judicial legislation—i.e. the guidance of future court decisions by means of abstractly formulated *rationes decidendi*, as laid down by the Supreme Court itself in the headnote of a case—clearly warrants such a classification. Heinonen

[79] The three terms "headnote", "headline", and "rubrication" of a case are all intended to have the same sense and reference here, being a concise summary or abstract of the legal issue or issues that received the court's attention. The term "headnote" will be adopted in the present discussion, with some exceptions in citations.

[80] See Art. 22 of the Internal Rules of Procedure of the Supreme Court, as approved in the Plenum Session of the Supreme Court on 23 August 1994. According to Art. 46 of the Internal Rules of Procedure, "the Chief Justice [of the Supreme Court] will give detailed orders on the application of the Internal Rules of Procedure, and directives concerning the working methods in the Court, if such are needed" (translation from Finnish by the author).

[81] P. Dahlbohm (ed.), *KKO—Opas. Kokeilulaitos 7.11.1996* (Korkein Oikeus, Helsinki, 1996), 56 (translation from Finnish by the author).

[82] Heinonen was nominated as Chief Justice of the Supreme Court on 2 June 1989, and took office on 1 October of the same year.

[83] O. Heinonen, "*Kuka saa juttunsa Korkeimman oikeuden tutkittavaksi?*" (1985) *Lakimiesuutiset* 30–2.

even suggested a relatively straightforward analogy between the headnote of a case and a statutory norm.[84]

Justice Heinonen's line of argument was intended as a contribution to an idea presented somewhat earlier by Curt Olsson, then Chief Justice of the Supreme Court. Olsson had forcefully argued that since the law reform in 1980, where the new criteria for granting the leave of appeal to the Supreme Court were laid down, the Supreme Court rulings were to have mandatory binding force on the lower-level courts of justice. Olsson grounded his argumentation on the Internal Rules of Procedure of the Supreme Court: since the court itself cannot overrule its own prior case-law, except by having recourse to an enlargened panel or the full bench of the court, how could the lower courts legitimately deviate from rulings of the Supreme Court?[85] Olsson's reading of the binding force of precedents was met with severe criticism from legal scholars,[86] and was subsequently dropped. The discussion on the headnotes continued, however.

Justice Heinonen then argued that the binding force of a Supreme Court decision is attached to the headnote of a case: "The headnote of a precedent is a thoroughly reflected standpoint on the legal issue of the case".[87] The *ratio* of a case is "almost always", as he put it, expressed in the headnote, while the occasions on which the precedent-norm cannot for some reason be outlined in an abstract and concise manner form an exception thereto.[88] "At the moment, the main rule is that the *ratio* of a case is given in the headnote", he wrote.[89] Since the headnote is usually expressed on a higher level of abstraction than the outward reasoning of the case, the headnote may become detached from the facts and begin to lead a life of its own.

At the beginning of the 1990s, Chief Justice Heinonen notably reversed his position on the role of the headnote.[90] Since 1990, he has consistently argued that the headnote of a case ought not to be read as the court's own formulation of the *ratio decidendi* of that case. Instead, the headnote should be taken as (no more than) a concise description of the legal issue or issues which were being considered by the court. In a book review in 1990, Heinonen rejected his former

[84] O. Heinonen, "*Kuka saa juttunsa Korkeimman oikeuden tutkittavaksi?*" (1985) *Lakimies-uutiset* 32.

[85] C. Olsson, "*Om rättsutveckling genom dom*" (1984) *Lakimies* 1193–5, 1200.

[86] On the discussion, see P. Timonen, *Ennakkotapaukset ja niiden merkitys oikeuslähteenä* (Lakimiesliiton Kustannus, 1987), 76–81; I. Saraviita, "*Muutama sananen Korkeimman oikeuden ennakkopäätösten sitovuudesta*" (1985) *Lakimies* 373–6, where Olsson's position was criticised for lack of constitutional support.

[87] Heinonen, above at n. 83, 32 (translation from Finnish by the author).

[88] Ibid., 31–2.

[89] Ibid., 32 (translation from Finnish by the author). Heinonen continued by pointing out: "Even in the published precedents, the Court frequently needs to be take some stance to other legal issues as well, apart from the ones mentioned in the headnote. According to the opinion held by the Supreme Court, such legal rulings do not have sufficient precedential value, and are thus equal to legal rulings in those cases which are not published at all" (translation from Finnish by the author).

[90] It seems that Heinonen's change of opinion from normative to—no more than—descriptive function of headnotes took place at the same time as his nomination as Chief Justice of the Supreme Court of Finland.

idea that headnotes might have the status of abstract legal norms in quite explicit terms:[91]

> "The Supreme Court invariably decides the concrete case at hand only, and restricts itself to the justification of the decision given. In the headnote, a description is given of the individual legal question upon which the Court wishes to issue a precedent. For obvious reasons, such a description is often a concise summary of the reasons for the legal outcome reached. As far as I can see, there are no further intentions held by the Supreme Court [in this respect]."

Moreover, in 1991 he wrote:[92]

> "Today, there is all the reason to reject the opinion that the Supreme Court would aim at issuing "normative" headnotes; I refer to my earlier argument to the effect that the task of the Supreme Court is *not to create law, nor to produce* [*legal*] *norms*."

The headnote is a kind of "shorthand description" of the legal issue or issues of a case, and a straightforward equation of the *ratio* and the headnote—as previously defended by Justice Heinonen himself—is no longer warranted. The headnote no more than gives condensed information of the court's final ruling. Yet, it may be that Chief Justice Heinonen took one step too far in his new, "minimalist" stance towards the precedent ideology adopted by the court. He stated that the task of the Supreme Court is "not to create law, nor to produce [legal] norms". However, since the law reform of 1980, the Supreme Court evidently has the status of a precedent-issuing court.

Heinonen's withdrawal from his earlier conception of precedents was, no doubt, influenced by the criticism received from legal scholars. In 1989, Linna argued that there is no statutory support for the conception that the headnote of a case might have more binding force than the rest of a Supreme Court decision. She also criticised the element of forthright prospectivity entailed in such a doctrine of precedents, arguing that the function of the headnote ought to be reduced to that of mere indexing only.[93] In his 1991 article, Chief Justice Heinonen made an explicit reference to another essay by Linna,[94] and, in fact, Heinonen's novel stance towards the role of headnotes is fairly well in line with Linna's argument.

Linna pointed out that the headnote could have four functions: (1) the allocation of binding force or normative value within a case; (2) the indexing of cases; (3) the reporting of cases; and (4) the guiding or directing of subsequent

[91] O. Heinonen, Book Review on P. Timonen (ed.), *Johdatus Suomen oikeusjärjestelmään, 1–2*, in (1990) *Oikeus* 161–2 (translation from Finnish by the author). Heinonen also makes a reference to his earlier, openly normative account of headnotes, now expressly rejecting such a reading of the court's precedent ideology: "From the point of view of the Supreme Court, this is in my opinion a clearly by-gone phase of development": Heinonen, ibid., 161 (translation from Finnish by the author).

[92] O. Heinonen, "*Korkeimman oikeuden rooli muuttuvassa ympäristössä*" (1991) *Lakimies* 238 (emphasis added).

[93] T. Linna, "*Korkeimman oikeuden päätösten otsikoista*" (1989) *Lakimies* 772, esp. 776–82.

[94] Above at n. 92, 238, with reference to T. Linna, "*Korkeimman oikeuden päätösotsikkojen tehtävistä*" (1990) *Lakimies* 969. Cf. Linna, above at n. 93.

judicial adjudication.[95] The allocation of normative binding force within a Supreme Court decision and the guiding of future adjudication, with reference to points (1) and (4) above, might be called the *normative* or *normative-guiding* function of the headnote of a case. On the other hand, the indexing and reporting of decisions, with reference to points (2) and (3) above, might be called the *descriptive* or *descriptive-informative* function of the headnote of a case. Finally, Linna rephrased her earlier contention that the normative role of the headnotes should be rejected, since it could not find adequate support in the statute-based legal system in Finland.[96]

Although Chief Justice Heinonen gave up the normative conception of headnotes in explicit terms in the early 1990s, his former stance has gained ground in Finland because the leading scholar of the field, Aarnio, has at least partially adhered to it even after Chief Justice Heinonen's change of opinion. In his contribution to the standard reference work on the subject matter, *Interpreting Precedents: A Comparative Study* by the *Bielefelder Kreis*, Aarnio singles out the normative-guiding function and the descriptive-explanatory function of headnotes, placing the decisive weight of emphasis on the former:[97]

> "The intention of the Supreme Court is not only to solve the individual cases but to give abstract and general *guiding information* for the future. . . . In Finland the decisive *guiding information* of a precedent is included in the so-called "rubrication". It includes a description of the legal norm (a rule or a principle) that has to be applied to the facts described in the case. A rubrication is thus not exclusively a description about a solution, but one wants, by its means, to influence the subsequent application of the law. It is thus a *normative instruction*. A rubrication contains an indication of the relevant facts as decided on; an explicit holding on an issue of law, or *ratio decidendi*; an explicitly formulated (or implicit) rule; and, sometimes, an explicitly formulated (or implicit) principle. It is the *ratio decidendi*, whether in the form of a rule or a principle—Consequently, a judge solving a subsequent case receives the *guiding information* expressly from the rubrication. In many cases, the normative guiding information is, however, expressed only implicitly and has to be rationally reconstructed on the basis of the rubrication and the other parts of the precedent."

In Aarnio's account of the doctrine of precedents in Finland, the headnote of a case, as expressly laid down by the Supreme Court itself, is prima facie regarded as the true *ratio* of that case. The terminology adopted by Aarnio, i.e. abstract and general *guiding information* and *normative instruction*, clearly implies such a normative-guiding function accorded to the headnote. The doctrine of judicial legislation and the intended prospectivity of Supreme Court rulings[98] may yet have to be modified or supplemented by elements drawn from judicial exegesis,

[95] Linna, above at n. 94, 971–981.

[96] Ibid., 974–6, 980–1.

[97] Aarnio, above at n. 75, 92 (emphasis on "normative instruction" and "guiding information" added).

[98] "The Supreme Court of Finland has adopted a clearly prospective function. It aims, by the published solutions it has defined as precedents, to guide the application of the law of the lower court of justice—and, on certain conditions, also its own subsequent decision-making activity": ibid., 80.

if the headnote of a case is found lacking in precision, or if, for some other reason, it cannot provide an adequate normative ground for subsequent adjudication.[99]

Finally, Aarnio criticises the recent phenomenon of *case-law positivism* among the legal profession, i.e. the inclination of some lawyers to completely detach the abstract headnote of a case from its factual and legal context, and to ground their legal reasoning on such context-free normative information only.[100] However, the emergence of headnote-oriented judicial positivism is, in fact, a forthright consequence of the doctrine of precedent-identification which holds the *ratio* of a case equal to its headnote. If the headnote were indeed taken as the primary point of reference for the *ratio decidendi* of a case, such a short-cut to the binding element of a case would be greeted as an entirely legitimate move in the 'game' of legal reasoning. That such is not the case, but a purely headnote-based method of precedent-identification is met with severe criticism from legal scholars, is a clear sign of the ideological defects of the doctrine.

6.3 A Critique of headnote-oriented judicial positivism

The emphasis laid on the headnote of a Supreme Court decision is probably due to the overarching positivist frame of the Finnish legal system. At the same time, it is one of the obvious reasons for the relatively underdeveloped state of truly case-bound legal reasoning in it. Under the positivist premises acknowledged, all judicial reasoning generally follows the familiar patterns of statutory interpretation, in the sense of deductive reasoning from abstract legal norms, possibly as modified by some less formal and more content-oriented tenets. Despite a clear move towards a more open style of argumentation in the 1980s and 1990s, the style of reasoning and the internal structure of Supreme Court decisions is still described as, in essence, syllogistic.[101] Because of the all-encompassing positivist frame of legal adjudication, there will be no incentive for members of the legal profession to learn to master the techniques of genuinely case-bound reasoning, in the sense of backward-looking judicial exegesis, realignment of the *ratio* of a case by the constant interplay of analogy and distinguishing, systemic construction of the underlying reasons from a line of precedents, or a dynamic revaluation of the merits of the prior case, to name just four different approaches to precedent-following.

As Linna rightly pointed out, there is no legislative or constitutional support for allocating the binding force (*ratio decidendi*) of a case to its abstract headnote.

[99] On a backward-proceeding, reconstructive reading of the *ratio* of a case, see ibid., 78 *in fine*.

[100] Ibid., 93; cf. 82. Cf. also Linna's argument to the effect that the abstractly formulated headnotes may begin to 'lead a life of their own', detached from their initial context: Linna, above at n. 93,778.

[101] Aarnio, above at n. 75, 72. Cf. A. Aarnio, "Statutory Interpretation in Finland", in D.N. MacCormick and R.S. Summers (eds), *Interpreting Statutes: A Comparative Study* (Dartmouth, 1991), 155.

Self-evidently, the institutional support provided by the Court's Internal Rules of Procedure, decreed by the Supreme Court for and by itself, cannot possibly provide the legislative backing needed. Therefore, any remnants of a normative-guiding doctrine of headnotes, as may still be found among the legal profession in Finland, should be discarded, and the relation between the headnote and the *ratio* of a case must be (re)defined in more modest terms. In consequence, the headnote of a case may have no more than a descriptive—and not normative—function under the current legal and institutional frame of precedent-following in Finland. A headnote may serve to attract the subsequent court's attention to the specific legal issues considered by the prior court, but it cannot be held equal to the *ratio decidendi* of that case, as Chief Justice Heinonen has consistently argued since his "descriptive turn" in 1990.

To put it concisely: the precedent ideology internalised by the Supreme Court in Finland bears most affinity to a weak version of judicial exegesis, where the *ratio* of a case is to be reconstructed from the court's normative and factual premises for the outcome reached. The attribute "weak" is due to the lack of adequate professional self-understanding and precedent-specific argumentative skills among the judiciary and the legal profession in Finland. Apart from the—in my opinion slightly misplaced—discussion on the role of headnotes, there has been no professional self-reflection among Finnish lawyers on *how to read precedents*, in the sense of trying to develop some operative criteria for distinguishing the *ratio* from the *dicta* in a case, nor on the precedent-specific patterns of argumentation required thereto. Since the proper tools for genuinely case-bound reasoning are generally lacking, the predominant ideology of statutory positivism has tended to "spill over" its legitimate domain of statutory reasoning and conquer the realm of precedent-based reasoning, as well. The judicial experience drawn from Italy would seem to lend strong support to a similar conclusion.[102]

6.4 The author's preference: case-by-case reasoning by analogy and distinguishing

In conclusion, the inherent necessities of case-law adjudication would seem to turn the scales in favour of the analogical approach of precedent-following, possibly as modified by some elements drawn from the field of judicial exegesis. My own preference for the Finnish system of precedent-following *de sententia ferenda*[103] is, in other words, based on the constant realignment of the *ratio/dicta* distinction of the prior case in subsequent judicial adjudication, resulting in the

[102] Cf. Corla's critical remarks on the Italian style of argumentation in the context of precedents, in Taruffo and La Torre, above at n. 4, 182–3.

[103] On the notion of *de sententia ferenda* and its relation to the "scientific statements of the valid law", in the sense of predictions put forth by legal science, see A. Ross, *Om ret og retfærdighed: En indførelse i den analytiske retsfilosofi* (Nyt nordisk forslag, 1953), 60 ff.

gradual unfolding of the *ratio* in terms of the shifting interplay of analogy and distinguishing.

No statutory provisions have so far been enacted on the legality or illegality of some particular precedent ideology to be enforced in Finland. However, some approaches to precedent-identification and precedent-following may be ruled out as quite self-evidently contrary to the prevalent notion of law in Finland, i.e. the idea of absolutely bound decision-making under judicial reference ideology, a full-scale retreat to the axiological and/or teleological background premises of law under the substantive approach to legal adjudication, and the "Solomonic" or merely arbitrary idea of a judge's semantic freeplay under the judicial hunch model of legal adjudication. Moreover, the wide field of judicial discretion enjoyed by the (subsequent) court under the overtly pragmatic judicial revaluation ideology would not find adequate support in the positivist frame of judicial adjudication acknowledged in Finland. The same would be true of the Herculean task of constructing a "seamless web of reasons" in law, as professed by the Dworkin-inspired underlying reasons approach to precedent-following.

In contrast, the current Finnish legal system does not appear to place any obstacles to the adoption of the analogy-based approach to precedent-following. Under such similarity—and—dissimilarity oriented premises, the "Supreme Court invariably decides the concrete case at hand only, and restricts itself to the justification of the outcome given", as Chief Justice Heinonen has consistently argued since the beginning of the 1990s.[104] The Supreme Court of Finland thus lays down (no more and no less than) a *model rule* or *paradigm case* to be followed analogically in subsequent adjudication. Even the idea of a set of *model reasons*, as set out by the prior court in support of the decision rendered, could function quite satisfactorily in the Finnish legal system. Judicial experience drawn from the reasons-oriented system of legal adjudication in the Federal Republic of Germany, the field of constitutional jurisdiction notwithstanding, may be worth serious consideration in that respect. While the current practice of furnishing a court's ruling with a relatively detailed fact-description would make such a realignment of the current precedent ideology of Finnish judges possible, the specific reading skills *vis-à-vis* precedent-following, or the argumentative techniques of *how to do things with precedents*, would still need to be substantially improved among the judiciary and the legal profession, so as to make the prevalent system of precedent-following a truly well-functioning one.

7. CONCLUSION: FROM PURE TYPES OF PRECEDENT IDEOLOGY TO THE LAW IN ACTION IN PRECEDENT-FOLLOWING (A TALE OF GRASSHOPPERS, BEEHIVES AND ANTHILLS)

The sum total of pure types of precedent ideology presented above may be read as a would-be all-encompassing scheme of *possible worlds semantics* for a judge

[104] Heinonen, above at n. 91, 161.

who is constrained by the formal doctrine of *stare decisis*, whether in a relatively strong or weak sense of the term. The total outcome of feasible ideological fragments discerned is equal with the contents of a judge's *intellectual toolbox vis-à-vis* precedent-identification and precedent-following on the level of legal source ideology. Due to their status as pure types or rational reconstructions of precedent-following, the models function as approximations or abstractions of judicial reality only, without putting forth any claim of perfectly corresponding the actual phenomena of judicial reality "out there". The internal coherence and theoretical purity of such a modelling approach is bought at the relatively high price of having to overlook the contingent elements of case-law adjudication, as well as the internal divergence entailed in the precedent ideologies adopted by various judges in a given legal system. The methodological strictures entailed in modelling judges' feasible precedent ideologies were concisely commented upon above in chapter 1 at p. 29ff.

Therefore, the law in action in precedent-following will not always follow the sharp-edged categories and neatly labelled classifications of a legal scholar's well-ordered universe of theory-construction. However, without first having recourse to such a clear-cut frame of analysis, there could be no conceptual distance drawn from the contingent and possibly discordant world of actual judicial phenomena which make up the "law in action". The main advantage of having such an abstract theoretical scheme of analysis is, exactly, to provide for an external ground of reference or a fixed yardstick of jurisprudential analysis in light of which any truly empirical or sociological claims on the use of precedents in the courts may then be evaluated. In other words, the somewhat *still life* picture of the norm-constitutive and signification-aligned fragments of judges' precedent ideology must be placed into a fruitful contrast with actual case-law adjudication, so as to attain a more dynamic, pragmatic and realist view of "precedents in action".[105]

An extensive empirical account of the precedent ideology in fact adopted by the judiciary of a legal system would necessitate having to probe into the voluminous set of precedents in it, each woven into the evolving texture of the legal outcomes thereby effected and the state of mind of the individual judge or judges at each occasion of judicial decision-making. As I see it, it is a task for theory-laden legal sociology, and not jurisprudence as such, to probe into the contingent, divergent and empirical world of "precedents in action"; while the proper task for jurisprudence and legal philosophy is, instead, to rationally *reconstruct* and—with equal right—to *deconstruct* the deep-reaching theoretical and philosophical premises involved in each occasion of legal adjudication. Disregarding

[105] Somewhat surprisingly, Hart described his *The Concept of Law* as "an essay in descriptive sociology" (Clarendon Press, Oxford, 1961), V. Rather than descriptive sociology, Hart's landmark treatise should be labelled a contribution to linguistically oriented jurisprudence, echoing the methodological credo of the Oxford philosophy of ordinary language in the context of law. There are few assertions which might be classified genuinely "descriptive" or "sociological" in Hart's book, unless the empirical facets entailed in his master rule, i.e. the ultimate rule of recognition, are taken to warrant such an overarching classification.

here any truly sociological or empirical endeavours into the state of mind of the judge or judges in question, one could argue that, at least in the presence of a weakly articulated tradition and theory of precedents in the legal system concerned, the precedent-ideology in fact adopted by the judiciary is a *cluster* or a loosely ordered set of *ideological fragments*, probably drawn from the field of several, though usually affiliated models of precedent ideology, instead of having any direct correspondence to some pure type of precedent ideology.

Accordingly, the search for the prior court's authentic intentions under judicial exegesis may become modified by a countervailing effort to attain some degree of legal systemic coherence in a set of precedents, whether on a Herculean or more modest scale. Equally, the search for an adequate reason to extend the scope of a prior decision analogically or cut down its coverage by distinguishing might be modified by elements drawn from backward-proceeding judicial exegesis or a more-or-less radical judicial revaluation of prior case-law. The officially proclaimed ideology of future-oriented, small-scale judicial legislation may have to yield to a far less formal conception of the *ratio* of a case in the law in action, if the subsequent courts simply refuse to lend their support to such quasi-legislative pretensions held by the highest national court or courts, as the judicial experience drawn from Italy clearly bears witness to. Moreover, even in the presence of a self-proclaimed professional stance *vis-à-vis* precedent-identification and precedent-following by the judiciary, certain fragments of a fully-developed precedent ideology may still be lacking in their professional understanding of *how to do things with precedents*, as the situation in France and Finland would seem to imply. In consequence thereof, the specific reading skills required may not be adequately mastered by judges and the legal profession. Even a relatively undiscriminating or openly eclectic array of divergent ideological fragments, extending from tenets of small-scale judicial legislation to open-ended judicial pragmatism in terms of a radical revaluation of the merits of the *ratio* of a case, is fully conceivable, as the judicial evidence drawn from the Court of Appeals of the State of New York affirms.

Thus, relaxing the theoretical confines of the various pure types of precedent-ideology, the resulting cluster of ideological fragments *vis-à-vis* precedent-identification and precedent-following can be illustrated with Figure 4.

In the widest terms possible, the precedent ideology in fact internalised by a judge may be based on, for example, the ideas of judicial exegesis and judicial analogy/distinguishing, with elements occasionally drawn from judicial legislation, systemic construction of underlying reasons from a line of cases, and more-or-less radical revaluation of the merits of a prior decision, while certain tenets derived from judicial consequentialism or rightness reasons may also have an impact thereupon. Such an ideological constellation held by a judge is, of course, subject to the restrictions laid down by the prevalent legal source doctrine and other legal systemic constraints of precedent-following, as analysed above. No judge could possibly have a purely idiosyncratic conception of the prevalent legal source material, since there must be some effected overlap in the

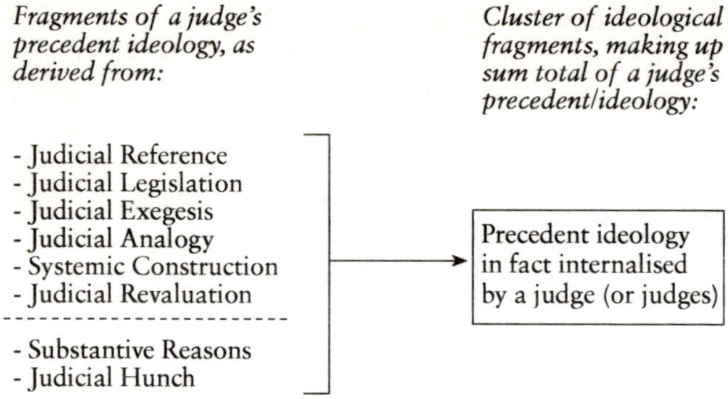

Figure 4: Ideological fragments and effected precedent ideology of a judge

conception of law and legal sources of the judiciary in a given legal system. Otherwise, the very idea of having a legal system would collapse and disperse into an array of instances of a Leibnizian solipsistic monadology. However, the presumably neat division between a judge's purely personal, idiosyncratic motives, which are left out of the concept of law and legal analysis, and the common, institutional elements derived from the prevalent legal source ideology, which are taken into account in such analysis, might prove to be less than clear-cut or self-evident for a legal scholar who has endeavoured to outline the collection of ideological stances held by the judiciary.[106]

It might even be the case that the subsequent court makes use of what may be called the *grasshopper technique* of legal argumentation, trying out and then rejecting, one by one, the various formally structured models of precedent-following, finally ending up in entirely non-formal judicial consequentialism. Accordingly, the idea of retracing the prior court's original intentions in terms of judicial exegesis may first be tried, only to be rejected because of the deeply-felt inadequacy of the outcomes that would be effected thereby; to be followed by a quest for the underlying legal systemic criteria in the line of prior cases so far gathered, only to be rejected for lack of systemic coherence in the cases under scrutiny; to be followed by a search for possible grounds of fact-based analogy between the two court cases, again to be rejected because of some essential and legally relevant dissimilarity in the court decisions in question. Finally, once all the formal reasons of precedent-following have been exhausted, the subsequent

[106] The intellectual distance between Ross' and Kennedy's intellectual positions may not prove to be so vast after all, as was argued above in chapter 1 at p. 8. Cf. Ross, above at n. 103, 49, where reference is made to such idiosyncratic factors as part of scholarly predictions concerning the future course of legal adjudication; and D. Kennedy, A *Critique of Adjudication {fin de siècle}* (Harvard University Press, 1997), 191–200, where the *bad faith argument* is introduced, with reference to the judges' effective even if officially denied ideological motives in legal adjudication.

judge may take recourse to open-ended judicial consequentialism, where the criteria of social expediency and means-end rationality are held to be decisive.

In fact, such a sequential model of legal argumentation, given in terms of formally valid legal rules, a coherent set of underlying principles, arguments based on analogy and, finally, judicial consequentialism, is defended by MacCormick in *Legal Reasoning and Legal Theory*.[107] In terms of the present discussion, a judge's reasoning may then be said to proceed from judicial exegesis via systemic construction of the underlying reasons of the case-law, to (coherence-seeking) judicial analogy and, eventually, to entirely non-formal judicial consequentialism.[108] Such a pattern of argumentative moves from strictly drawn legal formalism towards consequentialist non-formalism in legal adjudication plainly follows the "grasshopper technique" of legal argumentation. However, the focus of MacCormick's analysis is on the premises of judicial argumentation in general, and not on precedent-based argumentation in specific. To my knowledge, no systematic effort has been made to unveil the internal structure of precedent-based reasoning.[109]

However, the judicial material gathered from the six legal systems considered (United Kingdom, United States (State of New York), France, Italy, Federal Republic of Germany and Finland) would not seem to lend support to such a grasshopper effect in precedent-following. Instead, the vast and divergent American experience of precedents possibly notwithstanding, the methods of identifying and following the *ratio* of a case, and the argumentative weight to be attached to the *ratio*, are more-or-less strictly preframed or predetermined by the prevalent source doctrine and other legal systemic constraints upon precedent-following, as was argued in chapter 4 above at 4.1. Typically, there is at least a vague idea of the precedent ideology internalised by the judge or judges concerned, in the sense of a set or cluster of affiliated ideological fragments of precedent-identification and precedent-following among the judiciary.

[107] N. MacCormick, *Legal Reasoning and Legal Theory* (Oxford University Press, 1978), 250–1.

[108] Similarly, Aarnio has defended a sequential pattern of legal reasoning where the consequentialist arguments (in Aarnio: "practical reasons") are taken to have the final say, once the more formally framed arguments have been exhausted and found non-conclusive for the case: A. Aarnio, *The Rational as Reasonable: A Treatise on Legal Justification* (D. Reidel Publishing Co., 1987), 89–95, 98–101, 122–36.

[109] In his *Examiner's Preliminary Report on A Theory of Precedent*, submitted to the Law Faculty of the University in Helsinki, MacCormick, as the officially nominated opponent of the present (doctoral) thesis, pointed out (at p. 3) that such a sequential pattern of argumentation can, in fact, also be detected in a common law judge's precedent-based reasoning, given in terms of judicial exegesis, "guided by the ideas of legal coherence and integrity", to be followed by arguments from analogy, with a recourse to the (underlying) principles involved, finally ending up in openly consequentialist premises for judicial decision-making. In "Precedent in the United Kingdom" (above at n. 1), co-authored by Bankowski, Marshall and MacCormick himself, no such claim is put forth, however, with respect to the content of the precedent ideology of an English judge, unless the short *dictum* (on p. 319), to the effect that "(r)ules come first, but these are bedded in grounds of principle and, where appropriate, substantive elements of value or policy", is taken to convey such a specific meaning.

Rather than following the grasshopper technique of legal argumentation—or a sequence of argumentative leaps and jumps[110] from a highly formal conception of the *ratio* of a case under judicial exegesis or judicial legislation, proceeding towards less legal formalism under judicial analogy or systemic construction of underlying reasons from a line of cases, ending up finally in judicial consequentialism—precedent-based arguments find their proper place within a prestructured system of law that is formed in the image of a *beehive* or an *anthill*, if the insect world metaphor is extended to the constructive capacities of such creatures; while grasshoppers notably build no nests whatever. A well-formed and relatively rigid system of precedent-following, as, for example, in the United Kingdom, is structured in the image of a beehive, where the argumentative weight of the *ratio* of a case is preframed by the doctrine of *stare decisis* and the relatively well-defined meta-rules of how to read precedents among judges and the legal profession. A relatively weakly formed and easily malleable system of precedent-following, as, for example, in Italy, is shaped in the image of an anthill, where novel precedents, like the needles and straws carried onto the anthill by the hard-working ants, get piled up, without any properly reflected idea of the techniques of how to read precedents, nor of the argumentative weight of the *ratio* of a case or line of cases, among the judges and the legal profession.

The proper allegory for precedent-following is, accordingly, not the *grasshopper technique* of legal argumentation, where the strictures of initial legal formalism and the doctrine of *stare decisis* are gradually loosened in favour of open-ended judicial consequentialism but, instead, the process of a patient extraction of arguments from a prior case in accordance with the meta-rules of backward-looking judicial exegesis and the formal doctrine of *stare decisis*, giving effect to the *beehive model* of precedent-following (United Kingdom); or, alternatively, a flood of discordant precedents under a "let loose" conception of precedent-following, where "lines", "chains" or "strings" of mutually discordant or conflicting precedents are gradually piled up without any pre-defined internal structure or pattern, giving effect to the *anthill model* of precedent-following (Italy). The two legal systems of United Kingdom and Italy are, of course, the two extremes of legal formalism and non-formalism *vis-à-vis* precedent-following, while any other system of precedent-following is likely to be situated somewhere in-between two end poles.

110 On "jumps" in moral and legal reasoning, see A. Peczenik, *On Law and Reason* (Kluwer, 1989), 114–18, 130–1.

Part B

A Theory of the Multi-Level Structure of Law

6

Towards a Rule of Law Ideology for Precedents

1. PROLOGUE: SURFACE-STRUCTURE LEVEL OF OPERATIVE PRECEDENT-IDENTIFICATION AND PRECEDENT-FOLLOWING

The surface-structure level of law is no more than a visible *tip of the iceberg*, or a set of individual court rulings which are observable even by the Holmesian "bad man", only interested in knowing "what the Massachusetts or London courts will do in fact". At the operative surface-structure level of law, the *ratio* of a prior case is claimed to be duly identified by the subsequent judge or judges, as distinct from mere *dicta*, or argumentative context, of that *ratio*. However, the exact content of a judge's precedent ideology need not be very self-reflected or openly articulated even by the judiciary itself.

The remaining part of the "iceberg", i.e. the deep-reaching ideological, discourse-theoretical, and infrastructure level preconditions of precedent-norm formation, is "underwater", in the sense of the latent deeper-structure level preconditions of precedent-identification and precedent-following (or precedent-evading). The discourse-theoretical frame of law comprises the axiomatic postulates of legal validity and legal rationality. It is not common for judges to expressly restate the validity and rationality conditions of law on each occasion of judicial decision-making, while the existence of such criteria is a necessary prerequisite of rational legal argumentation in the first place.[1] The parallel requirement of legal rationality is materialised in the outward justification of a legal decision. Again, the meta-rules of legal discourse rationality are not generally displayed in open terms by judges in the course of judicial adjudication.[2]

With reference to the operative *ratio/dicta* distinction and the operative reading of the *ratio*, an authoritative judicial ruling is brought into effect *vis-à-vis* the facts of a new case. Following Hart's linguistic usage, one could say that the

[1] If the contrary were the case in legal practice, judicial decisions would invariably contain a validity clause to the following effect: "Legal norm N—which is valid since it was enacted by the Queen in Parliament, and is not in conflict with valid constitutional provisions, and finds further support in a line of precedents, etc.—is to be interpreted so-and-so in the novel case at hand".

[2] If the contrary were the case, judicial decisions would invariably contain a rationality clause to the following effect: "Since the commonly acknowledged precepts of legal discourse rationality—i.e. no speaker may contradict himself in the discourse, and every speaker must give reasons for what he asserts when asked to do so, unless he can cite reasons which justify a refusal to provide a justification, etc.—have been duly observed in the court proceedings and legal deliberation of the court, legal norm N is to be interpreted so-and-so in the novel case at hand".

operative surface-structure level of law, as it materialises in the gradual unfolding of precedent-identification and precedent-following in day-to-day legal adjudication, "exists only as a complex, but normally concordant, practice of the courts, officials, and private persons in identifying the law by reference to certain criteria".[3] Beneath such presumed judicial uniformity, there extends the deep-structure level edifice of a judge's normative ideology, the axiomatic postulates of legal validity and legal rationality, and the identity-evading infrastructures of law, language and philosophy under the theoretical premises of analytical positivism.

2. GENERAL OUTLINE OF THE MULTI-LEVEL THEORY OF LAW AND ITS RELATION TO TUORI'S CONCEPTION OF LAW

2.1 The three levels of law, presented in the form of a diagram

Conceptual analytics of precedent-norm formation is defined by the two categories of *legal norm constitution* and *judicial signification*, and the three levels of analysis, i.e. the surface-structure, deep-structure and infrastructure levels of law. The *surface-structure* level of precedent-based law consists of the *operative* preconditions of the *ratio* of a case. The *deep-structure* level of law consists of the *ideological*, on the one hand, and *discourse-theoretical* or *conceptual*, on the other, preconditions of the *ratio* of a case, and of a legal norm in wider terms. Finally, the *infrastructure* level of law consists of the *prelogical* and *preconceptual* preconditions of legal norm constitution/disintegration and the production/dissolution of a specific meaning-content within law. The surface-structure level of law is "glossed" by practice-oriented *legal dogmatics*, in the sense of providing for the interpretation and systematisation of valid legal rules and principles; the deep-structure level of law is analysed by theory-laden *jurisprudence*; and the infrastructure level of law is reflected upon by *legal philosophy*.

Thus, the formative premises of the *ratio* of a case, i.e. a precedent-norm, may be concisely presented in the form of the following conceptual scheme:

(1) *Surface-structure level of law*: operative preconditions of the identification and interpretation of the *ratio* of a case
= *level of legal dogmatics*.

(2) *Deep-structure level of law*: ideological and discourse-theoretical, or conceptual, preconditions of the *ratio* of a case:

(a) precedent ideology: identification and interpretation of the *ratio* of a case in light of the set of ideological fragments involved, as further qualified by the specific rule of law criteria for precedent-following,

[3] H.L.A. Hart, *The Concept of Law* (Clarendon Press, Oxford, 1961), 107. Hart was, of course, speaking of the rule of recognition in more general terms in the text extract cited.

(b) discourse-theoretical frame: the axiomatic ground of legal validity and legal rationality, plus the two conceptual claims effected and the felicity conditions of adjudication involved
= *level of jurisprudence (i.e. theory of law).*

(3) *Infrastructure level of law*: the prelogical and preconceptual preconditions of legal norm constitution and judicial signification under precedent-following
= *level of legal philosophy.*

The exact number of the levels of law is three or four, depending on whether a judge's ideological commitments and the discourse-theoretical frame of legal validity and legal rationality are gathered under the common heading of the deep-structure level of law, or whether they are treated as two distinct levels of law. Whether the infrastructures of law and legal discourse can be treated as a distinct level of law of their own is also contestable, since they operate from within the deep-structure (and surface-structure) level phenomena of law and, moreover, lack any constant metaphysical identity which could then be conceptualised.

The prerequisites of legal norm constitution define the *form*, and the prerequisites of judicial signification define the *content* of a legal norm. In the context of precedents, the prerequisites of legal norm formation bring into effect the formal *ratio/dicta* distinction, or the operative conception of the *ratio* of a case, as detached from its particular meaning-content in case-law adjudication, on the surface-structure level of operative adjudication; while the parallel prerequisites of judicial signification ascribe a specific meaning-content to the norm thus constituted. The two categories of norm constitution and judicial signification exemplify, apart from the basic categories of *form* and *content* in law, the two factors of *institutionalised use of power*, as effected in the law's self-declared claim to legal authority or binding force, and *correctness under the premises of legal rationality*, as effected in the inherent claim to correctness in legal statements issued by the legislator and judges.

Conceptual analytics of precedent-norm formation on the four levels of legal analysis is presented in Figure 5 below. The two columns denote the categories of legal norm constitution and judicial signification, respectively. The vertical categories denote the surface-structure, deep-structure and infrastructure levels of law and legal analysis. The figure may be read from the top downwards, i.e. from the surface-structure to the infrastructure level, or vice versa. The distinct premises of the *ratio* of a case, and partly of any legal norm, are elucidated on each level of analysis. Arrows indicate the direction of influence, and the boxed elements at the centre of the figure are the outcome of analysis on each level of law. The "linguistic precedent-norm (and reasons) formulation" is the starting point of legal analysis, if the diagram is read from top to bottom, and the end result of such conceptual derivation if the diagram is read from bottom to top, i.e. starting from the "production of the same/different within the context of norm/fact".

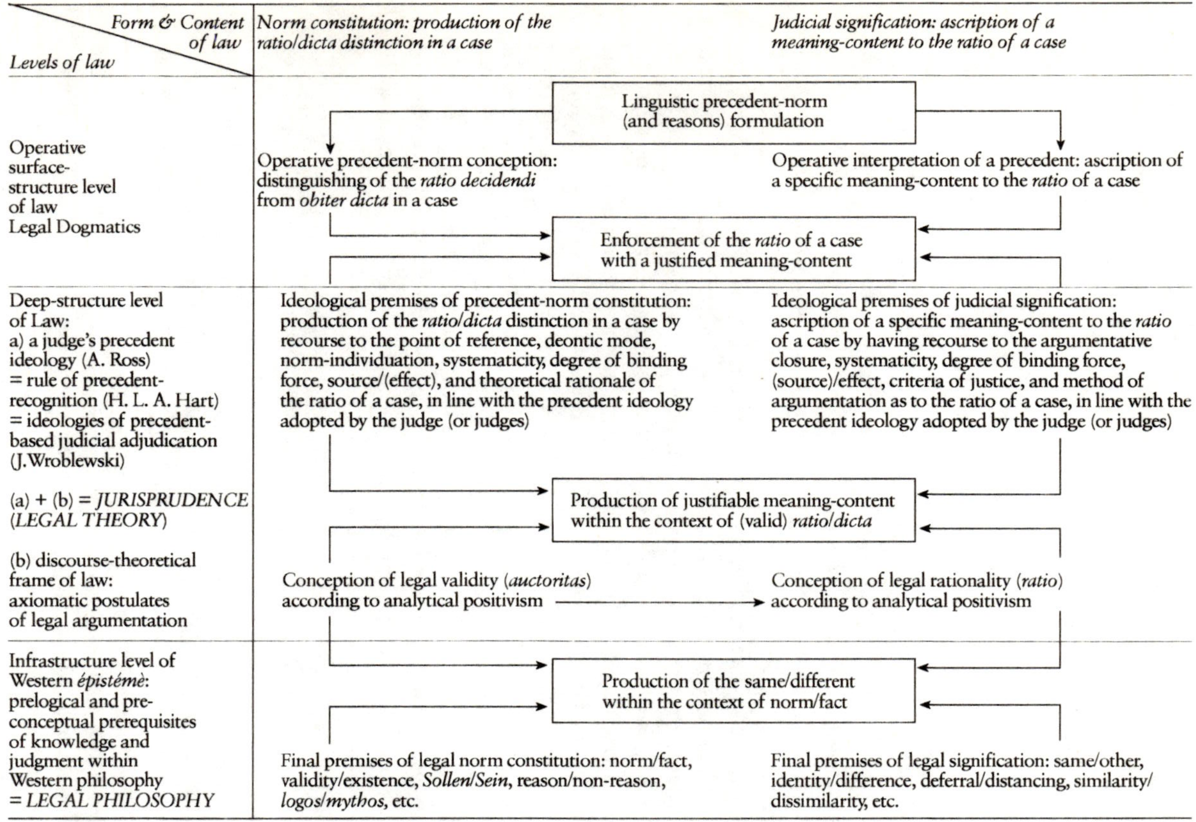

Figure 5: Sum total of the premises of legal norm constitution and judicial signification under precedent-following on the surface-structure, deep-structure and infrastructure levels of law

2.2 Tuori on the multi-layered structure of law

The present conception of the multi-level theory of law and the corresponding formative prerequisites of the *ratio* of a case have been greatly inspired by Tuori's theory of the multi-layered structure of law.[4] The exact content of his conception of law has, however, to some extent been modified here.

Tuori argues that there are three levels of law to be discerned: the *surface level*, the (level of) *legal culture*, and the *deep structure* of law.[5] The surface level comprises statutes, court decisions and statements on the correct interpretation of statutes and judicial decisions as produced by legal science, in the sense of legal dogmatics. The mid-level of legal culture is defined as a combination of the expert culture of legal professionals and the general legal culture of ordinary citizens, while the former is deemed more important in framing the legal phenomena. The expert culture of law comprises general doctrines of law, i.e. general principles and basic concepts in different branches of law. In addition, it includes canons of interpretation, such as the meta-rules of *lex superior*, *lex posterior*, and *lex specialis*, plus the patterns of argumentation applied in legal decision-making. Finally, the deep structure of law is said to correspond to Foucault's notion of the *épistémè* or "historical *a priori*" in the context of law.[6]

"Historical *a priori*" is Foucault's term for the *a priori* of Kant's *First Critique* "historicised". It refers to the formal-logically contingent, but historically and culturally determined conditions of possibility of a certain "order of things" in the (external) world in some historical epoch of the Western *épistémè*.[7] Foucault's (and Tuori's) historical epochs are defined in relatively broad terms, having reference to, for instance, antiquity, renaissance and the classic period in Foucault's epochs, and to traditional, liberal and social law in Tuori's theory. According to Tuori, the prevalent *épistémè* opens up the conceptual space for the categories of modern legal thought, ruling out the impact of alternative ways of legal thinking, argumentation and regulation. Tuori's deep structure of (modern) law is said to comprise the *basic legal categories* of law, like the notion of a legal subject or subjective right, the specific *type of rationality* entailed in modern law, like Weber's formal rationality conception, and the *fundamental*

[4] Chomsky may also be mentioned, with reference to the division of the surface structure and deep structure of language in his theory of linguistic grammar, but his ideas will not be elaborated in the present context. See, in general, N. Chomsky, *Knowledge of Language: Its Nature, Origin and Use* (Praeger, New York, 1986).

[5] K. Tuori, "Towards a Multi-Layered View of Modern Law", in A. Aarnio, R. Alexy and G. Bergholtz (eds), *Justice, Morality and Society: A Tribute to Aleksander Peczenik on the Occasion of his 60th Birthday 16 November 1997* (Juristförlaget i Lund, 1997), 432–6; K. Tuori, "Legal Systems as/and Social Science" (1997) 70 *ARSP* Beiheft 127, 128–30.

[6] Tuori, "Towards a Multi-Layered View of Modern Law", above at n. 5, 434.

[7] M. Foucault, *L'Archéologie du savoir* (Éditions Gallimard, Paris, 1969), 166 ff. Cf. M. Foucault, *Les Mots et les choses: Une Archéologie des Sciences Humaines* (Éditions Gallimard, Paris, 1966). Foucault's archeology of knowledge and the "historical *a priori*" will be commented upon in more detail in the context of the infrastructures of law, in Chapters 8 and 9 below.

normative principles of law, like the basic rights and principles of the *Rechtsstaat*.[8]

Initially, the theoretical frame for Tuori's three-level theory of law was derived from Hänninen's Marxist interpretation of society.[9] The terminology then used by Tuori consisted of the following categories: (1) the law form (*Gesetzform*) at the surface level, (2) the legal ideology (*Rechtsideologie*) at the mid-level, and (3) the legal form (*Rechtsform*) at the deep level of society. Each level of law was determined by the specific subject structure and the corresponding form of consciousness involved, essentially in line with Hänninen's Marxist orientation.[10] The original Marxist frame is lifted in Tuori's later versions of the theory. The change in the theoretical background rationale is already hinted at in "The General Doctrines in Public Law",[11] while in "Legal Systems as/and Social Science" and "Toward a Multi-Layered View of Modern Law"[12] the original Marxist frame recedes, giving room for a combination of ideas drawn—somewhat eclectically, as Tuori himself admits[13]—from Foucault, Ewald, Habermas, and the French Annalist school of historical studies. Now, the differing rate of change is held to be decisive as to the classification of legal phenomena on the three levels: the deep-structure level phenomena are the most resistant to change, whereas it takes no more than "three words from the legislator" or from a judge, i.e. a legislative enactment or a judicial precedent, to change the surface structure of law completely. On the mid-level of legal culture, the velocity of change is somewhere between the two extremes.

Eventually, Tuori has adopted the term *critical legal positivism*, in order to denote the conceptual distance drawn between the initial Marxist frame and the current version of the theory, and to underscore the link established with a Kelsenian type of legal positivism and the critical theory of law. The point of reference of such critique is now said to be found in the inherent contradictions that exist between the three levels of law. By adopting such a modified positivist stance towards the law, any direct allusions to the Marxist conception of society, where the surface structure of society is thought more or less passively to reflect the fundamental economic relations and forces of production operative at the deep-structure level of society, are rejected. At the same time, Tuori, in

[8] Tuori, "Towards A Multi-Layered View of Modern Law", above at n. 5, 434–5.

[9] S. Hänninen, *Aika, paikka, politiikka: Marxilaisen valtioteorian konstituutiosta ja metodista* (Tutkijaliiton julkaisusarja 17, 1981).

[10] K. Tuori, "The General Doctrines in Public Law" (1987) 31 *Scandinavian Studies in Law* 177, 184. See also K. Tuori, *Valtionhallinnon sivuelinorganisaatiosta, 1* (Suomalaisen lakimiesyhdistyksen julkaisuje, Helsinki, 1983), 74–7; K. Tuori, *Valtionhallinnon sivuelinorganisaatiosta, 2* (Suomalaisen lakimiesyhdistyksen julkaisuje, Helsinki, 1983) 12–13; Tuori, *Oikeus, valta ja demokratia* (Lakimiesliiton kustannus, Helsinki, 1990), 26–7.

[11] Tuori, "The General Doctrines in Public Law", ibid.,184, n. 22: "The present author's proposal regarding levels of law has been developed on the basis of Marxist social theory . . . However, it would seem that a separation of legal phenomena into levels with different rates of change along the lines presented here does not necessarily require the acceptance of Marxist theory".

[12] Tuori, "Towards A Multi-Layered View of Modern Law", above at n. 5, 432–6. Cf. Tuori, "Legal Systems as/and Social Science", above at n. 5, 128–30.

[13] Tuori, "Towards a Multi-Layered View of Modern Law", above at n. 5, 435.

pinpointing the very possibility of critique of the inherent inconsistencies in the formal edifice of law, casts off the idea of a fully coherent system of law, as recently defended by Dworkin and MacCormick, among others. Some post-Marxist remnants of the original frame of analysis may still be seen in Tuori's methodological self-reflection on critical legal positivism, however.[14]

2.3 Confrontations with Tuori's theory of law

The key difference between Tuori's theory of law and the present conception of law concerns the very subject matter of analysis. Here, the focus is on the theoretical prerequisites of (legal and) precedent-norm formation on the different levels of law. Tuori, in turn, depicts legal phenomena, or the law understood as "a phenomenon of the cultural normative sphere",[15] in more general terms, without restricting the scope of analysis to the constitutive factors of a legal norm. However, the present unfolding of the down-reaching edifice of the deeper-structure level premises of law by necessity widens the scope of analysis. Whereas the operative precedent-norm conception and the ideological premises of precedents are still aligned with the identification and subsequent interpretation of the *ratio* of a case, the discourse-theoretical level of law entails the conceptual premises of legal discourse in general. The infrastructures of law, in turn, lean on the infrastructures of Western philosophical tradition in general. There is also a terminological difference to take notice of: the surface level of law, the (level of) legal culture, and the deep structure of law are adopted in Tuori's theory of law. In the present discussion, the following levels of law are discerned: the operative surface-structure level, the ideological and discourse-theoretical deep-structure level and, finally, the prelogical and preconceptual infrastructure level of law. The linguistic-positivist surface-structure level of law is more or less identical in both theories of law, however. In contrast, there is no (Derrida-inspired) infrastructure level of law acknowledged in Tuori's conception.

In Tuori's theory, the difference between the three levels of law is outlined in quantitative terms.[16] In the present theory, on the other hand, there is a qualitative difference between the different levels of law. Tuori locates, for example, fundamental normative principles of law among the deep structure level phenomena of law. However, such a stipulation signifies an open deviation

[14] K. Tuori, "*Ideologiakritiikistä kriittiseen positivismiin*", in J. Häyhä (ed.), *Minun metodini* (Werner Söderström Oy, Helsinki, 1997), 312–19 and esp. 319.

[15] Tuori, "Towards a Multi-Layered View of Modern Law", above at n. 5, 433.

[16] In contrast, in the earlier Marxist version of Tuori's theory, the difference between the three layers of law was outlined in openly qualitative terms so as to find a parallel with the distinct subject structure and form of consciousness involved at each level. The later, "post-Marxist" shift in Tuori's theory of law signifies, among other things, the fact that the distinction drawn between the two deeper levels of law, i.e. the level of legal culture and the deep structure level of law, is under a constant threat of collapsing, resulting in a dualist model of manifest legal positivity and the—broadly conceived—critical elements of the deeper level(s) of law.

from the concept of *épistémè*, or the historical *a priori*, as introduced by Foucault and by means of which Tuori describes the deep structure of law. By importing overtly content-bound elements into it, Tuori's deep structure of law is eventually broken into two distinct segments, i.e. those based on Habermas' and Foucault's ideas, respectively, with an unbridgeable methodological gap in-between. The fundamental normative principles of (modern) law, like the basic rights and principles of a *Rechtsstaat*, belong to the Habermas-inspired, content-bound category in Tuori's deep structure of law; while the more formal notions of basic legal categories and the type of rationality of (modern) law yield to the precepts of a Foucauldian *épistémè*, or the historical *a priori*, of law.

I, instead, argue that the formal character of law increases constantly as one proceeds downwards from the surface-structure towards the deep-structure and infrastructure levels of law, and vice versa. The constituents of operative adjudication and of a legal or precedent ideology are, in other words, predominantly content-bound in character. The discourse-theoretical frame of legal validity and legal rationality, along with the conceptual claims and felicity conditions of adjudication thereby effected, are increasingly formal in character. Finally, the infrastructure level prerequisites of legal norm constitution and judicial signification under precedent-following are purely formal and, indeed, even without any constant metaphysical or conceptual identity.

The term *a priori* will be employed in the present treatise with reference to the ultimate premises of legal norm *constitution* (and *disintegration*) and the *proliferation* (and *dispersement*) of meaning under precedent-following, respectively. Apart from the influence of the Foucauldian notion of *épistémè*, or the "historical *a priori*", the present unfolding of the infrastructures of law has been greatly inspired by Derrida and the philosophy of deconstruction. Any theoretical link with the reconstructive elements of Habermas' theory of society, as are found in Tuori's conception of the deep-structure level of law, is thereby cut off, as the inclusion of such content-bound, normative elements into the infrastructure level of law has the effect of turning Foucault's "historical *a priori*" into an uneven combination of the "historical *a priori*" and the "historical *a posteriori*", the latter laden with a distinctively Habermasian undertone. The term *infrastructure* is derived from Derrida's (and Gasché's) conceptual usage, and there is no functionally equivalent to it in Tuori's theory of law.

2.4 Relations between the levels of law: condition of possibility, professional morality of aspiration and relation of restructuring

Tuori describes the vertical relations which prevail between the three levels of law in terms of sedimentation, constitution, concretisation, limitation, criticism and justification.[17] *Sedimentation* refers to the impact which positivist surface

[17] Tuori, "Legal Systems as/and Social Science", above at n. 5, 129–30; Tuori, "Towards A Multi-Layered View of Modern Law", above at n. 5, 436–42; Tuori, above at n. 14, 322–4.

level manifestations of law have on the deeper levels of law, in the sense that each individual legal enactment or judicial ruling may, at the same time, produce, reproduce and modify the level of legal culture and the deep-structure level phenomena of law. *Constitution* signifies the fact that deeper levels of law function as the grounding condition of possibility of the higher levels of law, in the sense that deeper-level phenomena of law provide the legislator, judges and legal scholars with the conceptual, normative and methodological tools by means of which they can produce statutory norms, judicial rulings, and statements on the interpretation of the former two. *Concretisation* refers to the materialisation of deeper levels of law in the form of surface-level manifestations. *Limitation* refers to the specific restrictions imposed on the surface level by the deeper-level phenomena of law. *Criticism* denotes the impact of "normative censorship effected through legal principles" on the surface level of law. Finally, *justification* refers to the finding of reasons for the surface-level phenomena of law from among elements situated at the level of legal culture and the deep structure level of law.

In the present context, the number of such vertical relations between the levels of law has been reduced to three, based on ideas put forth by Tuori, Fuller and, in the case of the infrastructures of law, Derrida.

The infrastructure level of law is the *condition of possibility* (and *impossibility*) of the discourse-theoretical frame of law, *grounding/cancelling* and *effecting/effacing* the deep-structure level phenomena of law. The infrastructures of law will be tackled in detail in chapters 8 and 9 below.

The discourse-theoretical level of law is the *condition of possibility* of legal phenomena prevalent at the level of legal ideology, to the effect that a judge's consistent ideological stance towards the identification and interpretation of the *ratio* of a case is conditional on the two deeper notions of legal validity and legal rationality, plus the conceptual, institutional and mental felicity conditions of adjudication. The relation between the level of legal ideology and the level of operative adjudication, in turn, is one of professional *morality of aspiration* only, appealing to "the pride of the craftsman" or "excellence in legality" in Fuller's terminology,[18] with allusion to the ideal of an attentive and prudent judge who strives for professional perfection or, at least, tries his best to avoid professional blame and censure in legal adjudication.

The down-reaching, feedback-oriented relations between the different levels of law *requalify*, *realign*, or *restructure* the deeper-level phenomena of law, once a profound enough change has taken place on the level of operative adjudication or on the level of legal ideology. If the operative mode of judicial adjudication has gone through some radical change, resulting in, for example, the breakthrough of the human rights argument in the courts of justice, then after some delay the discourse-theoretical frame of law will be forced to change, so as to restore a balance between the two levels of law. In principle, the same holds true

[18] Lon L. Fuller, *The Morality of Law* (Yale University Press, 1969), 41–3.

of the infrastructure level of law, if the discourse-theoretical frame of law has gone through some profound enough change. However, the infrastructures are, somewhat paradoxically, remarkably constant, despite their prelogical and preconceptual status of self-evasive "non-identity", since they are aligned with the basic postulates and ultimate limits of Western metaphysics.

Thus, the relation between the preconceptual/conceptual and the conceptual/ideological levels of law is one of a condition of possibility (and impossibility) *vis-à-vis* legal norm constitution and judicial signification, while the relation between the ideological/operative levels of law is equal to the Fullerian "morality of aspiration" only. That difference is materialised in the form of the *felicity conditions* of adjudication on the discourse-theoretical level of law, on the one hand, and the specific *rule of law ideology* on the level of legal ideology, on the other. The two conceptual claims effected at the discourse-theoretical frame of law, i.e. the claim to legal correctness and the claim to legal authority, necessitate avoiding a conceptual anomaly or performative contradiction in a judge's speech act of rendering a judicial decision; while a failure to meet with the ideological criteria involved would only make the decision "less than perfect", or defective as to its reasoning structure and a target for criticism from the legal profession. The normative impact of legal ideology is thus materialised in judges' professional ethics only.

Figure 6 illustrates the vertical relations between the levels of law.

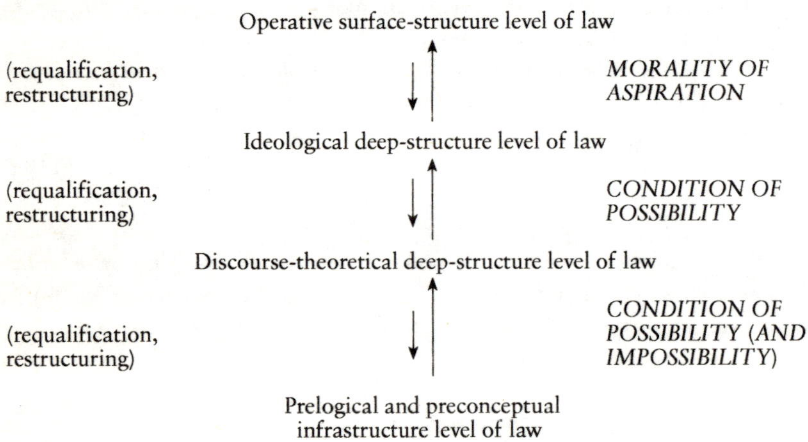

Figure 6: Vertical relations between the levels of law

3. REFRAMING THE IDEOLOGICAL PREMISES OF PRECEDENT-FOLLOWING

3.1 Fragments of a judge's precedent ideology reconsidered

The deep-structure level of law *vis-à-vis* precedent-following may be divided into two distinct subcategories: (1) a judge's *precedent ideology* (Ross) or the *rule of precedent-recognition* adopted by him (Hart), as placed within the context of the feasible *ideologies of precedent-based judicial decision-making* (Wróblewski), and (2) the *discourse-theoretical frame* of law, which, under the theoretical premises of analytical positivism, consists of the axiomatic postulates of legal validity (*auctoritas*) and legal rationality (*ratio*), plus the conceptual, institutional and mental felicity conditions of a judges' performance of specific speech acts in legal adjudication. The two concepts of a judges' precedent ideology (Ross) and the rule of precedent-recognition acknowledged by the judiciary (Hart) are here defined as functionally equivalent, having reference to the specific ideological fragments entailed in the identification and subsequent reading of the *ratio* of a case *vis-à-vis* the facts of the novel case at hand.

The sum total of the various models of precedent ideology make up the *possible worlds semantics* for a judge *vis-à-vis* precedent-identification and precedent-following. In the ideal world of rational model construction, the models may and, in fact, even should be defined as consisting of an internally coherent set of premises.[19] As was argued above, the law in action of precedent-based judicial adjudication may well be based on a more-or-less incoherent set of ideological premises, to which the judicial experience drawn from, for example, Italy, France and Finland bears witness. Yet, such an empirical inquiry into the divergent phenomena of the law in action is left out of the present discussion, to be pursued by the collective efforts of a theory-sensitive legal sociology.

The ideological fragments of precedent-norm constitution include, first, the *point of reference* in a court case by allusion to which the formal *ratio/dicta* distinction is brought into existence in the first place. *Argumentative closure* is its parallel in legal interpretation, with reference to the sources of law to which a judge has legitimate access in judicial decision-making. The *deontic mode* accorded to the *ratio* of a case, in the sense of the qualification of the deontic operator *S* in Kelsen's definition of a norm "if p, then *S*q", may be taken as part of formal norm constitution, due to the essentially ontological or "logical" character of the rule/principles dichotomy in Dworkin's conception of law.[20] The deontic mode of the *ratio* of a case may be manifestly expressed at the surface-structure level of law, but that need not be the case. In the three approaches to precedent-following which are based on a deontically prima facie indeterminate relation of social facts and legal consequences—i.e. material facts model, paradigm case model, and requalified facts model—the *ratio* of a case is only subsequently specified as to its deontic mode. *Precedent-norm individuation* is

[19] Cf. Peczenik on the requirement of coherence of legal ideology: "Legal ideology is a theoretical construction that aims at making a coherent totality of fragmentary practices and norms performed and internalised by courts, authorities, lawyers and some laymen. These people act and speak *as if* they were accepting legal ideology": A. Peczenik, *The Basis of Legal Justification* (Infotryck AB, 1983), 105. Cf. also ibid., 111, where the author refers to the task of legal ideology as an effort to bring some internal order within "an ever-changing cluster of normative and cognitive convictions".

[20] "The difference between legal principles and legal rules is a logical distinction": Dworkin, *Taking Rights Seriously* (Harvard University Press, 1978), 24.

determined by the relative degree of either sky-soaring abstractness or, alternatively, case-bound contextuality in the formal constitution of the *ratio* of a case.

The requirement of legal *systematicity* in a set of precedents is a defining feature of the Dworkinian underlying reasons model of precedent-following, where the notion of observing a high degree of legal coherence is acknowledged in terms of the *law as integrity* doctrine, both in legal norm constitution and judicial meaning-production. In all other approaches to precedent-following, loose casuistics prevails over any efforts of an overtly systemic kind. The *binding force* of the *ratio* of a case equally has an effect on both norm constitution and the ascription of a meaning-content to the norm thereby brought into effect. The *source/effect* of the *ratio* may be taken as part of formal precedent-norm constitution or as part of legal signification. A more formal reading would place the emphasis on a norm's source of origin in the prior court's or the subsequent court's legal discretion, while a more content-oriented reading of the issue would emphasise the normative effects a precedent exerts on later adjudication. The *method of argumentation* adopted in a precedent ideology covers the specific readings skills or precedent-sensitive techniques of ascribing a specific meaning-content to the *ratio* of a case, as outlined in terms of judicial exegesis, constant realignment of the *ratio* of a case in the interplay of analogy and distinguishing, the "best constructive interpretation of past legal decisions" under the Dworkinian doctrine of law as integrity, or a thorough revaluation of the merits of the prior decision, to name just four distinct alternatives to the reading of a precedent. The *theoretical background rationale* of a given precedent ideology is the "ideological cement" which holds together the various elements of precedent-norm constitution in a coherent manner. The *criteria of justice* adopted have a similar position, insofar as the internal coherence of the various tenets of legal signification is concerned.

The operative and ideological premises of the *ratio* of a case both deal with the criteria which create and sustain the formal *ratio/dicta* distinction in a case and the specific criteria for ascribing a specific meaning-content to the *ratio* thereby brought into effect. The distinction between the two levels of operative adjudication and legal ideology is drawn on the ground of the presence or lack of *theoretical self-reflection vis-à-vis* such fragments of precedent ideology on the part of judges and the legal profession generally. The operative surface-structure level of law, comprising the operative precedent-norm conception and the canons of operative interpretation *vis-à-vis* the *ratio* of a case, concerns the *pragmatics* of precedent-based judicial adjudication, where the prevalent doctrine and tradition of *how to read precedents* is taken as more or less granted by judges and other law-applying officials. Access to the ideological deep-structure level phenomena of law is, in turn, conditional on the degree of professional understanding and self-reflection attained by the judiciary and legal profession *vis-à-vis* such ideological premises of adjudication.

3.2 A formal definition of the rule of precedent-recognition

In Hart's theory of law, a somewhat simplified model of the rule of recognition for a system of statutory rules was given in the form of the *Queen rule*, i.e. "what the Queen in Parliament enacts is law". Hart, like Ross in his account of judges' normative ideology, makes room for the impact of a variety of legal sources in a modern legal system. When placed in the specific context of precedent-identification, the Hartian *rule of precedent-recognition* may be defined in the following, slightly formalised manner:

> A norm that is defined C_m as to its constitutive structure and S_n as to its structure of signification is valid law under the conception of precedent ideology I_p.

C_m refers to the various elements of formal precedent-norm constitution, i.e. point of reference, deontic mode, norm-individuation, systematicity, degree of binding force, source/(effect) and theoretical rationale of the *ratio* of a case. The variable *m* may hold the values defined above, e.g. the different degrees of legal formality under a precedent-norm's deontic mode, the degree of malleability in terms of its mandatory force, etc. S_n refers to the various elements of meaning-production in the context of precedents, i.e. argumentative closure, systematicity, degree of binding force, (source)/effect, criteria of justice and method of argumentation adopted in reading the *ratio* of a case. The variable *n* may hold the values defined above, e.g. formal predictability and substantive correctness in terms of the criteria of justice, etc. I_p refers to the cluster or sum total of the ideological fragments of precedent-identification and precedent-following adopted by the judge or judges concerned.

The rule of precedent-recognition may be defined broadly, with coverage of the constitutive and signification-aligned elements of precedent-norm formation alike. An alternative conception of the rule of precedent-recognition would entail only the constitutive elements of the *ratio* of a case, excluding the "sense-making" or meaning-constituting facets of legal signification. The wider notion of the rule of precedent-recognition will be followed here, since the form-oriented and content-oriented elements of the *ratio* of a case are thought to be relatively closely intertwined at the level of legal ideology.

The formal definition given of the rule of precedent-recognition above refers to the constituents of a judge's precedent ideology only. The operative premises of precedent-following may also be included in the notion of the rule of precedent-recognition, since the surface-structure level of operative adjudication reflects the deep-structure level phenomena of a precedent ideology, although in a less-than-fully self-reflected manner on the part of judges and other law-applying officials. The inclusion or exclusion of such operative elements of adjudication in the formal definition of the rule of precedent-recognition depends on whether Hart's master rule is taken primarily as a theoretical (re)construction of judges' professional understanding *vis-à-vis* the various fragments of a precedent ideology whose external effects are then materialised in the (claimed) uniformities of operative, day-to-day legal adjudication; or whether the rule of recognition is, instead, taken in the sense of an operative tool of rule-identification whose exact relation to the various fragments of the prevalent legal source ideology need not be fully reflected by the judges themselves.

Although Hart, being bred to the theory-aversive Oxford philosophy of ordinary language, usually underscores the actual, not necessarily self-reflected use of the rule of recognition by judges and other law-applying officials when identifying the valid law by reference to certain operative criteria, in the image of the *Queen rule* of the English legal system, instead of raising up the more theory-laden tenets involved in his master rule, the equation of the rule of precedent-recognition with the constituents of a judge's precedent ideology has, however, been adopted here. While a judge may be content with a less-than-fully self-reflected and articulated conception of the prevalent criteria of valid rule-recognition, as are conveyed to him by the pragmatics-laden doctrine and tradition on precedent-following in the legal system concerned, the specific theory-laden elements which stem from the legal source ideology—and from the discourse-theoretical frame of law and the infrastructures of law, as well—will have an essential impact on judicial adjudication, no matter whether or not the judges have fully grasped the influence of such deeper-structure level preconditions of law. Still, a judge who has gained an insight into such inherent, latently functioning laws of precedent-following will be far better equipped in meeting the challenge of *how to read precedents*, in comparison to his more pragmatics-minded colleague who has nothing but the legal tradition to rely on. Judicial experience drawn from the legal systems of the United Kingdom, United States, France, Italy, Federal Republic of Germany and Finland clearly bears witness thereof.

Moreover, the reconstructive element entailed even in a legal practitioner's operative outline of the (claimed) uniformities of judicial adjudication, which the present conception of the rule of precedent-recognition intends to capture with more intellectual rigour and scholarly coverage, will eventually necessitate a recourse to the contested and theory-laden insights of jurisprudence, since the criteria and the very concept of judicial uniformity cannot be read on the face of legal phenomena. Instead, judgment as to the presence or absence of uniformity or coherence in a set of cases cannot be achieved without drawing support from a rational reconstruction of such essentially theory-laden tenets of law. Moreover, such a definition of the rule of precedent-recognition has better compatibility with Ross' conceptual usage, in the sense of quite perfectly matching with the said constituents of a judge's precedent ideology.

4. A RULE OF LAW IDEOLOGY FOR PRECEDENTS?

The legal source doctrine adopted in a legal system provides for the wider ideological frame or context of precedent-following, laying down the *transcategorical context* of legal adjudication by fixing the higher (and lower) limits of the binding force the *ratio* of a case may legitimately have in a given legal system. However, even the presence of a fully consistent set of such ideological premises among the judiciary will not, as such, guarantee the legitimacy of the outcome of adjudication in society, and the fulfillment of a further set of ideological preconditions is needed. The sum total of such legitimacy-inducing qualifications of legal adjudication may be concisely called a *rule of law ideology* for precedent-following. It is only on the condition that a fully self-reflected notion of a precedent ideology, as further qualified by the specific rule of law criteria for a system of precedents, is commonly acknowledged as a professional standard by the judiciary and other legal professionals engaged in precedent-based legal adjudication that a consistent *pursuit of legitimacy* for the outcome of precedent-following is possible in the first place. In what follows, an effort will be made to define such a set of criteria in light of Fuller's famous idea of the *internal morality of law*.

4.1 Fuller, *The Internal Morality of Law*

In *The Morality of Law*, Fuller argued that there is a set of inherent or moral requirements imposed upon the law-giver, to the effect that a total failure to comply with any of the eight criteria identified by Fuller would lead to "something that is not properly called a legal system at all".[21] In his fictitious example of *King Rex*, who commits all "eight ways to fail to make law",[22] Fuller is mainly concerned with the enactment of legislative norms, but there are some hints towards judicial law-making as well, at least in relation to the issue of legal non-retroactivity. Fuller's list of the *morality that makes law possible* comprises the following eight criteria:[23]

(1) generality of laws (in rejection of *ad hoc* decision-making);
(2) due promulgation of laws;
(3) non-retroactivity of laws;
(4) (semantic) clarity and intelligibility of laws;
(5) non-contradictoriness of laws;
(6) that laws should not require conduct beyond the powers of the norm-addressees;

[21] Fuller, above at n. 18, 33–94, esp. 39.
[22] Ibid., 33 ff.
[23] Ibid., 38–94, esp. 39.

(7) relative constancy of laws through time; and
(8) congruence between official action and the declared rules of law.

Fuller's contention would seem to endorse the claim that a failure to meet with any of the criteria would deprive a legal system of its legally binding character, i.e. legal validity.[24] However, a few pages later Fuller concedes that—with the one exception of making laws known or duly available to those concerned, i.e. the requirement of due promulgation—such criteria have the status of only a *morality of aspiration vis-à-vis* the law-giver, not a morality of duty. Fuller's seven remaining elements thus lay down a professional ideal for the legal profession, making an appeal to "a sense of trusteeship and to the pride of the craftsman";[25] while the requirement of due promulgation is said to yield to the criteria of formalisation and, presumably, the morality of duty.

Fuller's line of argumentation bears some obvious affinity to J.L. Austin's famous example, "*the cat is on the mat but I do not believe it is*", to Habermas' universal-pragmatic preconditions of successful speech acts, and to Alexy's claim to legal correctness (and my corresponding claim to legal authority), which will be elaborated and analysed in more detail below, under the discourse-theoretical frame of law. Yet, while Austin, Habermas and Alexy are concerned with the grounding conditions of possibility of certain types of speech acts, Fuller no more than delineates the preconditions of a "morality of aspiration" or "perfection in legality" in his internal morality of law, the requirement of due promulgation of laws being the only exception thereto. Fuller is thus dealing with issues of the *ideological* deep-structure level of law in terms of the present discussion, while Austin, Habermas and Alexy focus instead on the deeper, *discourse-theoretical* level of law and society when putting forth the inherent validity claims of intelligible linguistic communication (Habermas, Alexy) or the felicity conditions of the performance of certain kinds of speech acts (Austin). Fuller outlines the preconditions for the pursuit of legitimacy in legislation (or jurisdiction); while Austin, Habermas, Alexy (and myself) set out essentially stronger claims to correctness and authority *vis-à-vis* the outcome of legislation and/or jurisdiction.

Taken at face value, precedents would seem to rank poorly indeed under the Fullerian standard of a judge's morality of aspiration. Precedents are, first, usually highly *context-bound*, tailor-made or even *ad hoc*, and not general in scope, since they are concerned with the specific topics of case-law adjudication. Second, precedents need not be given any authoritative or uniquely correct norm formulation, as Hart acutely pointed out,[26] and so the requirement of due *promulgation* might not be fulfilled in the case of precedents. Third, with the one exception of the strictly positivist models of precedent ideology, i.e. the

[24] Fuller's argumentation is thick with rhetoric. He talks of the "eight routes to disaster", in stark contrast to the declared aim of "legal excellence", "perfection in legality" or the "pride of the craftsman": ibid., 39–43.

[25] Ibid., 43–4.

[26] Hart, above at n. 3, 131.

ideologies of judicial legislation and judicial reference, precedents have a more-or-less *retroactive effect* on the litigants' legal position. Fourth, the need for semantic *clarity* is related to the requirement of promulgation of laws. If there is no expressly given or authoritative precedent-norm formulation, the requirement of semantic clarity cannot be satisfied either. Fifth, there is no guarantee of inherent *non-contradictoriness* in a line of precedents, except under the somewhat non-standard premises of the underlying reasons ideology of precedent-following where the Dworkinian "law as integrity" doctrine is adhered to by the judiciary.

Sixth, the requirement that the laws *should not require conduct beyond the powers of the norm-addressees* holds equally true for precedents as for statutory norms. However, the possible lack of any expressly given precedent-norm formulation may cause uncertainty as to what is, in fact, required from judges and citizens by the valid set of precedents.[27] Seventh, the idea of sustaining *constancy through time* would not seem to be a specific virtue ascribable to a system of precedents, the positivist ideologies of judicial reference and judicial legislation notwithstanding. Instead, a well-functioning system of precedents is more often taken to display the virtues of flexibility, legal dynamics and responsiveness to the needs for social change, as illustrated by the no-more-than loosely defined techniques of distinguishing, modifying or departing from a valid precedent. Finally, the requirement of having *congruence between official action and declared rule*, or between the "law in action" and the "law in books", may affect statutory norms and precedents alike, the latter, of course, on the condition that there is some expressly stated or otherwise identifiable *ratio* of a case to be observed in the first place. Due to the strongly case-bound character of precedent-based judicial adjudication, and to the element of retroactivity involved therein, precedents would seem to rank even better than their statutory counterpart under the last criterion.

With the exception of the two rather self-evident criteria that laws should not require what is impossible from norm-addressees and that there should be congruence between official action and declared rule, precedents would not seem to satisfy the Fullerian standards of law. To put it concisely, precedents are or, at least, may often: (1) be context-bound or even *ad hoc*, and not general or abstract, in character; (2) lack any express norm formulation, or even lack a widely acknowledged method of distinguishing the *ratio* of a case from its argumentative context or *dicta*, thus failing to satisfy the requirement of due promulgation of laws; (3) be retroactive as to their legal effect; (4) lack semantic precision, in consequence of point (2) above; (5) not be particularly resistant to

[27] As is well known, Bentham lauched a vehement and lifelong attack on the "sinister interests of Judge & Co." and the thoroughly retroactive character of the English common law system. He made a frequent request for the codification of English laws, in the image of the codes enacted, for instance, in France at that time. See J. Bentham, *Justice and Codification Petitions* (Fred B. Rothman & Co., 1992), where the author's age—Bentham was over 80 when drafting the said petitions—had not diminished his wit of argumentation in the least.

inherent contradictions in a line of precedents; and 6) not be particularly constant over time, due to the various means of distinguishing, modifying or departing from a precedent.

The specific reading skills needed for distinguishing the *ratio* of a case from the *dicta* may not be fully mastered even by the legal profession, at least not in civil law systems. Therefore, the external controllability of a system of precedents may seem weak, indeed, from a civilian lawyer's point of view. Is the resulting system of precedents, therefore, "something that is not properly called a legal system at all, except perhaps in the Pickwickian sense in which a void contract can still be said to be one kind of contract", as Fuller argued with respect to a law-giver's failure to meet with any one of the eight criteria which constitute the internal morality of law?[28] The answer is, of course, negative, as Fuller himself would seem to admit. Only the criterion of an efficient promulgation of laws is taken to have a *definitional* or validity-grounding effect on law. The seven remaining criteria, on the other hand, no more than specify the *qualifying* preconditions of well-functioning legislation, given in terms of "an appeal to the pride of the craftsman", an "aspiration toward perfection in legality", or striving after "excellence in legality".[29]

However, in light of the above analysis of precedents, not even the requirement of due promulgation may be regarded as a definitional criterion of law, the violation of which would deprive law of its validity or binding force, but as a qualifying criterion only. Therefore, Fuller's criteria for a morally sound law-making may be read as an effort to lay down ideological preconditions for the *pursuit of legitimacy* in law. Yet, Fuller's conception of law was outlined mainly with an eye on legislation and the resulting system of statutory norms. In the context of precedents, such legitimacy-inducing criteria will need to be substantially modified.

4.2 Six facets of a rule of law ideology for precedent-following

There are six general rule of law criteria for precedent-following which frame the pursuit of legitimacy for the outcome of such legal adjudication:

(1) appositeness (expediency) and adequacy of normative and factual information;
(2) fair predictability;
(3) systemic balance (congruence);
(4) ideological commitments and argumentative skills;
(5) respect for the basic conceptions of justice and fairness in society; and
(6) integrity in argumentation.

Below, each criterion will be considered individually.

[28] Fuller, above at n. 18, 39.
[29] Ibid., 41–3.

(1) Appositeness (expediency) and adequacy of normative and factual information

The appositeness or expediency and adequacy of the normative and factual information entailed in a precedent or line of precedents comprises two distinct feature—one quantitative, the other qualitative:

(a) *quantitative* criterion: adequate coverage of real and hypothetical cases of the information put forth in a precedent or line of precedents; and
(b) *qualitative* criterion: appositeness (expediency) of the normative information provided by a precedent or line of precedents.

From a purely *quantitative* point of view, an excessive flood of precedents, as in the Italian *Corte di Cassazione*, may be as harmful for the proper functioning of a system of precedents as a shortage of cases and case-law material. In the former situation, the subsequent judge is given more information than he can possibly cope with. Moreover, the content of such legal information may be internally irreconcilable or even contradictory in nature, as cases and their rulings are gradually piled up, without being framed or supported by a well-formed conception of *how to read precedents*. In the other alternative, i.e. where there is a shortage of precedents, the subsequent judge is left without any adequate guidelines for legal decision-making, thus necessitating a recourse to over-extended analogy on the basis of the few cases in fact available to him.

I would argue that the relative volume of precedents issued in any legal system should be roughly in balance with the impact of the following three factors: (1) the overall velocity of change in society; (2) the state of the art of legal doctrine *vis-à-vis* the complexity of society; and (3) the institutional setting of law, especially the balance of power between the legislator and the courts of justice. Thus, rapid and profound change affecting the very foundations of social structures, a poor and stagnant state of legal doctrine, and the relative weakness or passivity of the legislator in introducing legal instruments needed for mastering the dynamics of social change would all be arguments in favour of strengthening the relative position of the courts of justice, and in favour of increasing the volume of precedents produced by the courts each year in the legal system concerned. The adverse situation would be true of a static society where legal science has been able to provide an extensive and internally coherent set of well-reasoned legal solutions, with coverage of practically all the conceivable fact-situations that might emerge in society, and where, moreover, there is no specific need for judicial activism because of an all-encompassing scheme of social regulation that is being put into force by the legislator.

The *qualitative* aspect of appositeness or expediency of the normative information extracted from precedents deals with the quality of reasons given in their support. This is partly related to defects found in the quantitative side of the issue. The reasons given for a ruling should be extensive, elaborate, and detailed enough so as to enable the subsequent judge, advocates and all of the legal community to extract relevant legal arguments from them. Precedent-based argumentation may prove to deviate from the ideal state of legal reasoning in various ways. Apart from the obvious shortcomings induced by laconic, highly technical and oracle-like reasons for a judicial decision, in the style of the *Cour de Cassation* in France or the *massime* extracted from the court rulings by the *Ufficio del Massimario* in Italy, all too lengthy and elaborate chains of judicial reasoning may also be a judicial vice, at least if combined with a less than fully reflected or disciplined use of arguments. The English style of argumentation may be thought to bear some elements of such a judicial vice. In all, overdue legal formalism and the lack of internal structure, coherence and discipline in legal argumentation will count for the most obvious defects in judicial reasoning.

(2) *Fair predictability*

The requirement of fair predictability in case-law adjudication is related to the idea of seeing law as an instrument of social regulation in the sense of deliberate *social engineering*, by means of which the various process values of stability, cohesion, predictability or even "transparency" may be produced in society. At the same, law should be open to the adverse demand of social dynamics, flexibility and fair responsiveness to the demands of social change. The litigants of a case, and the citizens at large, have a right to expect that legal disputes are settled in a consistent and rational manner, so that the future course of judidial adjudication can—with considerable certainty, as Ross put it[30]—be predicted by the collective efforts of legal science. If the courts of justice frequently produce abrubt, "zig-zagging" or whimsical changes in the institutional structure of society, affecting citizens' rights and duties *vis-à-vis* the state and their fellow citizens, without giving fair warning or, at the least, some adequate reasons for the change effected, the process value of fair predictability in judicial adjudication will not be duly satisfied.

The requirement of reasoned continuity in case-law adjudication is all the more important in a system of precedents, because of the inherent element of retroactivity involved. Such retroactivity has some impact within the precedent ideology based on judicial exegesis; it is an essential element in the analogical and systemic models of precedent-following; and it has a predominant role in the ideology based on judicial revaluation. Thus, the idea of giving fair warning before changing the "rules of the game" in society cannot be fully achieved under a system of precedents, unless the strictly positivist premises of judicial legislation, or even of judicial reference, have been adopted by the judiciary. Such a positivist frame of precedent-following, however, would fail to attain the elements of flexibility and responsiveness to social change which are yet often affiliated with a well-functioning system of precedent-based judicial adjudica-

[30] A. Ross, *On Law and Justice* (University of California Press, 1958), 43.

tion. Thus, courts ought to pay increased attention to their line of reasoning in such cases where the prevalent *status quo* in legal and social affairs is suddenly changed, in addition to the more general requirement of giving adequate reasons for any judicial outcome reached.

(3) Systemic balance (congruence)

The systemic balance of a legal system concerns the inherent congruence which ought to prevail between the legal systemic factors exerting influence on *how to do things with precedents*. A precedent is framed by the following five elements: (1) a judge's professional understanding of the constituents of the distinct precedent ideology in fact acknowledged by him; (2) doctrine and tradition on precedents, or the relative determinacy and articulation of the conception on precedents among the judges and the legal profession; (3) the prevalent legal source doctrine, which sets the higher and the lower limits of a precedent's legitimate binding force within a legal system; (4) the discourse-theoretical frame of legal validity and legal rationality, plus the two conceptual claims and felicity conditions of adjudication thereby effected; and, finally, (5) the wider context of legal culture, comprising the essential choice between a positivist, pragmatic, historicist or naturalist definition of law. The requirement of systemic balance is equal to the criterion that a proper systemic congruence ought to prevail between the said determinants which frame the binding force of a precedent in a legal system.

Figure 3 (in chapter 4 above at 4.1, on p. 112) may now be supplemented with a set of broken arrows which denote the requirement of systemic balance in a legal system.

The binding force of the *ratio* of a case should not exceed, nor fall significantly below, the limits set by the prevalent legal source doctrine and the specific constraints derived therefrom upon a judge's legal discretion. Thus, if precedents are qualified as having no more than persuasive, weakly binding force in a given legal system, a judge should not deviate from such a transcategorical frame of adjudication, in the sense of either treating precedents as a mandatory, strictly binding legal source material or, alternatively, giving them no argumentative significance whatever in case-law adjudication. However, as was argued above, a judge's pursuit of legitimacy for the outcome of adjudication at the level of legal ideology deals only with "the pride of the craftsman" or a judge's professional "morality of aspiration", and not the stronger conceptual claims to be found at the discourse-theoretical level of law.

While the higher limit of the binding force of the *ratio* of a case may not be transgressed at the risk of systemic imbalance, the binding force of a precedent may occasionally be allowed to fall below the level it would ordinarily reach, if there are adequate reasons induced by the facts of the new case. If judges deviate from such strictures imposed upon them in the use of precedents, treating precedents as strictly mandatory premises of legal adjudication or as having no

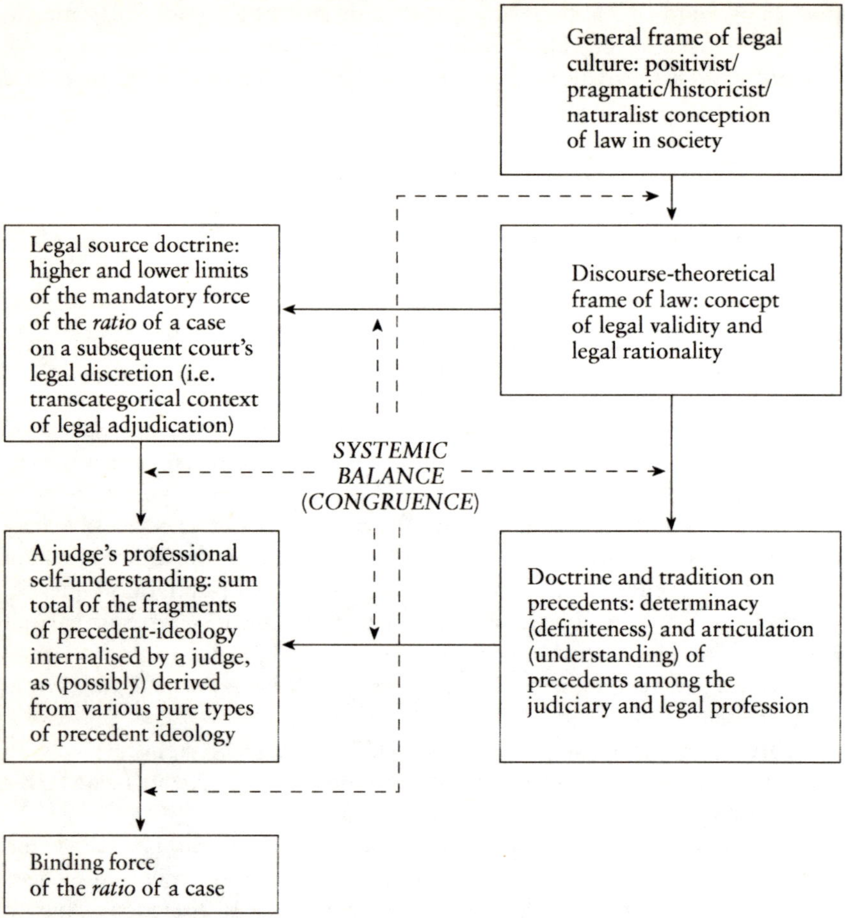

Figure 7: Systemic balance (congruence) between the various determinants of the binding force of a precedent

argumentative weight whatsoever, while the prevalent legal source doctrine would accord a weakly binding or persuasive effect to them, a legitimacy crisis or, alternatively, a profound change in the legal source doctrine will be effected.

Such a legitimacy crisis may have emerged if the arguments put forth by (then) Chief Justice Olsson had been accepted by the Finnish appellate courts and the courts of first instance in the mid-1980s. In stark contrast to the then (and now) prevailing legal source doctrine and the conception and tradition of precedent-following among Finnish judges, Olsson argued that the decisions given by the Supreme Court were to have mandatory, strictly binding force on lower courts' legal discretion. Had Chief Justice Olsson's stance towards precedent-following gained sufficient ground among the Finnish judiciary, the prevalent legal source doctrine would have been forced to change, turning the justices of the Supreme Court into small-scale legislators on the side of Parliament proper. Thus, the end result would have been the emergence of two competing norm-giving authorities of an equal institutional standing and equal request for norm-observance, both supported by a hypothetical Kelsenian *Grundnorm* of its own kind within the Finnish legal system.

A similar situation, verging on the edge of non-legitimacy, may have taken place by force of the landmark decisions issued by the European Court of Justice since the mid-1960s. If the Danish scholar Rasmussen's reading of the issue is accepted, the European Court took up the role of a "court of politics" on a European scale, issuing bold and unexpected quasi-legislative rulings which did not find adequate support in the articles of the Treaty of Rome.[31] From a slightly different angle of approach, such conflict may be described as a potential case of systemic incongruence between the Court's rulings and the constraints derived from the legal source doctrine then prevalent within the legal system of the European Communities.

With due caution, the argument for systemic balance or congruence can be extended to cover all legal systems, no matter what conception of law has been adopted on the level of legal culture. Given that a legal system is based on (moderately) positivist premises, a judge with a strong personal inclination towards the maxims of natural law theory, or with an equally strong ideological profile of a realist or historicist kind, would not pay adequate respect to the prevalent legal systemic constraints of law, and systemic imbalance would be effected.

(4) Ideological commitments and argumentative skills

Unless there is a specific set of ideological commitments and argumentative skills present among the judiciary and legal profession, a system of precedent-following cannot function properly. In other words, the operative notion of the *ratio* of a case should be supported by a consistent and self-reflected conception of the constituents of *precedent ideology* on the part of judges and other officials engaged in legal adjudication. The exact content of such a precedent ideology need not be articulated in the minutest detail, but there should be, at least, a common and widely shared understanding of the role and function of precedents as a source of legal argumentation. A more profound understanding of the inherent premises of precedent-based judicial adjudication would include detailed knowledge of the individual ideological fragments involved in precedent-following.

As was argued above, the prior court must provide subsequent courts with an adequate amount of legally relevant information in the form of the fact-description and legal evaluation of the case ruled upon, so that a relation of precedent-following may be established between the two courts and the two

[31] H. Rasmussen, *On Law and Policy in the European Court of Justice* (Martinus Nijhoff Publishers, 1988).

cases in the first place. Yet, it is really no use having detailed normative information available, if the essential reading skills are not mastered by the judiciary and legal profession in a given legal system. In other words, the argumentative techniques of *how to do things with precedents* are required from all those involved in precedent-based judicial adjudication and argumentation. Above, such precedent-specific techniques of argumentation were outlined in terms of backward-proceeding judicial exegesis, a constant realignment of the *ratio* of a case in terms of analogy/distinguishing, systemic construction of underlying reasons from a prior case or line of cases, and more-or-less radical revaluation of the merits of the prior case.

(5) Respect for the basic conceptions of justice and fairness in society

The social outcomes brought into effect by precedent-following in case-law should comply with the *basic conceptions of justice and fairness in society*. The exact meaning given to such content-bound terms of legal adjudication may—and will—vary in different social contexts. The idea of not violating the moral foundations of society in case-law adjudication may be taken as a functional parallel to Hart's idea of the *minimum content of natural law*, whereby Hart sought to outline the necessary moral criteria of legal regulation in a "non-suicidal" society, based on certain truisms of human nature and human condition. Moreover, such criteria bear some affinity to Fuller's requirement that laws should not require conduct that is beyond the powers of the citizens. The ideas of social equality among citizens of a comparable position and the equitableness of the final outcome of judicial decision-making may be given as two examples of the requirement of observing social justice and fairness in precedent-based legal adjudication.

(6) Integrity in argumentation

While no direct reference to Dworkin's theory of law is intended by the term "integrity", the sixth and final legitimacy criterion for a system of precedents may be called *integrity in argumentation*. Integrity, or honesty and openness in precedent-based legal argumentation, is an ideological safeguard against any reductive efforts of turning the law into interest-laden politics, as argued by some adherents of the Critical Legal Studies movement, or universal morals, as argued by the scholars affiliated with natural law theory. Notably, some of the *Crits* have restated the specific intellectual stance initially put forward by the American Legal Realists, to the effect that the express reasons for a judicial ruling are often nothing more than an empty façade, raised only *ex post facto* so as to conceal the impact of the judge's own ideological motives or bias on the outcome of legal adjudication. Integrity in argumentation may be defined as a set of meta-rules that is imposed upon the judiciary, with the plain intention of ruling out the overt malpractices of legal adjudication, such as the distinguishing of a prior case on purely imaginary or false grounds,[32] excessive distinguishing where a prior judicial ruling is confined to the facts of that particular case only, effected divergence between "saying" and "doing" in case-law adjudication,[33] or *sub silencio* overruling where the act of overruling is not openly acknowledged by the subsequent judge. Without such legitimacy-inducing preconditions in legal argumentation, all judicial reasoning would eventually be based on mere judicial hunch, in the sense of informal guesswork concerning the particular judge's personal preferences and motives.

5. THE "VIEW FROM THE BENCH": A RULE OF LAW IDEOLOGY FOR PRECEDENTS CONTESTED BY THE BAD FAITH ARGUMENT

The cogency of the present, Fuller-inspired rule of law ideology for precedent-following, and the analytical conception of a judge's *view from the bench* in general, can effectively be challenged by the criticism launched by the Critical Legal Studies (CLS) movement. Duncan Kennedy is without doubt one of the leading figures of the CLS movement.[34] I will make use of his recent contribution, *A Critique of Adjudication {fin de siècle}*, in order to contest the analytical conception of law and legal adjudication. Kennedy describes his own ideological position as part of the leftist, modern/postmodern critique of the mainstream doctrine of law, drawing freely—read: eclectically—on the intellectual legacy of the various schools of philosophy and social research on the continent.[35] To a great extent, his line of argumentation would seem to reincarnate the revolt against legal formalism initiated by the American Legal Realists in the 1920s and 1930s.

In the discussion of the various models of precedent ideology above, the term *ideology* was used in a technical sense, having reference to the identification and interpretation of the *ratio* of a case by the judge concerned. The frame of reference was anchored in the analytical and positivist conception of law, as outlined above by Wróblewski, Ross and Hart. Now, in the context of the CLS movement, the term "ideology" has a manifest political undertone, with reference to the officially denied premises of legal adjudication and the influence of the *bad faith argument*: despite judges' denial of the fact, judicial decision-making often entails elements of ideological preference or personal bias on the part of the judiciary. By force of the prevalent legal source doctrine and other formal tenets of legal adjudication, such ideological motives are officially denied and concealed behind the false veil of formal legal validity and rationality. Whereas the

[32] Cf. the notion of "excessive distinguishing" in R.S. Summers, "Precedent in the United States (New York State)", in D.N. McCormick and R.S. Summers (eds), *Interpreting Precedents: A Comparative Study* (Ashgate/Dartmouth, 1997), 392–4 and in MacCormick and Summers, ibid., 559 (Appendix: common questionnaire).

[33] On "saying" and "doing" in judicial adjudication, see Summers, above at n. 32, 401–3 (New York Court of Appeals) and in MacCormick and Summers, above at n. 32, 561 (Appendix: common questionnaire).

[34] R.M. Unger may be mentioned as another key representative of the CLS.

notion of a judge's precedent ideology, as delineated above with allusion to Wróblewski's, Ross' and Hart's analytical theories of law, is taken to encompass a more-or-less coherent set of ideological premises of precedent-identification and precedent-following, Kennedy underscores the essentially incoherent character of any ideology, contrasting the two motives of judicial decision-making in terms of "legality" and "ideology".[36]

Kennedy defines the concept of an ideology as a universalisation project, or textual mediation between the individual interests and universal claims of a social group. Any ideology is, by definition, committed to certain limitations derived from its specific subject matter.[37] An ideological conflict is different from both Socratic dialogue, where the truth of the contested issue is pursued, and from strategic, "arms-length" bargaining, where the only reason for someone to take part in the discourse is the wish to avoid the bad consequences of not attending to it. Ruling out the traditional distinction of the "deductive mode" and the "policy mode" of argumentation as too crude, Kennedy then introduces a tripartite division of arguments into the domains of *law*, still legally qualified but interest-impregnated *policy*, and openly extra-legal *ideology* or "politics". Policy arguments are claimed to be grounded on the universal, not particular, interests of the parties concerned, whereas ideological arguments are based only on the particular interests of the parties. Because of their relatively soft-edged character *vis-à-vis* ideologies proper, policy arguments are often treated as a potential "Trojan horse" for the importation of ideological arguments into law.[38]

Kennedy argues that judges frequently act out of idiosyncratic ideological motives, while the formal constraints of judicial adjudication have the effect of concealing their role in the judges' discretion. No straightforward equation of law and judge-specific ideology or politics is claimed by Kennedy, but law is under a constant threat of being infiltrated by ideological bias which cannot find adequate support in the prevalent legal source doctrine. Therefore, judges often take resort to what Kennedy labels *strategic behavior*, in seeking to give effect to some ideological motives of their own preference under the false veil of formal legality. A consistent denial of the ideological stakes involved in case-law adjudication accords the prevalent *status quo* in society an appearance of reified naturalness, false necessity and feigned justice.[39] At the same time, an ideological gap is opened up between the official ideology of jurisdiction and the judges'

[35] Kennedy's methodological self-reflection is not uncommon in the CLS approach to law in general: "This book is methodologically eclectic. It uses concepts, techniques, and models of performance drawn from technical legal analysis, jurisprudence, neo-Marxism, Weberian sociology, semiotics and structuralism, psychoanalysis, historicist narration, Lewinian field theory, phenomenology, modernist fiction, and deconstruction": D. Kennedy, *A Critique of Adjudication {fin de siècle}* (Harvard University Press, 1997), 15.

[36] Ibid., 52–3.

[37] Ibid., 42–3.

[38] Ibid., 109–11.

[39] Ibid., 2ff.

professional self-understanding, so that judges run the constant risk of losing their moral and professional integrity in legal adjudication. Such ideology-denying judges have three different behaviour strategies to choose from: constrained activism, difference-splitting, and bipolarity in adjudication.[40]

A *constrained activist* seeks to promote the ideological goals or motives he personally believes in, while not violating the semantic boundaries set by the law in force. An activist judge will make full use of the areas of open discretion left unspecified by the law-giver, in order to advance his own ideological preferences. If the relevant legal source material will not permit the desired outcome to be attained, a constrained activist will refrain from transgressing the boundary between the realms of formal legality and extra-legal ideology, and will make the decision against his own ideological conviction or preference. A *difference-splitting judge* is characterised by the tendency he has always to choose an intermediate or tempered position between the two extreme alternatives pursued by a constrained activist, whether radically liberal or radically conservative. Finally, a *bipolar judge* is said to combine elements from the two types of ideology-conscious judges described. On one occasion he may act as a constrained activist of either end of political topography, whereas in the next case he may take the part of a difference-splitting judge, seeking to enforce a dispassionate compromise between the extreme alternatives.

Above, a judge's ideological stance towards precedent-identification and precedent-following was framed by extending Wróblewski's three ideologies of judicial decision-making, Ross' account of a judge normative ideology, and Hart's rule of recognition to the specific domain of precedent-following. Kennedy's three judicial strategies of constrained activism, difference-splitting, and bipolarity in legal adjudication may be read as a disillusioned, or even sarcastic, parallel to such an analytical and positivist frame of law, where the loose-edged methodological credo of judicial pragmatism is given decisive priority over the postulates of an analytical and positivist theory of law. Instead of the feasible ideologies of precedent-based judicial decision-making (Wróblewski), a judge's precedent ideology (Ross) or the rule of precedent-recognition (Hart), we would then have informed guesswork as to the ideological preferences and personality traits of the judge or judges concerned, to be then evaluated in light of Kennedy's three strategies of legal adjudication and the *bad faith argument*. However, the argumentative potential of Kennedy's contention must be left pending for a while, and will be tackled anew at the end of chapter 7.

[40] Ibid., 180–6.

7

Discourse-Theoretical Frame of Law: Ratio *and* Auctoritas, *and the Felicity Conditions of Legal Adjudication*

1. THE DISCOURSE-THEORETICAL IDENTITY OF LAW UNDER ANALYTICAL POSITIVISM

The identification and subsequent interpretation of the *ratio* of a case at the surface-structure level of operative adjudication and at the level of legal ideology would not be possible without presuming the existence of still "deeper-level" prerequisites of law which provide the ground for rational legal argumentation. The identity of legal discourse under the premises of analytical positivism is determined by the following three criteria: (1) *legal validity* and *legal rationality*, as the two theoretical cornerstones of law, constitute the *axiomatic ground* of law; (2) the two conceptual claims, i.e. the *claim to legal authority* and the *claim to legal correctness*, are brought into effect with reference to the postulates of legal validity and legal rationality; and, finally, (3) the wider notion of the *felicity conditions* of legislation and judicial adjudication is determined by the relative success or failure of the legislator or judge to satisfy the *conceptual*, *institutional* and *mental* prerequisites involved in the performance of their specific speech acts, with reference to the avoidance of the various infelicities of a speech act as discerned by Austin (and Alexy). The felicity conditions of adjudication, in other words, comprise the fulfillment of the two conceptual claims, plus the specific institutional and mental prerequisites of legislation and judicial adjudication. As will be argued below, legal discourse may be classified as a "special case" of general practical discourse, thus resting on the theoretical premises laid down by the postulates of speech act theory.

2. THE AXIOMATIC GROUND OF LEGAL DISCOURSE: *RATIO* AND *AUCTORITAS*

Under the theoretical premises of analytical positivism, legal discourse can be defined as a more-or-less well-ordered set of statements, sentences or assertions where the *validity* and *rationality* of a legal norm or set of legal norms is either expressly affirmed, or the validity and rationality of a legal norm or set of legal norms is at least silently presupposed when such a statement, sentence or assertion is voiced. The validity and rationality of legal norms is, by necessity, presupposed in every norm-creating speech act of either legislative or judicial kind. Legal rationality (*ratio*) might be characterised as "reason(ing) in the shades of institutionalised coercion", or bounded rationality framed by the legal source doctrine and the constraints derived from the valid rules of judicial procedure. This conception of legal rationality then sets out a *claim to (legal) correctness*. The feasible alternatives to this conception of legal reason would comprise a vast range of options, i.e. a judge's free-flowing intuition or hunch, a sequence of non-rational emotions, workings of the subconscious mind, sheer madness, recourse to pure volition, or non-reason in general. Legal validity (*auctoritas*), in turn, might be described as sanction-based, legally enforceable ought (*Sollen*) that is conceptually detached from the "politics in disguise" claim of American legal realism and the later Critical Legal Studies movement, and also from the claim of enforcing some universal or transcendental morals that is put forth by the adherents of natural law theory. Such a positivist conception of legal validity then sets out a *claim to (legal) authority*.

A judge cannot reject either of the two postulates of legal validity and legal rationality, and still claim to adhere to the positivist (and analytical) premises of law.[1] The validity and rationality preconditions of a legal norm are, in other words, the given *axiomatic ground* of legal discourse under the theoretical premises of analytical positivism, since they cannot themselves be grounded on any further premises of "meta-validity" or "meta-rationality". Legal rationality is a "basic value which is not further justifiable in the legal discourse",[2] and questioning the rationality of legal rationality itself would signify a self-defeating effort of "saying the unsayable".[3] Similarly, the final validity ground of law is based on normative premises that are to be found within legal discourse itself, following the methodological credo of Kelsen's *Pure Theory of Law*: "The reason for the validity of a norm can only be the validity of another norm".[4] The final validity ground and final rationality ground of law will be investigated in detail in chapters 8 and 9 below.

The relative independence of the two postulates of legal validity and legal rationality is supported by the fact that they cannot be defined with reference to one another. Although legal reason is curbed by constraints derived from the prevalent legal source doctrine, and the binding force of law must be transformed into an outward legal justification in order to gain legitimacy, it would make no sense to question the "rationality of legal validity", nor the "validity of legal rationality", under the analytical and positivist premises recognised. Thus, it would be nonsensical to extend the validity claim of law to the ultimate ratio-

[1] Cf. Peczenik's remark that a judge or some other law-applying official cannot reject all or almost all of the legal sources and still be engaged in legal argumentation: A. Peczenik, *Vad är rätt? Om demokrati, rättssäkerhet, etik och juridisk argumentation* (Nordstedts juridik, 1995), 226, *in fine*.

[2] J. Wróblewski, *The Judicial Application of Law* (Kluwer, 1992), 306.

[3] A. Peczenik, *The Basis of Legal Justification* (Infoutryck AB, 1983), 91. Cf. ibid., 97.

[4] H. Kelsen, *Pure Theory of Law* (Peter Smith, 1989), 193.

nality ground of law. A similar Rylean *category mistake* would be effected, if the claim to legal correctness were extended to the ultimate criteria of legal validity, such as Kelsen's *Grundnorm*. But nor can the rationality of a legal norm be defined as a distinct subcategory of legal validity, or vice versa, by force of the enforced separation between the existence of law and its merit or demerit,[5] between law and "everything that is not strictly law",[6] between law and universal morals,[7] or between *ratio* and *auctoritas* in legal discourse, within the legal positivist tradition. The more any content-bound elements of rational justifiability are imported into the formal notion of legal validity, the less the outcome bears affinity to the axiomatic postulates of legal positivism, strictly defined. A purely axiological conception of legal validity, outlined in terms of legal principles and/or policies, would signify an open deviation from such a positivist definition of law. As Dworkin has convincingly argued, no formal rule of recognition can be extended to comprise legal principles.

Legal discourse may be divided into several subcategories, such as *legislative* discourse, *judicial* discourse and *legal scholarly* discourse.[8] The discourse-theoretical frame of legal validity and legal rationality is common to both the genuinely norm-creating discourse formations, i.e. legislative and judicial discourse. Legal scholarly discourse cannot satisfy the inherent claim to legal authority that is put forward by the two genuinely norm-creating discourse formations, since no valid legal norm is ever produced by the collective efforts of legal science.[9] The relative fulfilment of the claim to legal correctness in legal science, in turn, depends on the legal scholar's professional commitment to or, alternatively, critical deviation from the judge's epistemic stance towards the law. If a legal scholar accepts the judge's point of view as the normative frame of reference *vis-à-vis* the prevalent legal source ideology, the claim to correctness is meant to be satisfied. Such a notion of legal science was set out by, for example, Ross in his ideology-aligned prediction theory of law. If, on the other hand, a legal scholar has adopted a self-consciously critical stance toward the judges' legal source doctrine, seeking to give effect to an *uso alternativo del diritto* or some other ideological project of his own preference, the claim to correctness will not be satisfied, nor will it even be striven for.

[5] J. Austin, *The Province of Jurisprudence Determined* (Cambridge University Press, 1995), 157.

[6] Kelsen, above at n. 4, 1.

[7] Hart, "Positivism and the Separation of Law and Morals", in *Essays in Jurisprudence and Philosophy* (Clarendon Press, Oxford, 1983).

[8] The present discourse on legal discourse might be called *discourse-theoretical discourse*, following Alexy's conceptual usage: A. Alexy, *A Theory of Legal Argumentation: The Theory of Rational Discourse as Theory of Legal Argumentation* (Clarendon Press, Oxford, 1989), 187.

[9] Kelsen made the distinction between "authentic" and "non-authentic" interpretation, with reference to a judge's and a legal scholar's act of legal interpretation: the former creates an individual legal norm, but not the latter. See Kelsen, *Reine Rechtslehre. Mit einem Anhang: Das Problem der Gerechtigkeit* (Verlag Franz Deuticke, Wien, 1960), 346–54.

2.1 The concept of legal validity

Wróblewski has argued that in "practical legal language" a statement on the validity of a legal norm refers to its binding character: if deemed valid, a judge *ought* to apply a certain legal norm in judicial adjudication.[10] In theoretical reflection on law, in turn, there are (at least) three different interpretations of the concept of legal validity. Wróblewski made use of the tripartite division of legal validity into systemic validity, factual validity, and axiological validity.[11] *Systemic* validity is defined with reference to a legal norm's formal source of origin and consistency with other valid norms in the legal system in question,[12] essentially in line with Kelsen's and Merkl's idea of the hierarchical *Stufenbau* structure of a legal system. *Factual* validity is defined with reference to the operative and efficacious law in action in legal adjudication, i.e. the set of legal norms in fact recognised and duly enforced by the courts of justice. Finally, *axiological* validity is defined in terms of a norm's acceptability in light of certain extra-legal norms and/or values. Following Wróblewski, Aarnio has adopted a similar classification of legal validity conceptions.[13] The terms (formally) *positivist*, *sociological*, and *naturalist* validity conception may also be introduced, with reference to basic postulates of legal positivism, legal realism and natural law theory, respectively.

Although Aarnio would appear to write as if the different validity conceptions were equal in importance, the prevalent Nordic legal source doctrine determines their mutual priority order in judicial decision-making: (1) statutory enactments, which satisfy the criteria of formal systemic validity, are qualified as strongly binding, mandatory reasons in law; (2) prior court decisions or precedents, which satisfy the criteria of factual validity, are qualified as weakly binding, persuasive reasons in law; and (3) general legal principles, moral principles, and consequentialist arguments, which satisfy the criteria of axiological validity, are permitted reasons in law, according to Aarnio's tripartite division of a judge's legitimate legal source material.[14] In a similar manner, Wróblewski regarded systemic validity as the basic mode of legal validity in the civilian, statute-based systems of law, although without having recourse to such a tripartite hierarchy of legal sources. The two notions of factual validity and axio-

[10] Wróblewski, above at n. 2, 76.

[11] Ibid., 75–85.

[12] "According to the concept of systemic validity a rule *R* is valid in legal system LS if the following conditions are fulfilled: (a) *R* is enacted according to the rules valid in LS and thus has come into force; or (b) *R* is an acknowledged consequence of the rules valid in LS; (c) *R* has not been formally repealed ('derogated'); (d) *R* is not inconsistent with the rules valid in LS; (e) if *R* is inconsistent with any rule valid in LS then (ea) *R* is not treated as invalid according to the rules about conflict between legal rules or (eb) *R* is interpreted in such a way as to eliminate the inconsistency in question": ibid., 77.

[13] See A. Aarnio, *The Rational as Reasonable: A Treatise on Legal Justification* (D. Reidel Publishing Co., 1987), 33–46; ibid., 167–74, where he speaks of the "variety of validity notions".

[14] See the concise diagram of the relative binding force of the various sources of law in Aarnio, ibid., 93.

logical validity are said to be exceptionally applicable, as a corrective to the predominant systemic conception of validity.[15] The decisive priority accorded to the formal-systemic validity conception is, of course, in perfect accord with the basic postulates of a positivist conception of law. If, instead, the sociological or axiological validity notion were given priority over such formal-systemic considerations, the concept of legal validity would need to be framed in line with the specific premises of legal realism or natural law theory, respectively.

In the operative law in action, the systemic validity conception of law may be further supported by arguments derived from a norm's sociological efficacy and/or axiological acceptability, while the formal-systemic criteria of validity are still taken as primary, as Wróblewski argued above. But what kind of a legal norm could be said to fulfil only the criteria of axiological validity, with total exclusion of systemic validity and at least partial exclusion of factual validity? In light of what was argued in chapter 2 above, it is plain that the axiological validity conception of law overlaps with the notion of legal principles and/or legal policies. Moreover, the very notion of "validity" proved to be misplaced when applied to legal principles and policies, since their impact on the outcome of adjudication is based on a certain *sense of appropriateness* and *institutional support* only in society, reflecting the low level of legal formality entailed in such "proto-norms".

If legal validity is defined as a combination of a precedent-norm's *constitutive* and *mandatory* formality traits—i.e. its formal source of origin and point of reference, together with its level of mandatory force—then the degree of legal validity gradually decreases as one proceeds from the top left-hand corner of Figure 2 in chapter 2 above (on p. 61), downwards and to the right, i.e. from fully formal rules (judicial reference, quasi-legislative model) to weak, defeasible legal rules (reinterpreted rule model) and highly persuasive legal standards (binding reasons model), ending with weakly formal legal principles and/or policies (revalued reasons model) at the bottom right-hand corner of Figure 2. Thereby, the initially strictly positivist conception of a precedent's validity is gradually modified and replaced by elements drawn from the historical school of law, legal realism, and natural law theory. The "systemic deviation" entailed in Dworkin's later theory of legal principles would follow the model of weakly formal legal principles and/or policies in this respect, as modified by the high level of systemic formality involved (underlying reasons model).

2.2 The concept of legal rationality

The concept of legal rationality can be divided into the two subcategories, *L-rationality* and *D-rationality*.

[15] Wróblewski, above at n. 2, 76.

L-rationality stands for *logical* rationality, with reference to the rules of formal logic and the criteria of logico-inferential correctness in legal argumentation.[16] The rules of L-rationality may be formulated in terms of syllogistic logic. If L-rationality is duly followed in legal argumentation, an abstractly formulated legal norm of either legislative or judicial origin is taken as the general clause in the logical syllogism under which the proven facts of a novel case are to be subsumed. The end result will be a highly case-bound legal norm which is then derived from the said combination of the normative and factual premises of a syllogism by force of sheer logic. *D-rationality*, in turn, stands for *discursive* rationality where the idea of observing formal logico-inferential correctness is relaxed in favour of *pro et contra* argumentation. Under D-rationality, Habermas' notion of ideal speech situation, or some functional equivalent to it, is taken as the fixed point of reference for reasoning, to be then approximated in all legal argumentation. The set of such premises provides a judge or legal scholar with a yardstick by means of which he can either justify or criticise the state of argumentation in a legal system.[17]

The ideology of judicial legislation satisfies the criteria of *L-rationality*, since the outcome of a new case is to be inferred from the combination of the *ratio* of a prior case, as authoritatively and abstractly formulated by the prior court itself, and the facts of the new case by means of logical deduction. The classification of the reference ideology is slightly problematic in this regard. From the point of view of the prior court, reference ideology is an extreme case of judicial legislation where all powers of legal interpretation are jealously withheld at the norm-issuing authority. From the point of view of the subsequent court, however, the issue is judged differently, since it is entitled to do no more than passively read the *ratio* of the prior case, with no elements of legal discretion involved. Thus, the reference ideology would seem to fall short of satisfying even the formal criteria of L-rationality.

The distinct precedent ideologies based on judicial exegesis, judicial analogy, systemic construction of underlying reasons of law, and judicial revaluation

16 On L-rationality in general, see Aarnio, above at n. 13, 189–90. Aarnio speaks of rationality *sensu stricto* and rationality *sensu largo*, where the former refers to L-rationality and the latter to a combination of L-rationality and D-rationality. In addition to the rules of logical consistency, Peczenik places linguistic correctness under L-rationality. Here, however, the term L-rationality is reserved for the logico-inferential properties of a legal norm, while linguistic issues belong to the surface-structure level of law. See A. Peczenik, *On Law and Reason* (Kluwer, 1989), 56.

17 Peczenik still distinguishes the notion of *S-rationality*, i.e. *substantial* or *supportive* rationality, which is based on the concept of coherent justification, as defined in terms of a logical inference from a highly coherent set of premises. D-rationality, in turn, is defined by Peczenik more rigorously, with reference to elements of reasoning which cannot be refuted even in a "perfect discourse". Yet, if D-rationality were defined as the attainment of Habermas' ideal speech situation in legal discourse, it could function only as a utopian discursive ideal, devoid of any genuine impact on actual legal discourse. If, on the other hand, D-rationality is defined with less rigour, with allusion to legal argumentation which approximates to the Habermasian ideal and adopts it as a normative yardstick for reasoning, it will have much more argumentative force in the context of law. Therefore, only the two categories of L-rationality and D-rationality will be sustained in the present context, and not the notion of S-rationality. Cf. Peczenik, *On Law and Reason*, above at n. 16, 57.

plainly cannot satisfy the inferential criteria of L-rationality, but they do satisfy the less-strictly-defined meta-rules of *D-rationality*. The exact content given to such discourse rationality varies in accordance with the inherent tenets of the particular ideology in question: backward-proceeding reasoning in search of the original intentions of the prior court (judicial exegesis), realignment of the *ratio* of a prior case in the constant interplay of analogy and distinguishing in case-law adjudication (judicial analogy), coherence-seeking *law as integrity* approach to precedents (systemic construction of underlying reasons), or a thorough rejudgment of the merits of the prior decision (judicial revaluation). However, adherence to the meta-rules of D-rationality is the common denominator of the four approaches to precedent-based legal reasoning. The concept of D-rationality may be defined widely, so as also to comprise openly axiological and teleological argumentation. Finally, the judicial hunch ideology exemplifies *non-rational* argumentation in law, as possibly based on mere idiosyncratic prejudice, passion, arbitrariness or personal bias on the part of the judge or judges. The idea of such methodological anarchism, as envisioned by Feyerabend, is simply *anything goes*, with no traits of intended rationality involved.

In all, the domain of legal rationality extends between the two end poles of the *slot-machine judge* of judicial reference ideology, and the *coin-tossing judge* of judicial hunch ideology, with the approaches based on "legal and rational" judicial decision-making situated in-between, if Wróblewski's terminology is followed.—Having laid down the axiomatic ground of legal discourse in terms of the two postulates of legal validity and legal rationality, the speech act theoretical prerequisites of such a conception of law will now be discussed.

3. FELICITIES AND INFELICITIES OF LEGAL DISCOURSE

3.1 J.L. Austin on misfires and abuses of speech acts

As the very title of his main contribution to linguistic philosophy reveals, John L. Austin was intrigued by *how to do things with words*,[18] i.e. how certain convention-based outcomes could be brought into effect in society by (merely) expressing a few words in a specific social setting. A priest who says to a couple standing at the altar, "I pronounce you man and wife"; a statesman who breaks a bottle of champange against a ship's stem, saying, "I name this ship the *Queen Elizabeth*"; or a judge who says in the course of criminal law proceedings, "I sentence the accused to life imprisonment for murder", are all involved in performing speech acts of different types. The outcomes of such speech acts will then be effected in the form of a marriage, the naming of a ship, and a judicial verdict rendered by a court of justice, respectively.[19]

[18] J.L. Austin, *How To Do Things With Words* (Oxford University Press, 1986).

[19] Austin's conception of the various uses of language notably resembles the idea of language-games put forward by L. Wittgenstein in his *Philosophische Untersuchungen—Philosophical Investigations* (Basil Blackwell, Oxford, 1967).

Although Austin seems to have begun his inquiry into language and social phenomena with the intention of framing some relatively simple criteria for distinguishing the constative and the performative modes of language, he soon had to reject such a forthright venture.[20] Eventually, Austin divided the performance of various types of speech acts into the three categories of the locutionary, the illocutionary and the perlocutionary.[21] The performance of a *locutionary* act signifies the act of saying or stating something, with a certain sense and reference. The performance of an *illocutionary* act signifies the act of doing something—such as informing, ordering, warning, praying, arguing, sentencing, etc.—*in* saying something. Such linguistic utterances may be said to have conventional force, i.e. their illocutionary character is supported by a pre-existing convention to the said effect in society. Finally, the performance of a *perlocutionary* act denotes the act of successfully bringing about or achieving something *by* saying something. The relative priority of the illocutionary mode of language *vis-à-vis* the locutionary mode can be seen in the fact that even the act of stating or saying something is finally shown to follow the illocutionary mode of language usage in Austin's analysis.[22]

Within the realm of Austinian speech acts and the social consequences brought into effect by force of valid social conventions, various performative failures may occur, leading to the non-fulfilment of the social outcomes initially aspired for. The failures affecting a "less than happy" performance of a speech act are called *infelicities* by Austin. There are two main types of such infelicities, as discerned by Austin: "misfires", or acts purported but void, and "abuses", or acts professed but hollow.[23] *Misfires* are caused by a failure or some deficiency in the institutional setting required for a successful performance of the speech act in question. The person who announces a judicial verdict on behalf of a court of justice must be the judge who is presiding over the court proceedings, and not an actor in the midst of a Shakespearean or other drama, if such an infelicity of the speech act of judicial sentencing is to be avoided. Similarly, the statement "I pronounce you man and wife" is void of effect if it is said by someone else than a duly appointed minister in the course of a marriage ceremony. In the present analysis of legal adjudication, the fulfilment of the institutional preconditions of such linguistic performance will be presumed.

Abuses of speech acts, in turn, are caused by defects in the inner attitude or conviction of the speaker of a linguistic utterance, concerning for example the

20 Austin, above at n. 18, 55: "We must ask: is there some precise way in which we can definitely distinguish the performative from the constative utterance? And in particular we should naturally ask first whether there is some *grammatical* (or lexicographical) criterion for distinguishing the performative utterance". Cf. ibid., 67, 94 ff. At ibid., 4, n. 1, the provisional character of the analysis presented in the first sections of the book is stated in open terms.

21 On the distinction between locutionary, illocutionary and perlocutionary acts, see ibid., 94–103, 109 ff.

22 Ibid., 134.

23 Ibid., 12 ff., and esp. the diagram on p. 18. "Misfires" are treated at length from p. 25 onwards, and "abuses" from p. 39 onwards, in Austin, above at n. 18.

mental state of a judge when he announces a verdict on behalf of a competent court of justice. If a judge—i.e. a judge in a non-jury system of criminal adjudication where he is required to take a stance on the evidence presented before the court, besides being required to evaluate the legal side of the issue—finds the evidence as *not* beyond reasonable doubt and yet decides to inflict punishment based on such falsely grounded premises, the abuse of a speech act will take place. As Austin points out in his two ingenious examples, one cannot say *the cat is on the mat but I do not believe it is*,[24] or *I promise to do X but I am under no obligation to do it*,[25] without inducing conceptual failure, performative anomaly or inherent contradiction. Below, such performative failures or infelicities will be investigated in the specific context of legal adjudication.

3.2 Alexy on the meta-rules of rational legal discourse

> "Alexy's rationality norms can be interpreted as guaranteeing that the outcome of the debate solely depends on reasons, that is, on coherence, not on violence or emotions."[26]

> "Although the legal reasoning, too, is ultimately dependent upon feelings and will . . ."[27]

According to Habermas' theory of communicative rationality, there are four types of *validity claims* involved in linguistic utterances. The sum total of such validity claims is equal to the universal-pragmatic preconditions of communicative action: "claims as to the *intelligibility* of the utterance, of the *truth* of its propositional element, the *correctness* or suitability of its performative element, and the *veracity* of the speaker".[28] The *claim to intelligibility* is made each time a speech act of any kind is performed by a speaker. The *claim to truth* is made *vis-à-vis* the constative or propositional element of a speech act, the *claim to correctness vis-à-vis* the regulative or performative element of a speech act, and the *claim to veracity vis-à-vis* the sincerity of the speaker.[29] Thus, the truth of the statement is proclaimed each time something is asserted to be the case, and the correctness of normative interpretation is proclaimed each time a specific reading of some moral, legal or other kind of norm is put forward.

Based on Habermas' theory of communicative rationality, Alexy has argued that legal discourse is a *special case* or subcategory of general practical discourse. Both equally share the inherent claim to correctness, while legal

[24] Ibid., 48.
[25] Ibid., 54.
[26] Peczenik, above at n. 16, 191.
[27] Ibid., 238.
[28] Quoted in Alexy, above at n. 8, 107 (emphasis added); cf. J. Habermas, "*Wahrheitstheorien*", in *Vorstudien und Ergänzungen zur Theorie des kommunikativen Handelns* (Suhrkamp, Frankfurt am Main, 1989), 138.
[29] Alexy, above at n. 8, 107–8.

discourse is further modified by a set of criteria derived from its specific subject matter. According to Alexy, the meta-norms of general practical discourse comprise the following six types of rules or other elements:[30]

(1) *Basic rules*: for example, no speaker may contradict himself, and every speaker may only assert what he actually believes.
(2) *Rationality rules*: for example, every speaker must give reasons for what he asserts when asked to do so, unless he can cite reasons which justify a refusal to provide a justification (i.e. general justification rule). Everyone who can speak may take part in discourse, everyone may problematise any assertion, and no speaker may be prevented from exercising his rights laid down in these rationality rules by any kind of coercion internal or external to the discourse.
(3) *Rules for allocating the burden of argument*: for example, whoever has put forth an argument is obliged to produce further arguments only in the event of counter-arguments.
(4) *Argument forms*, having reference to some valid rule or the consequences of action.
(5) *Justification rules*: for example, the principle of generalisation of arguments presented in the discourse, and the possibility of critically testing the moral rules adopted by the speakers in terms of their historical and individual genesis.
(6) *Transition rules*: for example, it is possible for any speaker at any time to make a transition from practical discourse into theoretical (empirical) discourse or discourse-theoretical discourse.

Legal discourse is drawn apart from general practical discourse by force of a set of limiting conditions operative within the former. Such restrictions are derived from the prevalent *legal source doctrine*, on the one hand, and from the valid *rules of judicial procedure*, on the other. Alexy refers to the statute-bound character of legal argumentation, the essential role of precedents in it, its involvement with the doctrinal studies on law as achieved through the collective efforts of an institutionally organised legal profession, and its subjection to the specific ordinances and regulations dealing with the judicial procedure.[31] Legal source doctrine has a key position among such constraints of legal discourse, reflecting the axiomatic postulates of legal validity and legal rationality on the level of legal ideology in terms of the present treatise. The other subject-specific constraints mentioned by Alexy are either of a less definitional character or, alternatively, are restricted to some individual branch of law. Such features comprise the valid rules of legal procedure, the distribution of burden of proof between litigants, time limits placed for legal matters, the specific motivation ground of the parties of a case, and the asymmetry of their roles in criminal proceedings.[32]

[30] Ibid., 188–206.
[31] Ibid., 16.
[32] Cf. ibid., 16, 18–19, 218.

In legal discourse, Alexy's meta-rules of legal rationality are effected in the claim to legal correctness, signifying the requirement of rational justifiability of the outcome of legal adjudication and ruling out the impact of the judge's non-rational emotions and free-flowing intuition in judicial decision-making.[33] In consequence thereof, Alexy outlines the bounded rationality conception of legal discourse as follows:[34]

> "This, then, is the core of the special case thesis: the *claim to correctness* is indeed also raised in legal discourse, but this claim, unlike that in general practical discourse, is not concerned with the absolute rationality of the normative statement in question, but only with showing that it can be *rationally justified* within the framework of the validly prevailing legal order."

The discourse-theoretical identity of legal discourse is, in other words, structured by the claim to legal correctness, as effected in the requirement of rational justifiability of the outcomes of judicial adjudication. However, the axiomatic ground of law was also seen to comprise the element of legal validity as well, under the theoretical premises of analytical positivism.

3.3 Claim to correctness, claim to authority, and pursuit of legitimacy

The two conceptual claims to legal correctness and legal authority lay down the necessary preconditions of legislation and judicial adjudication. Each time some specific reading of a statute, precedent or some other relevant legal source material is authoritatively set out by the judiciary, the correctness of the outcome of legal interpretation is presumed by it. In a similar manner, each time some constitutional provision is enacted by a Parliament, the correctness of the enactment, in the sense of matching the prevalent criteria of justice in society, is silently presupposed by the it.[35] A failure to satisfy such preconditions of constitutional legislation or of judicial adjudication would lead to a conceptual failure or performative self-contradiction, in close analogy to Austin's two examples, *the cat is on the mat but I do not believe it is* or *I promise to do X but I am under no obligation to do it.*[36] Below, the focus of analysis will be on the discourse-theoretical prerequisites of (precedent-based) judicial adjudication, leaving constitutional issues outside the scope of the study. It will be argued that Alexy's claim to legal correctness, which frames the necessary preconditions of legal rationality, has its functional counterpart with respect to legal validity, as outlined in terms of the *claim to legal authority* or *claim to normative binding force* ascribed to a judicial decision.

[33] Cf. Peczenik, above at n. 16, 191, 238.

[34] Ibid., 220 (emphasis added). On the claim to correctness in general practical discourse, see ibid., 127 ff., where the requirement of rational justifiability is presented in the context of law.

[35] See Alexy, "On Necessary Relations Between Law and Morality" (1989) 2 *Ratio Juris* 167, 177–82; R. Alexy, *Begriff und Geltung des Rechts* (Verlag Karl Alber, 1992), 64–70.

[36] Austin, above at n. 18, 48, 54.

Let us consider the following examples. Examples on the right are from Alexy's theory of law; those on the left are of the present author's invention.

Legal validity	*Legal rationality*
Legislator: It is hereby decreed that so-and-so ought to be the case, but the enactment is to be devoid of normative binding force.	"X is a sovereign, federal, and unjust state."[37]
Judge: (Based on what is a correct interpretation of valid law) the defendant is sentenced to life imprisonment, but the judgment is to be devoid of normative binding force.	"Based on what is an incorrect interpretation of valid law, the defendant is sentenced to life imprisonment."[38]
➔ *Claim to legal authority*	➔ *Claim to legal correctness*

Alexy puts forward the argument that there is a necessary relation between law and morality, as illustrated by the two examples on the right of the table above. I would, instead, defend the argument that the two conceptual claims to legal authority and legal correctness, as effected through the two grounding postulates of legal validity and legal rationality at the discourse-theoretical level of law, lay down the *conceptual* preconditions of legal adjudication, in the sense of framing a judge's successful performance of the speech act of pronouncing a legal verdict. There is no moral element involved, but the issue is one of a conceptual necessity, sanctioned by the threat of a conceptual anomaly or performative contradiction, if such criteria are not duly complied with in law-enforcement. In the present discussion, all morals-based elements of legal adjudication are placed on the level of legal ideology. However, even there they—no more than—define the preconditions of the judges' professional *morality of aspiration* in Fuller's terminology, and not the grounding conditions of possibility of the speech act of giving a legal judgment. Evidently, an assertion concerning such a conceptual relation between law and morality would be in plain contradiction to the legal positivist's *separation thesis*, as defended by Austin, Kelsen and Hart, but not, of course, by Alexy in the present context.

[37] Alexy, "On Necessary Relations Between Law and Morality", above at n. 35, 178. Cf. Alexy, *Begriff und Geltung des Rechts*, above at n. 35, 65.

[38] In the German original: "*Der Angeklagte wird, was eine falsche Interpretation des geltenden Rechts ist, zu lebenslanger Freiheitsstrafe verurteilt*": Alexy, *Begriff und Geltung des Rechts*, ibid., 68. The English translation of the text, as found in Alexy, "On Necessary Relations Between Law and Morality", above at n. 35, 179, has been slightly modified here. Alexy makes a reference to Austin's "cat on the mat" example in Alexy, *Begriff und Geltung des Rechts*, above at n. 35, 68 n. 45; and Alexy, "On Necessary Relations Between Law and Morality", above at n. 35, 179, n. 15.

Examples on the left of the table have the following implications. A legislator which would self-defeatingly deny its own norm-giving competence by adding a specific qualification clause to a statute, to the effect that the enactment be devoid of any normative effect or binding force, would commit a performative failure of the Austinian kind, i.e. "a promise with no obligation involved". Similarly, a judge who would attach a specific provision to a judgment, to the effect that the court ruling is to have no binding force whatever *vis-à-vis* the litigants of the case and the *res judicata*, would equally commit a conceptual failure.

The *claim to legal correctness* lays down the discourse-theoretical preconditions of rational legal argumentation, in the sense that a judge cannot possibly contest the correctness of the specific reading of law put forward by him in a court ruling, without committing a conceptual failure or performative contradiction. The parallel *claim to legal authority* has an equal function in relation to the discourse-theoretical preconditions of the binding force of a judgment, in the sense that the court rulings are to be duly observed by the litigants at the threat of a legal sanction.

The constituents of a judge's legal ideology have a crucially different function in legal adjudication than the "deeper", discourse-theoretical premises of legal validity and legal rationality. The ideological prerequisites of legal discourse concern the winning or losing of *empirical legitimacy* for the outcome of adjudication in society. In fact, the very idea of reading the outcome of adjudication in light of a specific set of ideological premises, in the sense of the fragments of a judge's precedent ideology and the specific rule of law criteria for a system of precedents, is to raise the legitimacy of the outcome of jurisdiction: the more consistent and better reflected a judge's conception of the various ideology-oriented premises of legal adjudication is, the easier it will be for him to convince the parties of a legal dispute of the correctness and fairness of the decision rendered. The "ideological cement" provided by the theoretical background rationale of the precedent ideology in question and the leading criteria of justice entailed it would seem to have key importance here.

Thus, in stark contrast to the *power-wielding* claim to legal authority and the *hunch-dispelling* claim to legal correctness at the discourse-theoretical frame of law, the ideological premises of judicial adjudication are able to put forward no more (and no less) than the *pursuit of legitimacy vis-à-vis* the outcome of legal decision-making. A judge's precedent ideology, as further modified by the specific, Fuller-inspired rule of law criteria for a well-functioning system of precedent-following, will thereby provide judges with a presumably effective, *legitimacy-proliferating* argumentation strategy *vis-à-vis* the litigants of the case and the legal community at large.

4. THE "VIEW FROM THE BENCH" REVISITED: THE FELICITY CONDITIONS OF LEGAL ADJUDICATION AND THE QUEST FOR EMPIRICAL LEGITIMACY

Kennedy's *bad faith argument* was considered above in chapter 6, with reference to the impact which the ideological motives, preferences, or personal bias of a judge have on the outcome of adjudication. By force of the formal constraints of adjudication derived from the prevalent legal source doctrine and other law-specific strictures imposed upon a judge, the influence of such idiosyncratic, judge-specific factors is officially denied and ruled out from the acceptable premises of judicial decision-making. Thereby the outward judicial argumentation and the "true" motives of judicial decision-making are made to radically diverge from each other, according to Kennedy. In consequence thereof, judges run the constant risk of losing their moral and professional integrity. Kennedy's argument concerning the ultimately non-legal premises of adjudication may seem in the last resort irrefutable, since even a judge's self-proclaimed adherence to a specific set of legal premises of adjudication can always be contested by arguing that the decision was, in fact, induced by some conscious or subconscious ideological motives operative in the judge's mind at the time of making the decision. The impact of any subconscious motives on adjudication must be left out of scope of a jurisprudential—and not psychoanalytical—analysis of legal discourse, as being *per definitionem* beyond the reach of rational control. With regard to the impact of the consciously held ideological preferences of a judge, Kennedy's bad faith argument can be challenged by having recourse to the conceptual and ideological consequences brought into effect by the deep-structure level phenomena of law.

Evidently, there can be no absolutely foolproof or genuinely scientific means of either verifying or falsifying the validity of Kennedy's bad faith argument, nor of its antithesis, the term "falsification" taken in the Popperian sense here. Therefore, a much less resolute account of the issue will have to suffice. The bad faith argument can still be challenged by the degree of *empirical legitimacy* gained by the outcome of legal adjudication in society.

I will argue that the *key to the science of jurisprudence* is not to be found in the idea of coercive orders, as issued by the sovereign ruler and backed by the threat of physical force, as Austin boldly claimed in *The Province of Jurisprudence Determined*;[39] nor in a combination of the primary rules of obligation and secondary rules of change, adjudication and recognition, as Hart defines the preconditions of a legal system in *The Concept of Law*;[40] nor still in judges' and other lawyers' transcendental-logical presupposition of the hypo-

[39] Above at n. 5, 21.

[40] H.L.A. Hart, *The Concept of Law* (Clarendon Press, Oxford, 1961), 6, 79. Hart wittily pointed out that Austin's definition of law is equal to the *gunman situation writ large*, or the case of a bank robber with a loaded gun and a request for quick compliance: ibid., 18–25.

thetical *Grundnorm*, as Kelsen framed the ultimate ground of legal validity in *Pure Theory of Law*.[41] Austin, in his "sanction and sovereign" account of law, paid no respect to the role of citizens in the definition of law, in the sense of the empirical legitimacy criteria of law, and the same holds true of Hart's judge-centred conception of law. For Kelsen, the question of the legitimacy of law was quickly transformed into one concerning the formal *Stufenbau* structure of valid legal norms. Therefore, the core of legal analysis under the theoretical premises of analytical positivism will need to be (re)defined with reference to the *felicity conditions* of adjudication and the *rule of law criteria* for precedent-following which, in turn, give effect to the two *conceptual claims* and specific *ideological aspirations* involved at the deep-structure level of law.

The *authority-wielding, hunch-dispelling* and *legitimacy-inducing* criteria of precedent-based judicial adjudication are as follows: (1) the requirement of *legality*, giving effect to the *claim to legal authority* with respect to the outcome of adjudication, is duly satisfied; (2) the requirement of *legal rationality*, giving effect to the *claim to legal correctness* with respect to the outcome of adjudication, is duly satisfied; and (3) a fully self-reflected conception of a judge's normative *precedent ideology*, as further qualified by the specific *rule of law* criteria for a well-functioning system of precedent-following, is taken as a professional standard for the judiciary, giving effect to the *pursuit of legitimacy* with respect to the outcome of adjudication. The first two criteria are situated on the discourse-theoretical level of law. They lay down the axiomatic, conceptual ground of adjudication under the positivist and analytical premises acknowledged: a judge who paid no respect to either of the two criteria of validity and rationality of law would fail to produce a legal norm in the first place. Such conceptual claims are part of the *felicity conditions* of legal adjudication, which determine the relative success or failure of a judge to satisfy the *conceptual, institutional* and *mental* preconditions involved in his speech act of pronouncing a legal decision. The third criterion of observing a consistent conception of the judge's precedent ideology and a set of specific rule of law criteria for precedent-following, in turn, concerns the "morality of aspiration" or the "pride of the craftsman" only, in the sense of providing a professional yardstick for "judging the judges", and for evaluating the outcomes of judicial adjudication. The resulting jurisprudential triangle of effected *claim to authority, claim to correctness* and *quest for empirical legitimacy* in law is, in the last resort, conditional on the infrastructures of law, still "beneath" the deep-structure level phenomena of law. Such "ultimate" preconditions will be analysed in detail in chapters 8 and 9 below.

Whether legal discourse can withstand the *political, not legal* outcry voiced by the Critical Legal Studies (CLS) movement, and the—somewhat less frequently heard—*moral, not legal* critique professed by the natural law theory, will depend on the relative well-functioning or ill-functioning of the deep-structure level prerequisites of legal discourse and judicial adjudication. If the

[41] Above at n. 4, 201–5.

outcome of legal adjudication fails to gain an adequate degree of empirical legitimacy in society, despite the judges' observance of the felicity conditions of adjudication in the sense of the conceptual, institutional and mental criteria involved, and despite their commitment to the specific rule of law criteria for a well-functioning system of precedent-following, then nothing could prevent a disbelieving *Crit* from tearing down the empty façade of *false legality*, *failing rationality* and the *faltering quest for legitimacy* in front of what is no more than the "enforcement of politics" in the thin disguise of law. On the other hand, if the pursuit of empirical legitimacy proves to be fairly successful in society, as judged in light of the specific rule of law criteria for precedents and the conceptual, institutional and mental felicity conditions of adjudication, then I see no reason why legal discourse could not survive relatively intact, and even prosper, on side with the various competing means of conceptualising the effected "order of things" in society, in Foucault's terminology. The conclusion is, accordingly, more or less in line with Weber's contention that the effected legitimacy of law is ultimately based on the citizens' *Legitimitätsglaube*, having reference to the commonly shared belief in the satisfaction of a set of formal, legitimacy-inducing validity and rationality conditions of law among citizens.[42]

Evidently, there is no *view from nowhere*, as Nagel insightfully put it,[43] or some privileged angle of approach or scholarly stance which would be free from all kind of ideological orientation and metaphysical commitment. The formal edifice of law, as outlined in terms of the felicity conditions of adjudication and the judges' pursuit of legitimacy for the outcome of adjudication, may well be taken to frame and structure the formal edifice of law—on the one key condition that judges are not held to be consciously *acting in bad faith*, involved in a haphazard *coin-tossing rationality* of the judicial hunch ideology, *playing hide-and-seek* with the true normative premises of judicial argumentation, or engaged in what Hart called the *game of scorer's discretion*. If such a fraudulent, Janus-faced model of adjudication were, in fact, adopted by the judiciary, the resulting divergence of official action and professional self-reflection of the judiciary would soon become evident even to a disinterested external observer or the Holmesian "bad man", who is only interested in predicting the material consequences of his evil deeds. The judicial experience drawn from the French system of adjudication would seem to be provide sufficient evidence thereof. In consequence, if the CLS alternative is rejected as a *nightmare vision of law,* since it has no place for law outside the realm of interest-laden politics, while the *noble dream* of Dworkin's "law as integrity" doctrine is equally rejected,[44] since it

[42] M. Weber, *Wirtschaft und Gesellschaft* (JCB Mohr, Tübingen, 1972), 19–20. Cf. J. Habermas, "*Wie ist Legitimität durch Legalität möglich?*" (1987) 20 *Kritische Justiz* 1.

[43] T. Nagel, *The View from Nowhere* (Oxford University Press, 1986).

[44] Cf. H.L.A. Hart, "American Jurisprudence through English Eyes: The Nightmare and the Noble Dream", in *Essays in Jurisprudence and Philosophy* (Clarendon Press, Oxford, 1983). Cf. also Wróblewski's comments on the "ultra-rationalistic fallacy" of the ideology of bound judicial decision-making and the "irrationalistic fallacy" of the ideology of free judicial decision-making, as

provides no effective safeguards for citizens against judges' Solomonic or less virtuous discretion, then the judge's *view from the bench* might well be framed in terms of the analytical and positivist theory of law, as expounded by, for example, Wróblewski, Ross and Hart.[45]

5. LIMITS OF THE DISCOURSE-THEORETICAL FRAME OF LAW: META-RULES, SPEECH ACTS AND SOCIAL INSTITUTIONS

The meta-rules of rational legal discourse proved to signify a deviation from the rationality rules of general practical discourse, due to the constraints derived from the prevalent legal source doctrine and the valid rules of legal procedure. But how could such meta-rules of legal rationality themselves be justified? Alexy singles out four possible candidates for a "deeper" justification of legal discourse: technical, empirical, definitional and universal-pragmatic modes of justification.[46] Although Alexy would not openly state his own intellectual stance *vis-à-vis* the different modes of justification, his actual preference for a *universal-pragmatic* justification of legal discourse can be inferred from the general frame of analysis adopted by him.

But how far can a universal-pragmatic justification of legal discourse rationality be extended? Such a frame of legal discourse is said to signify the "reconstruction of general and unavoidable presuppositions of possible processes of understanding",[47] essentially in line with Habermas' theory of communicative action and the inherent claims to intelligibility, truth, correctness and veracity constitutive of such linguistic practices. Alexy's own, "weaker" version of the universal-pragmatic justification of discourse rationality consists of proving the cogency of the following two-fold argument: (1) the validity of certain meta-rules of discourse rationality is the condition of possibility of such speech acts whereupon the institutions of society are grounded; and (2) those specific speech acts cannot all be rejected, save by giving up the distinct forms of behaviour which we regard as peculiarly human or essential to society.[48]

contrasted with the ideology of "legal and rational" decision-making, in *The Judicial Application of Law*, above at n. 2, 306.

[45] However, Ross' conception of law bears some obvious affinity to Kennedy's *bad faith thesis*, as was argued above in chapter 1. Ross writes that the idiosyncratic motives held by a judge cannot be taken as part of judges' normative ideology, since the law is, in essence, a social or collective phenomenon which cannot be allowed to disperse into an array of the judges' personal, idiosyncratic motives. Yet such factors must—or merely, may?—be taken into account by anyone who seeks to predict the future course of adjudication, as Ross himself admits. Cf. A. Ross, *Om ret og retfærdighed: En indførelse i den analytiske retsfilosofi* (Nyt nordisk forslag, 1953), 48–49.

[46] Alexy, above at n. 8, 180–7.

[47] Habermas is cited in ibid., 185.

[48] Cf. ibid., 185. The present emphasis on the institutional side of the issue is derived from Searle, whereas Alexy speaks only of the constitutive rules of linguistic communication and the corresponding forms of human behaviour. Yet, the social or institutional dimension of language is of most importance, in the sense of being equal to the external outcomes brought into effect by a successful performance of such speech acts in legislation and jurisdiction.

The two postulates of legal validity and legal rationality constitute the axiomatic ground of legal discourse at the deep-structure level of law, under the analytical and positivist premises acknowledged. In line with Searle's philosophical argument, such a conception of law cannot withstand a total rejection of either of the two axiomatic premises involved, nor a total disregard of the two conceptual claims thereby effected. However, Alexy never posits the question of the ultimate grounds of law. The meta-rules of legal discourse rationality—or the basic foundation of rules, speech acts and social institutions, if Searle's conceptual usage is rather preferred—are simply taken as given, in the sense of providing for a meaningful starting point of linguistic and socio-legal analysis.[49] But what would be the "*law of the law*" or the "*law preceding the law*"[50] beneath the surface-structure level of operative adjudication, the deep-structure level of a judge's normative ideology and the discourse-theoretical frame of legal validity and legal rationality, if the quest for the final premises of law were ruthlessly pushed beyond such pre-given limits of legal discourse?

[49] Alexy, above at n. 8, 187. Cf. J.R. Searle, *Speech Acts: An Essay in the Philosophy of Language* (Cambridge University Press, 1992).

[50] F. Ewald, "The Law of Law", in G. Teubner (ed.), *Autopoietic Law: A New Approach to Law and Society* (Walter de Gruyter, 1988).

8

The Quest for the Final Premises of Law—I: The Infrastructures of Legal Norm Constitution

1. PROLOGUE: HOW LONG IS THE STANDARD METRE?

Wittgenstein wrote in *Philosophical Investigations*:[1]

> "There is *one* thing of which one can say neither that it is one metre long, nor that it is not one metre long, and that is the standard metre in Paris. But this is, of course, not to ascribe any extraordinary property to it, but only to mark its peculiar role in the language-game of measuring with a metre-rule. Let us imagine samples of colour being preserved in Paris like the standard metre. We define: 'sepia' means the colour of the standard sepia which is there kept hermetically sealed. Then it will make no sense to say of this sample either that it is of this colour or that it is not."

The dilemma taken up by Wittgenstein deals with the reference of length measurement: how long is the *standard metre* which is—or rather was[2]—used as an indispensable criterion of all length measurement, and what would be the colour of "*standard colours*" if such had also been established and placed in Paris? Wittgenstein, in effect, argues that the length of the standard metre cannot be defined, since that would necessitate having to apply the criterion of length measurement self-referentially upon itself. Devoid of any reference outside of the thing measured, nothing but utterly nonsensical or meaningless results could be gained by such a hollow act of "quasi-measurement", where the boundaries of the language-game of "measuring with a metre-rule", that of "defining colours with a set of standard colours", or their functional parallels in other fields of judgment, would be grossly violated.

However, in light of the subsequent philosophical discussion on the rule-bound, institutionally established facts, Wittgenstein is plainly mistaken in his *standard metre argument*. The standard metre bar is *per definitionem* exactly one metre long, by force of an explicit convention to that effect made within the community of length measurement. The same would be true of the imaginary

[1] L. Wittgenstein, *Philosophische Untersuchungen—Philosophical Investigations* (Basil Blackwell, 1967), § 50 (p. 25/25[e]).

[2] Nowadays, the length of the metre is defined with reference to the distance travelled by light in a vacuum in 1/299,792,458 of a second, but that will not, of course, affect the validity of the philosophical argument.

"standard colours" in Wittgenstein's other example, if a similar convention had indeed been made of the definition of colours. The standard metre is, in other words, an *institutional fact*[3] whose definitional properties have been laid down by an express convention to that effect within the community of length measurement.

Refusing to accept the convention-based status of the standard metre and the definitional properties derived from the convention—to the effect that the length of the standard metre is exactly one metre—would not qualify as an instance of outstanding philosophical erudition and caution. Rather, the situation is analogical to the fictitious dialogue which took place between the *Tortoise* and *Achilles* (of Zeno's paradox) in Lewis Carroll's insightful philosophical essay, "What the Tortoise said to Achilles". The (paradox-loving) tortoise consistently refused to accept the final conclusion of a logical inference, despite the fact that it had accepted all the premises of that inference which Achilles had patiently laid down before it, insisting on ever further premises before accepting the conclusion. As Winch rightly points out, questioning the act of drawing a valid conclusion from a set of premises is simply a sign of not having grasped the very idea of a logical inference.[4] Equally, questioning the (exact) length of the standard metre bar would imply that the speaker has not fully understood the inherent "logic" of such institutional facts and the role of social (or legal) conventions in their logico-conceptual constitution.

There is a grain of truth in Wittgenstein's line of argument, however. The length of the standard metre cannot be accounted for *within* the language-game of "measuring with a metre-rule". Yet, since the totality of the various kinds of language-games do not constitute a set of hermetically closed, solipsistic worlds of a Leibnizian monadology, but are likened to an open-ended set of tools by the Austrian philosopher himself, each with a different kind of usage and function, there is no reason *not* to cross the soft-edged border from the language-game of *measuring with a metre-rule* to that of *instituting a rule-bound, conventional fact*, whereby the length of the standard metre, or the definition of "standard colours" in Wittgenstein's other example, has conclusively been settled.

There is a valid social or legal rule behind the "metricity" of the standard metre by means of which any haze of mystery can be effectively dispelled from around it, but the truly aporetic philosophical question is not answered thereby. When "measuring" the rule behind the "metricity" of the standard metre, or—in more general terms—the ultimate validity and rationality ground of law, things are far more complicated. The question, what is valid law and how can it be identified from among other social phenomena?, cannot be settled by ref-

[3] On institutional facts, see, e.g. E. Anscombe, "On Brute Facts" (1958) 18 *Analysis* 69; J.R. Searle, *Speech Acts: An Essay in the Philosophy of Language* (Cambridge University Press, 1992), 50–3; and in the field of law, N. MacCormick and O. Weinberger, *An Institutional Theory of Law: New Approaches to Legal Positivism* (D. Reidel Publishing Co., 1986).

[4] P. Winch, *The Idea of a Social Science and its Relation to Philosophy* (Routledge & Kegan Paul, 1958), 55–7, where Lewis Carroll's (i.e. Charles Dodgson's) philosophical argument is cited.

erence to some widely acknowledged, convention-based *standard norm*, hermetically sealed and placed in a *Museum of Normativity*, in Paris or elsewhere. The situation is, instead, as if there were several "standard norms" of a mutually incompatible kind—one, for example, in Paris, London, New York, Moscow and Tokyo—and each with a different conception of legal validity (and legal rationality) under the divergent theoretical premises of legal positivism, legal realism, natural law theory, historical school of law, the Critical Legal Studies movement, etc. Instead of the concrete, standard metre bar placed in Paris, the far less tangible case of imaginary "standard colours" would be better matched with the key question of what would count as the "standard norm" for law, or the ultimate criterion of legal validity and legal rationality.

The nature and function of law have often been illustrated with the *game metaphor* in legal theoretical literature. Ross draws the analogy between law and chess in *Om ret og retfærdighed*,[5] and Hart, no doubt inspired by Wittgenstein's original idea of the various language-games, refers to the analogy of law and cricket in *The Concept of Law*.[6] The leading idea or objective striven for is usually well predetermined in most, if not all, games: to score more goals than the opposing side in football in accordance with the rules of the game; checkmate in chess in accordance with the constitutive rules of the game, etc. Still, as Morawetz insightfully points out,[7] there is one key element which effectively distinguishes the law from any ordinary game like chess, football or cricket, i.e. the lack of a widely shared understanding or common consensus as to the social outcomes to be attained and the methods to be employed in legal deliberation. There is, in other words, no *standard norm* in the domain of law which might function as an equivalent to Wittgenstein's tangible standard metre bar, the existence of which may be ascertained simply by paying a visit to Paris.

The game metaphor would be most telling of law if, indeed, there existed a convention-based *standard norm* or an operative yardstick of legal validity and legal rationality somewhere, but that is not, of course, the case. Far from being a non-contested and trivial, game-like pursuit whose institutional goals and methods of argumentation have been laid down in advance, legal discourse is an instance of a *deliberative practice*, in which the very concept of law, or what will qualify as a valid and rational argument in legal deliberation, is highly disputed and, most probably, will remain as such even after a full round of confrontations in legal discourse.[8] Morawetz gives an illustrative counter-example to the game metaphor in law: "From the point of view of the theorist, the situation is paradoxical. A player of chess plays with a player of Chinese checkers, and they

[5] A. Ross, *Om ret og retfærdighed: En indførelse i den analytiske retsfilosofi* (Nyt nordisk forslag, 1953) 22–8, 41ff.

[6] See Hart, *The Concept of Law* (Clarendon Press, Oxford, 1961), 9, 34, 58, 99, 138–41. The idea of a language-game is said to have come to Wittgenstein when watching a game of football. See N. Malcolm, *Ludwig Wittgenstein. Muistelma* (WSOY, Juva, 1990), 85.

[7] T. Morawetz, "Epistemology of Judging. Wittgenstein and Deliberative Practices", in D.M. Patterson (ed.), *Wittgenstein and Legal Theory* (Westview Press, 1992), 3–27.

[8] Ibid., 19–23.

in turn play with a third who is playing bridge. Each justifies her moves by appealing to her particular game".[9] There is, in other words, always room for consensus-defying disagreement as to the social goals to be attained and the methods to be employed in legal deliberation. In consequence, even the institutional theory of law fails to give a satisfactory account of the ultimate premises of law and legal discourse behind such effected institutional arrangements.[10]

The contested nature of law is beautifully depicted at the very beginning of Hart's *The Concept of Law*, where the key question "what is law?" is presented. As Hart points out, no vast literature is dedicated to questions like "what is chemistry?" or "what is medicine?". The standard textbooks on medicine do not begin with a definition of the said discipline as "what doctors do about illness" or "a prediction of what doctors will do", but in legal literature such definitions are put forth.[11] Nor do textbooks on chemistry rule out some standard part of that branch of study, for example the study of acids, as "not really" a part of chemistry at all, but in legal literature such stipulations are indeed made.[12] In football, chess or cricket, there is usually no wide disagreement among the players, umpire or spectators about the very idea of the game. In legal discourse, on the other hand, the innocent-sounding question of "what is law?" is bound to raise ideological strife and controversy, as it is the theoretical watershed which distinguishes the different schools of law from each other. Nor is there any promise of widely shared understanding on the concept of law in the foreseeable future.

The judges of a legal system hold a privileged—or merely burdened—institutional position in society, since they are placed under an obligation somehow to identify valid legal rules and accord a justifiable meaning-content to them, even if there is no uncontested criterion of rule-recognition, nor any unchallenged methods of legal interpretation available. A resigned, defeatist judgment of a *non liquet* is not permitted to judges in a modern society. In the past, the law was anchored in the will of God, the immutable precepts of human reason, or the legally unbound will of the sovereign ruler, with reference to the doctrines of classical natural law theory, the law of reason in the enlightenment era, and Austin's classic version of legal positivism, respectively. However, if the grounding axioms of modern analytical positivism are observed in a fully consistent manner, the external confines of law must ultimately be drawn in a self-referential manner, letting the law "work itself pure" and free from any external ground point of reference. Only then is the methodological credo of Kelsen's *Pure Theory of Law* duly followed.[13]

[9] *Wittgenstein and Legal Theory* (Westview Press, 1992), 6–7.

[10] On the institutional theory of law, see MacCormick and Weinberger, above at n. 3.

[11] Hart, above at n. 6, 1. Hart, of course, refers to the definitions of law by Llewellyn and Holmes, respectively.

[12] Ibid., 1 ff. However, one may wonder whether issues of a similar kind might not be encountered in more philosophically-oriented literature on medicine or chemistry.

[13] "It is called a 'pure' theory of law, because it only describes the law and attempts to eliminate from the object of this description everything that is not strictly law: Its aim is to free the science of

Wittgenstein was puzzled by the inescapable dilemmas of self-referentiality and the contestable status of any final reference for knowledge and judgment in *Philosophical Investigations*[14] and *On Certainty*.[15] In chapters 8 and 9, the Wittgensteinian methodological request for "leaving everything as it is"[16] will be deliberately rejected, defying the seductive call of the Oxford philosophy of ordinary language and its thoroughly pragmatics-laden conception of language and the world. Instead, the persistent dilemmas encountered at the ultimate edges of law will be tackled by pointing out a set of Derridean *infrastructures* whose decisively *prelogical* and *preconceptual* status provides for the "ultimate" criteria of norm/fact, validity/existence, *Sein/Sollen*, identity/difference, *logos/mythos*, etc., as *effected* and—with equal force—*effaced* within Western metaphysics.

2. THE INFRASTRUCTURES OF LEGAL NORM CONSTITUTION: THE CONSTITUTIVE *A PRIORI* OF LAW

In the relentless, uncompromising quest for the final premises of law—or of philosophy, for that matter—there is *absolutely nothing* that could claim immunity or sheltered position from Derrida's obstinate request of retaining an "unlimited right to ask any question, to suspect all dogmatism, to analyze every presupposition, even those of the ethics or the politics of responsibility".[17] In consequence, not even the axiomatic postulates of legal validity and legal rationality may be taken as the irrefutable end point or solid bedrock of legal and philosophical analysis. How valid is the ultimate validity ground of law? How rational is the ultimate ground of legal rationality? How is the rule of recognition itself identified, by means of a still higher meta-level criterion, or by means of the very rule of recognition itself? Is the rule of recognition then a valid norm, endowed with the claim to legal validity, or is it no more than a social fact, endowed with the property of effectiveness in society? Such questions are accounted for by constitutive infrastructures of law and legal discourse. In all, the following four questions will be reflected upon in more detail:

(1) *final validity ground of legal validity*
 = the ultimate criteria of legal ontology;
(2) *final rationality ground of legal rationality*
 = the ultimate criteria of legal methodology;
(3) *recognition of the rule of recognition*;

law from alien elements. This is the methodological basis of the theory": H. Kelsen, *Pure Theory of Law* (Peter Smith, 1989), 1.

14 Above at n. 1.

15 L. Wittgenstein, *Über Gewissheit—On Certainty* (Harper & Row, New York, 1972).

16 Wittgenstein, above at n. 1, § 124 (p. 49/49e).

17 J. Derrida, *On the Name* (Stanford University Press, 1995), 28.

(4) *norm/fact character of the rule of recognition*
= the ultimate criteria of legal epistemology (3) and (4)).

The "ultimate" *grounds*, *edges*, *criteria* or *premises* of law will be outlined in light of the prelogical and preconceptual infrastructures of law. The infrastructures of law may be divided into two main categories: the prerequisites of legal norm *constitution* (and *disintegration*), which account for the condition of possibility (and impossibility) of the validity and rationality claims in law, and the prerequisites of judicial signification, which provide for the *production* (and *dissolution*) of meaning within a system of legal norms or precedents. The latent impact of such infrastructures is, by necessity, silently presupposed in all statements concerning the validity and/or rationality of a legal norm, or set of legal norms, in legal discourse. Since the infrastructures cannot be grounded on any further premises of an even "deeper" or more basic character, they might be called the *a priori* element of legal norm constitution and meaning-production in law. The infrastructures of legal signification will be considered in separate terms in chapter 9 below.

The idea of the *a priori* of legal norm constitution is derived from Foucault's *archeology of knowledge*, where the French philosopher analysed the historically changing conditions of possibility of the human sciences. In a self-consciously drawn contrast to Kant's formal *a priori,* or the transcendental-logical and immutable conditions of possibility of human knowledge as expounded in Kant's *Critique of Pure Reason*, Foucault's *a priori historique*[18] concerns the contingent positivity of the various discourse formations which surface in the realm of the human sciences: not the validity ground of a set of judgments, but the condition of possibility of their existence; not the legitimacy ground of certain assertions, but the condition of possibility of their emergence, co-existence, transformations, and, finally, disappearance from the positivity of a discourse formation.[19] There are some inherent restrictions on what can conceivably be said, asserted or denied within a given discursive formation, as determined by what Foucault called the "historical *a priori*".[20] By introducing the concept of the historical *a priori*,

[18] M. Foucault, *L'archéologie du savoir* (Éditions Gallimard, Paris, 1969), 166–73 ("*l'a priori historique*"). That book is Foucault's theoretical self-reflection on the methodological issues related to the birth of the human sciences, as delineated in his earlier work *Les Mots et les choses: Une Archéologie des Sciences Humaines* (Éditions Gallimard, Paris, 1966).

[19] Foucault, *L'Archéologie du savoir*, ibid., 167: "... *un a priori qui serait non pas condition de validité pour des jugements, mais condition de réalité pour des énoncés. Il ne s'agit pas de retrouver ce qui pourrait rendre légitime une assertion, mais d'isoler les conditions d'émergence des énoncés, la loi de leur coexistence avec d'autres, la forme spécifique de leur mode d'être, les principes selon lesquels ils subsistent, se transforment et disparaissent. A priori, non de vérités qui pourraient n'être jamais dites, ni réellement données à l'expérience; mais d'une histoire qui est donnée, puisque c'est celle des choses effectivement dites*". On the term "discourse formation" or "discursive formation", see ibid., 44–54 ("*les formations discursives*").

[20] The theoretical limits of the "historical *a priori*" of the prevalent Western philosophy may be challenged by trying to find analogies to the non-Linnaean classification of animals found in a "Chinese encyclopædia" in J.L. Borges' insightful fiction. Borges' short story notably provided the source of inspiration for Foucault's inquiry into the "order of things" in the (external) world. See Foucault, *Les Mots et les choses*, above at n. 18, 7 ff.

Foucault "historicised" Kant's *Critique*, by showing the historically transforming character of Kant's transcendental-logical conditions of possibility of human knowledge and judgment, which are are then unfolded in the Western *épistémè*, or the historically evolving "order of things" in the (external) world.

The Derridean supplement to, or rather deviation from, the Foucauldian archeology of knowledge is captured in the *infrastructures* of human knowledge and judgment. Infrastructures of the Western *épistémè* might be characterised as the *quasi-transcendental* prerequisites of knowledge and judgment within the Western philosophical tradition, since they are the radically ambivalent *grounding/cancelling* or *effecting/effacing* condition of possibility and impossibility of such an order of things imposed upon the (external) world—"quasi-transcendental" and not truly transcendental, since they make an allusion to the conditions of knowledge and judgment "beyond" or "before" the existing positivity of legal, social, human or any other discourse, while lacking any constant metaphysical identity or conceptual essence of their own to which such an attribute might be attached. Therefore, they fall short of being qualified as the *a priori* of knowledge in the Kantian/Foucauldian sense of the term, dwelling endlessly in the realm of the "pre-metaphysical" and "quasi-transcendental". However, their external effects "take place" and unfold in time on the common coordinates of two-valued logic and linguistic conceptuality, as effected (and effaced) through such infrastructures of human judgment. Even the discourse on law leans ultimately on the silent operation of the infrastructures of Western metaphysics.

Constitutive infrastructures of law frame and structure the issues of legal ontology, legal epistemology and legal methodology in terms of the basic categories of norm/fact, *Sein/Sollen*, validity/existence, *logos/mythos*, reason/non-reason, sensible/intelligible, etc. Infrastructures of linguistic and legal signification, on the other hand, frame and structure the key issues of identity/non-identity, same/other or similarity/difference in the production of meaning-content for a linguistic sign or a legal norm based on such linguistic premises. Since the constitutive infrastructures of law are the *effecting* condition of possibility and, with equal force, the *effacing* condition of impossibility of the phenomena concerned, they should, in fact, be called the infrastructures of legal norm *constitution/disintegration.*

Infrastructures of norm constitution are held in common by all valid legal norms. Infrastructures of judicial signification, in turn, are "precedent-specific", or aligned with the production (and dissemination) of meaning in the context of precedent-following. Similar infrastructures of meaning-production could, of course, also be pointed out for statutory norms (defined in close analogy to the legislative paradigm of precedent-following which will be considered in detail in chapter 9), but such models of statutory reasoning will not be entered into in the present discussion. Besides framing the ultimate ontological, epistemological and methodological prerequisistes of legal validity and legal rationality, the constitutive effects of infrastructures of law are also reflected on the ideological level of law.

The *deontic mode* of the very criterion used for classifying legal norms into rules and principles (or policies) may be presented as an illustration of the impact of infrastructures of norm constitution on the level of legal ideology. The rule/principle dichotomy was said to reflect a deeper ontological or, in Dworkin's terms, "logical" distinction. The division of legal norms into the two categories of legal rules and principles (or policies) evidently requires a distinct criterion with reference to which such a dichotomy can be drawn and sustained. Is the criterion behind the rule/principle dichotomy itself a binary, rule-like criterion of the *on/off* or *either/or* type, or is it a graded, principle-like criterion of the *more-or-less* type? If the rule/principle dichotomy is based on a binary criterion, the conceptual boundary between the two types of norms is drawn in a clear-cut manner of the either/or type, like railroad tracks which can either be followed or not followed, but which cannot be followed more-or-less without falling off the tracks. In such a case, there is a genuinely qualitative difference between legal rules and principles (or policies). If, on the other hand, the rule/principle dichotomy is based on a graded criterion, there is a soft-edged transition from the realm of formally constituted legal rules to that of legal principles (and policies), with the domain of norms with a mixed profile of legal formality extending in-between.

Dworkin's and Alexy's theory of legal principles is based on an *either/or* distinction between the two norm types, since they both view the dichotomy as a categorical and qualititative one, resting ultimately on a binary code. On the other hand, Hart's account of legal rules and principles is based on a graded, *more-or-less* or principle-like criterion, since there is a soft-edged, quantitative transition from one norm type to another. The same holds true of Aarnio's fourpartite scheme of (1) legal rules, (2) rule-like principles, (3) principle-like rules, and (4) legal principles proper, with soft borders in-between the different categories of norms.[21]

3. THE FINAL VALIDITY GROUND OF LAW: VALIDITY OF LEGAL VALIDITY

As was noted above in chapter 1, a fully consistent positivist stance towards the law would seem rather hard to maintain and defend. Both Peczenik and MacCormick finally took recourse to the moral and/or political background premises of law, thereby crossing the line between formally legal and extra-legal discourse formations. Even Kelsen, in his bold effort to purify the cognition of law from all non-legal elements, eventually had to make room for the "by and large" empirically observable effectiveness of the *Grundnorm*, and of the system

[21] A. Aarnio, *Reason and authority: A Treatise on the Dynamic Paradigm of Legal Dogmatics* (Ashgate/Dartmouth, 1997), 179ff.; A. Aarnio, "Taking Rules Seriously" (1989) 42 *ARSP Beiheft* (Franz Steiner Verlag, 1989), 184.

of legal norms enacted under its presumed authority.[22] The tenets of modern natural law theory notwithstanding, the purely norm-based validity ground of law has been defended by the theory of *legal autopoiesis*, which defines the concept of law in essentially circular, self-referential terms under the normativistic and methodological premises of Kelsen's *Pure Theory of Law*[23] fully evolved and taken to extremes. By force of the present analytical and positivist frame of analysis, any forthright retreat to the moral and/or political background premises of law, as openly professed by (some) adherents of natural law theory and the Critical Legal Studies movement, respectively, is ruled out from among the feasible candidates of the final validity ground of law. There are three options left to be considered in more detail:

(1) formal legal validity, based on the transcendental-logical precondition of the hypothetical *Grundnorm*, supported by its empirical effectiveness or efficacy[24] in society (Kelsen);
(2) formal legal validity, based on the ultimate source norm or the underpinning reasons of law (Peczenik, MacCormick);
(3) formal legal validity, based on the positivity of the law itself (Aarnio, and the theory of legal autopoiesis).

3.1 Validity in Kelsen's *Pure Theory of Law*

(1) Validity based on the transcendental-logical presupposition of the Grundnorm

In his widely influential *Pure Theory of Law*, Kelsen sought to maintain a strict separation between the two realms of the *Is* (*Sein*) and the *Ought* (*Sollen*), or the world of facts and the world of values and norms, respectively. Kelsen's original inspiration for legal philosophy was drawn from the neo-Kantian philosophy of science, where the loosely defined field of human sciences (*Geisteswissenschaften*), or the studies on human intention, meanings and cultural artefacts, was to be distinguished from the field of natural sciences by force of their different subject matter and, therefore, different method or methods employed.[25] In Kelsen's classification of scientific inquiry, legal science was

[22] H. Kelsen, *Reine Rechtslehre. Mit einem Anhang: Das Problem der Gerechtigkeit* (Verlag Franz Deuticke, Wien, 1960), 219: "*Grund der Geltung . . . ist die vorausgesetzte Grundnorm, derzufolge man einer tatsächlich gesetzten, im grossen und ganzen wirksamen Verfassung und daher den gemäss dieser Verfassung tatsächlich gesetzten, im grossen und ganzen wirksamen Normen entsprechen soll. Setzung und Wirksamkeit sind in der Grundnorm zur Bedingung der Geltung gemacht . . .*". Cf. Kelsen, above at n. 13, 212.

[23] Above at n. 13.

[24] "Effectiveness" and "efficacy" are both used as English equivalents to, or, rather, approximations of, the German original term *Wirksamkeit*, which is the functional counterpart to the term *Geltung*, or the validity of a legal norm, in the legal context.

[25] On Kelsen's relation to the neo-Kantian philosophy of science, see Kelsen, "*Rechtswissenschaft und Recht: Erledigung eines Versuchs zur Überwindung der 'Rechtsdogmatik'*", in

characterised as a norm science (*Normwissenschaft*), to the effect that its task was to describe the valid legal norms which constitute a legal order.[26] All non-legal elements, no matter whether of a sociological, economical, moral or any other kind, were to be cleaned out of legal science thus "purified".[27]

Kelsen was very explicit in his contention that a norm's validity cannot be derived from the existence of some fact, framing the issue in Humean terms:[28]

> ". . . the question why a norm is valid, why an individual ought to behave in a certain way, cannot be answered by ascertaining a fact, that is, by a statement that something *is*; that the reason for the validity of a norm cannot be a fact. From the circumstance that something *is* cannot follow that something *ought* to be; and that something *ought* to be, cannot be the reason that something *is*. The reason for the validity of a norm can only be the validity of another norm."

In Kelsen's *Pure Theory of Law*, valid norms of a given legal order may be presented in the form of a norm-pyramid (*Stufenbau*), where the validity of an individual legal norm is invariably derived from the validity of another norm with a higher status in the norm hierarchy.[29] Administrative decrees and ordinances of varying hierarchical status derive their validity from a statutory norm, while the validity of a statutory norm is grounded on the currently valid constitution. Moreover, the validity of the current constitution is derived from the historically first constitution of the legal system concerned. Finally, the ultimate norm upon which the validity of the historically first constitution is grounded is called the *Grundnorm*, or *basic norm*, by Kelsen: "All norms whose validity can be traced back to one and the same basic norm constitute a system of norms, a normative order. The basic norm is the common source for the validity of all norms that belong to the same order—it is their common reason of validity".[30] The *Grundnorm* thus grounds the validity and internal unity of the legal order in question.

Kelsen's scholarly preoccupation with the thematics of the *Pure Theory of Law* extended well over half a century, with a gradual shift taking place from the initial neo-Kantian premises of the first edition of *Reine Rechtslehre* (1934) to the fragments of full-fledged normative irrationalism[31] in the posthumously published, unfinished manuscript, *Allgemeine Theorie der Normen*. The apt description *from Kant to Hume* has been suggested by Hartney with reference

F. Sander and H. Kelsen, *Die Rolle des Neukantianismus in der Reinen Rechtslehre: Eine Debatte zwischen Sander and Kelsen* (Scientia Verlag, 1988), 279–411, and the other essays included in Sander and Kelsen, ibid.

[26] Kelsen, above at n. 13, 70 ff.

[27] See ibid., 1, where the methodological purity of the pure theory is explicated.

[28] Ibid., 193.

[29] The idea of a norm hierarchy stems from Merkl's writings on legal theory. See, e.g., A.J. Merkl, "*Prolegomena einer Theorie des rechtlichen Stufenbaues*", in *Gesammelte Schriften. Erster Band: Grundlagen des Rechts, Teilband 1* (Duncker and Humblot, Berlin, 1993).

[30] Kelsen, above at n. 13, 195.

[31] The term *Normenirrationalismus*, or normative irrationalism, is suggested by O. Weinberger in *Normentheorie als Grundlage der Jurisprudenz und Ethik: Eine Auseinandersetzung mit Hans Kelsens Theorie der Normen* (Duncker & Humblot, Berlin, 1981), 94 ff.

thereto.[32] As the general theoretical frame of the *Pure Theory of Law* became modified, the concept of the *Grundnorm* went through a series of corresponding changes as well.[33] In *Allgemeine Staatslehre* (1925), the *Grundnorm* was described as a "hypothetical norm".[34] In the first edition of *Reine Rechtslehre* (1934), it was called "the basic presupposition" of all cognition concerning a legal system, as being grounded on the same constitution.[35] In *General Theory of Law and State* (1945), the *Grundnorm* was described as "the postulated ultimate rule according to which the norms of this order are established and annulled, receive and lose their validity", and as "a juristic hypothesis" which is said to "really exist in the juristic consciousness".[36] In the second edition of *Reine Rechtslehre* (1960), the *Grundnorm* is identified as the "transcendental-logical presupposition" with reference to which the subjective meaning of a constitution-creating act and other norm-creating acts based on the constitution is accorded the objective meaning of legal validity.[37] Finally, in the posthumous *Allgemeine Theorie der Normen* (1979), the *Grundnorm* is characterised as no more than a fiction, in the sense of Vaihinger's *als ob* philosophy.[38] In the present context, Kelsen's intellectual position of the second edition of the *Pure Theory of Law* (1960) will be taken as the primary reference of analysis.

In essence, the main function of the *Grundnorm* is to ground the validity of the historically first constitution upon which the validity of all the subsequent legal norms of a given legal order is based, whether of a constitutional, legislative or judicial kind.[39] In *Pure Theory of Law*, the question of a legal norm's validity ground is posited within the epistemic frame of a neo-Kantian philosophy of science. According to Kelsen, any assertion as to the validity of some legal

[32] M. Hartney, "Introduction: The Final Form of The *Pure Theory of Law*", in H. Kelsen, *A General Theory of Norms* (Oxford University Press, 1991), IX–LIII, esp. LII–LIII.

[33] See generally, R. Walter, "*Entstehung und Entwicklung des Gedankens der Grundnorm*", in R. Walter (ed.), *Schwerpunkte der Reinen Rechtslehre* (Manz Verlag, Wien, 1992), 54–7; Weinberger, above at n. 31, 132–5. Cf. also S.L. Paulson, "*Die Unterschiedlichen Formulierungen der 'Grundnorm'*", in A. Aarnio *et al.*, *Rechtsnorm und Rechtswirklichkeit: Festschrift für Werner Krawiez zum 60 Geburtstag* (Duncker & Humblot, Berlin, 1993), 53–74, esp. 58–63.

[34] That is: "*eine hypothetische Norm . . . nicht gesetzte, sondern vorausgesetzte*", H. Kelsen, *Allgemeine Staatslehre* (Österreichische Staatsdruckerie, 1993), 104. On the characterisation of the *Grundnorm* as "*die Verfassung in einem rechtslogishen Sinne*", see ibid. 249.

[35] In the German original: "*die Grundvoraussetzung, von der alle Erkenntnis der auf dieser Verfassung beruhenden Rechtsordnung ausgeht*": Kelsen, *Reine Rechtslehre* (1934), 65. Cf. H. Kelsen, *Introduction to the Problems of Legal Theory* (Oxford University Press, 1992), 57. Despite the somewhat misleading title, the said book is a translation of the first edition of *Reine Rechtslehre*.

[36] H. Kelsen, *General Theory of Law and State* (Harvard University Press, 1949), XV, 113, 116.

[37] Kelsen, above at n. 13, 201–3. Cf. Kelsen, above at n. 22, 204–6.

[38] Kelsen, above at n. 36, 256.

[39] Alexy has discerned three separate functions of the *Grundnorm*: (1) *Kategorietransformation*, which provides for the "category transformation", or the transition from the world of the *Sein* to the world of the *Sollen*; (2) *Kriterienfestlegung*, which determines the particular criteria of legal validity by reference to which the law-constituting facts are distinguished from facts which are irrelevant from the legal point of view; and, finally (3) *Einheitsstiftung*, which constitutes the unity of the norms of a given legal order: R. Alexy, *Begriff und Geltung des Rechts* (Verlag Karl Alber, 1992), 170–3.

norm is ultimately based on the *transcendental-logical precondition* that the validity of the *Grundnorm* is first silently presumed, providing for the validity ground of the historically first constitution and of all legal norms which have subsequently been enacted under its presumed authority.[40] But what is the ontological status of Kelsen's master criterion of legal validity, i.e. the *Grundnorm*, itself? Is it a legal norm, endowed with the same property of normative validity as the set of legal norms the validity of which is ultimately conditional upon its presumed validity/existence, or is it no more than a social fact, itself subjected to the criterion of social effectiveness?

Kelsen, as we saw, was very explicit in his claim that the validity of a legal norm cannot be derived from the existence of some social or other kind of fact, since that would be in gross violation of the Humean principle: "The reason for the validity of a norm can only be the validity of another norm".[41] Thus, the *Grundnorm* is defined as a norm, but one whose validity is only of a "presupposed" or "hypothetical" kind. Because of Kelsen's quick retreat to the safer realm of legal epistemology under the premises of a neo-Kantian philosophy of science, the question of the ontological status of the *Grundnorm* is left unanswered.

However, eventually even Kelsen had to reject his initial quest of purifying the realm of law from all non-legal or non-normative elements, and make room for the "by and large effectiveness" of the *Grundnorm*, of the valid constitution, and of the system of legal norms whose validity is based on those two.[42] The criterion of *by and large effectiveness* now accorded to the *Grundnorm* provides for an operative yardstick—or a feasible candidate for a *standard norm* in law—for distinguishing the system of valid legal norms from the commands issued by Mafia or any other system of unauthorised and illegitimate coercion, and also from the merely imaginary norms which may dwell in a legal philosopher's noble dreams of a perfectly just and fair society. The requirement of such effectiveness breaks down the pure normativity of Kelsen's *Pure Theory of Law*, since issues of a factual or empirical kind are given the final say on the concept of legal validity.

What is perhaps even more upsetting in Kelsen's *Pure Theory of Law* is the fact that his argumentation proceeds in a logical circle, since he is forced to presuppose the validity of the "*law before the law*" or the "*law preceding the law*", using Ewald's apt terminology, when framing the final validity conditions of law.[43] The validity of the *Grundnorm* is conditional on the contingent fact that

[40] Kelsen, above at n. 22, 200–9, 224–5.

[41] Kelsen, above at n. 13, 193.

[42] "*Grund der Geltung, das ist die Antwort auf die Frage, warum die Normen dieser Rechtsordnung befolgt und angewendet werden sollen, ist die vorausgesetzte Grundnorm, derzufolge man einer tatsächlich gesetzten, im grossen und ganzen virksamen Verfassung und daher den gemäss dieser Verfassung tatsächlich gesetzten, im grossen und ganzen virksamen Normen entsprechen soll. Setzung und Wirksamkeit sind in der Grundnorm zur Bedingung der Geltung gemacht; . . .*" Kelsen, above at n. 22, 219. Cf. Kelsen, above at n. 13, 212.

[43] F. Ewald, "The Law of Law", in G. Teubner (ed.), *Autopoietic Law: A New Approach to Law and Society* (Walter de Gruyter, 1988), 36: "The law presupposes itself; it necessary precedes itself",

there exists a "by and large" effective practice of norm-enforcement in the competent courts of justice in a given legal order. However, the judgment as to what will qualify as a court of justice, as distinguished from the putative "law-enforcement" organs of the Mafia or some other, possibly highly effective system of unauthorised coercion, is itself conditional on the pre-existence of some legally qualified criteria. What will count as a competent court of justice—in other words, what is law—is resolved with reference to a set of criteria which themselves presuppose the pre-existence of the laws of court organisation and formal judicial procedure. Thereby, the law conceptually precedes itself in Kelsen's *Pure Theory of Law*.

Theoretical dilemmas induced by the introduction of the hypothetical *Grundnorm* into law are not exhausted by the facets of ultimately failing legal normativity and the predicaments involved in the identification of law. In the mutual co-existence of statutory and precedent-based law in a legal system, there is still another theoretical pitfall to take notice of.

(2) *A theoretical dilemma affecting Kelsen's* Grundnorm *in a system of statutory and precedent-based norms*

Under the precedent ideology based on judicial legislation, the prior court is taken as a small-scale legislator with powers of interstitial and future-oriented norm-giving, in the image of the legislator proper. Yet, the adoption of such an approach to precedent-following by the judiciary will inevitably upset the balance of norm-giving powers between the legislature and the judiciary, unless the *transcategorical context* of adjudication, as provided by the prevalent legal source doctrine in the legal system concerned, is able to strike an equilibrium between the two norm-givers. The parallel impact of statutory norms with mandatory binding force on adjudication and precedent-norms with an equally strong, "quasi-legislative" claim for norm-observance *vis-à-vis* judges, would ultimately break the Kelsenian *Stufenbau* into two distinct and, possibly, mutually conflicting normative systems, since both systems of norms equally put forth an exclusive claim to legal supremacy. Under the Kelsenian premises thus logically extended, statutory norms would ground their validity on a statute-grounding *Grundnorm*$_s$, to the effect that statutory norms, as duly issued by Parliament, are (valid and) supreme in the legal system concerned. Precedent-norms, on the other hand, would ground their validity on a parallel precedent-grounding *Grundnorm*$_p$, to the effect that precedent-norms, as issued by the highest national court of justice, are (valid and) supreme in the legal system concerned.[44]

[44] Kelsen himself devoted some consideration to precedents in *Pure Theory of Law*, 250–6. He tackled the possible incompatibility of the two kinds of (systems of) general norms in passing in ibid., 251, while ignoring the potentially system-disintegrating impact of precedent-norms which are claimed to be endowed with an equally general and supreme status as norms of a statutory origin in the legal system concerned. Under the theoretical premises of Kelsen's *Pure Theory of Law*, there can, of course, be only one genuine *Grundnorm*.

In a conflict situation between the two systems of norms and the corresponding meta-level *Grundnormen*,[45] i.e. the statute-grounding *Grundnorm*$_s$ and the precedent-grounding *Grundnorm*$_p$, a judge would have no other option but to have recourse to a radically equivocal or unclassifiable statute-grounding/precedent-grounding *Grundnorm*$_{s/p}$, endowed with a still higher meta-meta-level status, in order to resolve the persistent conflict between the two normative systems and the respective *Grundnormen*. Introduction of the novel *Grundnorm*$_{s/p}$ would then signify an effective "overruling" or invalidation of either *Grundnorm*$_s$ or *Grundnorm*$_p$, giving decisive priority to norms of either statutory or precedential origin. Evidently, *Grundnorm*$_s$ and *Grundnorm*$_p$ cannot be sustained simultaneously, since there can be only one *Grundnorm* of the last resort under the theoretical premises of Kelsenian normativism. However, the novel *Grundnorm*$_{s/p}$ must remain radically undecidable *vis-à-vis* the two options available, by force of the line of argumentation which will be discussed in detail below.

If the statute-grounding *Grundnorm*$_s$ were privileged at the cost of the precedent-grounding *Grundnorm*$_p$ and the corresponding system of precedent-norms, the resulting outcome would be a legal system where judicial norms may be overruled by a statutory enactment to the said effect. Such a system of law can be said to follow the rule of law ideology under the auspices of parliamentary sovereignty. If, on the other hand, the precedent-grounding *Grundnorm*$_p$ were given decisive priority over the statute-grounding *Grundnorm*$_s$ and the corresponding system of statutory norms, a gradual erosion of legislative supremacy and a corresponding growth in the courts' norm-giving power would be effected. Such a legal system could be described by the German term *Richterstaat*, or a state governed by the judiciary and judge-made law. In most, if not all, national legal systems the will of the Parliament is held to be decisive, and any quasi-legislative court rulings may be overruled by subsequent legislative measures. It is only outside the domain of municipal law, i.e. in international law and legal systems which are functionally parallel to it, that the court-oriented model of a *Richterstaat* may easily become realised. In multinational legal relations, there is frequently no sovereign legislator, and the court of justice which has been granted jurisdiction to rule over such issues may try to invade the "no-man's-land" that is left unoccupied by the lack of a sovereign legislator. That, at least, might be one interpretation of the highly activist phase of the European Court of Justice since the late-1960's to mid-1980s.[46]

The emergence of a radically unresolvable conflict between the norms of legislative origin and the norms of judicial origin is usually prevented by having reference to the transcategorical context of adjudication, i.e. the prevalent legal source doctrine that sets the degree of legitimate binding force of a precedent

[45] *Grundnormen* is the plural mode of (a) *Grundnorm*.

[46] Cf. H. Rasmussen, *On Law and Policy in the European Court of Justice* (Martinus Nijhoff Publishers, 1986); cf. M. Cappelletti, *The Judicial Process in Comparative Perspective* (Clarendon Press, Oxford, 1989), 383–401, where Hjalte Rasmussen's arguments are critically evaluated.

below that of a statutory norm, or vice versa. In the contrary case, i.e. in a *Richterstaat* where the highest court or courts of justice would have supremacy to issue rulings in disregard of the will of the Parliament, the constraints derived from the legal source doctrine would be lifted *vis-à-vis* precedents, and equal restraints would be placed upon the normative force of statutes. Yet, in the absence of such a frame of constraint to either effect, a judge's legal ideology would be left radically unresolved, oscillating between the two incompatible options of parliamentary sovereignty and judicial sovereignty, with no state of equilibrium in-between.

3.2 Validity based on a moral and/or political validity conception: Peczenik and MacCormick on the final validity ground of law

Meta-level norms which determine the relative binding force of various source material, from among which a judge may then derive the normative premises of judicial decision-making, are called *legal source norms* by Peczenik. But what is the status and final validity ground of such source norms themselves? In Peczenik's theory of law, source norms, which determine the order of preference of legal sources in terms of their *must-*, *should-* or *may*-standing, are themselves classified as legal norms, despite their meta-level status *vis-à-vis* the primary, first-level legal norms proper.[47] Peczenik's conception of law may be criticised on the ground that it extends the notion of a legal norm too wide, to cover also some rules of rational legal argumentation. In terms of the present discussion, the sum total of such source norms would be placed among the formative premises of a judge's legal or precedent ideology, and not among legal norms themselves.

Since the validity of legal source norms is said to be derived from customary law, such a customary norm, or set of customary norms, has the status of a third-level criterion of legal validity *vis-à-vis* primary, first-level legal norms. As to the validity ground of customary norm or norms, Peczenik refers to the background reasons of law in terms of the moral and/or political conceptions of democracy, legal security and legal tradition in society. Finally, when reflecting upon such fourth-level background reasons of legal validity, Peczenik makes a reference to von Wright's assertion, to the effect that a norm's validity is in the last resort based on another norm's *existence*, not upon the latter's validity.[48] von Wright has argued as follows:[49]

> "A norm is valid, if at all, *relative to* another norm permitting its issuing or coming into existence. This relativity of the notion of validity, however, must not be

[47] "From the logical point of view, the source-norms are meta-norms, determining the legal status of other norms": A. Peczenik, *On Law and Reason* (Kluwer, 1989), 324.

[48] A. Peczenik, *Vad är rätt? Om demokrati, rättssäkerhet, etik och juridisk argumentation* (Nordstedts juridik, 1995), 226; cf. Peczenik, above at n. 47, 322–3.

[49] G.H. von Wright, *Norm and Action: A Logical Enquiry* (Routledge & Kegan Paul, 1963), 196. von Wright would seem to refer to Merkl's and Kelsen's idea of a formal norm hierarchy (*Stufenbau*).

misinterpreted. It does *not* mean that the issued norm is valid *if* the norm permitting its issuing is *valid*. The first norm does not 'get' its validity from the validity of the second. The validity of a norm, in the sense now under discussion, is not validity relative to the *validity* of another norm. It is validity relative to the *existence* of another norm, hierarchically related to the first in a certain way."

Thus, ultimately Peczenik grounds the validity of law on arguments found relevant in the moral and/or political discourse formation in society: a fifth-level source norm, to the effect that "what promotes such values as historical continuity, legal security and democracy is to be taken into account in legal argumentation", is said to *exist* in moral-political discourse.[50] Thereby, the endless regress to ever higher meta-level norms of nth degree is avoided, but the initial legal frame of reference is transformed into one of moral and/or political discourse. But how could such an ultimate source norm exist, without being first qualified as valid? An assertion to the effect that there exists an *absolutely non-valid* norm, in the sense of a norm which fails to satisfy the validity criteria of any normative system whatever, but which would still somehow "exist" in society, would be a plain *category mistake* in the Rylean sense of the term.[51]

When reflecting upon the deeper-level justification of legal validity, MacCormick similarly makes use of the notion of *underpinning reasons of law*. Underpinning reasons are said to be the "reasons for accepting the system's criteria of validity",[52] as given in terms of "*consequentialist* arguments which are essentially *evaluative* and therefore in some degree *subjective*".[53] Such justificatory criteria, like Peczenik's moral and/or political background reasons of law, provide for the very final premises of legal validity. However, they import moral and/or political consideration into the (initially) formal edifice of law, in open disregard of the methodological strictures imposed by Kelsen's *Pure Theory of Law*, strictly defined.

3.3 Validity based on normative validity itself: Aarnio and the theory of legal autopoiesis on the final validity ground of law

A theoretically fully consistent, but still problematic, account of legal validity under the auspices of legal positivism is given—in separate terms—by Aarnio and the theory of legal autopoiesis. Aarnio would seem to follow Kelsen's

[50] Peczenik, above at n. 48 226 (translation from Swedish by the author).

[51] See G. Ryle, *The Concept of Mind* (Penguin/Peregrine Books, 1963), 17ff., 75–7. Cf. Lon L. Fuller, *The Morality of Law* (Yale University Press, 1969), 39, where an allusion is made to the "Pickwickian" sense in which a void contract might be said to be one kind of a contract.

[52] N. MacCormick, *Legal Reasoning and Legal Theory* (Oxford University Press, 1978), 64. On the notion of "underpinning reasons", see ibid., 62–5, 106, 138–40, 240–6, and 275–92. "Only in some few cases . . . do the underpinning reasons come overtly to the surface in litigious argument and judicial opinions. Only in these rare cases are the underpinning reasons necessarily offered as essential to the explicit justification of a decision": ibid., p. 64.

[53] Ibid., 106 (emphasis in original). Cf. also ibid., 138–9.

methodological request down to its stern logical conclusions. When pondering upon the final validity ground of law, Aarnio takes resort to a notably self-referential argument, to the effect that the criteria of legal validity have been expressly laid down by the legislator in the case of statutory (and customary) law. He writes concerning statutory law, which is thereby classified as having mandatory force in the Finnish legal system, that the "law text . . . has been 'made official', as it is a source of law which is specifically mentioned in . . . the Finnish Code of Judicial Procedure. This means that the law text has the greatest authority as justification".[54] In the Finnish Act of Judicial Procedure, two separate articles indeed regulate the binding character of statutory law in judicial decision-making. The Act of Judicial Procedure, Chapter 1, Article 11 decrees as follows:[55]

> "A judge shall carefully study the true purpose and rationale of the law, and give the judgment accordingly, but not against it, at his own will. Customary law, unless it is deemed inequitable, shall also guide him in adjudication, if there exists no statutory law [on the issue]."

The Act of Judicial Procedure, Chapter 24, Article 3 places the following requirements on judicial decisions:

> "Each judicial decision shall be grounded on reasons and law, and not on [the judge's] arbitrary whim; and the main reasons for the decision, and the article of law upon which it is based, shall be clearly presented therein."

Such an express recognition of the binding force of statutory (and customary) norms in Finnish legislation has the double function of, first, providing the ultimate validity ground of law, given in such self-referential terms, and, secondly, providing the ultimate criteria for the identification of mandatory legal source material in the Finnish legal system. The argument is, of course, a classic example of a *petitio principii*, begging the question and neatly reflecting the ultimately self-referential identity of analytical positivism as concerns its ontological, epistemological and methodological foundation.

The theory of *legal autopoiesis*, as put forth by, for example, Teubner[57] and Luhmann,[58] seeks to give a theoretical account of such circular phenomena of systemic self-constitution, self-identification, and self-legitimation in law. The theory of legal autopoiesis stems from a systems-theoretical approach to society, where the German term *Selbstreferenz* has been adopted with reference to

[54] A. Aarnio, *The Rational as Reasonable: A Treatise on Legal Justification* (D. Reidel Publishing Co., 1987), 92. See also ibid., 99 ff. Cf. Peczenik, above at n. 48, 227–9; A. Aarnio, *Laintulkinnan teoria* (WSOY, Juva, 1989), 220; A. Aarnio, *Oikeussäännösten tulkinnasta* (Juridica, Helsinki, 1982), 94–5.

[55] The Act of Judicial Procedure 1:11 (translation from Finnish by the author).

[56] The Act of Judicial Procedure 24:3 (translation from Finnish by the author).

[57] G. Teubner, *Law as an Autopoietic System* (Blackwell Publishers, 1993), 13–46; G. Teubner, "How the Law Thinks: Towards a Constructivist Epistemology in Law" (1989) 23 *Law and Society Review* 727.

[58] N. Luhmann, *Das Recht der Gesellschaft* (Suhrkamp Verlag, 1993), 188 ff.

the effects of the self-constituting and self-organising processes in law and society.[59] Legal autopoiesis defines a legal system in terms of *operative closure* and *cognitive openness vis-à-vis* its social environment,[60] with the aim of producing "legal order from social noise".[61] Legislation and jurisdiction account for the self-constitution of a legal system, whereas legal self-description, or self-observance, is left to be pursued by legal doctrine.[62]

Teubner's theory of legal autopoiesis exemplifies a radically constructivist approach to law and society,[63] where the logical consequences of a truly normativistic conception of law are fully evolved. As in Aarnio's theory of law, the source of legal validity is found within the notion of valid law itself. The seeds of such a circular validity conception of law can be traced back to Kelsen's *Pure Theory of Law*, where the Austrian legal philosopher set out the methodological claim that the validity of a legal norm can only be grounded on another norm with a hierarchically higher status in the *Stufenbau* structure of law.[64] Kelsen cut down the menacing circle of full-fledged logical self-referentiality by means of the hypothetical *Grundnorm* which functions as the transcendental-logical presupposition of all cognition concerning the valid norms of a given legal system. Legal autopoiesis, on the other hand, bluntly rejects any futile longing for some external reference or end point of justification in the law, as found outside the realm of valid legal norms themselves.

3.4 The inherent limits of the legal positivist frame

The discovery of the inherent shortcomings affecting the ultimate premises of legal validity should not be read as nihilistic "trashing" of the grounding axioms of law as professed by the school of analytical positivism. My intention is, instead, to identify the *theoretical limits* of the analytical and positivist frame, so as eventually to reach beyond such self-imposed methodological constraints. In a careful close-reading of Kelsen's, Peczenik's, MacCormick's and Aarnio's theories of law, the final validity ground of law proved to be one of the *blind spots* of legal analysis which cannot be accounted for by means of the same conceptual tools provided by analytical positivism itself.

[59] Ibid., 77, where the dichotomy *Selbstreferenz—Fremdreferenz* is explicated.

[60] Teubner, *Law as an autopoietic System*, above at n. 57, 69–71; Luhmann, above at n. 58, 77, 83.

[61] The apposite phrase "order from noise" is derived from von Förster's systems-theory. See Teubner, *Law as an Autopoietic System*, above at n. 57, 71; N. Teubner, "How the Law Thinks: Towards a Constructivist Epistemology in Law", above at n. 57, 740.

[62] Teubner, *Law as an Autopoietic System*, above at n. 57, 39. Other reflexive notions of a Teubnerian origin would include self-production, self-organisation and self-regulation: ibid., 16 ff. The notion of self-constitution may yet be taken to comprise all the three terms.

[63] On legal constructivism in general, see *Teubner*, "How the Law Thinks: Towards a Constructivist Epistemology in Law", above at n. 57.

[64] "For it is a most significant peculiarity of law that it regulates its own creation and application." Kelsen: above at n. 13, 71. Cf. ibid., 255.

Kelsen's bold effort to purify the law of all non-legal elements ended up in having to presuppose the existence of the *law before the law* or the *law preceding the law*, since the by and large effective enforcement of legal norms by the competent courts of justice proved to be a decisive criterion of their legal validity. Peczenik and MacCormick, in order to stop the endless regress to the ever higher validity criteria of the nth degree, both made a recourse to the moral and/or political background criteria behind the law: Peczenik to the values of democracy, legal security and legal tradition, and MacCormick to the underpinning reasons of law. However, the positivist frame became thereby transformed into one of moral and/or political discourse, whereby Kelsen's idea of safeguarding the purity of legal science from non-legal elements was decisively rejected. Finally, Aarnio's unfeigned positivist conception of law, where the validity ground of law was derived from an express statutory provision to that effect, leads to a full-fledged logical circle of argumentation. Such circular processes of self-constituting self-referentiality have been further analysed by the systems-theoretical endeavours of legal autopoiesis (Luhmann, Teubner).

If the positivist conception of law is to be sustained in a consistent manner, to the effect of rejecting any retreat to the moral, political, or otherwise non-legal premises of legal validity, the predicaments encountered at the ultimate edges of law must be tackled with the self-effacing *infrastructures* of law. Such self-evading phenomena will be reflected upon in detail, once the final rationality ground of legal rationality, the recognition of the ultimate rule of recognition, and the norm/fact character, or validity/existence, of the rule of recognition, have first been considered.

4. RATIONALITY OF LEGAL RATIONALITY: THE ULTIMATE GROUND OF LEGAL JUSTIFIABILITY

4.1 Wróblewski and MacCormick on the final premises of legal rationality

Wróblewski has defined legal rationality as a function of the epistemic and axiological premises for a judicial decision.[65] According to the Polish legal philosopher, the different levels of judicial decision-making rationality can be presented as follows:[66]

(1) consistency of the justificatory premises of the decision with the outcome reached, as judged in light of the rules of justificatory reasoning adopted, or the *internal* rationality of the decision;
(2) justification of the premises of reasoning from a critical, *external* point of view;

[65] J. Wróblewski, *The Judicial Application of Law* (Kluwer, 1992), 114, 210.
[66] Ibid., 210–11 (emphasis added).

(3) evaluation of the rules of justificatory reasoning adopted, with respect to whether they are justified and/or correctly used, or the *logic of justification*;
(4) identification of the *presuppositions* necessary for any justification on the first three levels above; and
(5) identification of the *ultimate premises* which justify or explain the justification made on the four preceding levels.

Wróblewski seems to suddenly change the frame of analysis between points (3) and (4), from legal justification in terms of internal consistency (point (1)), external criticism (point (2)), and evaluation of the method of reasoning adopted (point (3)) to the self-referential question of the identification of the reasoning premises required for the prior three levels (point (4)) and, ultimately, for all the prior four levels of analysis discerned (point (5)). The ultimate nature of the fifth level premises of judicial decision-making rationality is simply taken as given. The question from where such "ultimate" premises are derived is never posited by Wróblewski, who confines his analysis explicitly to the first and second levels of justification only, along with some "fragments", as he puts it, of the third level.[67] Rationality is, as Wróblewski writes, a "basic value which is not further justifiable in the legal discourse".[68] He makes a reference to MacCormick's similar contention of the non-justifiability of the concept of rationality: "My belief that I ought to be rational is not a belief which I can justify by reasoning".[69]

Kant's *Kritik der reinen Vernunft* may be read as an effort to give a solid foundation for human reason, as judged by the faculties of that reason itself. The quest for the final ground of legal rationality faces a parallel dilemma: how to give a pertinent (self-)legitimation to the categories of legal reason. Wróblewski's "analytical scalpel" cuts through the tissues of law and reason with exceptional sharpness and precision, but the status of that analytical instrument itself is never questioned, nor explicated by him. Wróblewski cut down the endless regress to ever higher premises of justification by a mere *fiat*, violently ending the backward-proceeding proliferation of novel arguments at the fifth, "ultimate" level of justification, but the legitimacy of such a stipulation is far from evident, and the exact content of the fifth level of legal argumentation is left unspecified. The same is true of MacCormick's *dictum* of the non-justifiability of the reason's dictate to be rational. Since the scholars identified with analytical positivism have been rather laconic on the "rationality of legal rationality", a few remarks will suffice before considering Hart's rule of recognition anew.

[67] J. Wróblewski, *The Judicial Application of Law* (Kluwer, 1992), 211.
[68] Ibid., 306.
[69] Wróblewski, above at n. 65, 313, n. 5; MacCormick, above at n. 52, 268.

4.2 From the meta-rules of legal rationality to a Wittgensteinian form of life: Aarnio and Peczenik on the final premises of legal rationality

Above, Alexy argued for the *special case thesis*, to the effect that legal discourse is a distinct subcategory of general practical discourse, differentiated from the latter by its inherent claim to legal correctness and the constraints derived from the legal source doctrine and the rules of legal procedure. Aarnio, on the other hand, would seem to defend an exceptionally strong rationality thesis in his *Reason and Authority*.[70] He sees the concept of legal rationality as deeply embedded in our most profound culture-laden expectations concerning law, legal adjudication, and legal argumentation.[71] As was argued above, legal rationality may be defined in the sense of logical *L-rationality*, strictly defined, or discursive *D-rationality*, in approximation of Habermas' notion of an ideal speech situation in legal discourse. The idea of legal rationality is then materialised in citizens' warranted request for legal predictability, equality, and justice before the law. Aarnio's key idea of *rational and reasonable* legal decision-making is based on a reconstructive reading of Western legal culture where the formal tenets related to the decision-making procedure and the substantive requirements placed upon the outcome of such deliberation are held in balance by reference to the criteria of rational acceptability.

In framing the meta-rules of rational legal decision-making, Aarnio incorporates four kinds of theoretical constructions into his theory of law: Habermas' *ideal speech situation*,[72] Perelman's and Olbrechts-Tyteca's *universal audience* at which the outcome of legal argumentation is directed;[73] Alexy's *meta-rules of legal discourse rationality*, given in terms of consistence, efficiency, coherence, generalisability, sincerity and support in argumentation;[74] and Rawls' *veil of ignorance* behind which rational legal deliberation is thought to take place.[75] Alexy's rationality rules of legal discourse were touched upon above. The notion of an ideal speech situation, in turn, is an essential part of Habermas' universal-pragmatic theory of language. In the ideal speech situation, all contingent and coercive elements which might have effect on the free presentation of arguments in discourse have been eliminated. In consequence, each speaker may freely put forth arguments, challenge the validity of counter-arguments presented by others, and either justify or question the premises of arguments employed in the discourse.[76] In the ideal speech situation, arguments have neither less, nor more weight than their inherent argumentative potential admits

[70] Above at n. 21.
[71] Aarnio, above at n. 54, 193–5.
[72] Aarnio, *Reason and Authority*, above at n. 21, 209 ff.
[73] Ibid., 220 ff.; Aarnio, above at n. 54, 220–9.
[74] Aarnio, above at n. 54, 195–201; Aarnio, *Reason and Authority*, above at n. 21, 214–16.
[75] Ibid., 228.
[76] J. Habermas, "*Wahrheitstheorien*", in *Vorstudien und Ergänzungen zur Theorie des kommunikativen Handelns* (Suhrkamp, 1989), 174 ff., esp. 177–8.

them to have, free from all external coercion or interference of non-rational elements.

According to Perelman and Olbrechts-Tyteca, the idea of universal audience is based on the distinction drawn between merely persuasive and truly convincing argumentation. Persuasive argumentation is affected by the contingent characteristics, personal interests, and ideological motives of the members of some concrete audience, and less-than-fully rational arguments may accordingly be utilised in it. Convincing argumentation, by contrast, is directed at the universal audience (*l'auditoire universel*) where the impact of all other types of arguments, except for those which are fully rational, have been ruled out of the discourse.[77] The two authors point out that the support eventually gained for an argument in the universal audience is not an empirical issue (*question de fait*), but a normative one (*question de droit*).[78] The universal audience is, in other words, a normative yardstick or criterion by reference to which the rationality of arguments presented in some actual discourse may be evaluated.[79]

In Rawls' widely influential book, *A Theory of Justice*, the *veil of ignorance* was introduced as a novel tool of philosophical analysis, deviced for the purpose of framing the hypothetical original position which is thought to prevail before making an (imaginary) social contract and entering a well-ordered society under its terms. Behind the veil of ignorance, parties to the discourse of initial social contracting are deprived of any knowledge concerning their own individual or personal qualities, values and interests.[80] Such Musilian *Männer ohne Eigenschaften*, or "men without properties", are then thought to reach an agreement concerning the basic principles of justice and the institutional frame of society. Now, Aarnio places legal deliberation behind such a conceptual device.

Rawls' veil of ignorance is a powerful conceptual tool when applied to the *tabula rasa* type of situation of initial social contracting, whether conceived of in truly historical and actual or merely imaginary and hypothetical terms. However, once the institutional frame and basic principles of justice have been established in society, the veil of ignorance must be raised to make room for an efficient system of law-making and law-application under such terms as consented to by the parties of the social contract. At the least, the veil of ignorance must be made "thin" enough to allow the prevalent legal source doctrine and the institutional frame of court organisation and judicial procedure to have full effect on judicial deliberation, while the essential elements of non-partiality and objectivity in decision-making are still retained. If that is not the case, i.e. if the veil of ignorance is defined as "thick" enough to cancel the impact of such an institutional and legal frame of judicial deliberation, it will have the negative

[77] C. Perelman and L. Olbrechts-Tyteca, *La nouvelle Rhétorique: Traité de l'Argumentation* (Éditions de l'Université du Bruxelles, 1988), 34–40. Cf. also ibid., 634, 40. According to the authors, the distinction *persuader/convaincre* is derived from Kant: ibid., 37.

[78] Ibid., 41.

[79] On the concept of a universal audience, see ibid., 40–6.

[80] J. Rawls, *A Theory of Justice* (Oxford University Press, 1976), 136–7. On the veil of ignorance in general, see ibid., 136–42.

side-effect of erasing all that might have genuinely legal significance for the issue under consideration. Behind the veil of ignorance, as outlined by Rawls in *A Theory of Justice*, the parties to a legal dispute are made to forget temporarily their expectations and aspirations as to the outcome of the case, in addition to their overall state of oblivion on the particular conditions of human history and society. But how could a judicial decision be legally and rationally justified under such Rawlsian premises?

Rawls, like others before him, has convincingly argued that "one must distinguish between justifying a practice as a system of rules to be applied and enforced, and justifying a particular action which falls under these rules".[81] The inadequacy of the Rawlsian device in judicial decision-making is induced by the essential difference in the context of justification in the two situations. When negotiating a (hypothetical) social contract on the basic principles of justice and institutional frame in society, all that might have relevance for the bargaining position of the parties is included in their knowledge of general laws of justice and human society. In a concrete legal dispute before a court of justice, in turn, the ideological stakes, preferences and personal motives held by the parties are at the very heart of the legal issue, once their expectations as to the final outcome of the case have been transformed into a set of formal rights/ duties, privileges/"no-rights", powers/liabilities, and immunities/disabilities, if Hohfeld's slightly artificial but sharp-edged analytical terminology is employed.[82]

There is simply not enough conceptual room for rational legal argumentation, if the Rawlsian veil of ignorance is permitted to fall down again, cutting litigants off from their legal and ideological stakes in the outcome of a case. Aarnio's theory may be saved by redefining the Rawlsian veil of ignorance as "thin" enough to no more than guarantee the observance of certain general criteria of impartiality and objectivity on the part of the judge concerned, without any further commitment to the abstracting tenets entailed in Rawls' original idea of social contracting and the veil of ignorance.

When seeking to give an account of the "deeper-level" premises of legal argumentation, Aarnio tries to avoid an endless regress to ever higher meta-level criteria of rationality by taking resort to Wittgenstein's late philosophy, as set out in *Philosophical Investigations*[83] and *On Certainty*.[84] According to Aarnio, the chain of argumentation simply needs to be brought to an end at some time, since the constant interplay of questioning the premises so far presented and then finding some further support for the preferred outcome in the case just cannot

[81] J. Rawls, "Two Concepts of Rules" (1955) LXIV *The Philosophical Review* 3 ff. According to Rawls, the distinction is an old one, employed by, e.g., Hume, Austin, Mill, Mabbott and Toulmin before Rawls himself: ibid., 3, n. 2.

[82] W.N. Hohfeld, *Fundamental Legal Conceptions as Applied in Judicial Reasoning* (Yale University Press, 1964), 36.

[83] Above at n. 1.

[84] Above at n. 15.

go on infinitely.[85] In consequence, the line of reasoning may be legitimately stopped when the premises for the outcome are thought to be "strong enough" in the *particular ideal audience* at which the chain of argumentation is directed.[86] The ultimate premises of legal justification are thus left to be determined by the meta-level criterion of *rational acceptability* in the legal community, or form of life, concerned.[87] The notion of a form of life is an allusion to a shared *Weltanschauung* or common cultural background[88] operative behind a particular notion of legal rationality in society.

Peczenik, in turn, has made use of two distinct levels of legal justification: a "contextually sufficient legal justification" is more or less equal to the surface-structure level operative and the deep-structure level ideological premises of law in terms of the present treatise, while the "deep", "deepest" or "fundamental" justification of law refers to the ultimate level of legal justification, in the sense of what is "as fundamental as possible in the optimal conditions of discourse".[89] Peczenik makes an allusion to the ideal preconditions of a fully rational legal discourse, in the sense defined above by Alexy and Habermas. But what are the very final prerequisites of legal rationality behind or beneath Peczenik's "deepest" justification of law? Again, the end point of legal reasoning is anchored in the notion of a form of life, characterised as *a reification of the unknown end-points of justification* by Peczenik,[90] and the avoidance of chaos in society.[91]

The final premises of rational legal argumentation are thus deeply embedded in the prevalent form of life. Any effort to give the final preconditions of rational argumentation some precise linguistic formulation would imply "saying the unsayable",[92] while legal source norms and other meta-norms of legal reasoning provide the legal profession with no more than a set of *vague yardsticks of rationality*.[93] Yet, the Wittgensteinian form of life, defined as the common cultural background or a widely shared *Weltanschauung* in society, cannot provide

85 Aarnio *The Rational as Reasonable*, above at n. 54, 214–15.

86 On the notion of a "particular ideal audience", see ibid., 224–5.

87 Ibid., 213–29. In Aarnio's more recent contribution, *Reason and Authority: A Treatise on the Dynamic Paradigm of Legal Dogmatics*, above at n. 21, 188–93, the criteria of legal rationality similarly concern citizens' warranted expectations of legal certainty and, thereby, the concepts of legal community and democracy.

88 Aarnio, ibid., 117.

89 A. Peczenik, *The Basis of Legal Justification* (Infotryck AB, Lund, 1983), 1 ff. Cf. Peczenik, above at n. 47, 157, where the author speaks of "a *deep (fundamental) justification* which provides support or criticism to the premises that the lawyer takes for granted" (emphasis in original).

90 Peczenik, above at n. 89, 98. Cf. ibid., 101: "But *how* deep can the deep justification reach? The ultimate point is determined by our form of life. This end-point is not logical in the traditional sense but factual" (emphasis in original). On the form of life in Peczenik's theory of law, see also his *On Law and Reason*, above at n. 47, 147–50.

91 Peczenik, *On Law and Reason*, ibid., 206–8. On the chaos argument and the form of life, see A. Aarnio and A. Peczenik, "*Suum Cuique Tribuere*: Some Reflections on Law, Freedom and Justice" (1995) 8 *Ratio Juris* 145, 167–71. The chaos argument is put forward already in A. Aarnio, R. Alexy and A. Peczenik, "The Foundation of Legal Reasoning, II: The Justification of Legal Transformations by Rational Legal Discourse:" (1981) 12 *Rechtstheorie* 257, 278–9.

92 Peczenik, above at n. 89, 91. Cf. ibid., 97.

93 Ibid., 91.

for the "ultimate" premises of law and legal reasoning, since the concept of a form of life is no less ambiguous than that of legal rationality itself. If a form of life is defined as "a reification of the unknown end-points of justification", as Peczenik put it, we are entrapped in a logical circle where one contested term is elucidated by reference to another, with no more explanatory power or self-evident character than the one to be explicated. How could the prevalent form of life in the field of law be specified, except by having reference to the judicial practice itself? The problem is analogical to the philosophical dilemma encountered by Hart when he reflected upon the eventually self-evasive character of the ultimate rule of recognition on the law/fact dimension.

5. RECOGNITION OF THE RULE OF RECOGNITION

In addition to the *ontological* question of the final premises of legal validity and the *methodological* question of the grounding premises of legal rationality under the theoretical premises of analytical positivism, an equally self-referential question of legal *epistemology* is left to be considered: how is the ultimate rule of recognition itself identified, i.e. by means of some second-level rule of recognition, whereby an endless regress to ever-higher-order criteria of norm-identification of nth degree would be launched, or alternatively, with reference to the initial rule of recognition itself, with the inevitable end result of full-fledged logical circularity and the theoretical perplexities resulting therefrom?

In *The Concept of Law*, the question of the identification of the rule of recognition is left unanswered—and, in fact, even unposited—by Hart, who refers merely to the (claimed) uniformities of judicial practice as an indirect proof of the existence of some common criterion of rule-recognition among the judiciary. A "deeper" philosophical analysis of the element of self-referentiality entailed in the recognition of the prevalent rule of recognition would follow the line of argumentation presented above in the context of the final validity and rationality grounds of law. In order to avoid repetition, I will not rephrase such argumentation here. The identification of the ultimate rule of recognition will be reconsidered briefly below, since the ontological identity of Hart's master rule and the epistemological criteria used in its identification are intertwined in Hart's jurisprudential and philosophical thinking.

6. NORM/FACT CHARACTER OF THE ULTIMATE RULE OF RECOGNITION

6.1 Between Kelsen and Borges: is the ultimate rule of recognition a norm or a fact?

Above, the content of a judge's *rule of precedent-recognition* was defined as the sum total of the various fragments of *precedent ideology* internalised by him.

Both theoretical terms, as derived from Hart's and Ross' theories of law, respectively, comprise a judge's ideological stance on the subsequent identification of the *ratio* of a case, as distinguished from its argumentative context or *dicta*, and possibly also the criteria for reading the *ratio* in the novel context. An all-encompassing definition of the rule of recognition in a modern, diversified system of law will comprise constitutional provisions, statutory norms, customary norms, *travaux préparatoires* and other feasible sources of law, in addition to precedents;[94] but what is the ontological status of the rule of recognition itself on the *norm/fact* dimension?

Is Hart's ultimate rule of recognition itself a valid legal norm, in the image of legal rules proper which are claimed to be identified with reference to it by the judiciary? For Peczenik, the meta-level source norm which directs a judge's discretion in his use of prevalent legal source material was classified as a legal norm, so there is no self-evident reason why the ultimate criterion of rule-recognition may not itself qualify as a legal rule. One might also argue that under the (analytical and) positivist premises acknowledged, the final edges or criteria of law must be qualified as "legal", since otherwise the sphere of law would ultimately be framed and defined by essentially non-legal factors. Alternatively, is Hart's master rule a social fact, as contingently present in the judges' (presumably) uniform practice of legal source identification, and which is—unlike Kelsen's *Grundnorm*—devoid of any normative binding force or validity claim *vis-à-vis* the judiciary and other officials engaged in norm-application?[95]

First, Hart very explicitly ruled out the possibility that his master rule—despite the rule-aligned terminology consistently employed by him—might itself be qualified as a valid rule:[96]

> "We only need the word 'validity', and commonly only use it, to answer questions which arise *within* a system of rules where the status of a rule as a member of the system depends on its satisfying certain criteria provided by the rule of recognition. No such question can arise as to the validity of the very rule of recognition which provides the criteria; *it can neither be valid nor invalid but is simply accepted* as appropriate for use in this way."

The decisive influence of Wittgenstein's late philosophy can be discerned there, since the great Austrian philosopher had a similar *dictum* on the length of the Parisian standard metre bar in *Philosophical Investigations*.[97] According to Wittgenstein's philosophical argument, which was yet challenged above, no meaningful assertion can be made on the length of the standard metre bar, since

[94] Hart, above at n. 6, 98. *Travaux préparatoires*, are not mentioned by Hart, due to the characteristics of the English legal system.

[95] Similarly, with respect to Ross' theory of law: is the set of criteria which make up a judge's normative ideology itself a valid (legal) norm imposed upon the judge, or is it no more than a collection of contingent, though presumably uniform (social) facts, devoid of any validity claim?

[96] Hart, above at n. 6, 105–6 (emphasis on "within" in original; further emphasis added).

[97] Wittgenstein, above at n. 7, § 50 (p. 25/25^{e}), and as cited at the beginning of this chapter.

there is no external reference for such an act of quasi-measurement. Even more so, there are no means of "measuring" the validity (or invalidity) of the ultimate rule of recognition, if the cogency of Hart's argument is accepted.[98] Hart states that when faced with the ultimate rule of recognition, "we are brought to a stop in inquiries concerning validity: for we have reached a rule which, like the intermediate statutory order and statute, provides criteria for the assessment of the validity of other rules; but it is also unlike them in that there is no rule providing criteria for the assessment of its own legal validity".[99]

Hart sought carefully to distinguish the ultimate rule of recognition from the no-more-than hypothetical validity ground accorded to Hans Kelsen's *Grundnorm*.[100] He argued, first, that the terminology used by Kelsen—i.e. a "juristic hypothesis" or a "hypothetical", "postulated ultimate rule"—obscures, or is perhaps even inconsistent with, the essentially factual character of the rule of recognition. According to Hart, the existence of the rule of recognition in the practice of courts, officials and private persons in identifying valid law is simply a "matter of fact".[101] Secondly, Kelsen speaks consistently of the validity of the *Grundnorm*, whereas "no question concerning the validity or invalidity of the generally accepted rule of recognition as distinct from the factual question of its existence can arise".[102] Thirdly, the content of the *Grundnorm* is always the same, having reference to the dictates of the historically first constitution, whereas the content of the rule of recognition may, and actually will, vary in different legal systems, in accordance with the prevalent legal source doctrine acknowledged in each. Finally, and again in contrast to Kelsen, no assertion is made as to the non-conflicting relation of legal and moral rules in Hart's theory of law.

In addition, any straightforward reference to universal morals, as claimed by natural law theory, is ruled out by the essentially positivist premises of Hart's conception of law, as he argued in explicit terms under the *separation thesis* of

[98] Hart, in fact, makes a brief reference to the standard metre bar. Cf. Hart, above at n. 6, 106. Cf. N. MacCormick, *H.L.A. Hart* (Edward Arnold, London, 1981), 109–10.

[99] Hart, above at n. 6, 104.

[100] For some reason, the key comparison between Hart's rule of recognition and Kelsen's *Grundnorm* is placed in a footnote to the book: Hart, above at n. 6, 245–6, n. to 97. Hart refers to Kelsen's *General Theory of Law and State*, above at n. 36, since the English translation of the second edition of *Reine Rechtslehre* (1960), published in 1967, was not available at the time of writing *The Concept of Law*. The notion of a "juristic hypothesis", in particular, is peculiar to the conceptual usage of *General Theory of Law and State*.

[101] Hart, above at n. 6, 107.

[102] Hart's argument is, however, in contradiction with his own assertion that the attribute of validity cannot be ascribed to the ultimate rule of recognition: ibid., 104, 105–6. Cf. also ibid., 110, where Hart writes: ". . . they [the judges] must generally share, accept, or *regard as binding* the ultimate rule of recognition specifying the criteria in terms of which the validity of laws are ultimately assessed" (emphasis added). The idea of the normatively binding status of the ultimate rule of recognition *vis-à-vis* judges would seem to imply the judge's internal point of view as to the master criterion's validity, but the attribute of validity is expressly ruled out by Hart himself with respect to the rule of recognition: ibid., 104, 105–6.

law and morals.[103] For the same reason, MacCormick's idea of the underpinning reasons of law, or Peczenik's moral and/or political background reasons of law, cannot possibly provide a final validity ground for Hart's master rule. However, there is a somewhat confusing "natural law deviation" in Hart's theory of law, outlined in terms of the *minimum content of natural law.* A legal order which paid no respect to the contingent, but still no-less true, facts concerning for example, human vulnerability, limited degree of altruism, approximate equality and limited level of understanding and strength of will among humans, could not rely on their voluntary norm-compliance and co-operation with respect to any other norms. One could plausibly argue that such meta-rules are no more than a set of technical rules for efficient norm-giving in a "non-suicidal society", as Hart put it, with no allusion to the immutable principles of natural law proper. Thus, no stronger claim of the enforcement of universal or ideal morals is ever put forth by Hart, who was quick to blame Fuller for holding such vain pretensions. Hart even wittily compared Fuller's *internal morality of law* to the "morality of poisoning": only a set of technical rules of an efficient legal system is involved in Fuller's misconceived quest for the "morality that makes law possible".[104]

MacCormick relates the contingent fact of actual judicial uniformity, as effected by the judges' adherence to a commonly shared rule of recognition, to the rationality conditions of judicial adjudication in a rather straightforward manner:[105]

> "Since only a madman would frame and adopt such a standard [i.e. rule of recognition] without conscious animadversion to the standards he sees and understands others in a like position of responsibility to be using, there are strong reasons to expect a high degree of agreement and conformity among the judiciary in this matter . . ."

MacCormick's *madman argument*, apart from privileging judicial conformity for mere conformity's sake,[106] plainly accords some degree of normativity or profession-specific compelling effect to the rule of recognition, and the source of such uniformity is said to be derived from the concept of a rational judge and his professional self-image.[107] But upon what is such normative pressure for judi-

[103] H.L.A. Hart, "Positivism and the Separation of Law and Morals", in *Essays in Jurisprudence and Philosophy* (Clarendon Press, Oxford, 1983), 49–87.

[104] Hart, above at n. 6, 189–95; H.L.A. Hart, "Lon L. Fuller: *The Morality of Law*", in *Essays in Jurisprudence and Philosophy*, above at n. 103, 350. Cf. Fuller, above at n. 51, 33–94.

[105] MacCormick, above at n. 52, 241.

[106] If all the judges of a given legal system, except one, have the constant habit of overlooking, for example, the human rights argument, why should the dissenting judge, who is perhaps more open-minded and responsive to the dynamics of legal development, be labelled a madman? One could also refer to the institutional frame of adjudication under a totalitarian regime, as, e.g., in the former Soviet Union, and the situation of a more liberal-minded judge within it.

[107] Jellinek described the common tendency of ascribing a normative impact to the prevalent state of affairs in society by the term *die normative Kraft der Faktischen*, in G. Jellinek, *Allegemeine Staatslehre* (Hermann Gentner Verlag, 1960), 337 ff. and 339–40. Jellinek's stance towards the binding character of law is, however, a psychological assertion, and not one wherefrom the ultimate validity ground of law may be derived in the philosophical sense of the term.

cial uniformity ultimately grounded? Hart firmly rejected any validity claim that might be attached to the rule of recognition, by force of the analogy drawn from Wittgenstein's standard metre argument. However, Hart argues that the existence of a common standard of rule-identification among the judiciary is "a necessary condition of our ability to speak of the existence of a single legal system".[108] Thereby the actual state of uniformity in legal adjudication is turned into a conceptual criterion of our linguistic usage *vis-à-vis* the existence of a legal system. Since no validity claim can be accorded to the rule of recognition, by force of Hart's own argument to the effect described, the ultimate rule of recognition can be only an empirical fact, in the image of the tangible standard metre bar in Paris, but far more complex because of the more diversified or divergent character of the array of social phenomena covered by it.

In consequence, Hart argued that throughout *The Concept of Law*, the existence of the rule of recognition is regarded "as an empirical, though complex, matter of fact". If challenged, its existence "could be established by appeal to the facts, i.e. to the actual practice of the courts and other officials of the system when identifying the law which they are to apply".[109] The outward effects of the rule of recognition can be seen in the generally uniform conception of valid legal rules in a given legal system and the rarity of occasions when the validity of some would-be legal rule is, in fact, questioned. But which of the two phenomena is logico-conceptually prior to the other: the ultimate rule of recognition of a legal system, or, alternatively, the judicial practice whose presumably consistent operative functioning has been brought into effect with reference to the former? If the rule of recognition "exists only as a complex, but normally concordant, practice of the courts, officials, and private persons in identifying the law by reference to certain criteria",[110] how can it be drawn conceptually apart from court practice?

In the absence of any external point of reference for the rule of recognition, the identification of valid legal rules (or other legal source material) and the identification of the rule of recognition itself are given in interlocking, circular terms in Hart's theory of law: the valid rules of a given legal system are identified with reference to the rule of recognition, while the rule of recognition itself cannot be identified, except by having recourse to the same judicial practice which was claimed to be identified by reference to the rule of recognition, and so on *ad infinitum*. Hart's line of argumentation, in other words, proceeds in a logical circle. This predicament bears obvious affinity to that encountered at the ultimate edges of law in Kelsen's *Pure Theory of Law*, where the infrastructure level phenomena of the *law preceding the law* eventually had to be presumed by Kelsen himself.

The perplexities affecting Hart's rule of recognition, taken as a shorthand description of "the actual practice of the courts and officials of the system when

[108] Hart, above at n. 6, 112–13.
[109] Ibid., 245–6, n. to 97.
[110] Ibid., 107.

identifying the law", can be illustrated by the fictitious "imperial cartographers" in Borges' short story "On Exactitude in Science" (*Del rigor en la ciencia*):[111]

> "In that Empire, the craft of Cartography attained such Perfection that the Map of a Single province covered the space of an entire City, and the Map of the Empire itself an entire Province. In the course of Time, these Extensive maps were found somehow wanting, and so the College of Cartographers evolved A Map of the Empire that was of the same Scale as the Empire and that coincided with it point for point."

Borges' idea of the natural-size map of "the Empire" applies also to Hart's rule of recognition of a positivist's "Law's Empire". If the rule of recognition cannot be distinguished from the judicial practice upon which it is claimed to have some unifying effect, in the sense of providing for the ultimate criteria of valid rule-identification, the rule of recognition and the judicial practice neatly converge with each other, and Hart's master rule ceases to exist as an external reference for legal rule-identification. Ultimately, the rule of recognition is, like the life-sized map of "the Empire" in Borges' fiction, identical with judicial practice itself.

In consequence, Hart is caught between the conflicting criteria of validity-constituting normativity, shaped in the image of Kelsen's hypothetical *Grundnorm*, and validity-free, one-to-one descriptivity, outlined in close analogy to the accomplishment of the "imperial cartographers" in Borges' insightful fiction. Neither of the two alternatives could provide the rule of recognition with a satisfactory, self-sufficient ontological ground which could be drawn conceptually apart from its subject matter or point of reference in valid legal norms, or sources of law in more general terms. Hart rejected the validity-constituting alternative in explicit terms, to the effect that the rule of recognition "can neither be valid nor invalid but is simply accepted" (by judges).[112] On the other hand, a purely descriptive account of Hart's master rule, with no element of normativity involved, will leave no independent conceptual space for the said criterion as distinct from the sum total of judicial practice. However, is there still a third alternative?

6.2 A Shift from ontology to epistemology: external statements of fact and internal statements of validity

Hart was well aware of the perplexities which are likely to emerge if the ultimate rule of recognition, in the sense of the criterion with reference to which the

[111] J.L. Borges, "On Exactitude in Science", in *Universal History of Infamy* (Penguin Books, New York, 1972), 131. Cf. "*Del rigor en la ciencia*", in *El hacedor* (Alianza Editorial, Madrid, 1987), 143–4. The story continues (and ends) as follows: "Less attentive to the study of Cartography, succeeding Generations came to judge a map of such Magnitude cumbersome, and, not without Irreverence, they abandoned it to the Rigors of sun and Rain. In the western Deserts, tattered Fragments of the Map are still to be found, sheltering an occasional Beast or beggar; in the whole nation, no other relic is left of the Discipline of Geography".

[112] Hart, above at n. 6, 105. Cf. ibid., 104.

ultimate edges of *law/fact* or *norm/fact* are drawn, is itself qualified either as a valid norm or as an efficacious social fact. Hart's reflection on the issue is worth citing at length, since he identifies the dilemma acutely and tries fervently to find his way out of it:[113]

> "The first difficulty is that of classification; for the rule which, in the last resort, is used to identify the law escapes the conventional categories used for describing a legal system, though these are often taken to be exhaustive. . . .[114] Plainly the rule that what the Queen in Parliament enacts is law does not fall into either of these categories. . . . This aspect of things extracts from some a cry of despair: how can we show that the fundamental provisions of a constitution which are surely law are really law? Others reply with the insistence that at the base of legal systems there is something which is '*not law*', which is '*pre-legal*', '*meta-legal*', or is just '*political fact*'. The uneasiness is a sure sign that the categories used for the description of the most important feature in any system of law are too crude. The case for calling the rule of recognition '*law*' is that the rule providing criteria for the identification of other rules of the system may well be thought a defining feature of a legal system, and so itself worth calling 'law'; the case for calling it '*fact*' is that to assert that such a rule exists is indeed to make an external statement of an actual fact concerning the manner in which the rules of an 'efficacious' system are identified. Both these aspects claim attention but we cannot do justice to them both by choosing one of the labels 'law' or 'fact'. Instead, we need to remember that the ultimate rule of recognition may be regarded from two points of view: one is expressed in the *external statement of fact* that the rule exists in the actual practice of the system; the other is expressed in the *internal statement of validity* made by those who use it in identifying the law."

One can almost sense the dizziness experienced by Hart, when he realises that there is no solid ground to be found for law, although he is quick to re-establish his intellectual balance. According to Hart, there are reasons in favour of adopting either of the two alternatives on the law/fact dimension, but neither is said to do full justice to the peculiar status of the ultimate rule of recognition. In order to avoid having to enter the suspicious realm of the "law preceding the law", Hart chooses to recast the *ontological* question of the contested law/fact character of the rule of recognition in terms of *epistemology* of law. The rule of recognition, as rules in general, may be viewed from two different angles of approach: the one internal and the other external.[115]

External statements of fact are statements concerning the actual or empirical existence of a rule in court practice or in society, seen from the point of view of legal sociology or a disinterested external observer of law who has no stakes or interest in the ongoing judicial proceedings, nor any commitment to the validity

[113] Hart, above at n. 6, 107–8 (emphasis added).

[114] In the text extract omitted from the citation here, Hart points out that in English constitutional law a division has been made, post-Dicey, between "laws strictly so called (i.e. statutes, orders in council, and rules embodied in precedents)" and "conventions which are mere usages, understandings or customs". Instead of such conventions, usages, understandings or customs, one could speak of social facts which are unable to impose legal duties upon the authorities (or citizens).

[115] Ibid., 83, 86–8, 96, 99.

of the rules of the legal system concerned. Hart's textbook example of an external statement of fact is as follows: "In England they recognise as law . . . whatever the Queen in Parliament enacts . . .".[116] *Internal statements of validity*, in turn, are statements where some commonly shared set of rules is used as a normative standard or yardstick for the evaluation of one's own or others' conduct, giving effect to requests for norm-conformity, plus normative blame and censure if such standards are not complied with. The vocabulary used, i.e. normative phrases like "ought", "must", and "should", is expressive of the internal perspective of the law, and the function of such linguistic usage is to draw attention to the specific demands imposed upon citizens and officials by the legal rules in force. Hart's own example of an internal statement of validity, as expressed by a judge, other law-applying official or private citizen involved in a legal dispute, is as follows: "It is the law that . . .".[117]

By force of Hart's own definition, an internal statement of validity by necessity entails the idea that the attribute of *validity* can be accorded to the rule in question. Yet in the case of the ultimate rule of recognition, the question of validity was explicitly denied by Hart: the master criterion is "neither valid nor invalid but is simply accepted" by the judges.[118] However, if the attribute of validity cannot be bestowed upon the rule of recognition without inducing a Rylean *category mistake* under the terms of Hart's legal philosophy, neither could an "internal statement of validity" legitimately be made of it. Once the possibility of such a normative impact of Hart's master rule is denied, the ultimate rule of recognition will equally fall short of providing a "standard for the appraisal" of one's own and others' behaviour, "the basis of criticism", and the "justification of demands for conformity, social pressure, and punishment".[119] The idea that judges may have a truly internal point of view to the ultimate rule of recognition is, in other words, rejected by Hart himself, by force of the very definition given by him of the internal point of view to law and the ultimate criterion of rule-identification in a legal system.

Therefore, the inadequacy of the two-fold *law/fact* classification, in terms of Hart's legal philosophy, cannot be resolved by an evasive move in philosophical argumentation where the discourse on issues of legal ontology is changed into one concerning the two feasible epistemic stances towards the law. Both alternatives, in the sense of external statements of fact and internal statements of validity, are laden with theoretical aporias, if the philosophical inquiry is relentlessly pursued beyond the claimed "final" criteria of law, as the Kelsen/Borges dilemma above intended to prove. On Hart's own account of the issue, no internal claim of validity can be accorded to the ultimate rule of recognition as it is accepted and used by the judiciary. On the other hand, a fully external point of view to Hart's master rule will lead to perplexities which are analogical to those

[116] Hart, above at n. 6, 99.
[117] Ibid.
[118] Ibid., 105.
[119] Ibid., 96.

encountered by the fictitious cartographers in Borges' philosophical short story: the rule of recognition—in the sense of having one-to-one correspondence to the topography of a legal positivist's "law's empire"—loses its conceptual identity *vis-à-vis* the judicial practice.

Hart, in fact, points out a third alternative to the qualification of the ultimate ground of a legal system, while ruling out its potential significance for the issue. This third option, or the *triton genos* "between", "behind" or "beyond" the two categories of "law" and "fact", is said to have been framed, by some authors, in terms of what is *not law*, what is a *pre-legal* or *meta-legal* phenomenon, or what is just a *political fact*. The recourse taken to such phrases which clearly evade taking any conclusive stance on the identity of the ultimate criteria of law, bears witness to the inadequacy of the conventional categories of legal analysis, when pushed to—and eventually beyond—the ultimate *edges*, *grounds*, *criteria*, or *premises* of law and legal discourse. To tackle this aporetic situation, some novel tools of philosophical analysis are needed; these will be outlined in terms of the constitutive (and disintegrating) *infrastructures of law* which account for the "law preceding the law".

7. CONCLUSION: IS THERE A "STANDARD NORM" FOR LAW?

The identity of law under the theoretical premises of analytical positivism, as structured by the axiomatic postulates of validity and rationality in law plus the institutional and mental felicity conditions of legal adjudication, is ultimately conditional on a set of inherently volatile, identity-evading phenomena which successfully defy any effort at being conceptualised. Above, the ultimate premises of legal ontology, legal epistemology and legal methodology were identified with Kelsen's hypothetical *Grundnorm* and its necessary allusion to the "law preceding the law"; the indefinability or inexpressibility of the final criteria of rationality in Wróblewski's, MacCormick's, and Peczenik's conceptions of law; the suspicious element of self-referentiality entailed in the identification of the ultimate rule of recognition itself; and the self-evasive character of Hart's ultimate rule of recognition as to its ontological status on the law/fact or validity/existence dimension. Such philosophical perplexities are bound to emerge if the quest for the very final premises of law is relentlessly pursued even after the self-stipulated reference ground of analytical positivism has been reached, and the philosopher's spade is turned back by force of the "argumentative bedrock" of common sense and linguistic analysis, as Wittgenstein would have it.[120] While there can be no external point of reference for the law under the analytical and positivist premises adopted, the two-fold predicament of logical self-referentiality or an infinite regress to ever-higher meta-level criteria of knowledge and judgment will finally be set off, by force of Kelsen's request for

[120] Cf. Wittgenstein, above at n. 1, § 217 (p. 85/85e).

methodological purity: "The reason for the validity of a norm can only be the validity of another norm".[121]

In a legal philosopher's closed, logico-conceptual universe consisting of (legal) norms and (social) facts only, the ontological status of the ultimate grounds of legal validity cannot be accounted for, except in terms of the *per definitionem* all-encompassing, mutually exclusive *law/fact* dichotomy. However, as soon as some tentative ruling is made on the law/fact status of, for example, Kelsen's *Grundnorm* or Hart's rule of recognition, the ultimate criteria of law are drawn within the very same law/fact dualism which is initially brought into existence with reference to the said "ultimate" prerequisites of judgment. Moreover, once some tentative ruling is made on the ultimate criteria of legal validity, the law/fact status of the very criterion utilised in the latest classification must still somehow be accounted for, rephrasing the initial law/fact predicament on a still higher meta-level of philosophical argumentation. Therefore, the ultimate criteria of law—whether given in terms of Kelsen's *Grundnorm*, Hart's ultimate rule of recognition, or some functional equivalent to them—cannot themselves be ascribed the status of a legal norm or social fact, without cancelling and levelling off their function as the "ultimate" criteria "behind" the effected law/fact dichotomy.

The terminology Hart so decisively rejected in his philosophical reflection on the law/fact status of the ultimate criteria of law, i.e. the *not-legal*, *pre-legal* or *meta-legal* phenomena at the basis of a legal system, can be read as a self-conscious effort to reach beyond the manifest positivity of law and touch upon the evasive "final" grounds of law. However, the very "ultimate" grounds, edges, criteria or premises of law cannot themselves be accounted for without having recourse to the identity-evading *infrastructures* of legal discourse which reflect an inherent predicament of Western philosophical tradition. Such *prelogical* and *preconceptual* prerequisites of human knowledge and judgment were introduced above in chapter 1 and in this chapter at p. 201. As mentioned, such infrastructures defy any effort at being conceptualised or drawn within the metaphysics-laden conceptuality of the Western *épistémè*, since they are the *effecting/effacing* condition of possibility and impossibility of such reality-constituting and sense-making endeavours within Western philosophical tradition.

Following Derrida's linguistic usage, the infrastructures of judgment, which equally ground/cancel, effect/efface or establish/level off the ultimate criteria, premises, grounds or edges of law represent radical *undecidability*,[122] *indefinability* or *equivocality* in law: the infrastructures of law, which ground (and level off) the basic categories of norm/fact, validity/existence, *Sein/Sollen*, reason/non-reason, legal/non-legal, *logos/mythos*, etc., within legal discourse, cannot themselves be ascribed any constant identity from among the sheaf of

[121] Kelsen, above at n. 13 193.

[122] J. Derrida, *Dissemination* (The Athlone Press, London, 1993), 220; R. Gasché, *The Tain of the Mirror: Derrida and the Philosophy of Reflection* (Harvard University Press, 1986), 7, 95, 240–4.

two-fold conceptual categories established and sustained with reference to such "ultimate" criteria, without erasing and cancelling their infrastructure level status as the ultimate preconditions of the "order of things" in the (external) world. However, within the closed sphere of Western metaphysics there is simply no other option available for a legal philosopher who has boldly taken up the "Linnaean"—and eventually futile—task of (re)producing an absolutely all-encompassing classification of the various phenomena found within and on the very edges of legal discourse, except for the very law/fact, validity/existence, *Sein/Sollen*, *logos/mythos*, etc., dualism. In more general terms, no system of metaphysics can be ontologically, epistemologically or methodologically closed without inducing the radically unresolvable question of the ontological, epistemological and methodological status of the ultimate premises or edges of such an "order of things" in the (external) world.

Therefore, the only candidates for a *standard norm* in law, drawn in the image of the tangible standard metre bar of Wittgenstein's philosophical argument, are equal to the identity-less infrastructures of knowledge and judgment within Western philosophical tradition, as *effected/effaced* in the dislocated "ultimate" premises of legal ontology, legal epistemology and legal methodology. Endlessly dwelling in the realm of the *prelogical* and *preconceptual*, the infrastructures cannot be accorded any constant metaphysical identity without committing a logico-conceptual fallacy, begging the question by pushing the very predicament up to a still higher meta-level of philosophical argumentation, and levelling off their infrastructure level status and function as the "ultimate" criteria of knowledge and judgment in legal discourse. If such infrastructures are said to have any identity of their own, it is unfolded in their endlessly self-evading and self-effacing self-referentiality. The term "constitutive *a priori*" of law is therefore laden with a slightly ironic sense, since the Derridean constitutive *a priori* of human knowledge and judgment is also, and with equal force, the "disintegrating *a priori*" of such knowledge and judgment, expressive of the decisive shift of philosophical argument from Kant's "formal *a priori*" to Foucault's "historical *a priori*" and, finally, to the Derridean "dislocating *a priori*", with its allusion to the radically equivocal *constitutive/disintegrating* forces within the Western *épistémè*.

9

The Quest for the Final Premises of Law—II: The Infrastructures of Judicial Signification under Precedent-Following

1. PROLOGUE: "AN INFALLIBLE PARADIGM OF IDENTITY"?

In *Philosophical Investigations*, Ludwig Wittgenstein wrote:[1]

> "215. But isn't *the same* at least the same?—We seem to have an infallible paradigm of identity in the identity of a thing with itself. I feel like saying: 'Here at any rate there can't be a variety of interpretations. If you are seeing a thing you are seeing identity too.'—Then are two things the same when they are what one thing is? And how am I to apply what the *one* thing shews me to the case of two things?
> 216. 'A thing is identical with itself'—There is no finer example of a useless proposition, which yet is connected with a certain play of the imagination. It is as if in imagination we put a thing into its own shape and saw that it fitted.—We might also say: 'Every thing fits into itself.' Or again: 'Every thing fits into its own shape.' At the same time we look at a thing and imagine that there was a blank left for it, and that now it fits into it exactly."

Above, Wittgenstein put forward the argument that the length of the standard metre (or the colour of the standard colours) cannot be defined since there is no external point of reference outside of the tangible standard metre bar (or the imaginary standard colours) which could provide a yardstick for such a self-referential act of quasi-measurement. The standard metre argument was, however, contested in chapter 8 by pointing out the convention-based character of the standard metre and its constitutive properties, i.e. its exact length.

When judging the parallel criteria of *identity/difference* within the conceptual "order of things" in the (external) world thereby established, there are no effective legal or social conventions available, nor any external reference of *standard identity* for things tangible and intangible, unless the self-evident identity of a thing with itself is taken to provide for such an absolute, non-contestable criterion of identity. Mapping the domain of absolute identity is, however, an endeavour as absurd as that of the cartographers in Borges' insightful short

[1] Wittgenstein, *Philosophische Untersuchungen—Philosophical Investigations* (Basil Blackwell, Oxford, 1967), § 215–16 (p. 84–85/84e–85e) (emphasis in original).

story "On Exactitude in Science".[2] An immense, life-sized map of "the Empire" was finally produced by the collective efforts of Borges' fictitious cartographers, only to be abandoned to the "rigors of sun and rain" by the succeeding generations who were less devoted to such intellectual precision, in disregard of the obvious scientific breakthrough achieved by their predecessors, i.e. the attainment of the ultimate level of exactitude in scientific representation or the discovery of an irrefutable criterion of absolute identity. The *infallible paradigm of identity* can be based only on the criterion provided by the very object of knowledge itself, if any deviations from scientific precision of a Borgesian scale are to be evaded.

The argument from absolute identity is, as Wittgenstein correctly notes, devoid of any argumentative potential or meaningful discursive context within the realm of ordinary language. Stating the identity of a thing with itself is like saying "all green things are green", "each triangle has three angles", or "all tangible things are extensional", i.e. expressing an analytical truth where the truth of an assertion is *per definitionem* entailed in its premises. To rephrase the issue in Wittgensteinian terms, one might say that there is no use for the "language-game of (absolute) identity", nor for that of affirming—or denying—the identity of a thing with itself in any non-artificial discourse formation or language-game in society. No operative system of meaning-production could be grounded on such premises of absolute identity-alignment either.

The language-game of absolute identity is left "homeless", without a meaningful discursive context in the linguistic community. The same can be said of its negation or opposite, i.e. the language-game of absolute alterity or radical difference, where the initial premises of judgment are refuted by an act of radical exclusion or absolute denial, leaving the outcome of judgment without any reference within the semantic confines of the discourse formation concerned. Between the two end poles of absolute identity and absolute alterity, which equally fail to set out a well-functioning system of sense-differentiation in a discourse formation—the former because of the unyielding requirement to reproduce the original identity of the "order of things" in the (external) world in all subsequent occasions of that discourse formation, and the latter because of its absolute denial of any affiliation with the initial discursive order—there extends the domain of "fading identity", where allusion is made to the unfolding of divergent facets of relative (dis)similarity in the objects constituted within a discourse formation. Under such premises, the production of meaning for a sign is conditional on the ever-present possibility of meaning-differentiation or sense-variation. The term "language-game of (relative) difference" may be employed with reference thereto.

In a sense, Wittgenstein is of course right in attaching the "infallible paradigm of identity" to the identity of a thing with itself, and in pointing out the futility

[2] J.L. Borges, "On Exactitude in Science", in *Universal History of Infamy* (Penguin Books, New York, 1972). Borges and the short story "*Del rigor en la ciencia*", in *El hacedor* (Alianza Editorial, Madrid, 1987), were commented upon in chapter 8 above where the norm/fact character of Hart's ultimate rule of recognition was reflected upon.

of such an assertion within the ordinary uses of language. However, the "infallible paradigm of identity" can be challenged by the Derridean reflections on the "ultimate" preconditions of knowledge and judgment within Western philosophical tradition. Devoid of any constant metaphysical identity or fixed conceptual core, the *infrastructures* "behind" the conceptual "order of things" in the (external) world cannot be extended on the resulting coordinates of two-valued logic and linguistic conceptuality without instantly levelling off their infrastructure level status, since they are the radically equivocal *effecting/effacing* condition of possibility and impossibility of Western metaphysics, and of the array of divergent discourse formations grounded on such "reality-constituting" (and disintegrating) premises. Thus, because of their fugitive, identity-evading character, Derridean infrastructures cannot be qualified as the proper subject matter of even a trivial judgment of (absolute) identity. The only "Pickwickian" identity they might be said to possess consists of the two-fold prelogical and preconceptual movement of endlessly self-effacing self-referentiality, on the one hand, and spacing/temporisation or self-deferral/self-distancing, on the other, with allusion to the two "strings" or "cords" of infrastructures of radical *undecidability* and *différance*.

"Constantly disappearing as they go along", infrastructures of knowledge and judgment "cannot, in classical affirmation, be affirmed without being negated".[3] Thus, the "logic of difference" cannot be captured by the affirmative logic of conventional Western philosophy which is committed to the "metaphysics of presence", the conceptualised "order of things" in the (external) world, and the inherent claims to common intelligibility, truth, correctness and veracity entailed in linguistic utterances.[4] Instead, the "infallible paradigm of difference" is found in the "logic of *différance*", which accounts for the incessant realignment of meaning-constitution, or the constant interplay of the proliferation/dissemination of meaning-content, in a discourse formation.

2. *DIFFÉRANCE* ("THIS ALMOST NOTHING OF THE UNPRESENTABLE")

Différance—"neither a word nor a concept",[5] having neither presence, nor absence,[6] "neither existence, nor essence",[7] "not yet language or speech or

[3] J. Derrida, *Dissemination* (The Athlone Press, London, 1993), 157.

[4] The "order of things" in the (external) world, of course, refers to Foucault's idea of the Western *épistémè*, while the four claims to intelligibility, truth, correctness and veracity in linguistic utterances refer to the universal-pragmatic preconditions of communicative rationality as outlined by Habermas. The "metaphysics of presence" may be taken to refer to any philosophical stance which privileges present intentions, meanings or ideas over (merely) potential, latent, deferred or distanced alternatives to them.

[5] "[D]*ifférance* . . . is neither a word nor a concept": Derrida, "*Différance*", in *Margins of Philosophy* (Great Britain: The Harvester Press, 1982), 3, 7.

[6] Derrida, *Points . . . Interviews, 1974–1994* (Stanford University Press, 1995), 79, 346–7.

[7] Derrida, above at n. 5, 6. As Rorty and Caputo point out, the fate of *différance* is to be turned into an ordinary concept, once it is brought into common linguistic usage and its prelinguistic mode

writing or sign", and therefore irredeemably beyond the reach of binary logic and linguistic conceptuality[8]—is a neographic "quasi-concept" of Derrida's philosophical invention. It is derived from the fact that the Latin root *differre*[9] opens up into two divergent directions, one diachronic-temporal (*defer*) and the other synchronic-spatial (*differ*), if *différance* as an infrastructure precondition of signification is drawn violently within the sphere of ordinary linguistic presentation. The verb *defer* and its conceptual derivatives, like *deferral* and *deferred*, signify the delaying of something in a diachronic-temporal sense; while the verb *differ* and its conceptual derivatives, like *differing*, *difference*, and *differentiation*, refer to the conceptual space opened up between individual "things" or signs in a synchronic-spatial sense. *Différance* is the infrastructure level precondition of sense-differentiation in language or any specific discourse formation based on such linguistic premises.

Derrida's line of argumentation has been greatly inspired by de Saussure's *Cours de linguistique générale*, where the Swiss scholar outlined a model of linguistics based on the essentially *arbitrary* and *differential* character of a sign.[10] The production of meaning for an individual sign is not determined by some inherent elements of that sign, but by its differential and, therefore, arbitrary relation to all the feasible alternatives to it within the system of signs concerned. For instance "white" is not defined by some inherent property or essence of "whiteness" or of "being white", but by its differential relation to the alternatives of "black", "grey", "red", etc. The proper meaning of a linguistic sign is never "there" or entirely present since it is determined by factors which lie outside of it in a system of differentially ordered signs.

Différance, written with an inaudible "*a*" instead of the grammatically correct "*e*" in the third syllable, remains endlessly unresolved or radically equivocal between the active and passive modes of representation,[11] i.e. as something that is passively deferred/different, but also as something that is itself active in the process of deferring/differing (something else).[12] With the introduction of *différance,* a sheaf of theme-related concepts such as difference/different/differing/deferring/deferred/differentiated/distinguished/distanced (etc.) is opened up within the conceptual grid of language. *Différance* may be likened to *khōra* in Plato's *Timaeus*, described as neither "sensible", nor "intelligible" by the great Greek philosopher, but as belonging to a "third genus" (*triton genos*) of its own which effectively transcends the two categories of Plato's otherwise dualist

of operation is forgotten and erased or, one might add, simply misunderstood. See J.S. Caputo, "On Not Circumventing the Quasi-Transcendental: The Case of Rorty and Derrida", in G.B. Madison (ed.), *Working through Derrida* (Northwestern University Press, Illinois, 1993), 159.

[8] Derrida, above at n. 6, 79.

[9] In French: *différer*. Cf. R. Gasché, *The Tain of the Mirror: Derrida and the Philosophy of Reflection* (Harvard University Press, 1986), 195–6.

[10] Derrida, above at n. 5, 10; F. de Saussure, *Cours de linguistique générale* (Grande Bibliothèque Payot, Paris, 1995), 100–2.

[11] The "*a*" in *différance* would signify an active mode of presentation, if there were such a term as "*différance*" in French as acknowledged in standard dictionaries.

[12] Derrida, above at n. 5, 7–9.

ontology.[13] Plato's *khōra*—which remains endlessly undecided, oscillating between the two alternatives of double exclusion (*neither/nor*) and all-encompassing inclusion (*both/and*) *vis-à-vis* the categories of sensible/intelligible, visible/invisible, form/substance, destructible/immutable, *logos/mythos*, etc., of Plato's dualist ontology[14]—is the "place", "location", "imprint-bearer", or "immense and indeterminate spatial receptacle"[15] in which the sensible parallels of Platonic pure forms are inscribed or engendered (by the Demiurge). Dwelling outside the sphere of ordinary logic and metaphysics-laden linguistic conceptuality, the strange attributes *prelogical* and *preconceptual* may be applied to Plato's *khōra* and Derrida's *différance* alike.

Différance accounts for the primordial extension/unfolding of the two indispensable coordinates of spacing/temporisation behind the effected emergence, subseqent alterations or transformations, and eventual disappearance of a sign's meaning-content on the surface-structure level of language or discourse, providing for the ceaseless movement of synchronic distancing or spacing (*differentiation*) and diachronic span or delay (*deferral*) in linguistic signification. The two-fold impact of *différance* as the "*almost nothing of the unpresentable*",[16] or the *trace* of non-presence and radical alterity in a sign whose meaning-content is never fully present since it is in a constant state of transition under the two-fold spell of deferral/distancing, is then materialised in the unfolding of sense on the two dimensions or axes of language. Since there is no fixed end point of reference, nor any transcendental signified to which the meaning of a (linguistic) sign could be definitively anchored, the Derridean double-gesture of deferral/distancing should, in fact, be called the "ultimate" precondition for the *production/dissemination*, or *proliferation/dispersement*, of sense in a system of signs. There is an element of profoundly sense-dislocating *différance* at the very heart of linguistic and judicial signification, operative even behind Hart's pragmatics-laden semantics of the common core of "plain cases and settled meanings".[17]

[13] Plato, *Timaeus*, in *The Dialogues of Plato* (Clarendon Press, Oxford, 4th ed. 1953), § 49a (p. 735) and § 52a–c (pp. 738–9); Derrida, *On the Name* (Stanford University Press, 1995), 89–127, esp. 89, 96. Cf. Caputo's comments thereupon in J. Derrida and J.D. Caputo, *Deconstruction in A Nutshell* (Fordham University Press, New York), 82–105, esp. 83–5.

[14] Derrida, above at n. 13, 91.

[15] Ibid., 93.

[16] "How could the desire for presence let itself be destroyed? It is desire itself. But what gives it, what gives it breath and necessity—what there is and what remains thus to be thought—is that which in the presence of the present does not present itself. Différance or the trace does not present itself, this almost nothing of the unpresentable is what philosophers always try to erase. It is this trace, however, that marks and relauches all systems": Derrida, above at n. 6, 83.

[17] H.L.A. Hart, *The Concept of Law* (Clarendon Press, Oxford, 1961), 121–50, esp. 123–5, 140–2.

3. SYNTAGMATIC AND PARADIGMATIC DIMENSIONS OF LANGUAGE, AND THE *A PRIORI* OF A DISCOURSE FORMATION

The determinants of linguistic signification are located on the two distinct axes or dimensions of language: one *syntagmatic* and the other *paradigmatic*. The syntagmatic/paradigmatic dichotomy stems from the postulates of structural semiotics as envisioned by de Saussure, who introduced the distinction between syntagmatic and "associative", or paradigmatic, relations in language.[18]

Syntagmatic relations are based on a sequence or combination of signs, as effected in the linear succession of linguistic elements in the resulting positivity of language or some specific discourse formation based on such linguistic premises. The syntagmatic dimension, in other words, follows the logic of conjunction ("x *and* y"). *Paradigmatic* relations, on the other hand, are based on the ever-present possibility of effecting a selection from among a set of mutually exclusive signs, where one linguistic element may always be substituted or replaced by another, endowed with an equivalent or parallel standing or function within the discourse formation in question. The paradigmatic dimension thus follows the logic of disjunction ("x *or* y").[19] Jakobson has called the syntagmatic dimension of language the "axis of combination", and the paradigmatic dimension the "axis of selection".[20] The issue could also be rephrased in terms of linear positivity (speech, *parole*) and vertical substitutability (writing, *langue*) in a discourse formation, respectively.

Foucault's archeology of knowledge may be read as an effort to "historicise" the Kant of *Critique of Pure Reason* and the notion of the "formal *a priori*" of human knowledge entailed therein. By means of the "historical *a priori*"[21] Foucault sought to describe the historically changing conditions of possibility of the conceptual "order of things" in the (external) world, i.e. the emerging, gradually transforming, and eventually disappearing discourse formations within Western *épistémè*. Now, the scales could be turned, and Foucault's archeology of knowledge could equally be "formalised" by pointing out the inherent, formal or—even—transcendental-logical element that is by necessity entailed in any discourse formation. However, the mutual relation between the three philosophers Kant, Foucault and Derrida is now more complicated than in the

[18] de Saussure, above at n. 10, 170–5.

[19] W. Nöth, *Handbook of Semiotics* (Indiana University Press, 1990), 195; A.J. Greimas and J. Courtés, *Sémiotique: Dictionnaire raisonné de la théorie du langage* (Hachette Livre, Paris, 1993), 266–7, 376–7 (entries on *paradigmatique*, *paradigme*, *syntagmatique* and *syntagme*).

[20] Nöth, ibid., 195. Cf. R. Jakobson, "Linguistics and Poetics", in T.A. Sebeok (ed.), *Style in Language* (The M.I.T. Press, 1960), 358: "The selection is produced on the basis of equivalence, similarity and dissimilarity, synonimity and antonymity, while the combination, the build up of the sequence, is based on contiguity".

[21] M. Foucault, *Les Mots et les choses: Une Archéologie des Sciences Humaines* (Éditions Gallimard, Paris, 1966), *passim*; M. Foucault, *L'archéologie du savoir* (Éditions Gallimard, Paris, 1969), 166–73 (*l'a priori historique*). Foucault's historical *a priori* was also tackled in chapter 8 above.

context of the infrastructures of formal legal norm constitution above where the outer edges of human knowledge and Western metaphysics were drawn within the discourse on law. There, the Kantian formal *a priori* gave room for the historical *a priori* of Foucault's archeology of knowledge, to be modified by the Derridean allusion to the "quasi-transcendental" or pre-metaphysical preconditions of knowledge and judgment, thereby giving effect to the radically equivocal "dislocating *a priori*" within Western philosophy.

The *syntagmatic/paradigmatic* axes of language, as discerned by de Saussure and the school of structuralist linguistics, is the formal or "Kantian" element in Foucault's archaeology of knowledge, the existence of which is, by necessity, presumed in any discourse formation, no matter what exact shape the historical *a priori* takes in it. Any assertions concerning the conceptualised order of things in the (external) world are unfolded on the two coordinates of linear, syntagmatic positivity or narrativity and vertical, paradigmatic substitutability, alternativity or replaceability, providing for the two-fold condition of possibility of any subsequent transformations of the specific discourse formation in question. However, since the two dimensions of language or discourse ultimately instantiate and reflect the possibility of a synchronic/diachronic differentiation of the meaning of a sign, the historical *a priori* in Foucault's archeology of knowledge is ultimately premised on a Derridean *différance* which accounts for the preconceptual movement of spacing/temporisation or deferral/distancing in linguistic meaning-production.

In the context of precedent-based law, the *syntagmatic* axis of signification is concerned with the linear unfolding of the *ratio* in case-law adjudication and the resulting interplay of continuity and change in judicial meaning-production. The *paradigmatic* axis of signification is, in turn, concerned with the selection of meaning-constituting elements for a particular court ruling from among a set of ideological alternatives of a mutually exclusive standing, situated "beneath" the resulting linear positivity of law. However, the argument of the necessary syntagmatic/paradigmatic elements involved in any actual discourse formation may, at least partially, be relaxed in the context of the four paradigms of judicial signification under precedent-following discussed below, due to their status as scientific reconstructions or ideal types. For the present purpose, the two coordinates of linguistic signification may, therefore, be partly detached from each other.

4. AN OUTLINE OF THE FOUR PARADIGMS OF JUDICIAL SIGNIFICATION UNDER PRECEDENT-FOLLOWING AND RELATED JUDICIAL IMAGERY

The infrastructures of judicial signification under precedent-following consist of the "ultimate" preconditions of meaning-production in a system of precedents, i.e. the ascription of a specific meaning-content to the *ratio* of a case. Such infrastructures are equal to the *a priori* element of judicial signification which is silently presumed in all "sense-making" discourse on *how to read precedents*.

Moreover, the different types of judicial signification under precedent-following may be collected conveniently under four distinct *paradigms*.

A paradigm of meaning-production under precedent-following comprises a set of precedent ideologies which all share a common ground of meaning-constituting prerequisites at the infrastructure level of law, along with a common judicial imagery. In all, four such judicial paradigms may be discerned: (1) *legislative* paradigm, (2) *dispute-solving* or *contextualist* paradigm, (3) *systemic*, *constructive* or *legal scholarly* paradigm, and (4) *extra-legal* or *non-formal* paradigm of adjudication.

The *legislative paradigm* of precedent-following comprises the ideologies of judicial reference and judicial legislation, as outlined above in Part A of this treatise. The *dispute-solving* or *contextualist paradigm* of precedent-following comprises the ideologies of judicial exegesis, judicial analogy and judicial revaluation, where the *ratio* of a case is defined in a strictly context-bound manner. The *systemic* or *constructive paradigm* of precedent-following comprises the underlying reasons approach to precedent-following. The term "legal scholarly paradigm" may also be used, since the idea of constructing a "seamless web" of underlying reasons from a line of prior cases is rather a task to be pursued by legal science, and not by individual judges in the course of judicial dispute-resolution. Finally, the *extra-legal* or *non-formal paradigm* of legal adjudication comprises ideologies based on judicial consequentialism, rightness reasons in adjudication and the judicial hunch model, where the legal decision is based on openly socio-political, moral or entirely free premises.

Judicial imagery, or the prevalent conception of the role and function of the judge in judicial adjudication, varies in accordance with the paradigm of judicial signification adopted.

Under the *legislative* paradigm of precedent-following, the judge of the prior court is regarded as a "small-scale" legislator, endowed with interstitial powers of judicial legislation. The role of the subsequent judge, on the other hand, is reduced to a mere passive reading of the letter of the law in the way envisioned by Montesquieu, or is reduced to (no more than) drawing the logical consequences out of the *ratio* of a case as explicitly formulated by the prior court. Thus, depending on whether the issue is seen from the point of view of the prior court or the subsequent court, the image of the judge is framed in terms of either "wild-running" judicial activism, or Montesquieu-inspired judicial passivism, respectively.

Under the *dispute-solving* or *contextualist* paradigm of precedent-following, the subsequent judge is regarded as an unbiased and dispassionate arbiter who renders a decision only on the individual legal disputes brought before the court. Notably, he is deemed to have no quasi-legislative pretensions which would extend beyond the individual case at hand, nor any genuinely systemic-constructive ambitions of a "Herculean" scale.

Under the *systemic* or *constructive* paradigm of precedent-following, the judge is regarded as "a lawyer of superhuman skill, learning, patience, and acumen",[22] in the image of Dworkin's fictitious superjudge, Hercules J. The task reserved for the judge is to probe into the latent signification structure beneath the manifest precedent-norm and/or reasons expression of the prior case, or line of cases, and to construct the meaning-content of the *ratio* in light of the Dworkinian doctrine of *law as integrity*.

Finally, under the *extra-legal* or *non-formal* paradigm of legal adjudication, the judge is regarded as a political and/or moral philosopher, seeking to realise some specific goals of social expediency or some distinct values of social justice and fairness, essentially unconstrained by any formal strictures derived from the prevalent legal source doctrine or the doctrine of *stare decisis*. Under such premises of judicial meaning-production, the judge is taken as an infallible authority of the prevalent state of political morality in society. In the extreme case of the judicial hunch ideology, the judge is left free to pursue the ideological objectives of his own preference, acting out of noble Solomonic motives or mere personal self-interest and prejudice.

To put it concisely, there are four main images of the judge: (1) a combined image of the judge as either a *small-scale legislator*, if acting in the role of the prior court, or a passive *reader* who recites the unambigious letter of the law, if acting in the role of the subsequent court; (2) the judge as a dispassionate *dispute-solver* or arbiter on a strict case-to-case basis; (3) the judge as a *legal scholar*, committed to the Herculean task of constructing a "seamless web" of reasons in law; and (4) the judge as a *political or moral philosopher*, with either Solomonic or less-noble intentions. In a trivial sense, all judicial adjudication is, of course, more or less committed to the resolution of individual legal disputes, but the present research interest is slightly different: it is concerned not with the final outcome of legal disputes as such, but with the variety of judicial imagery related to precedent-following or judicial adjudication in more general terms.

The *legislative* paradigm of precedent-following is, in principle at least, located on the syntagmatic axis of judicial signification, since the possibility of somehow altering the authentic meaning-content of the *ratio* of a case, as authoritatively laid down by the prior court, is ruled out. There is, in other words, no room for a non-positivist differentiation of the norm's meaning-content on the paradigmatic dimension of judicial signification. In fact, even the syntagmatic dimension of meaning-variation is reduced to a mere repetition of the norm's authentic meaning (judicial reference), or the unfolding of the logical consequences of the original norm and/or reasons formulation (judicial legislation). Therefore, the legislative discourse formation should instead be said to dwell "on the threshold" of the properly syntagmatic axis of judicial signification, since no genuine process of linear sense-differentiation is ever set off under such premises.

The *contextualist*, *dispute-solving* paradigm of precedent-following is located on both the syntagmatic and paradigmatic axes of judicial signification,

[22] R. Dworkin, *Taking Rights Seriously* (Harvard University Press, 1978), 105.

as the meaning-content of the *ratio* of a case is only gradually unfolded through the double-play of deferral/distancing in the course of subsequent adjudication. However, the weight of emphasis is placed on the syntagmatic axis of legal positivity and narrativity here, at the cost of ideological alternatives to such effected positivity. There is also some internal variation in the three distinct approaches to precedent ideology which belong to the contextualist paradigm—i.e. *retracing* of the prior court's original intentions in judicial exegesis, an incessant *realignment* of the original *ratio* in terms of judicial analogy/distinguishing, and a dynamic *rereading* of the *ratio* in judicial revaluation—but the idea of strictly context-bound meaning-constitution and meaning-variation in law is common to all three.

The *systemic*, *constructive* or *legal scholarly* paradigm of precedent-following is equally located on the syntagmatic and paradigmatic axes of judicial signification. However, the decisive weight of emphasis is placed on the paradigmatic dimension of legal discourse, since the true *ratio* of a case, or line of cases, is constructed by having recourse to the latent signification structure beneath the manifest precedent-norm and/or reasons expression of a prior case, substituting the effected positivity of law by its system-bound ideological alternatives.

Finally, the *extra-legal* or *non-formal* paradigm of judicial adjudication is, in principle at least, located on the paradigmatic axis of judicial signification, grounded on the idea of displacing the original legal premises of the *ratio* of a case by having recourse to the teleological, axiological or entirely unconstrained premises of judicial meaning-production. The syntagmatic axis of legal signification is *per definitionem* ruled out, in the sense of any formal or legally qualified premises of meaning-production in judicial adjudication. However, the extra-legal paradigm could also be said to be situated "on the outer edge" of the paradigmatic axis of legal signification, since the legally qualified frame of meaning-constitution is rejected as soon as the search for a meaning-content to be attached to the subsequent case is set off.

5. ASCRIPTION OF MEANING-CONTENT TO THE RATIO OF A CASE UNDER THE FOUR PARADIGMS OF JUDICIAL SIGNIFICATION UNDER PRECEDENT-FOLLOWING

5.1 Legislative paradigm of precedent-following: self-referentiality and the reproduction of original identity

Under the legislative paradigm of precedent-following, the infrastructure level preconditions of judicial signification aim at reproducing the *original identity* of the *ratio* of a case in subsequent jurisdiction. The exact meaning-content of the *ratio* of a case is defined in terms of circular self-referentiality and self-legitimation, if the issue is seen from the prior court's point of view, and in terms of total predetermination of the norm's meaning-content, if seen from the subsequent court's point of view. The identity-enhancing processes of judicial signification are then materialised in the prior court's own infallible announcement of what will count as the true *ratio* of the case.

Apart from full-fledged semantic closure and self-referentiality of judicial meaning-production under the judicial reference ideology, the legislative paradigm of precedent-following admits of only one legitimate pattern of legal reasoning, i.e. logical deduction, where the *ratio* of a prior case is taken as the general premise of a normative inference which is to be completed by the subsequent court. In the course of legal adjudication, the *ratio* of a case will gradually become concretised, so as to find a better match with the contingent, divergent features of the novel cases to be ruled upon. However, the subsequent court is not entitled to deviate from the original *ratio* of a precedent, nor to add any novel elements to it by means of genuine legal discretion. The original identity of the *ratio* of the prior court decision must be retained, despite the resulting decrease in the level of abstractness involved in subsequent court rulings. The legislative paradigm of precedent-following finds its parallel in a logician's or mathematician's formally closed and artificial system of signs, where the value or values which may be attached to some semantic variable are predetermined and fully unequivocal.

5.2 Dispute-solving paradigm of precedent-following: contextual sense-differentiation by an incessant interplay of deferral/distancing

Entering the domain of contextual sense-differentiation in precedent-following necessitates leaving behind the realm of logico-syllogistic deductions, self-referentially defined preconditions of meaning-production, and the reproduction of the original identity of the *ratio* of a case. Instead, the sense ascribed to the *ratio* of a case is aligned with the divergent facets of similarity and dissimilarity found in the facts of the two cases, thereby giving effect to a gradual realignment of the original *ratio vis-à-vis* the various novel fact-constellations to be ruled upon. Contextual—and also systemic—differentiation of a norm's meaning-content occupies the conceptual mid-area extending between the two end poles of absolute identity and radical alterity, as are materialised in the precedent ideologies of judicial reference and judicial legislation, on the one hand, and the judicial ideologies based on social consequentialism, rightness reasons in adjudication and free-flowing judicial hunch, on the other.

There are two "strings" or "cords" entailed in a contextual sense-differentiation of the *ratio* of a case: *deferral* and *distancing*. Deferral of sense, in contrast to a transient locking-up of a sign's meaning-content at a given point of time, accounts for the gradual realignment or reshaping of sense from one case or context of application to another. Distancing, or the production of meaningful differences in a system of signs, in contrast to a mere reciting of a sign's original meaning-content as under the legislative paradigm, accounts for the conceptual space extending between the relevant similarities and dissimilarities in two non-identical signs or cases at a given point in time. In the legal context, the two-fold process of deferral/distancing of a norm's meaning-content on the synchronic/diachronic or spatial/temporal dimensions finds a parallel with those patterns of legal reasoning where the semantic confines of the *ratio* of a case are in a constant state of change from one occasion of norm-application to another. Consequently, the *ratio* of a case is subject to be later reconstructed (*judicial exegesis*), realigned by means of analogy/distinguishing (*judicial analogy*), or redefined (*judicial revaluation*) in the context of a novel and, in some legally relevant aspect, different fact-constellation to be ruled upon.

The dispute-solving paradigm of precedent-following bears closest affinity with the process of meaning-production in ordinary language, despite the obvious fact that the institutional prerequisites of norm-giving and norm-enforcement, in analogy to the role and function of the legislator and courts of justice, are of course lacking. In ordinary language, there is no authoritative and pre-existing canon of predetermined linguistic meanings, in the image of the legislative paradigm; nor any recourse to some latent signification structure beneath the manifest surface-structure level of language, in the image of the systemic-constructive paradigm; nor still a retreat to some external reference beyond the domain of ordinary language, in the image of the extra-legal paradigm. Instead, the two-fold process of meaning-production by sense-variation is outlined in strictly context-bound terms, where the exact meaning-content of a linguistic sign may—and will—vary from one discursive context to another. The approach is thus in perfect accord with the structuralist premises of linguistic signification as laid down by de Saussure and Derrida, among others.

5.3 Systemic paradigm of precedent-following: sense-differentiation by privileging the latent signification structure beneath the manifest precedent-norm or reasons formulation

Under the systemic-constructive paradigm of precedent-following, any manifest precedent-norm or reasons formulations as put forth by the prior court may be disregarded, and the *ratio* of a case, or line of cases, is constructed from the latent signification structure beneath such positivity of law. The exact meaning-content ascribed to the *ratio* of a case is, in other words, brought into effect by reversing the priority order within the conceptual pairs involved in legal adjudication, as outlined in terms of what is *present/absent*, *manifest/latent*, *contingent/system-bound*, or *positivist/non-positivist* in precedent-based law. Although prima facie the former element of each conceptual pair would seem to have more bearing on the issue of meaning-production in precedent-following, the sense carried by the *ratio* of a case is still defined in accordance with the latter element. A convenient analogy to the systemic paradigm of precedent-following can be found in a system of encoded and decoded linguistic messages. To decode an encrypted message, one must have an insight into the underlying signification structure or internal "logic" of the system of signs in question from which the key of interpretation is to be derived. Like the dispute-solving paradigm, the systemic-constructive paradigm of precedent-following is ultimately conditioned on a Derridean *différance*, giving effect to the idea of meaning-production through sense-differentiation in legal discourse. However, here the emphasis is on the paradigmatic axis of signification, rather than the syntagmatic dimension of language.

The judgment of the presence or absence of some legally relevant aspect of similarity or dissimilarity in the prior case—subsequent case relation is, of course, affected by a reversal of the conceptual pairs and priorities involved. In consequence, some surface-structure level similarity between two cases may in fact turn out to be a sufficient reason to distinguish them, when the impact of the latent signification structure of law is taken into account. There is, in other words, a constant threat of a "systemic surprise" or *jack-in-the-box effect*,[23] since each novel case brought before the court might induce a radically novel reading of the line of prior decisions. A prior case may never be taken at its face value, in disregard of the latent *seamless web* of underlying reasons beneath the manifest surface-structure level of legal positivity. The argumentative consequences of such systemic differentiation of a norm's meaning-content are materialised in the Dworkin-inspired request for retaining a high level of systemic coherence under the doctrine of *law as integrity*.

A consistent privileging of the prima facie "weaker" element of the conceptual dichotomies involved may seem to have some affinity with the slightly misconceived "method of deconstruction" professed by the *Critical Legal Studies* (CLS) movement and the circles of literary criticism in the United States, as described—and criticised—above in chapter 1. However, there is a crucial point of divergence on the aim to be attained in the two approaches, i.e. the grounding of a seamless web of underlying reasons of law under the systemic-constructive paradigm of precedent-following, and a reductionist disbelief in anything like the formal edifice of law and legal systematicity in the CLS alternative.

5.4 Extra-legal paradigm of judicial adjudication: production of radical dissimilarity by displacement of the legal premises

Under the extra-legal or non-formal paradigm of judicial adjudication, the subsequent court is thought to reject any formal legally defined frame of judicial decision-making in the sense of the prevalent legal source doctrine and the doctrine of *stare decisis*. Decisive priority is, instead, given to the openly teleological, axiological or intuitive elements in a judge's process of decision-making.

[23] I owe this term to Wilhelmsson who uses it to describe the impact of the European law on municipal jurisdiction in his essay, "Jack-in-the-Box Theory of European Community Law", in L. Krämer, H.W. Micklitz and K. Tonner (eds), *Law and Diffuse Interests in European Legal Order* (Nomos Verlagsgesellschaft, Baden-Baden, 1997).

The inherent "logic" of judicial meaning-production is framed in terms of what was initially excluded from legal deliberation by force of its formal characteristics, i.e. the pre-legal background reasons of law. Such a displacement of the *ratio* and normative premises of a prior case aims at producing radical semantic alterity in subsequent case-law adjudication. In consequence, no direct inference is permitted from the *ratio* of a prior case to the facts of the novel case. Instead, the line of argumentation must pass through the pre-legal background reasons of law "beneath" the positivist surface-structure level of judicial signification, in order to ensure the correspondence of the outcome of adjudication with the teleological, axiological or entirely free, i.e. intuitive, premises of judicial decision-making.

6. IN CONCLUSION: *DIFFÉRANCE* AND OTHER INFRASTRUCTURES OF JUDICIAL SIGNIFICATION UNDER PRECEDENT-FOLLOWING

The infrastructures of judicial signification under precedent-following extend in logico-conceptual space and unfold in time on the two-fold grid of language, i.e. the *syntagmatic* and *paradigmatic* dimensions of language, resulting in the specific processes of meaning-constitution and sense-differentiation effected thereby. Such "sense-making" forces are defined in terms of self-referential, absolute identity (legislative paradigm), a constant interplay of relative similarity and dissimilarity, placing emphasis on either the syntagmatic or paradigmatic axis of language (contextualist and systemic paradigms, respectively), and radical alterity (extra-legal paradigm) in judicial meaning-production. The specific infrastructures of judicial signification each reflect their own "logic" or mode of operation:

(1) *circular self-referentiality* and reproduction of original identity on the syntagmatic axis of legal discourse in the legislative paradigm of precedent-following, where the role of the subsequent court is reduced to a mere unfolding of the necessary consequences of the *ratio* of a case by means of logical deduction;
(2) *contextual sense-differentiation* on the syntagmatic (and paradigmatic) axes of legal discourse, or the production of less than identity-invoking similarity and dissimilarity in the gradual realignment of the *ratio* of a prior case through an incessant interplay of deferral/distancing, under the auspices of a Derridean *différance* in the dispute-solving, contextualist paradigm of precedent-following, thereby giving effect to the distinct argumentative strategies of backward-proceeding judicial reconstruction (judicial exegesis), a "moving classification system" in gradual realignment (judicial analogy/distinguishing), and more or less radical judicial redefinition (judicial revaluation) of the *ratio* of a case;
(3) *systemic sense-differentiation* on the (syntagmatic and) paradigmatic axes of legal discourse by privileging the latent signification structure which

extends beneath the manifest precedent-norm and/or reasons expression in the systemic-constructive paradigm of precedent-following, with reference to the *best constructive interpretation of the community's legal practice*[24] and resting ultimately on a Derridean *différance*; and

(4) *radical displacement* of the formally legal premises of judicial adjudication and the production of radical alterity on the paradigmatic axis of "legal" discourse in the extra-legal non-formal paradigm of judicial adjudication, with reference to arguments of teleological (i.e. political), axiological (i.e. moral), or intuitive (i.e. Solomonic or merely arbitrary) kind.

Since the adoption of the extra-legal, non-formal paradigm of judicial adjudication would mean having to cast off the legal or formal frame of judicial meaning-production, there are three alternatives to be considered within the confines of a legally qualified discourse on precedents. The theoretical pre-eminence of the dispute-solving paradigm of precedent-following, as supported and framed by the inherent processes of spatial/temporal sense-differentiation in the sense of deferral/distancing (*différance*), can be defended against the two other alternatives. Adherence to a regressive self-referentiality in judicial meaning-production, as in the legislative paradigm, would deprive legal adjudication of all its dynamic and flexible facets, with the result of "freezing" or "petrifying" all subsequent jurisdiction. There is simply no room for context-sensitive sense-variation under the austere and rigid premises of meaning-production in judicial legislation, strictly defined. The dispute-solving paradigm and the systemic-constructive paradigm of precedent-following both avoid the pitfalls of such judicial self-referentiality and full-fledged semantic closure, by force of the sense-differentiating elements involved. However, the very idea of a systemic-constructive reading of prior case-law by necessity entails the constant threat of a "systemic surprise", or *jack-in-the-box effect*, since the "true" meaning of the *ratio* of a case can never be read on the face of a prior case; instead, recourse must always be taken to the latent signification structure beneath the potentially misleading linguistic precedent-norm and/or reasons expressions which are found on the surface-structure level of law.

In all, the four paradigms of precedent-following or judicial adjudication, the variants of judicial imagery, and the respective infrastructures of judicial signification may be presented in the form of the Figure 8 over.

[24] R. Dworkin, *Law's Empire* (Fontana Masterguides, 1986), 225 ff.

Paradigms of judicial signification in precedent-following	*Judicial imagery: conception of the judge in precedent-following*	*Infrastructures of judicial signification under precedent-following*
Legislative paradigm: – judicial reference – judicial legislation	The prior judge as a "small-scale legislator" endowed with interstitial powers of judicial legislation; while the subsequent judge is entitled to do no more than draw the logical consequences from a prior decision; judge as a *lawgiver, dressed in robe* along with a *slot-machine judge*	Self-referential signification: reproduction of original identity through unfolding of the logical consequences from the precedent-norm and/or reasons formulation on the syntagmatic axis of judicial signification
Dispute-solving paradigm (contextualist paradigm): – judicial exegesis – judicial analogy – judicial revaluation	Judge as an unbiased arbiter in the individual case brought before the court, giving effect to dispute-resolution on strictly contextualist basis: judge as a *dispute-solver*	Signification by contextual differentiation: production of relative similarity/dissimilarity through the interplay of deferral/distancing (*différance*) on the syntagmatic (and paradigmatic) axes of judicial signification
Systemic paradigm (constructive paradigm): – systemic construction of underlying reasons in law	Judge as Dworkin's Hercules, J., or "a lawyer of superhuman skill, learning, patience, and acumen", with the aim of constructing the latent signification structure of law beneath the manifest precedent-norm and/or reasons formulation: judge as a *legal scholar*	Signification by systemic differentiation: production of relative similarity/dissimilarity by having recourse to the latent signification structure of legal discourse on the (syntagmatic and) paradigmatic axes of judicial signification
Extra-legal paradigm (non-formal paradigm): – consequentialism – rightness reasons – judicial hunch	Judge as essentially unconstrained by the prevalent legal source doctrine and the doctrine of *stare decisis*, free to give effect to arguments of axiological, teleological or intuitive kind: judge as a *moral/political philosopher*, with Solomonic or less noble motives (i.e. *coin-tossing judge*)	Signification with reference to radical semantic alterity: production of extra-legal dissimilarity by having recourse to the political, moral or intuitive premises of adjudication on the paradigmatic axis of judicial signification

Figure 8: The four paradigms of judicial adjudication, types of judicial imagery, and the respective infrastructures of judicial signification (i.e. meaning-production) under precedent-following

10

Summary

1. HOW TO READ PRECEDENTS

A treatise on legal theory should not merely be "a book from which one learns what other books contain", as Hart and Fuller have—with all good reason—argued.[1] Apart from the common law discourse on "why cases have *rationes* and what these are",[2] precedents have not been analysed in depth in analytically oriented jurisprudential and legal philosophical literature. Therefore, an effort was made above to probe into the deep-reaching constitutive premises of the *ratio* of a case, along with the various ways of reading that *ratio* in subsequent judicial adjudication.

The frame of analysis adopted in this book was concisely presented in chapter 1, in terms of the object of inquiry, legal systemic frame, theoretical frame of reference and methods of analysis employed. The object of inquiry was focused on the formative premises of the *ratio* of a case on each of the three (or four) levels of law and legal analysis discerned, i.e. the operative *surface-structure*, the ideological and discourse-theoretical *deep-structure*, and the prelogical and preconceptual *infrastructure* levels of law. The legal systemic frame of this treatise was aligned with that of a civil law judge who is placed under the specific kind of constraints of precedent-identification and precedent-following. The doctrine of *stare decisis* was, however, detached from the common law context of precedent-following and affiliated to that of legal adjudication in more general terms. Since the techniques of *how to read precedents*, in the sense of genuine case-to-case reasoning, are frequently far better mastered in the common law tradition than in the statute-oriented civil law tradition, a significant portion of arguments that were utilised in analysing the feasible precedent ideologies of a judge was imported from the common law context.

A novel reading of Dworkin's well-known theory of legal rules and legal principles was presented in chapter 2. The neatly overlapping character of Dworkin's conception of legal rules and principles and Summers' categories of legal formality was discovered in a close cross-reading of the two theories of law. Legal principles were (re)defined as legal instruments which rank low in all five categories of legal formality discerned, i.e. *constitutive* formality, *systemic* formality, *mandatory* formality, *structural* formality, and *methodological*

[1] H.L.A. Hart, *The Concept of Law* (Clarendon Press, Oxford, 1961), VI; Lon L. Fuller, *The Morality of Law* (Yale University Press, 1969), 95.

[2] Cf. N. MacCormick, "Why Cases Have Rationes and What These Are", in L. Goldstein (ed.), *Precedent in Law* (Oxford University Press, 1991).

formality; while legal rules proved to rank uniformly high under such premises. Moreover, the quasi-Kelsenian notions of standard or *strong relation of imputation* and deficient or *weak relation of imputation* were utilised, with reference to the various categories of legal formality entailed in legal rules and legal principles or policies, respectively.

A legal principle or policy gives effect to no more than a weak relation of imputation between a set of facts *p* and consequences *q*, being of the type: "if *p*, then it *ought to* be that *q*, unless there are strong enough countervailing reasons present with reference to which *q* may be outweighed in the case at hand", or "if *p*, then it ought to be that more-or-less *q*, depending on the relative impact of other, countervailing reasons in the case at hand". The notion of *deontic formality* was introduced to denote the sum total of the categories of legal formality ascribed to a legal norm, no matter whether of legislative or judicial origin. Legal principles and policies, or *proto-norms* as they were also called in the analysis above, are situated on the conceptual edge or boundary of the legal and pre-legal discourse formations, to the effect of importing arguments of social expediency or social justice and fairness from the domain of the latter into the formally framed edifice of law. Legal principles and policies function, so to speak, as an intermediate link between what is and what is not law.

The source of inspiration for Part A of this treatise was based on Wróblewski's classification of the three ideologies of judicial decision-making, Ross' notion of a judge's normative ideology, and Hart's idea of judges' rule of recognition. None of the said masters of modern analytical and positivist legal theory, however, paid any specific attention to the role of precedents in judicial adjudication. That "missing piece" of analytical jurisprudence was therefore outlined in chapters 3–5 above, where the feasible *ideologies of precedent-based judicial decision-making* (Wróblewski), the various models of *precedent ideology* (Ross), and the content of a judge's *rule of precedent-recognition* (Hart) were analysed in detail. In addition, the ideological premises of legal adjudication were briefly reconsidered in chapter 6 above.

The present inquiry into the constitutive elements of a judge's ideology of precedent-identification and precedent-following may be read as a systemic effort to present the contents of a judge's *intellectual toolbox vis-à-vis* the doctrine of *stare decisis*, i.e. the identification and interpretation of the *ratio decidendi* of a case, as distinguished from the argumentative context, or *obiter dicta*, of that *ratio*. Precedent-ideologies were divided into the following six main categories and thirteen individual models or pure types of legal adjudication:

(1) judicial reference:
 (a) *reference model*;
(2) judicial legislation:
 (b) *quasi-legislative model*,
 (c) *binding reasons model*;

(3) judicial exegesis:
  (d) *reconstructed rule model,*
  (e) *material facts model,*
  (f) *material reasons model;*
(4) judicial analogy:
  (g) *model rule approach,*
  (h) *paradigm case model,*
  (i) *model reasons approach;*
(5) systemic construction of underlying reasons of law:
  (j) *underlying reasons model;*
(6) judicial revaluation:
  (k) *reinterpreted rule model,*
  (l) *requalified facts model,*
  (m) *revalued reasons model.*

In judicial reference ideology, the *ratio* of a case is given an express formulation by the prior court which, moreover, withholds all powers of legal interpretation at its own discretion. In judicial legislation, the *ratio* of a case is similarly laid down in a final and "canonised" form by the prior court, while the subsequent court is entitled to do no more than read out the logical consequences from the decision once authoritatively given. In judicial exegesis, the *ratio* of a case is reconstructed by the subsequent court from the normative and/or factual reasoning premises of that decision, with the aim of retracing—as authentically as possible—the prior court's original intentions. In judicial analogy, the prior decision is taken as a model rule, paradigm case or set of model reasons to be either extended analogically to cover the facts of the novel case, or cut down by distinguishing the two cases on some factual ground. In the Dworkin-inspired underlying reasons ideology of precedent-following, the *ratio* of a case or line of cases is read in light of the *best constructive interpretation of past legal decisions.* Finally, in judicial revaluation, the *ratio* of a case may be given a more-or-less radical reformulation, re-reading or reinterpretation by the subsequent court, in order to better match with the requirements of the facts of the novel case and changing social requirements.

Each pure type of precedent ideology was defined in terms of the following twelve individual facets or ideological fragments: operative precedent-norm conception, point of reference, deontic mode, norm-individuation, argumentative closure, degree of systematicity in a set of precedents, degree of binding force, source/effect of a precedent, method of argumentation, techniques of departure from a precedent, leading criteria of justice, and theoretical background rationale of the precedent ideology concerned. In chapter 4 above, some of the ideological fragments were systematically contrasted. Such constitutive fragments of a judge's precedent ideology were also briefly reconsidered in chapter 6, where the parallel function of a judge's normative source ideology (Ross), and the rule of recognition (Hart) was defended, and a formal definition of the judges' rule of precedent-recognition was given.

The precedent ideology in fact adopted by the highest court or courts of justice in the six legal systems chosen for the purpose (United States (State of New York), United Kingdom, France, Italy, Federal Republic of Germany and Finland) was analysed in chapter 5, in order to test the validity of the modelling approach employed, and to provide a direct link to the results reached by the international research group *Bielefelder Kreis* in their book, *Interpreting Precedents: A Comparative Study*.[3] Finally, the "law in action" in precedent-following was outlined briefly by relaxing the conceptual confines of the various pure types of precedent ideology, giving effect instead to a set or cluster of ideological fragments in actual case-law adjudication. Thereby, the "still life" image of precedent-following was transformed into a more dynamic conception of judicial reality.

Therefore, the idea of a *grasshopper technique* of judicial argumentation was suggested, with reference to a sequence of argumentative "leaps" and "jumps" which lead step-by-step away from a strictly formal definition of the *ratio* of a case towards a less-formal conception of the doctrine of *stare decisis*, and finally ending up in overtly non-formal judicial consequentialism where all the strictures of initial legal formalism have been discarded. However, such a notion of precedent-following did not gain adequate support from the precedent ideologies in fact acknowledged in the six legal systems included in the comparative section of the study, while the thoroughly pragmatic notion of precedent-following in the United States (State of New York) might be thought to entail some elements of such non-formalism, along with other tenets. Feasible alternatives to the grasshopper technique of precedent-following were outlined in terms of the beehive/anthill metaphor. A relatively rigid system of precedents, as in the United Kingdom, is formed in the image of a *beehive*, where the argumentative impact of the *ratio* of a case is prestructured by the formal constraints derived from the doctrine of *stare decisis*, strictly defined, and the relatively rigid techniques of precedent-based legal argumentation available to a judge, i.e. mainly backward-proceeding judicial exegesis. A relatively weakly structured system of precedents, as, for example, in Italy, is formed in the image of an *anthill*, where individual precedents, like the needles and straws carried to the anthill by the hard-working ants, become piled up loosely on top of one another, without being pre-framed by a well-defined notion of the argumentative weight to be ascribed to the *ratio* of a case, nor supported by well-functioning techniques of *how to read precedents* among the judiciary and legal profession.

Part B of the treatise then sought to deepen the frame of analysis by displaying the down-reaching edifice of the formative premises of the *ratio* of a case at the three levels of law discerned: the operative *surface-structure* level of law, as "glossed" by practice-oriented legal dogmatics; the ideological and discourse-

[3] D.N. MacCormick and R.S. Summers (eds) (Ashgate/Dartmouth, 1997).

theoretical *deep-structure* level of law, as analysed by theory-bound jurisprudence; and the prelogical and preconceptual *infrastructure* level of law, as reflected upon by the collective efforts of legal philosophy. The theoretical prerequisites of the *ratio* of a case were outlined in terms of the two categories of formal legal norm constitution, or the criteria for distinguishing the *ratio decidendi* of a case from its argumentative context or *obiter dicta*, and judicial signification under precedent-following, or the ascription of a specific meaning-content to the *ratio* of a case. Such an analysis was then undertaken on each "deeper" level of legal discourse discerned. The quest for the theoretical and philosophical premises of the *ratio* of a case is intended to account for the frequently unarticulated, latent deeper-structure level prerequisites of precedent-identification and precedent-following.

The manifest inadequacy of Fuller's *internal morality of law* was discovered when applied to precedent-following. A set of specific, tailor-made rule of law criteria for precedents was therefore outlined in terms of the following criteria:

(1) appositeness (i.e. expediency) and adequacy of normative and factual information entailed in precedents;
(2) fair predictability of precedent-based law;
(3) systemic balance (i.e. congruence), as effected through the multi-faceted relation prevailing between the effected binding force of the *ratio* of a case and the legal systemic constraints derived from:
    (a) professional self-understanding of the judge concerned *vis-à-vis* precedent-identification and precedent-following, in the sense of the specific precedent ideology internalised by him;
    (b) prevalent legal source doctrine in the legal system in question;
    (c) relative determinacy and articulation of the doctrine and tradition on precedents among the judiciary;
    (d) discourse-theoretical frame of law, giving effect to the conceptual, mental and institutional felicity conditions of legal adjudication; and
    (e) constraints derived from the general frame of legal culture and the specific conception of law entailed;
(4) ideological commitments (i.e. precedent ideology) and precedent-specific argumentative skills, as are required from judges and the legal profession;
(5) respect for the basic conceptions of justice and fairness in society; and
(6) integrity in argumentation, ruling out the impact of the "bad faith argument".

In all, the six elements of a rule of law ideology for precedent-following lay down (no more than) the preconditions of a judge's "morality of aspiration", framing the pursuit of empirical legitimacy for the outcome of legal adjudication, in addition to the requirement of being grounded on a consistent conception of precedent ideology.

As Austin argued in his book, *How To Do Things With Words*, one cannot say *the cat is on the mat but I do not believe it is*,[4] nor, *I promise to do X but I*

[4] J.L. Austin, *How To Do Things With Words* (Oxford University Press, 1986), 48.

am under no obligation to do it,[5] without committing a conceptual failure or performative contradiction. In the context of judicial argumentation, the resulting *claim to legal correctness* grounds a judge's inherent claim of having interpreted the law correctly when ruling upon a contested issue, as Alexy has argued. The claim to legal correctness deals with the rationality conditions of judicial adjudication. The novel *claim to legal authority*, introduced above as a validity-aligned parallel to the Alexian claim to legal correctness, gives effect to a court decision's quality of being endowed with binding force *vis-à-vis* the *res judicata* of the case and the litigants involved in it. On the level of legal ideology, the judge's *pursuit of legitimacy* with respect to the outcome of adjudication has a parallel function, giving effect to a judge's "morality of aspiration", as defined in terms of the "pride of the craftsman" and the avoidance of professional blame on the part of the judge, or judges, concerned.

The discourse-theoretical frame of law under the analytical and positivistic premises acknowledged was defined by means of the following factors: (1) the *axiomatic postulates* of legal rationality and legal validity, reflecting the two notions of *ratio* and *auctoritas* in law; (2) the two conceptual claims effected, i.e. the *claim to legal authority* and the *claim to legal correctness*, having reference to the validity and rationality conditions of law; and (3) the *felicity conditions* of legal adjudication, accounting for the satisfaction of the conceptual, institutional and mental preconditions of judicial adjudication. Kennedy's *bad faith argument*, or the contention that the law is being infiltrated constantly by the judges' ideological motives, idiosyncratic preferences or personal bias, was rejected by reference to the specific, legitimacy-proliferating *rule of law criteria* for precedent-following and the *felicity conditions* of legal adjudication on the deep-structure level of law. The felicity conditions of legal adjudication comprise the two *conceptual* claims mentioned, plus the *institutional* and *mental* preconditions imposed upon a judge's performance of the speech act of pronouncing a judicial decision. Taken together, the felicity conditions of legal adjudication, plus the specific, Fuller-inspired rule of law criteria for precedents, are equal to a judge's *view from the bench vis-à-vis* precedent-identification and precedent-following under analytical positivism.

A close-reading of Hart's rule of legal recognition in terms of its contested ontological status on the *law/fact* (*Sollen/Sein*) or *validity/existence* dimension led to the discovery that Hart's master rule, as defined by the great English legal philosopher himself, is caught between the two—both less-than-fully satisfactory—alternatives of validity-constituting normativity, shaped in the image of Kelsen's merely hypothetical *Grundnorm*, and one-to-one empirical descriptivity, shaped in close analogy to the immense, life-sized map produced by the imperial cartographers in Borges' insightful fiction, "On Exactitude in Science" (*Del rigor en la ciencia*).[6] Since Hart rejected the normative, validity-constitut-

[5] J.L. Austin ibid., 54.

[6] In *El hacedor* (Alianza Editorial, Madrid, 1987).

ing reading of the ultimate rule of recognition in explicit terms, to the effect that it "can neither be valid nor invalid but is simply accepted" by the judiciary,[7] Hart's master rule is defined in perfectly circular, interlocking terms: the set of valid legal rules, or the pertinent legal source material in general, is identified with reference to the rule of recognition, but the rule of recognition cannot itself be identified, except "by appeal to the facts, i.e. to the actual practice of the courts and officials of the system when identifying the law which they are to apply",[8] and so on, *ad infinitum*.

2. FROM ANALYTICAL POSITIVISM TO A DECONSTRUCTION OF LAW

In all, the present treatise proceeded from analytical jurisprudence, as elaborated and exemplified by Wróblewski, Ross and Hart, to the radically non-conventional philosophy of deconstruction by Derrida, with brief excursions taken to Fuller's internal morality of law, Tuori's theory of the multilayered structure of law, Austin's theory of speech acts, and Foucault's archaeology of knowledge. *Analytical positivism* was identified as the theoretical frame of analysis of the inquiry in a two-fold sense. Chapters 3–7 aimed at a *rational reconstruction* of a judge's ideological stance towards precedent-identification and precedent-following, i.e. the doctrine of *stare decisis*, along with the discourse-theoretical identity of law under the theoretical premises of analytical positivism. Moreover, chapter 2 provided some refined analytical tools for a further elaboration of the Dworkinian legal rule/principle dichotomy, seen through Summers' various categories of legal formality. However, the very final or ultimate *premises*, *grounds*, *edges* or *criteria* of law proved to be the "blind spot" of such analysis, irredeemably beyond the reach of the conceptual or methodological tools introduced by analytical jurisprudence. Therefore, in chapters 8–9 the initial analytical frame had to be rejected, giving room for a decisively *post-analytical philosophy of law*. The *critical unfolding* or *radical questioning* of the very "final" or "ultimate" premises of law eventually led to the discovery of the infrastructures of law.

The *infrastructures* of law have a two-fold relation to Foucault's "historical *a priori*", in the sense of the two "facets", "strings" or "cords" of legal discourse discerned, i.e. being related to legal norm constitution and judicial signification under precedent-following.

Foucault "historicised" the formal *a priori* entailed in Kant's *Critique of Pure Reason* by unveiling the historically changing conditions of possibility of Western *épistémè*, in the sense of the conceptual "order of things" in the (external) world. By "historical *a priori*" Foucault sought to describe the transcendental-logically contingent but historically determined conditions of possibility

[7] Hart, above at n. 1, 105–6.
[8] Ibid., 245, n. to p. 97. Cf. ibid., 107.

of the epistemological frame by reference to which "words" (*les mots*) and "things" (*les choses*) are linked together within a given discourse formation.[9] Unlike Kant's formal, universal and immutable conditions of human knowledge, Foucault's historical *a priori* leaves adequate room for historical change in such transcendental preconditions of human knowledge and judgment. In *Les Mots et les choses* Foucault gave a vivid presentation of the sequential historical transformations of the Western *épistémè* from the Renaissance through Classicism to Modernity. In the quest for the final premises of legal norm constitution above, Foucault's historical *a priori* was further relativised by pointing out the radically equivocal or unresolvable status of the final grounds, premises, criteria or edges of Western metaphysics. The infrastructures of knowledge and judgment proved equally to *ground/cancel*, *effect/efface* or *establish/level off* the basic categories of thought and language, being expressive of the deeply felt necessity and, at the same time, absolute impossibility of finding some solid ground or argumentative bedrock (Wittgenstein) for the "ultimate" preconditions of human knowledge and judgment.

Like Plato's *khōra*, which successfully defies the categories of his dualist ontology which is defined in terms of sensible/intelligible, visible/invisible, form/substance, destructible/immutable, *logos/mythos*, etc.,[10] the final premises or *infrastructures* of law cannot be classified under either of the two conceptual categories of law/fact, validity/existence, or *Sein/Sollen*, which are brought into effect with reference to such "ultimate" criteria in legal discourse, without levelling off their self-evading status as the "ultimate" preconditions of law, language and philosophy. Any effort at an all-encompassing classification of the phenomena found within the confines of legal discourse, inclusive of the very final grounds or ultimate edges of law, is bound to fail, leading to the perplexities of infinite regress or logical circularity, once the persistent question on the status of the "ultimate" criteria of law themselves is posited. As the radically equivocal *effecting* condition of possibility and—with equal force—the *effacing* condition of impossibility of knowledge and judgment within the domain of the Kantian "pure reason" of human knowledge, the infrastructures of law provide for the radically equivocal, *quasi-transcendental* condition of possibility and impossibility, or the Derridean "dislocating *a priori*", of Western philosophical tradition.

When probing into the infrastructures of signification in language and law, Foucault's archaeology of knowledge was "reformalised" by pointing out the necessary formal or "Kantian" element in it. The *syntagmatic/paradigmatic* grid of linguistic signification upon which any historical discourse formation is

[9] Foucault's main contribution to the "archeology of knowledge" is titled *Les Mots et les choses: Une Archéologie des sciences humaines* (Éditions Gallimard, Paris, 1966). The English translation, *The Order of Things*, may not fully capture the enigmatic relation between the "words" and the "things" so neatly depicted in the French title of the work.

[10] Plato, *Timaeus*, in *The Dialogues of Plato* (Clarendon Press, Oxford, 4th ed. 1953), § 49a (p. 735) and § 52 a–c (pp. 738–9); J. Derrida, *On the Name* (Stanford University Press, 1995), 89–127, esp. 89, 96.

extended in (conceptual) space and unfolded in time is the formal, inherent or "transcendental-logical" condition of possibility of any initially emerging, gradually transforming and eventually disappearing discourse formation within the Western *épistémè*, irrespective of the actual shape and terms of existence of the "historical *a priori*" in it. Since the syntagmatic/paradigmatic grid of language accounts for the indispensable element of synchronic/diachronic meaning-differentiation in a system of signs, such a necessary, inherently formal ingredient of a discourse formation leans ultimately on a Derridean *différance*, in the sense of the incessant preconceptual movement of spacing/temporization, or deferral/distancing, in linguistic and judicial signification.

The sum total of the two mutually intertwined facets of a discourse formation, i.e. the "sense-making" infrastructures of linguistic signification and the "reality-constituting" infrastructures of ontology and epistemology, accounts for the Western *épistémè* or the conceptual "order of things" in the (external) world, as it is then realised in, for example, the discourse on law. The sense-making infrastructures of linguistic signification are aligned with "words" or signs, and the reality-constituting infrastructures of ontology and epistemology are aligned with "things" or phenomena, in terms of the two-fold epistemic grid opened up by force of the Western will to knowledge. The connection between the two facets of a discourse formation is provided by the relation that the two types or "strings" of the infrastructures involved have *vis-à-vis* one another, i.e. the dislocating, radically equivocal *a priori* of reality-constitution and the difference-proliferating *a priori* of sense-making in linguistic and judicial signification, i.e. *différance*.

The transition from the analytical to the post-analytical frame of analysis was attained by reflecting on Wittgenstein's philosophical argument on the length of the standard metre bar in Paris. In *Philosophical Investigations*,[11] the great Austrian philosopher put forward the argument that no meaningful assertion can be made as to the length of the standard metre itself, since it provides for the fixed point of reference of all length measurement. As was argued above, Wittgenstein was mistaken in his standard metre argument because he ignored the institutional, convention-based status of the standard metre bar and the social consequences to be drawn from such a convention. Behind the "metricity" of the standard metre, there is a valid legal and/or social convention in which the constitutive properties of the standard metre bar, i.e. its exact length, have been conclusively defined. The truly perplexing question, however, still remains unanswered: what would be a parallel *standard norm* for the law, or an uncontested yardstick for the "measurement" of legal validity (and legal rationality) within a legal community?

The final validity ground of law, the final rationality ground of law, recognition of the rule of recognition itself, and the identity-evading status of the rule

[11] L. Wittgenstein, *Philosophische Untersuchungen—Philosophical Investigations* (Basil Blackwell, Oxford, 1967).

of recognition on the law/fact or validity/existence dimension, all denote the predicament affecting the ultimate criteria of legal ontology, legal methodology and legal epistemology under the constitutive premises of law and legal discourse. The deeply felt necessity and, at the same time, absolute impossibility of finding some solid reference ground, argumentative bedrock (Wittgenstein), or conclusive end point of justification denotes a parallel predicament for the production of meaning within law. A legal scholar who had set off for the "Linnaean"—and, eventually, futile—task of producing an all-encompassing conceptual and metaphysical scheme or an exhaustive "order of things" for the phenomena tangible and intangible alike, could not find a place in his classification for the highly unconventional phenomena encountered at the ultimate edges of legal discourse, or of Western metaphysics in more general terms. Within legal discourse, as framed by the self-imposed methodological credo of Kelsen's *Pure Theory of Law*[12] under the auspices of analytical positivism, a request for the "ultimate" premises of law will lead to the predicament of logical circularity or infinite regress, once the inevitable quest for the ontological, epistemological, and/or methodological status of the "ultimate" grounds, premises, edges or criteria of law is voiced. Therefore, the only candidates for a *standard norm* in the law, drawn in the image of the tangible standard metre bar in Paris or the imaginary "standard colours" of Wittgenstein's philosophical argument, were identified with the curiously identity-evading *infrastructures* of Western metaphysics.

The parallel transition to the infrastructures of judicial signification was achieved by reflecting upon Wittgenstein's argument concerning the *infallible paradigm of identity*, in the trivial sense of the identity of a thing with itself. The distinguished Austrian philosopher is self-evidently right in pointing out that the self-referential assertion of a thing's identity with itself is devoid of meaningful discursive context or effected language-game in any linguistic community. However, the *identity argument* cannot be extended to apply to the strange infrastructure level phenomena "behind" or "before" Western metaphysics. While providing for the prelogical and preconceptual preconditions of human knowledge, judgment and linguistic signification in the sense of the *almost nothing of the unpresentable*,[13] the infrastructures themselves lack any constant metaphysical identity or conceptual essence by force of their self-evading "definition".

Two "strings" or "cords" of such Derrida-inspired infrastructures of law were discussed in detail: radical *undecidability* in legal norm constitution, with allusion to their peculiar role in legal discourse whereby they *ground/cancel*, *effect/efface* or *establish/level off* the "ultimate" premises of legal ontology, legal epistemology, and legal methodology; and *différance*, i.e. deferral/distancing or spacing/temporisation in judicial signification, with allusion to the pro-

[12] Peter Smith, 1989.
[13] J. Derrida, *Points . . . Interviews, 1974–1994* (Stanford University Press, 1995), 83.

duction (and dissolution) of meaning-content under precedent-following. Accordingly, radical undecidability denotes the truly equivocal, unresolvable or self-evading status of the grounding premises of legal validity and legal rationality at the discourse-theoretical level of law under analytical positivism. Thus, the ontological, epistemological and methodological status of the "ultimate" premises of law cannot be conclusively defined without committing a logico-conceptual fallacy, cancelling their infrastructure level function as the final criteria of law, or begging the question. The endlessly unsettled status of Kelsen's *Grundnorm* and Hart's ultimate rule of recognition on the ontological law/fact dimension, along with the radical indefinability or inexpressibility of the ultimate criteria of human reason in, for example, Wróblewski's, MacCormick's and Peczenik's theories of law, denote the impact of such a predicament on the ultimate edges of philosophical analysis and judgment. *Différance*, in turn, denotes the self-evasive movement of sense-differentiation on the synchronic/diachronic dimensions of linguistic and judicial signification, whereby a norm's meaning-content is in an incessant movement of transition or flux under the meaning-constituting and meaning-dissolving forces of spacing/temporisation or deferral/distancing. The *infallible paradigm of difference* was therefore identified with the "logic of *différance*", written with an inaudible "*a*" in the third syllable instead of the grammatically correct "*e*".

Infrastructures of legal norm constitution are aligned with the grounding categories of legal ontology, legal epistemology and legal methodology, while their self-evadingly "*quasi-transcendental*" or "*pre-metaphysical*" status *vis-à-vis* the categories of two-valued logic and ordinary linguistic conceptuality is expressive of their inherent predicament of "non-identity". In order to be able to function as the "ultimate" preconditions behind the dualistic conceptual categories of norm/fact, *Sein*/*Sollen*, *logos*/*mythos*, etc., within legal discourse, the infrastructures must themselves remain endlessly deferred/distanced from the very outcomes effected (and effaced) through them at the level of manifest legal positivity, legal ideology, and the discourse-theoretical level of legal validity and legal rationality, thereby accounting for the self-evading and definition-defying lack of conceptual identity *vis-à-vis* the "ultimate" grounds of law. *Différance*, as the infrastructure level precondition of meaning-production through sense-differentiation, also entails an element of radical equivocality or undecidability, to the effect that the conceptual identity of *différance* cannot be locked up in either of the two "strings" or "cords" involved, i.e. spacing/temporisation or deferral/distancing. Thus, the two "strings" or "facets" of infrastructures involved, i.e. radical *undecidability* and *différance*, lean towards and presuppose each other, without being totally overlapping.

Radical undecidability draws the external boundaries of law in terms of legal ontology, legal epistemology and legal methodology; whereas *différance* is aligned with the internal functioning of law thus grounded/cancelled or effected/effaced within the conceptual confines defined by such philosophical equivocality. An insight into the infrastructures of law, as encountered at the ultimate edges of Western metaphysics and at the very heart of linguistic and legal signification, will eventually lead to a *deconstruction* of the final premises of law. Therefore, we will finally end up in twisting Wittgenstein: *Wovon man nicht sprechen kann, darüber muss man schreiben—Whereof one cannot speak, thereupon must writing be inscribed.*[14] The resulting positivity of language and the conceptual "order of things" in the (external) world thereby effected is ultimately conditional on the prelogical and preconceptual infrastructures of human knowledge and judgment within the Western philosophical tradition which, by force of their self-evading non-identity, are decisively beyond the reach of metaphysics and linguistic conceptualisation.

3. CONCEPTUAL ANALYTICS OF PRECEDENT-NORM FORMATION, PRESENTED IN THE FORM OF A TRIANGLE (OR "ICEBERG")

A legal norm may be divided into the two elements of *form* and *content*, reflecting the end result of the two-fold formative process of legal norm constitution, on the one hand, and the ascription of a specific meaning-content to the norm thereby established, on the other. The logico-conceptual distance which extends between the two elements of formal norm constitution (and disintegration) and the production (and dispersement) of meaning *vis-à-vis* the *ratio* of a case, is at its narrowest on the surface-structure level of legal positivity, and at its widest on the discourse-theoretical level of legal validity and legal rationality. In other words, the identification of the *ratio/dicta* distinction and the specific reading of the *ratio* are closely intertwined at the surface-structure level of operative adjudication. At the level of legal ideology, in turn, the theoretical prerequisites of legal norm constitution (and disintegration) and the production (and dissemination) of meaning are still thought to make up a relatively coherent whole under the unifying premises of the precedent ideology in fact adopted by the judiciary. The axiomatic postulates of legal validity and legal rationality at the discourse-theoretical level of law are essentially two-fold in structure, as can be inferred from the non-reducibility of the two criteria and the conceptual claims involved, i.e. the claim to legal authority and the claim to legal correctness, with respect to one another.

The question of such a logico-conceptual distance between legal norm constitution and judicial signification is, however, misplaced in relation to the infrastructure level prerequisites of law. The prelogical and preconceptual infrastructures of legal norm constitution which effect/efface the basic categories of norm/fact, validity/existence, *Sein/Sollen*, *logos/mythos*, reason/non-reason, etc., and the specific infrastructures of linguistic and judicial signification which

[14] Or: *Wovon man nicht sprechen kann, darüber muss man Schreiben gründen.* Cf.: "Wovon man nicht sprechen kann, darüber muss man schweigen"—"Whereof one cannot speak, thereof one must be silent": L. Wittgenstein, *Tractatus Logico-Philosophicus* (Routledge and Kegan Paul, 1986), § 7 (p. 188/189). Cf. ibid., Vorwort/Preface, 26/27.

provide for the production/dissolution of a norm's meaning-content in terms of the same/other, identical/different, synchronic/diachronic, deferral/distancing, etc., lean towards and presuppose each other, without totally overlapping or being identical. In consequence, Figure 5 which was presented at the beginning of Part B of this book, should, in fact, be drawn in the form of a triangle or, rather,

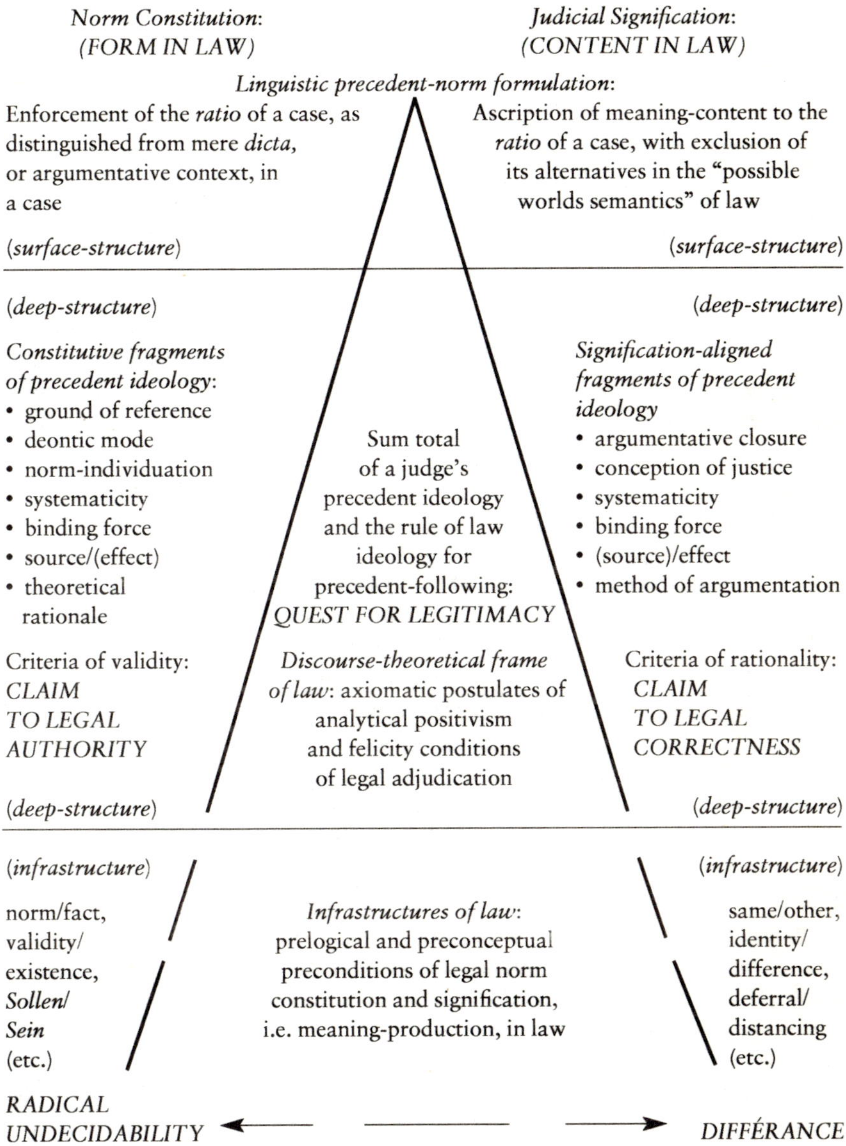

Figure 9: The logico-conceptual distance between the constitutive and signification-aligned premises of the *ratio* of a case, presented in the form of a triangle (or *iceberg*)

an *iceberg*, the base line and full extension of which cannot be seen from above the water line, i.e. the surface-structure level of operative adjudication.

4. THEORY AND PRACTICE OF PRECEDENTS

The present inquiry into the theoretical premises of precedent-following proceeded from a rational *reconstruction* of a judge's precedent ideology and the deep-structure postulates of legal validity and legal rationality entailed in the analytical and positivist conception of law, to a relatively complex *deconstruction* of the very "ultimate" or "final" prerequisites of law and legal discourse. Due to their highly theory-laden character, such outcomes of analysis might be thought to be without any genuine bearing on the course and content of law as it takes place on the surface-structure level of operative adjudication. As was argued in chapter 1, the surface-structure level of operative adjudication may function more or less satisfactorily even without a fully self-reflected conception of the deeper-structure level preconditions of precedent-identification and precedent-following among the judiciary, if only the tacit knowledge of "how to deal with precedents" is rich and detailed enough in the legal system concerned, conveying operative patterns of legal reasoning for judges. Even then, however, an insight into the latently functioning, deep-structure level preconditions of precedent-following will make the legal system far less vulnerable to the inherent threats of systemic volatility and instability that may be induced by the inherent shortcomings of some specific precedent ideology, or a cluster of ideological fragments drawn from several pure types of precedent ideology.

A legal system is even more exposed to the threat of such systemic imbalance and defects if there is no deeply rooted tradition on *how to do things with precedents* among the judiciary. A haphazard, blindfolded adoption of some specific precedent ideology, without first having gained an adequate insight into the theoretical and philosophical consequences which are, by necessity, entailed therein, may bring about grave systemic defects in the form of operative malfunctioning and systemic volatility. That was illustrated above by the Italian judicial experience with its overwhelming flood of precedents under the two sets of mutually discordant premises of legal positivist and legal pragmatic kind, and by the perplexities induced by the quasi-legislative "ruling by judicial headnotes" precedent ideology in Finland. In general, the relative success or failure of a legal system to produce and effectively maintain a well-functioning system of precedent-following is, to a great extent, conditional on whether judges and the legal profession have duly grasped the deeper-structure level premises of precedent-based legal adjudication and, in particular, the compatibility of the precedent ideology in fact adopted by them with the legal systemic constraints derived from the *transcategorical context* of precedent-following. To put it concisely, there are things that simply cannot be done with a set of precedents, not even with the best of a judge's noble intentions, if the inherent restrictions of precedent-following are not duly observed. The reflections put forth in the Part A of this treatise (chapters 1–5), may be read as a systemic outline of what can and what possibly cannot be done with precedents, if a certain conception of precedent-identification and precedent-following has been adopted by the judiciary.

To concretise the issue, some key fragments of the quasi-legislative precedent ideology in the form of headnote-oriented judicial positivism were detected in Finland. Such a doctrine of precedent-identification was semi-officially professed by some of the justices of the Supreme Court in the mid-1980s. Moreover, it was defended by the leading scholar of the field in a standard reference work in as late as 1997. Due to the existence of such ideological remnants in the Finnish doctrine of precedent-following, the criticism directed at the ideology of judicial quasi-legislation above will not count as "flogging a dead horse", or first raising and then knocking down some lifeless strawman, spun out of a legal scholar's wild-running philosophical fantasy. If precedent-based judicial adjudication is defined in terms of the abstract, canonised *ratio* of a case, as expressly laid down by the prior court in the headnote of the case, the advantages of judicial dynamics and quick responsiveness to the demands for social change, which are yet frequently associated with a well-functioning system of precedent-following, are irredeemably lost. Indeed, the overall impact of such quasi-legislative *rationes decidendi* will be one of "freezing" or "petrifying" the future course and content of judicial adjudication.

Moreover, the argumentative skills of *how to read precedents* will not be advanced among the judiciary and legal profession, if the deeper-level ideological premises of precedent-identification and precedent-following are not openly acknowledged, as the judicial experience drawn from Italy, France and Finland amply illustrates. On the theoretically barren or even inconsistent premises of precedent-following in those three civilian legal systems, there will be no proper incentive, nor any ideological or institutional support for the evolvement of genuine case-to-case reasoning on precedents among the judiciary and legal profession as a whole, no matter whether such reasoning is outlined in terms of backward-proceeding judicial exegesis, a realignment of the *ratio* of a case in the constant interplay of fact-based analogy and distinguishing, the "Herculean" task of constructing a seamless web of underlying reasons from a line of prior decisions, or a more-or-less radical revaluation of the merits of the prior decision—with reference to the leading ideas of *judicial exegesis*, *judicial analogy*, *systemic construction of underlying reasons of law*, and *judicial revaluation*, respectively. Instead, there may be a flood of discordant precedents under the inconsistent theoretical premises of legal positivism and legal pragmatism adopted both at the same time by different courts (Italy), a divergence of official action and the professional self-understanding of the judiciary (France), or a highly perplexed relation between the headnote of a case and the whole of judicial reasoning in it (Finland). In the absence of an adequate insight into the theoretical preconditions of how to read precedents, there will probably be unyielding resistance to any subsequent changes to the operative patterns of legal adjudication once taken into use.

The inherent properties of precedent-following will make judge-made law a highly responsive and dynamic instrument of social engineering and conflict-resolution, provided the doctrinal, institutional, ideological and discourse-theoretical determinants of legal adjudication are not permitted to place obstacles in its gradual evolvement. To my mind, a judge should not imitate the model of judicial activism effected by the legislator, nor yield to the *Montesquieu'ean* doctrine of absolute judicial passivism, as is professed by the *legislative paradigm* of precedent-following; nor should the judge take up the essentially legal scholarly task of constructing a seamless web of underlying reasons from a line of prior cases, as is professed by the Dworkin-inspired *systemic paradigm* of precedent-following; nor still should the judge reject the initial legal frame of analysis and, instead, take up the role of a moral and/or political philosopher, or even take resort to sheer semantic freeplay with truly Solomonic or less-noble intentions, as is professed by the *extra-legal paradigm* of adjudication. Instead, a judge—and especially a judge of the highest national court of justice—should be fully aware of the true potentials and, even more so, the inherent limitations of the feasible models of precedent-identification and precedent-following available to him, where the notions of judicial exegesis, reasoning based on fact-based analogy and distinguishing, or a thorough revaluation of the prior decision will have a crucial role to play in line with the theoretical premises of the *contextualist, dispute-solving paradigm* of precedent-following.

The resulting precedent-norm formulation is no more than a *tip of the iceberg*, supported and framed by the down-reaching edifice of the theoretical and philosophical premises of law at the deep-structure and infrastructure levels of legal discourse. The task left for jurisprudence and philosophy of law is, then, to bridge the logico-conceptual distance which extends between the urgent need for finality, certainty, authoritativeness and relative determinacy of law at the operative surface-structure level of legal adjudication, and the inherently volatile, fragmented or even fragile texture of the "ultimate" premises of law at the infrastructure level of the Western *épistémè*, as mediated by the fragments of legal ideology and the discourse-theoretical postulates of legal validity and legal rationality under analytical positivism. Unless the demands posited by the different levels of law are brought into balance in the context of judicial adjudication, systemic defects and malfunctioning is bound to emerge even at the operative surface-structure level of precedent-following.

5. READING THE LAW/SKATING ON THIN ICE

Under the self-imposed methodological rules of analytical positivism, the final reference of law is anchored in the sovereign's "orders backed by threats" (Austin), the transcendental-logical precondition of the hypothetical

Grundnorm (Kelsen), the ultimate rule of recognition (Hart), the "ultimate", fifth-level premises of legal justification (Wróblewski), a judge's normative ideology *vis-à-vis* the identification and interpretation of law (Ross), the ultimate legal source norm (Peczenik), underpinning reasons of law (MacCormick), the prevalent form of life, in the Wittgensteinian sense of the term, and avoidance of chaos in society (Aarnio, Peczenik), etc. The end point of justification is reached when the thread of argumentation is judged to be "strong enough" (Aarnio), in light of the specific meta-level rationality rules of legal discourse, taken as a special case of general practical discourse, and their universal-pragmatic mode of justification (Alexy). No inquiry is extended into the rationality ground of the concept of rationality itself, as that would signify "saying the unsayable" (Peczenik), questioning a "basic value" which cannot be further justified within legal discourse (Wróblewski), or casting doubt on a rationality conception that is culturally given to us (MacCormick). The final outcomes of analytical positivism are, in other words, equal to an insight into the surface-structure and deep-structure level phenomena of law in terms of the present treatise.

However, analytical positivism notably fails to give an adequate account of the *law behind the law* or the *law preceding the law*, i.e. the infrastructure level "ultimate" prerequisites of legal ontology, legal epistemology and legal methodology, which equally *effect/efface* or *ground/cancel* the resulting deep-structure level phenomena of legal validity (*auctoritas*) and legal rationality (*ratio*). Eventually, the self-imposed methodological confines of the analytical and positivist frame must be cast off, and the very concept of law must be (re)defined in more open-ended terms, in order to make room for the relentless quest for the "final" premises of law. Above, Derrida's deconstructive philosophy of *radical questioning* was taken to ground the "unlimited right to ask any question, to suspect all dogmatism, to analyze every presupposition, even those of the ethics or the politics of responsibility".[15] In obstinately "running up against the limits of language",[16] and trying to reach even beyond the "argumentative bedrock" of the claimed necessities of common sense and ordinary language, as laid down by Wittgenstein in his *Philosophical Investigations*[17] and the Oxford philosophy of ordinary language, Derrida's methodological request denotes that no individual tenet of a legal or philosophical theory, and not even the axiomatic postulates of analytical positivism, may successfully claim immunity or sheltered position before a critical inquiry into the "ultimate" prerequisites of such a discourse formation.

In the relentless quest for the final premises of law, the ontological, epistemological and methodological status of the ultimate grounds, edges, premises or criteria of law is endlessly dislocated, reframed, dissolved, deferred, distanced and redefined by force of the identity-evading infrastructures of formal norm

[15] Derrida, above at n. 10, 28.
[16] Wittgenstein, above at n. 11, § 119 (p. 48/48^{e}).
[17] Ibid., § 217 (p. 85/85^{e}).

constitution. Infrastructures of law successfully defy any effort at being conceptualised or drawn within the closed sphere of Western metaphysics, since they provide for the radically equivocal condition of possibility and impossibility of such metaphysics-laden conceptuality and the resulting "order of things" in the (external) world in the first place. In consequence, the infrastructures equally *effect/efface*, *ground/cancel* or *establish/level* off the resulting phenomena of legal validity and legal rationality within legal discourse.

Infrastructures of judicial signification, in turn, account for the production (and dissolution) of a specific meaning-content in law through the identity-aligned or *différance*-aligned infrastructures of "sense-making" within legal discourse, as ultimately defined in terms of: (1) *circular self-referentiality* and the reproduction of original identity of the *ratio* of a case in a subsequent case; (2) *syntagmatic differentiation* of a norm's meaning-content through case-to-case realignment or deferral/distancing of sense; (3) *paradigmatic differentiation* of a norm's meaning-content by recourse to the latent signification structure "beneath" the manifest positivity of law, in disregard of any expressly given precedent-norm and/or reasons formulation; and (4) *radical alterity* of meaning-content, with rejection of the formally legal frame of judicial decision-making and the preference given to the pre-legal, i.e. moral (axiological), political (teleological), or entirely free (intuitive) background premises of judicial decision-making.

Reading the law—like philosophy, literature, or any other specific discourse formation within the Western *épistémè*—is like long-distance *skating on thin ice* in the late springtime. There is no safe retreat from the vast, dazzling field of ice extending over a great forest lake or sea, once you have taken the hazardous effort of such skating/reading, calmly overlooking the well-intentioned warnings of the legal positivists, who prefer to stay on a solid ground or "argumentative bedrock" (Wittgenstein) of their own choice and definition, and the reductionist disbelief shared by the *Crits*, for whom the law is no more than "frozen politics" (Unger), or an inherently fragile and volatile mixture of social interests, power and ideology.

Guided only by the *song of the ice* underneath the skates and your own (hopefully) sharp sight and prudence, it would be foolish to simply close your eyes and naively ignore the cracks and fractures which may be there, on and below the visible surface of the ice/text. Due to such flaws in its inner composition and the external pressure now inflicted upon it, the ice/text may suddenly break, leaving you in the midst of the shattered premises of failing normativity, faltering rationality and the fragments of sense-dislocating textuality. Therefore, having the right equipment for the risky encounter with the ice/text is of critical importance, as provided by Derrida and the philosophy of deconstruction: a metal-pointed *ice-pike* to try the strength of the ice/text before and around you, and—once the ice/text has broken—a pair of needle-sharp *ice-prods* to get a firm grip of the edge of the ice/text/reality and to drag yourself out of the ice-cold water.

Rejecting the deceptive illusion of a predetermined reference ground, end point of legal justification, firm foundation of judgment, solid argumentative bedrock, or transcendental signified for the law, as all too hastily proclaimed by the legal positivists, and equally declining to accept the reductionist disbelief shared by the *Crits*, for whom the law is politics in thin disguise, legal discourse is ultimately premised on the *infrastructures* of Western metaphysics. In the last resort, the positivity of law is conditional on the two-fold prelogical and preconceptual movement of, first, self-effacing self-referentiality, as effected/effaced in the radical *undecidability* of the very final grounds, criteria or edges of law, and, second, the endless production/dissolution of novel sense in law through the fugitive double-play of spacing/temporisation or deferral/distancing, i.e. *différance*.

Bibliography

AARNIO, A. (1982) *Oikeussäännösten tulkinnasta* (Helsinki: Juridica).

——(1987) *The Rational as Reasonable: A Treatise on Legal Justification* (Dordrecht/Boston/Lancaster/Tokyo: D. Reidel Publishing Co.).

——(1989) *Laintulkinnan teoria* (Juva: WSOY).

——(1989) "Taking Rules Seriously", 42 *ARSP Beiheft* 180 (proceedings of the fourteenth IVR World Congress in Edinburgh, August 1989) (Stuttgart: Franz Steiner Verlag).

——(1991) "Statutory Interpretation in Finland", in D.N. MacCormick and R.S. Summers (eds), *Interpreting Statutes: A Comparative Study* (Aldershot: Dartmouth).

——(1997) "On the Predictability of Judicial Decisions", in M. Hyvärinen and K. Pietilä (eds), *The Institutes We Live By* (University of Tampere: Publications of the Research Institute for Social Science).

——(1997) "Precedent in Finland", in D.N. MacCormick and R.S. Summers (eds), *Interpreting Precedents: A Comparative Study* (Aldershot: Ashgate/Dartmouth).

——(1997) *Reason and Authority: A Treatise on the Dynamic Paradigm of Legal Dogmatics* (Aldershot: Ashgate/Dartmouth).

AARNIO, A., ALEXY, R, and PECZENIK, A. (1981) "The Foundation of Legal Reasoning, II: The Justification of Legal Transformations by Rational Legal Discourse", 12 *Rechtstheorie* 257.

AARNIO, A. and PECZENIK, A. (1995) "*Suum Cuique Tribuere*: Some Reflections on Law, Freedom and Justice", 8 *Ratio Juris* 145.

ALEXANDER, L. (1994) "Constrained by Precedent", 63 *Southern California Law Review* 3 (reprinted in M. Arnheim (ed.) (1994), *Common Law* (The International Library of Law and Legal Theory. Aldershot: Dartmouth)).

——(1996) "Precedent", in D. Patterson (ed.), *A Companion to Philosophy of Law and Legal Theory* (Blackwell Companions to Philosophy, Cambridge (Massachusetts) and Oxford: Blackwell Publishers).

ALEXY, R. (1985) *Theorie der Grundrechte* (Baden-Baden: Nomos Verlagsgesellschaft).

——(1989) *A Theory of Legal Argumentation: The Theory of Rational Discourse as Theory of Legal Argumentation* (Oxford: Clarendon Press).

——(1989) "On Necessary Relations Between Law and Morality", 2 *Ratio Juris* 167.

——(1992) *Begriff und Geltung des Rechts* (Freiburg/München: Verlag Karl Alber).

——(1992) "Individual Rights and Collective Goods", in C. Nino (ed.), *Rights* (The International Library of Law and Legal Theory. Aldershot: Dartmouth).

ALEXY, R. and DREIER, R. (1997) "Precedent in the Federal Republic of Germany", in D.N. MacCormick and R.S. Summers (eds), *Interpreting Precedents: A Comparative Study* (Aldershot: Ashgate/Dartmouth).

——(1991) "Statutory Interpretation in the Federal Republic of Germany", in D.N. MacCormick and R.S. Summers (eds), *Interpreting Statutes: A Comparative Study* (Aldershot: Dartmouth).

ALLEN, C.K. (1964) *Law in the Making* (Oxford: Oxford University Press, 7th ed.).

Andenas, M. (ed.) (1994) *Article 177 References to the European Courts—Policy and Practice* (London, Dublin, Edinburgh: Butterworths).

Anscombe, E. (1958) "On Brute Facts", 18 *Analysis* 69.

Arnaud, A.-J. *et al.* (eds) (1993) *Dictionnaire encyclopédique de théorie et de sociologie du droit* (Paris: LGDJ, 2nd ed.).

Atiyah, P.S. and Summers, R.S. (1987) *Form and Substance in Anglo-American Law: A Comparative Study of Legal Reasoning, Legal Theory, and Legal Institutions* (Oxford: Clarendon Press).

Audi, R. (ed.) (1995) *The Cambridge Dictionary of Philosophy* (Cambridge University Press).

Austin, J. (1995) *The Province of Jurisprudence Determined* (Cambridge: Cambridge University Press).

Austin, J.L. (1955) *How To Do Things With Words* (The William James Lectures delivered in Harvard University in 1955) (Oxford, New York: Oxford University Press, 2nd ed.).

Balkin, J.M. (1987) "Deconstructive Practice and Legal Theory", 96 *The Yale Law Journal* 743.

—— (1989/90) "Nested Oppositions", 99 *The Yale Law Journal* 1669.

—— (1993) "Tradition, Betrayal, and the Politics of Deconstruction", in S.J. Brison and W. Sinnott-Armstrong (eds), *Contemporary Perspectives in Constitutional Interpretation* (Boulder, San Francisco and Oxford: Westview Press).

—— (1996) "Deconstruction", in D. Patterson (ed.), A *Companion to Philosophy of Law and Legal Theory* (Blackwell Companions to Philosophy, Cambridge (Massachusetts) and Oxford: Blackwell Publishers).

Bankowski, Z. (1995) "Analogical Reasoning and Legal Institutions", in Z. Bankowski, I. White and U. Hahn (eds), *Informatics and the Foundations of Legal Reasoning* (Law and Philosophy Library, Vol. 21: Dordrecht, Boston and London: Kluwer).

Bankowski, Z. and MacCormick, D.N. (1991) "Statutory Interpretation in the United Kingdom", in D.N. MacCormick and R.S. Summers (eds), *Interpreting Statutes: A Comparative Study* (Aldershot: Dartmouth).

Bankowski, Z., MacCormick, D.N. and Marshall, G. (1997) "Precedent in the United Kingdom", in D.N. MacCormick and R.S. Summers (eds), *Interpreting Precedents: A Comparative Study* (Aldershot: Ashgate/Dartmouth).

Bayles, M.D. (1992) *Hart's Legal Philosophy: An Examination* (Law and Philosophy Library, Vol. 17: Dordrecht, Boston and London: Kluwer).

Bentham, J. (1992) *Justice and Codification Petitions: Being Forms Proposed for Signature by All Persons Whose Desire It Is To See Justice* No *Longer Sold, Delayed, or Denied: and To Obtain A Possibility of That Knowledge of the Law, in Proportion to the Want of Which They Are Subjected to Unjust Punishments, and Deprived of the Benefit of their Rights. Drafts for the Above Petitions* (Littleton, Colorado: Fred. B. Rothman & Co.).

Bingham, J.W. (1992) "What Is the Law?", XI *Michingan Law Review* 109 (reprinted in R.S. Summers (ed.) (1992), *American Legal Theory* (The International Library of Law and Legal Theory, Aldershot: Dartmouth)).

Borges, J.L. (1987) "*Del rigor en la ciencia*", in *El hacedor* (Madrid: Alianza Editorial).

—— (1972) "On Exactitude in Science", in *Universal History of Infamy* (New York: Penguin Books).

Brison, S.J. and Sinnott-Armstrong, W. (1993) An Introduction to Balkin's Essay

"Tradition, Betrayal, and the Politics of Deconstruction", in S.J. Brison, and W. Sinnott-Armstrong (eds), *Contemporary Perspectives in Constitutional Interpretation* (Boulder, San Francisco, Oxford: Westview Press).

CAPPELLETTI, M. (1989) *The Judicial Process in Comparative Perspective* (Oxford: Clarendon Press).

CAPUTO, J.D. (1993) "On Not Circumventing the Quasi-Transcendental: The Case of Rorty and Derrida", in G.B. Madison (ed.), *Working through Derrida* (Evanston, Illinois: Northwestern University Press).

CHOMSKY, N. (1986) *Knowledge of Language: Its Nature, Origin and Use* (New York: Praeger).

COOK, W.W. (1924) "The Logical and Legal Bases of the Conflict of Laws", 23 *The Yale Law Journal* 457 (reprinted in R.S. Summers (ed.) (1992), *American Legal Theory* (The International Library of Law and Legal Theory, Aldershot: Dartmouth)).

—— (1927) "Scientific Method and the Law", XIII *American Bar Association* 303.

CROSS, R. and HARRIS, J.W. (1991) *Precedent in English Law* (Oxford: Clarendon Press, 4th ed.).

DAHLBOHM, P. (ed.) (1996) *KKO—Opas. Kokeilulaitos 7.11.1996* (Helsinki: Korkein Oikeus).

DALTON, C. (1985) "An Essay in the Deconstruction of Contract Doctrine", 94 *The Yale Law Journal* 997.

DAWSON, J.P. (1978) *The Oracles of the Law* (Westport, Connecticut: Greenwood Press).

DE SAUSSURE, F. (1995) *Cours de linguistique générale* (Paris: Grande Bibliothèque Payot).

DE SOUSA SANTOS, B. (1987) "Law: A Map of Misreading. Towards a Postmodern Conception of Law", 14 *Journal of Law and Society* 279.

DERRIDA, J. (1972) *Positions: Entretiens avec Henri Ronse, Julia Kristeva, Jean-Louis Houdebine, Guy Scarpetta* (Paris: Éditions de Minuit).

—— (1976) *On Grammatology* (Baltimore and London: The Johns Hopkins University Press).

—— (1982) "Différance", in *Margins of Philosophy* (Great Britain: The Harvester Press).

—— (1987) "*Lettre à un ami japonais*", in *Psyché: Inventions de l'autre* (Paris: Éditions Galilée).

—— (1988) "Letter to A Japanese Friend", in D. Wood and R. Bernasconi (eds), *Derrida and Différance* (Evanston, IL: Northwestern University Press).

—— (1993) *Dissemination* (London: The Athlone Press).

—— (1995) *On the Name* (Stanford, California: Stanford University Press).

—— (1995) *Points . . . Interviews, 1974–1994* (Stanford, California: Stanford University Press).

DERRIDA, J. and CAPUTO, J.D. (1997) *Deconstruction in a Nutshell: A Conversation with Jacques Derrida* (New York: Fordham University Press).

DEVLIN LORD P. (1959) *The Enforcement of Morals* (Oxford: Oxford University Press).

DWORKIN, R. (1967) "The Model of Rules, I", (1978) in *Taking Rights Seriously*. With a New Appendix, a Response to Critics (Cambridge, Massachusetts: Harvard University Press).

—— (1972) "The Model of Rules, II", (1978) in *Taking Rights Seriously*. With a New Appendix, a Response to Critics (Cambridge, Massachusetts: Harvard University Press).

—— (1975) "Hard Cases", (1978) in *Taking Rights Seriously*. With a New Appendix, a Response to Critics (Cambridge, Massachusetts: Harvard University Press).

DWORKIN, R. (1978) *Taking Rights Seriously*. With a New Appendix, a Response to Critics (Cambridge, Massachusetts: Harvard University Press).

—— (1982) "Law as Interpretation", 60 *Texas Law Review* 527 (reprinted in A. Aarnio and D.N. MacCormick (eds), *Legal Reasoning, Vol. II* (The International Library of Law and Legal Theory. Aldershot: Dartmouth)).

—— (1986) *Law's Empire* (London: Fontana Masterguides).

EISELE, T.D. (1992) " 'Our Real Need': Not Explanation, But Education", in D.M. Patterson (ed.), *Wittgenstein and Legal Theory* (Boulder, San Francisco, Oxford: Westview Press).

EISENBERG, M.A. (1988) *The Nature of the Common Law* (Cambridge, Massachusetts and London: Harvard University Press).

EKELÖF, P.O. (1958) "Teleological Construction of Statutes", 2 *Scandinavian Studies in Law* 76 (reprinted in A. Aarnio and D.N. MacCormick (eds), *Legal Reasoning, Vol. II* (Aldershot: Dartmouth)).

EKELÖF, P.O. and BOMAN, R. (1990) *Rättegång. Första häftet* (Sjunde upplagan. Stockholm: Nordstedts Förlag).

ESSER, J. (1956) *Grundsatz und Norm in der richterlichen Fortbildung des Privatrechts* (Tübingen: JCB Mohr).

EWALD, F. (1988) "The Law of Law", in G. Teubner (ed.), *Autopoietic Law: A New Approach to Law and Society* (Berlin, New York: Walter de Gruyter).

FINNIS, J. (1980) *Natural Law and Natural Rights* (Oxford: Oxford University Press, Clarendon Law Series).

FISH, S. (1989) *Doing What Comes Naturally: Change, Rhetoric, and the Practice of Theory in Literary and Legal Studies* (Durham and London: Duke University Press).

FOUCAULT, M. (1966) *Les Mots et les choses: Une Archéologie des Sciences Humaines* (Bibliothèque des Sciences humaines. Paris: Éditions Gallimard).

—— (1969) *L'Archéologie du savoir* (Bibliothèque des Sciences humaines. Paris: Éditions Gallimard).

FRANK, J. (1930) *Law and the Modern Mind* (Gloucester, Mass.: Peter Smith).

FRIEDMANN, W. (1967) *Legal Theory* (London: Stevens & Sons, 5th ed.).

FULLER, L.L. (1934) "American Legal Realism", 82 *University of Pennsylvania Law Review* 429 (reprinted in R.S. Summers (ed.), *American Legal Theory* (The International Library of Law and Legal Theory, Aldershot: Dartmouth)).

—— (1969) *The Morality of Law* (New Haven and London: Yale University Press).

GARNER, B.A. (1995) *A Dictionary of Modern Legal Usage* (Oxford: Oxford University Press, 2nd ed.).

GASCHÉ, R. (1986) *The Tain of the Mirror: Derrida and the Philosophy of Reflection* (Cambridge, Massachusetts and London: Harvard University Press).

GOODHART, A.L. (1930) "Determining the *Ratio Decidendi* of A Case", *Yale Law Journal* (reprinted in A.L. Goodhart (1931), *Essays in Jurisprudence and the Common Law* (London, New York: Cambridge University Press).

—— (1959) "The *Ratio Decidendi* of a Case", 22 *Modern Law Review* 117.

GOLDSTEIN, L. (ed.) (1991) *Precedent in Law* (Oxford: Oxford University Press).

GREIMAS, A.J. and COURTÉS, J. (1993) *Sémiotique: Dictionnaire raisonné de la théorie du langage* (Paris: Hachette Livre).

HABERMAS, J. (1987) "*Wie ist Legitimität durch Legalität möglich?*", 20 *Kritische Justiz* 1.

—— (1989) "*Wahrheitstheorien*", in *Vorstudien und Ergänzungen zur Theorie des kommunikativen Handelns* (Frankfurt am Main: Suhrkamp).

HÄNNINEN, S. (1981) *Aika, paikka, politiikka: Marxilaisen valtioteorian konstituutiosta ja metodista* (Oulu: Tutkijaliiton julkaisusarja 17).

HART, H.L.A. (1961) *The Concept of Law* (Oxford: Clarendon Press).

——(1982) *Law, Liberty and Morality* (Oxford: Oxford University Press).

——(1983) "American Jurisprudence through English Eyes: The Nightmare and the Noble Dream", in *Essays in Jurisprudence and Philosophy* (Oxford: Clarendon Press, 1983).

——(1983) "Lon L. Fuller: *The Morality of Law*", in *Essays in Jurisprudence and Philosophy* (Oxford: Clarendon Press).

——(1983) "Positivism and the Separation of Law from Morals", in *Essays in Jurisprudence and Philosophy* (Oxford: Clarendon Press).

——(1994) *The Concept of Law* (Oxford: Clarendon Press, 2nd ed.).

HARTNEY, M. (1991) "Introduction: The Final Form of The *Pure Theory of Law*", in H. Kelsen, *A General Theory of Norms* (Oxford: Oxford University Press).

HEDEMANN, J.W. (1933) *Die Flucht in die Generalklauseln: Eine Gefahr für Recht und Staat* (Tübingen: JCB Mohr).

HEINONEN, O. (1985) "*Kuka saa juttunsa Korkeimman oikeuden tutkittavaksi?*", *Lakimiesuutiset* 30.

——(1990) Book Review on P. Timonen (ed.), *Johdatus Suomen oikeusjärjestelmään, 1–2*, in *Oikeus* 161.

——(1991) "*Korkeimman oikeuden rooli muuttuvassa ympäristössä*", *Lakimies* 229.

HELIN, M. (1988) *Lainoppi ja metafysiikka: Tutkimus skandinaavisen oikeusrealismin tieteenkuvasta ja sen vaikutuksesta Suomen siviilioikeuden tutkimuksessa vuosina 1920–1960* (Helsinki: Suomalaisen lakimiesyhdistyksen julkaisuja).

HOHFELD, W.N. (1964) *Fundamental Legal Conceptions as Applied in Judicial Reasoning* (New Haven and London: Yale University Press).

HOLMES, O.W. Jr. (1897) "The Path of the Law", 10 *Harvard Law Review* 457.

——(1992)"The Common Law" (extract) (reprinted in *The Essential Holmes: Selections from the Letters, Speeches, Judicial Opinions, and Other Writings of Oliver Wendell Holmes* (Chicago: The University of Chicago Press)).

HONDERICH, T. (ed.) (1995) *The Oxford Companion to Philosophy* (Oxford: Oxford University Press).

HUTCHESON, J.C. Jr. (1929) "The Judgment Intuitive: The Function of the 'Hunch' in Judicial Decision", 14 *Cornell Law Quarterly* 274.

JÄÄSKINEN, N. (1986) "*Ennakkopäätösten merkityksestä yleisen lain alalla*", in U. Kangas and K. Tuori (eds), *Liber Amicorum Carolo Makkonen Deditus* (Helsinki: Yliopistopaino).

JAKOBSON, R. (1960) "Linguistics and Poetics", in A.S. Thomas (ed.), *Style in Language* (Cambridge, Massachusetts: The M.I.T. Press).

JELLINEK, G. (1960) *Allgemeine Staatslehre* (Dritte Auflage, siebenter Neudruck. Bad Homburg vor der Höhe: Hermann Gentner Verlag).

JORI, MARIO: "Introduction", in M. Jori (ed.). *Legal Positivism* (The International Library of Law and Legal Theory. Aldershot: Dartmouth).

KANT, I. (1998) *Critique of Pure Reason*. Translated and edited by P. Guyer and A.W. Wood (United States: Cambridge University Press).

KELSEN, H. (1925) *Allgemeine Staatslehre* (Wien: Österreichische Staatsdruckerei).

——(1949) *General Theory of Law and State* (Cambridge, Massachusetts: Harvard University Press).

KELSEN, H. (1960) *Reine Rechtslehre. Mit einem Anhang: Das Problem der Gerechtigkeit* (Wien: Verlag Franz Deuticke).

—— (1965) "*Was ist Juristischer Positivismus?*", 20 *Juristen-Zeitung* (reprinted in H. Klecatscky, R. Marcic and H. Schambeck (eds) (1968), *Die Wiener Rechtstheoretische Schule. Schriften von Hans Kelsen, Adolf Merkl, Alfred Verdross* (Wien: Europa Verlag).

—— (1988) "*Rechtswissenschaft und Recht. Erledigung eines Versuchs zur Überwindung der 'Rechtsdogmatik'*", in F. Sander and H. Kelsen, *Die Rolle des Neukantianismus in der Reinen Rechtslehre. Eine Debatte zwischen Sander und Kelsen* (Aalen: Scientia Verlag).

—— (1989) *Pure Theory of Law* (Gloucester, Massachusetts: Peter Smith).

—— (1991) *General Theory of Norms* (Oxford: Oxford University Press).

—— (1992) *Introduction to the Problems of Legal Theory: A Translation of the First Edition of the Reine Rechtslehre or Pure Theory of Law* (Oxford University Press,).

—— (1994) *Reine Rechtslehre: Einleitung in die rechtswissenschafliche Problematik* (Aalen: Scientia Verlag).

KENNEDY, D. (1997) *A Critique of Adjudication {fin de siècle}* (Cambridge, Massachusetts and London: Harvard University Press).

KLAMI, H.T. (1980) *Anti-Legalism: Five Essays in the Finalistic Theory of Law* (Turku: Turun yliopiston julkaisuja).

—— (1980) *Finalistinen oikeusteoria* (Turku: Turun yliopiston yksityisoikeuden laitoksen julkaisuja).

—— (1983) *Ihmisen säännöt: Tutkimus oikeuden olemuksesta, synnystä ja toiminnasta* (Turku: Turun yliopiston julkaisuja).

KLECATSCKY, H., MARCIC, R. and SCHAMBECK, H. (eds) (1968) *Die Wiener Rechtstheoretische Schule: Schriften von Hans Kelsen, Adolf Merkl, Alfred Verdross.* (Wien: Europa Verlag).

KOSKENNIEMI, M. (1989) *From Apology to Utopia: The Structure of International Legal Argument* (Helsinki: Lakimiesliiton Kustannus).

—— (1990) "The Politics of International Law", 1 *European Journal of International Law* 4.

LA TORRE, M., PATTARO, E. and TARUFFO, M. (1991) "Statutory Interpretation in Italy", in D.N. MacCormick and R.S. Summers (eds), *Interpreting Statutes: A Comparative Study* (Aldershot: Dartmouth).

LEVI, E.H. (1949) *An Introduction to Legal Reasoning* (Chicago and London: The Chicago University Press).

LINNA, T. (1989) "*Korkeimman oikeuden päätösten otsikoista*", *Lakimies* 772.

—— (1990) "*Korkeimman oikeuden päätösotsikkojen tehtävistä*", *Lakimies* 969.

LLEWELLYN, K. (1991) *The Bramble Bush: On Our Law and Its Study* (New York: Oceana Publications).

LUHMANN, N. (1993) *Das Recht der Gesellschaft* (Frankfurt am Main: Suhrkamp Verlag).

MACCORMICK, N. (1978) *Legal Reasoning and Legal Theory* (Oxford: Oxford University Press).

—— (1981) *H.L.A. Hart*. Jurists: Profiles in Legal Theory (London: Edward Arnold).

—— (1991) "Why Cases Have Rationes and What These Are", in L. Goldstein (ed.), *Precedent in Law* (Oxford: Oxford University Press).

—— (1995)"Defeasibility in Law and Logic", in Z. Bankowski, I. White and U. Hahn (eds), *Informatics and the Foundations of Legal Reasoning* (Law and Philosophy Library, Vol. 21. Dordrecht, Boston and London: Kluwer).

——(1998) *Examiner's Preliminary Report on A Theory of Precedent*, by R. Siltala, candidate for the degree of Dr. Jur. Submitted to the Law Faculty of the University in Helsinki, for the Faculty Board Meeting, 28 May 1998.

——(1998) "Raimo Siltala, *A Theory of Precedent: From Analytical Positivism to A Post-Analytical Philosophy of Law*, Opponent's Review", in *Oikeus* 424.

MacCormick, D.N, and Summers, R.S. (1991) "Interpretation and Justification", in N.D. MacCormick and R.S. Summers (eds), *Interpreting Statutes: A Comparative Study* (Aldershot: Dartmouth).

——(1991) *Interpreting Statutes: A Comparative Study* (Aldershot: Dartmouth).

——(1997) *Interpreting Precedents: A Comparative Study* (Aldershot: Ashgate/Dartmouth).

MacCormick, N. and Weinberger, O. (1986) *An Institutional Theory of Law: New Approaches to Legal Positivism* (Law and Philosophy Library, Vol. 3. Dordrecht, Boston, Lancaster and Tokyo: D. Reidel Publishing Co.).

Malcolm, N. (1990) *Ludwig Wittgenstein. Muistelma* (Juva: WSOY).

Merkl, A.J. (1931) "*Prolegomena einer Theorie des rechtlichen Stufenbaues*", in *Gesammelte Schriften. Erster Band: Grundlagen des Rechts, Teilband 1* (Berlin: Duncker & Humblot).

Miettinen, M. (1979) "*Prejudikaattidispenssistä valituslupaan*", in *Korkein Oikeus 60 vuotta* (Helsinki: Valtion painatuskeskus).

Montesquieu, Baron de (1951) *L'esprit des lois*, in *Oeuvres Complètes, II* (Bibliothèque de Pléiade. Paris: Gallimard).

Morawetz, T. (1992) "Epistemology of Judging. Wittgenstein and Deliberative Practices", in D.M. Patterson (ed.), *Wittgenstein and Legal Theory* (Boulder, San Francisco and Oxford: Westview Press).

Nagel, T. (1986) *The View from Nowhere* (New York and Oxford: Oxford University Press).

Nöth, W. (1990) *Handbook of Semiotics* (Bloomington and Indianapolis: Indiana University Press).

Oliphant, H. (1928) "A Return to Stare Decisis: Stare Decisis—Continued", 14 *American Bar Association Journal* 159 (reprinted in R.S. Summers (ed.), *American Legal Theory* (Aldershot: Dartmouth)).

Olsson, C. (1985) "*Om rättsutveckling genom dom*", *Lakimies* 1182.

The Oxford Concise Dictionary (1995) (Oxford, New York: Oxford University Press, 9th ed.).

Paulson, S.L. (1993) "*Die Unterschiedlichen Formulierungen der 'Grundnorm'* ", in A. Aarnio, S.L. Paulson, O. Weinberger, G.H. von Wright and D. Wyduckel (eds), *Rechtsnorm und Rechtswirklichkeit: Festschrift für Werner Krawietz zum 60. Geburtstag* (Berlin: Duncker & Humblot).

Peczenik, A. (1983) *The Basis of Legal Justification* (Lund: Infotryck AB).

——(1989) *On Law and Reason* (Law and Philosophy Library, Vol. 8. Dordrecht, Boston and London: Kluwer).

——(1995) *Vad är rätt? Om demokrati, rättssäkerhet, etik och juridisk argumentation* (Stockholm: Nordstedts juridik).

——(1997) "The Binding Force of Precedent", in D.N. MacCormick and R.S. Summers (eds), *Interpreting Precedents: A Comparative Study* (Aldershot: Ashgate/Dartmouth).

Perelman, C. and Olbrechts-Tyteca, L. (1988) *La nouvelle Rhétorique: Traité de l'Argumentation.* (Bruxelles: Éditions de l'Université du Bruxelles, 5th ed.).

PLATO (1953) *Timaeus* (Oxford: Clarendon Press, 4th ed.).

POUND, R. (1910) "Law in Books and Law in Action", 44 *American Law Review* 12.

RASMUSSEN, H. (1988) *On Law and Policy in the European Court of Justice* (Dordrecht: Martinus Nijhoff Publishers).

——(1994) "Docket Control Mechanism, the EC Court and the Preliminary References Procedure", in M. Andenas (ed.), *Article 177 References to the European Courts—Policy and Practice* (London, Dublin and Edinburgh: Butterworths).

RAWLS, J. (1955) "Two Concepts of Rules", in LXIV *The Philosophical Review* 3.

——(1972) *A Theory of Justice* (London, Oxford and New York: Oxford University Press).

ROSS, A. (1953) *Om ret og retfærdighed: En indførelse i den analytiske retsfilosofi* (København: Nyt nordisk forslag).

——(1958) *On Law and Justice* (Berkeley, Los Angeles: University of California Press).

RUIZ M.A. and LAPORTA, F. (1997) "Precedent in Spain", in D.N. MacCormick and R.S. Summers (eds), *Interpreting Precedents: A Comparative Study* (Aldershot: Ashgate/ Dartmouth).

RYLE, G. (1949) *The Concept of Mind* (Middlesex: Penguin/Peregrine Books).

SANDER, F. and KELSEN, H. (1988) *Die Rolle des Neukantianismus in der Reinen Rechtslehre: Eine Debatte zwischen Sander und Kelsen* (Aalen: Scientia Verlag).

SARAVIITA, I. (1985) "*Muutama sananen Korkeimman oikeuden ennakkopäätösten sitovuudesta*", *Lakimies* 373.

SARTOR, G. (1995) "Defeasibility in Legal Reasoning", in Z. Bankowski, I. White and U. Hahn (eds), *Informatics and the Foundations of Legal Reasoning* (Law and Philosophy Library, Vol. 21. Dordrecht, Boston and London: Kluwer).

SCHAUER, F. (1988) "Formalism", 97 *The Yale Law Journal* 509.

SCHERMERS, H.G., TIMMERMANS, C.W.A., KELLERMANN, A.E. and WATSON, J.S. (eds) (1987) *Article 177 EEC: Experiences and Problems* (TMC Asser Instituut. The Hague, North Holland).

SCHLEGEL, J.H. (1995) *American Legal Realism and Empirical Social Science* (Chapel Hill and London: University of North Carolina Press).

SEARLE, J.R. (1992) *Speech Acts: An Essay in the Philosophy of Language* (New York: Cambridge University Press).

SILTALA, R. (1998) "The Quest for the Ultimate Premises of the Law", *Oikeus* 420.

SIMPSON, A.W.B. (1961) "The *Ratio Decidendi* of a Case and the Doctrine of Binding Precedent", in A.G. Guest (ed.), *Oxford Essays in Jurisprudence* (Oxford: Oxford University Press).

SMITH, C.S. (1995) "The Redundancy of Reasoning", in Z. Bankowski, I. White and U. Hahn (eds), *Informatics and the Foundations of Legal Reasoning* (Law and Philosophy Library, Vol. 21. Dordrecht, Boston and London: Kluwer).

SPIVAK, G.C. (1976) "Translator's Preface", in J. Derrida, *Of Grammatology* (Baltimore and London: The Johns Hopkins University).

STONE, J. (1959) "The *Ratio* of the *Ratio Decidendi*", 22 *Modern Law Review* 597.

SUMMERS, R.S. (1982) *Instrumentalism and American Legal Theory* (Ithaca and London: Cornell University Press).

——(1990) "Theory, Formality and Practical Legal Criticism", 106 *Law Quarterly Review* 407 (reprinted in R.S. Summers, *Essays on the Nature of Law and Legal Reasoning* (Berlin: Duncker & Humblot)).

——(1992) "Form and Substance in Legal Reasoning", in R.S. Summers, *Essays on the Nature of Law and Legal Reasoning* (Berlin: Duncker & Humblot).

——(1992) "The Formal Character of Law", 51 *Cambridge Law Journal* 242.

——(1992) "Statutes and Contracts as Founts of Formal Reasoning", in R.S. Summers, *Essays on the Nature of Law and Legal Reasoning* (Berlin: Duncker & Humblot).

——(1992) "Working Conceptions of the Law", in R.S. Summers, *Essays on the Nature of Law and Legal Reasoning* (Berlin: Duncker & Humblot).

——(1994) "*Der Formale Charakter des Rechts II*", 80 *ARSP* 66.

——(1994) "The Formal Character of Law III", 25 *Rechtstheorie* 125.

——(1995) "The Juristic Study of Law's Formal Character", 8 *Ratio Juris* 237.

——(1997) "Precedent in the United States (New York State)", in D.N. MacCormick and R.S. Summers (eds), *Interpreting Precedents: A Comparative Study* (Aldershot: Ashgate/Dartmouth).

TARUFFO, M. (1997) "Institutional Factors Influencing Precedents", in D.N. MacCormick and R.S. Summers (eds), *Interpreting Precedents: A Comparative Study* (Aldershot: Ashgate/Dartmouth).

TARUFFO, M. and LA TORRE, M. (1997) "Precedent in Italy", in D.N. MacCormick and R.S. Summers (eds), *Interpreting Precedents: A Comparative Study* (Aldershot: Ashgate/Dartmouth).

TEUBNER, G. (1989) "How the Law Thinks: Towards a Constructivist Epistemology in Law", 23 *Law and Society Review* 727.

——(1993) *Law as an Autopoietic System* (Oxford: Blackwell Publishers).

TIMONEN, P. (1987) *Ennakkotapaukset ja niiden merkitys oikeuslähteenä* (Helsinki: Lakimiesliiton Kustannus).

TROPER, M, and GRZEGORCZYK, C. (1997) "Precedent in France", in D.N. MacCormick and R.S. Summers (eds), *Interpreting Precedents: A Comparative Study* (Aldershot: Ashgate/Dartmouth).

TROPER, M., GRZEGORCZYK, C. and GARDIES, J.-L. (1997) "Statutory Interpretation in France", in D.N. MacCormick and R.S. Summers (eds), *Interpreting Statutes: A Comparative Study* (Aldershot: Dartmouth).

TUORI, K. (1983) *Valtionhallinnon sivuelinorganisaatiosta, 1: Julkisoikeudellinen tutkimus komiteatyyppisten elinten asemasta Suomen valtio-organisaatiossa. 1. nide: Teoreettinen ja historiallinen tausta* (Helsinki: Suomalaisen lakimiesyhdistyksen julkaisuja, A:159).

——(1983) *Valtionhallinnon sivuelinorganisaatiosta, 2: Julkisoikeudellinen tutkimus komiteatyyppisten elinten asemasta Suomen valtio-organisaatiossa. 2. nide: Positiivisoikeudelliset tarkastelut* (Helsinki: Suomalaisen lakimiesyhdistyksen julkaisuja, A:160).

——(1987) "The General Doctrines in Public Law", 31 *Scandinavian Studies in Law* 177.

——(1990) *Oikeus, valta ja demokratia* (Helsinki: Lakimiesliiton kustannus).

——(1997) "*Ideologiakritiikistä kriittiseen positivismiin*", in J. Häyhä (ed.), *Minun metodini* (Helsinki: Werner Söderström Lakitieto OY).

——(1997) "Legal Systems as/and Social Science", 70 *ARSP* 127.

——(1997) "Towards a Multi-Layered View of Modern Law", in A. Aarnio, R. Alexy and G. Bergholtz (eds), *Justice, Morality and Society: A Tribute to Aleksander Peczenik on the Occasion of his 60th Birthday 16 November 1997* (Lund: Juristförlaget i Lund).

UNGER, R.M. (1983) *The Critical Legal Studies Movement* (Cambridge, Massachusetts and London: Harvard University Press).

UNGER, R.M. (1987) *False Necessity: Anti-Necessitarian Social Theory in the Service of Radical Democracy*, in *Politics*, Part I (Cambridge: Cambridge University Press).

VON WRIGHT, G.H. (1963) *Norm and Action: A Logical Enquiry* (International Library of Philosophy and Scientific Method. London: Routledge & Kegan Paul).

WACHTLER, S. (1990) "Judicial Lawmaking", 65 *New York University Law Review* 1.

WALTER, R. (1992) "*Entstehung und Entwicklung des Gedankens der Grundnorm*", in R. Walter (ed.), *Schwerpunkte der Reinen Rechtslehre* (Wien: Manz Verlag).

WEBER, M. (1972) *Wirtschaft und Gesellschaft* (Tübingen: JCB Mohr).

——(1988) "*Die 'Objektivität' sozialwissenschaftlicher und sozialpolitischer Erkenntnis*", in M. Weber, *Gesammalte Aufsätze zur Wissenschaftslehre*. (Tübingen: JCB Mohr (Paul Siebeck)).

—— (1988) *Gesammelte Aufsätze zur Wissenschaftslehre* (Tübingen: JCB Mohr (Paul Siebeck)).

WEINBERGER, O. (1981) *Normentheorie als Grundlage der Jurisprudenz und Ethik: Eine Auseinandersetzung mit Hans Kelsens Theorie der Normen* (Berlin: Duncker & Humblot).

WILHELMSSON, T. (1997) "Jack-in-the-Box Theory of European Community Law", in L. Krämer, H. W. Micklitz and K. Tonner (eds), *Law and Diffuse Interests in the European Legal Order—Recht und diffuse Intressen in der Europäischen Rechtsordnung: Liber amicorum Norbert Reich* (Baden-Baden: Nomos Verlagsgesellschaft).

WILSON, C. (2000) *Swedish–English Skating Dictionary*, at http://www.sssk.se/english/dictionary.htm

WINCH, P. (1958) *The Idea of a Social Science and its Relation to Philosophy* (London: Routledge & Kegan Paul).

WITTGENSTEIN, L. (1967) *Philosophische Untersuchungen—Philosophical Investigations* (Oxford: Basil Blackwell 1967).

——(1972) *Über Gewissheit—On Certainty* (New York: Harper & Row).

——(1986) *Tractatus Logico-Philosophicus* (London and New York: Routledge & Kegan Paul).

WRÓBLEWSKI, J. (1974) "The Concept and Function of Precedent in Statute-Law Systems", VII *Archivum Juridicum Cracoviense* 7.

——(1984) "Informatics and Ideology of Judicial Decision-Making", X *Informatica e diritto* 117.

——(1992) *The Judicial Application of Law* (Law and Philosophy Library, Vol. 15. Dordrecht, Boston and London: Kluwer).

Index

Aarnio, 17–18, 30, 43, 66, 82, 99, 135–6, 140–1, 147, 155, 182, 204–5, 212–14, 218–20, 265
  legal rationality, 217–20
abductive reasoning, 87
Abel, 22
Achilles, 198
Aktenversendung, 78
Alexander, 67
Alexy, 17–18, 46–7, 55, 66, 79, 83, 112–13, 132, 134, 155, 166, 179, 181, 190, 195–6, 204, 207, 217, 220, 254, 265
  legal principles as Optimierungsgebote, 47
  meta-rules of rational legal discourse, 187–9
Allen, 73, 100, 102, 104
alterity, 25
  language-game of absolute alterity, 234
analogy, 91–5, 114, 116–17, 125, 128, 143
analytical jurisprudence, 1, 3,
  see also analytical positivism
analytical model construction, 29, 31–2, 67–78, 250–1
analytical positivism, 17–21, 37–9, 43, 54, 67, 152, 179–81, 189, 193, 200, 216, 229–31, 255–60, 265–7
  from analytical positivism to deconstruction of law, 255–60
  self-referential identity of, 213
  theoretical limits of, 214–15, 257–60
  see also legal positivism, positivism
analyticity, 19–21
  methodological constraints of, 32
  see also, analytical positivim, theoretical limits of
Andenas, 80
Anscombe, 198
anthill metaphor, 148, 252
anti-formalism, 5
aporia, 25, 28, 51, 198, 229
Aquinas, 106
archives of political morality, 55, 58–9, 62
argumentation, *see* legal reasoning
Aristotle, 33, 95
Arnaud, 19, 22, 47
Arnheim, 67
articles found inherently dangerous, 92–3
Atiyah, 47–9, 123–4
Aufhebung, 25
Austin (J), 3, 17–19, 43, 70, 83, 118, 181, 190, 192–3, 200, 219, 264
Austin (J L), 28–9, 166, 179, 185–7, 189, 191, 253–5
  misfires and abuses of speech acts, 185–7
autopoiesis, 205, 213–14
axiomatic grounds, 14, 37, 113, 151, 153–4, 161, 179–81, 185, 188, 193, 196, 210, 229, 254, 260-1, 265
axiomatic postulates, *see* axiomatic grounds

Baldwin, 87
Balkin, 23–4
Bankowski, 13, 91, 94, 117, 121–3, 147
Bayles, 9–10
beehive metaphor, 148
Begriffsjurisprudenz, 3, 121, 252
Bentham, 167
Bergholtz, 155
Bernasconi, 22
bias, 101, 107
Bielefelder Kreis, 16, 18, 30–1, 73, 111–13, 121, 124, 140, 252
binary/graded logical code, 42–4, 59–60, 62, 69, 204
binding force of a precedent, 111–15
  external determinants of, 112–14
  levels of, 111–12
Bingham, 68–9
Blackstone, 19
Bobbio, 20
Borges, 128, 202, 221, 229, 233–4, 254
  imperial cartographers, 226, 254
Brandeis brief, 13, 83–4
Bülow, 5

Cappelletti, 210
Caputo, 26, 33, 235–7
Carroll, 29, 198
category mistake, 181, 212, 228
Chomsky, 155
civil law systems, 13, 17, 66, 70, 112, 168, 249
claim to legal authority, 179, 189–91, 153, 254
claim to legal correctness, 179, 181, 189–91, 254
closure, 71, 78, 80, 82, 86, 94, 161, 243
command theory of law, 19–20, 43, 70, 83, 208–9
common law, 11, 13, 17, 19, 44, 65, 72, 87, 99, 113, 121, 123–4, 167, 249

concepts, 19
  conceptual analytics of precedent norm formation, 14–15, 152–4, 260–2
  conceptual anomaly, *see* conceptual failure; performative contradiction
  conceptual failure, 187, 189, 191, 254
    see also performative contradiction
  conceptual necessity, *see* conceptual failure; performative contradiction
  cluster concepts, 9, 19, 145–6, 161, 163, 252
constitutional jurisdiction, 79
contract law, 23, 124
  freedom of contract, 98
Cook, 69, 105–6
Corla, 142
Courtés, 238
Critical Legal Studies, 22–4, 29, 37–9, 67, 174–5, 180, 193–4, 199, 205, 245, 266–7
critical unfolding, *see* radical questioning
Cross, 65, 85–8, 123
customary law, 128, 213

Dalton, 23–4
Dawson, 78–9
deconstruction, 22–9, 37–8, 158, 176, 245, 255–60
  and methodology, 24, 26–9, 245
  manoeuvres or 'tricks' of, 27–9
  of law, 255–60
deductive reasoning, 73, 81, 90–1, 116, 122, 125, 127, 130–1, 132, 141, 171, 176, 187–5, 243, 246–8
defeasibility, 74, 117
definition:
  cluster definition, 9
  paradigm, 9
deferral/distancing, 24, 27, 36–8, 154, 235, 236–7, 239, 243–4, 276–7, 248, 257–9, 261, 266
  condition of possibility and impossibility, 27, 33, 36–7, 159–60, 202–3, 230, 235, 256, 266–7
deliberative practice, 199–200
Denmark, 11
deontic mode, 69–70, 75, 110, 161, 163, 204, 251
deontic operator, 41–2, 53–4, 69–70, 75, 161
Derrida, 15, 21–7, 29, 35, 37–8, 157–9, 230–1, 236, 238, 244, 255, 256, 258, 266–7
  as quasi-transcendental philosopher, 33
  différance, 27, 235–7, 239, 245, 257–9, 261–7
  dislocating a prior, 231
  infrastructures, *see* infrastructures
  logic of *différance*, 235
  neologisms of, 26
  pre-metaphysical question, 33
  quasi-concepts, 26–7, 36, 236–7, 239
  radical undecidability, 27, 27–8, 230, 235, 258–61, 267
  relentless quest for the ultimate premises, v, 32, 34–5, 37–9, 201, 265–7
  turn to singularity, 26
de Saussure, 236, 239, 244
  syntagmatic/paradigmatic dichotomy, 238–9
Descartes, 30
de Sousa Santos, 62
Dicey:
  post-Dicey, 227
différance, *see* Derrida
discourse—theoretical frame of law, 254
  limits of, 195–6
distinquishing, 12, 13, 31, 65, 73–4, 88, 91–5, 99, 109, 114, 116–7, 124–5, 131, 134, 136–7, 141–143, 145
Donoghue v. *Stevenson*, 89, 92
Dreier, 17, 66, 79, 112–13, 132, 134
Dworkin, 21, 28, 42–7, 49–53, 55, 58–60, 62, 75, 77, 81, 90, 96–100–1, 103, 110, 114–17, 134, 143, 157, 161, 174, 181, 183, 194, 204, 241, 244, 247, 249, 251, 255
  critique of Hart, 43–6
  institutional support, 45–6, 50, 53, 58–9, 61–2, 99, 103, 105, 117–8, 172, 183, 263
  law as integrity, 51, 58, 99, 115, 118, 162, 167, 185, 194, 245
  legal systematicity, 96–101
  seamless web of reasons, 51, 96–7, 110, 118, 135, 143, 240–1, 245, 263
  sense of appropriateness, 42, 45, 50, 53, 59, 103, 118, 183

école exégétique, 3
effecting/effacing, *see* condition of possibility and impossibility
Ehrlich, 5, 119
Eisenberg, 67
Ekelöf, 94
empiricism, 6, 30, 102
  logical empiricism, 6
épistémè, *see* Foucault, Western *épistémè*
epistemology, 27, 32, 38, 202–3, 208, 226–9, 231, 256, 258–9, 265
Esser, 43
European Court of Justice, 16, 79–80, 210
  as court of politics, 173
Ewald, 156, 196, 208
extra-legal discourse, 54, 63, 71, 77–8, 204, 240–2, 245–8

facts treated as material, 87–90
facts and consequences approach, 68–9
felicity conditions of adjudication, 21, 37, 153, 158–60, 161, 171, 185–91
feminism, 22

Feyerabend, 108, 185
Finland, 16, 72, 113, 121, 135–43, 161, 262–3
  Supreme Court of Justice, 82, 121, 135–43, 172–3
  use of headnotes, 136–42
Finnis, 106
Fish, 48, 97
football:
  rule of recognition for, 10
  Wittgenstein and language-games, 199
formalism, *see* legal formality
Foucault, 36, 155–6, 158, 194, 202–3, 231, 235, 255–6
  archaeology of knowledge, 155, 202, 238–9, 255–6
  épistémè, 33, 38, 154–5,158, 203, 230, 231, 235, 238, 255–6, 257, 264, 266
  historical *a priori*, 155, 158, 202–31, 238–9, 255–7
France, 16, 113, 122, 127–8, 161, 194, 263
  Cour de Cassation, 127, 170
  dispositif and *motif*, 127
  judicial function of French judges, 127
  system of adjudication, 4
Frank, 69, 102, 104, 107–8
Frankfurter J, 125
free–floating model of reasons, 134
free law movement, 4–5, 77, 117, 119
Freirechtsbewegung, see free law movement
French Annalist school of history, 156
French Revolution, 79, 127
Friedmann, 18
Führerstaat ideology, 4–5
Fuller, 21–2, 68, 159, 168, 174–5, 190–1, 224, 249, 253, 255
  application of ideas to precedent, 166–8
  internal morality of law, 165–8
  morality of aspiration, 159–60, 166, 171, 190, 193, 253

game metaphor, 199
Gardies, 4, 79
Gasché, 24–5, 27, 33, 37, 230, 236
Gény, 4–5, 77, 119
Germany, 16, 78–80, 132–5
  Federal Constitutional Court, 17, 83, 112, 132–5
  general grounding principles, 132
  tragende Gründe (supporting reasons), 133
giurisprudenza costante (ie. giurisprudenza consolidata), 113, 130
Goldstein, 65, 249
Goodhart, 85, 87–9, 123
grasshopper technique of augmentation, 146–8
gramme, 26
Greimas, 238
grounding/cancelling, *see* condition of possibility and impossibility
Grzegorczyk, 4, 13, 79, 113, 122, 127

Habermas, 156, 158, 166, 184, 194, 217, 220, 235
  ideal speech situation, 184, 217–8
  theory of communicative rationality, 187, 195, 235
  validity claims, 187
Hahn, 91, 94, 117
Hänninen, 156
Harris, 65, 85–7, 123
Hart, 4, 6, 8, 10–15, 17–19, 21, 28, 43, 46, 52, 67, 83, 94, 96, 101, 104–5, 108, 117–18, 144, 151–2, 154, 161, 164, 166, 175–7, 181, 190, 192, 194–5, 199–200, 222, 226–30, 234, 237, 249–51, 255
  critique of Fuller, 224
  critique of Dworkin, 46
  legal semantics, 9. 94, 237
  minimum content of natural law, 20, 174, 224
  model of law, 9
  Queen rule, 9–11, 151, 163, 227–8
  rule of recognition, 8–11, 14, 45, 83, 144, 152, 163–4, 177, 181, 201–2, 215–6, 221–31, 234, 250, 254–5, 257–9, 265
  three dilemmas of precedent–following, 12
Hartney, 207
Häyhä, 157
headnotes, 136–42
  functions of, 139–49
Heck, 4, 94
Hedemann, 5
Hegel, 25
Heinonen CJ, 137–40, 142–3
Helin, 6
Henningsen v. *Bloomfield Motors, Inc*, 43, 98–9
Henry IV, 90, 95
Hercules J, 96, 100, 241
hermeneutics, 6, 30
historical school of law, 117–18, 183, 199
Hobbes, 101
Hohfeld, 18, 219
Holmes, 84, 90, 94–5, 102, 104, 107, 151, 194, 200
Honderich, 20, 87
human rights, 159, 224
human sciences, 30–1, 202, 205
Hume, 206, 219
hunch, *see* judicial hunch
Hutcheson, 107

iceberg metaphor, 68, 151, 260–2, 264
ideal types, 30–1, 239
identity/difference:
  criteria of, 233–5
ideology:
  different senses of, 175

ideology (*cont.*):
ideological bias, 23–5
ideological cement, 191
ideological fragments, 21, 67–76, 144–7, 152, 161, 163, 173, 251,
see also precedent ideology
imputation (strong or weak), 41–3, 54, 55–8, 60–1, 75, 250
information:
adequacy of, 169, 253
appositeness of, 169–70, 253
infrastructures, 14–15, 21–2, 24–7, 152, 158, 160, 200, 203, 235
as final outcomes of philosophical analysis, 35, 255–61
nature of, 33–5, 37
of judicial signification, 246–8, 266
of law, 14–15, 21, 32, 36–7, 68, 152–4, 157, 159–60, 193, 215, 229, 255, 266
of legal discourse, 230–1
of legal norm constitution, 201–4
of precedent–following, 203, 233–48
of Western metaphysics, 35–7, 203, 258–60, 265–7
self effacing (and self-referential) character of, 25–9, 33, 35–6, 37–8, 215, 231, 235, 267
institutional fact, 198
institutionalised use of power, 153
institutional support, *see* Dworkin
institutional theory of law, 200
integrity in argumentation, 168, 174–5, 253
see also Dworkin, law as integrity
International Court of Justice, 16
international law, 23–4
interpretation, 48, 53, 60, 79, 114, 155
statutory interpretation, 94, 111, 115, 125, 141
intuition, *see* judicial hunch
Italy, 16, 79–80, 113, 122, 128–32, 148, 161, 262–3
conflicts in a line of precedents, 130–1
Corte de Cassazione, 81, 129–32, 169
massima, 129–31, 137,170
Ufficio del Massimario, 129, 131, 137, 170

Jääskinen, 72
jack-in-the-box effect, 245, 247
Jakobson, 238
Jellinek, 224
Jori, 19, 47
Joyce, 29
judges, 200
as tyrant dressed in robe, 101
bipolar judge, 177
bound judicial decision-making, 3–4
constrained activist, 177
difference–splitting judge, 177
discretion of, 4, 56, 90, 104, 132, 143, 171, 177, 195
dynamic role of, 4–5
evaluative role of, 5–6
free judicial decision-making, 4–5
ideological aspects, 3–6, 7–8, 67, 164, 173–4, 191
idiosyncratic motives of, 8, 146, 176, 185, 254,192, 195
intellectual toolbox, 15, 31, 67, 144, 250
judicial delay, 80
judicial hunch, 5, 107–8, 115, 117–9, 146, 180, 185, 191, 193,-4, 241, 248
judicial imagery, 240–2, 248
judicial skills, 101, 122, 142–3, 173–4
legal and rational judicial decision–making, 5–6
passive judge, 78, 80
professional ethics, 160
see also Fuller, morality of aspiration
professional understanding, 112–13, 127, 132, 145, 162
role of, 3–4
view from the bench, 11, 175, 192, 195, 254
judgment intuitive, 107–8
see also judges, judicial hunch
judicial analogy, 78, 91–5, 109–10, 114–16, 126, 128, 143, 145, 147, 170, 172–3, 184–5, 240, 248, 263, 251
model reasons approach, 91, 95, 128, 135, 143, 251
model rule approach, 91, 95, 143, 251
paradigm case model, 91, 95, 143, 251
judical exegesis, 78, 84–90, 109–10, 114–16, 121–3, 126, 136, 140, 142, 145, 147, 170, 184–5, 240, 248, 251, 263
material facts model, 85, 87–9, 251
material reasons model, 89–90, 251
reconstructed rule model, 85–7, 136, 251
judicial ideologies (general), *see* substantive approach, semantic freeplay
see also precedent ideologies
judicial legislation, 78, 80–4, 109–10, 114–15, 123, 126, 136–7, 140, 145, 184, 240, 248, 250–1
binding reasons model, 83–4, 250
quasi-legislative model, 80–4, 131, 136–7, 250
judicial procedure:
rules of, 188
judicial reference:
reference model, 78–80, 109–10, 114–15, 240, 248, 250–1
judicial revaluation, 78, 102–5, 109–110, 114–16, 125–6, 131–2, 145, 184–5, 240, 248, 251, 263
reinterpreted rule model, 103, 251
requalified facts model, 103, 251

revalued reasons model, 103, 135, 251
judicial signification, 21, 32, 246–8, 266
dispute solving paradigm, 240–4, 246–8, 264
extra-legal paradigm, 240–2, 245–8, 264
legislative paradigm, 240–3, 246–8, 264
paradigm of, 239–42, 264
systemic paradigm, 240–2, 244–8, 264
jurisprudence, 15, 144, 153, 164, 264
"key to the science of", 192
see also legal philosophy
jurisprudence constante, 113, 128
justice, 74, 76, 82, 87, 95, 98, 100, 103, 106, 174, 191
Kadi-Justiz, 8

Kant, 35, 155, 202–3, 216, 231, 238–9, 255–6
neo-Kantian philosophy, 41, 205–7
Kantorowicz, 5, 119
Kelsen, 3–4, 6–7, 17–19, 41–3, 47–8, 51, 53–4, 66–7, 71, 83, 118, 156, 161, 173, 180–2, 190, 192–3, 200–1, 204–5, 208–9, 211–12, 214–15, 221–3, 225–6, 228–30, 254, 258
dilemma of statutory and precedent–based norms, 209–11
effectiveness, 20, 205–9, 215
Grundnorm, 48, 173, 181, 192, 204–10, 223, 226, 229, 254, 259, 265
validity, 205–11
Kennedy, 22, 175, 177
bad faith argument, 8, 146, 175, 177, 192, 195, 254
ideology, 176
legality, 176
strategic behaviour of judges, 176–7
tripartite division of arguments, 176
Klami, 106
Koskenniemi, 23–4

language:
dimensions of, 238–9, 248
limits of, 26, 29, 33–4, 35–6, 265
see also de Saussuse
language-games, 28, 33–4, 185, 197–8, 233–4
Laporta, 79, 112
La Torre, 79, 113, 122, 129–32, 142
law:
as closed system, 3, 19–20, 51, 71, 75, 78–80, 154, 161, 163, 212–4, 243, 246–8, 251, 261
as "frozen politics", 38, 266–7
as integrity, *see* Dworkin
background reasons of, 20, 42, 57–58, 60–2, 78, 90, 105–6, 211–2, 224, 246
contested nature of, 200
doubts about coherence of, 156–7
formal character of law, 158
law/fact dichotomy, 228–30
preceding the law, 196, 208–9, 215, 225, 227, 229, 265
ultimate edges of, 36, 201–2, 263–7
ultimate premises of, 37–8, 201–2, 265
law in action, 17, 21, 31, 69, 114, 121, 128, 161, 183
law in books, 69
leave to appeal, 135, 138
legal authority, *see* claim to legal authority
legal correctness, *see* claim to legal correctness
legal culture, 112–14, 155–6
legal discourse, 38, 54, 60, 63, 179, 187–9, 193–4, 199, 217, 231
axiomatic ground of, 14, 37, 113, 151, 153–4, 161, 179–81, 185, 188–9, 193, 195–6, 201, 229, 254, 260–1, 265
distinct from general practical discourse, 188
felicities and infelicities of, 185–91, 253–4
subcategories of, 181
legal dogmatics, 15, 152, 155, 252
legal formality, 4, 37, 47–63, 79, 103, 132, 148
constitutive formality, 50–1, 56, 59, 249
degree of, 110
deontic formality, 53–4
kinds of, 60–3
levels of, 47–9
mandatory formality, 50–2, 56, 59–60, 249
methodological formality, 50, 53, 58–60, 62, 249–50
structural formality, 50, 52–3, 58–60, 249
systemic formality, 50–1, 56, 249
see also Summers
legal historicism, 75, 114, 117
legal philosophy, 15, 144, 153, 264
see also jurisprudence
legal policies, 55–63, 183
as proto-norms, 55–8
see also policy
legal positivism, 3, 38–9, 45, 48, 75, 83, 114, 118, 131, 137, 181–3, 199
legal principles, 21, 42–7, 55–63, 97, 103, 183
as proto-norms, 55–8
see also Dworkin; principles
legal profession, 188
legal rationality, 36, 112, 153, 179–81, 183–5, 190, 193, 196, 199, 201, 265
D-rationality, 183–5
L-rationality, 183–5
rationality of, 201, 215–21
S-rationality, 184
see also legal reasoning
legal realism, 4, 22, 69, 75, 102–4, 106–8, 114, 117–18, 125, 174–5, 180, 182–3, 199
legal reasoning, 115–16, 146, 162, 170, 243–4
argumentative loopholes, 28
case-bound reasoning, 84, 91–95, 125–6, 251
see also analogy
in Finland, 136, 141–2

legal reasoning (*cont.*):
in France, 128
in Germany, 132–5
in Italy, 131–2
integrity in, 168, 174–5, 253
in UK, 122–3
in US, 125–6
methods of, 61, 73, 75–6, 80–1, 87, 91–4, 97–9, 102–3, 106, 108, 115–6, 251
strong/weak imputation, 41–3, 53–8, 60–1, 75, 250
see also analogy, legal rationality
legal scholar, 181
legal scholarly paradigm, 240, 247–8
mere witty scholarly criticism, 101
see also professors of law
legal sociology, 144, 161
legal source doctrine, 7, 11, 82, 111–17, 121, 136, 145, 165, 171–3, 175–6, 180–1, 182, 188, 192, 209–11, 217, 218, 223, 241, 245, 248, 251
see also transcategorical context
legal systemic frame, 15–17
legal theory, *see* jurisprudence
legal theoretical literature, 16
legislation, *see* statute
legislative intentions, 111
legitimacy, 165, 168–75, 180, 191, 254
empirical legitimacy, 192–4
levels of analysis, 14–15, 21, 31–2, 152, 154, 249, 252–3, 260–2
deep-structure level, 14–15, 32, 68, 99, 151–2, 154–6, 192–3, 196. 260–1
discourse-theoretical frame, 14–15, 21, 151, 153, 159–60, 260–61
infrastructure level, *see* infrastructures
operative surface-structure, 14–15, 32, 68, 151–2, 154–6, 196, 260–1
precedent ideology, *see* precedent ideology
relations between levels, 158–60
Levi, 91–4, 99, 103, 115, 117, 124–5
lex iniusta non est lex, 106
libre recherche scientifique, 4
Linna, 139–41
Llewellyn, 89, 102–4, 118, 124, 200
logic, 107, 184
fuzzy logic, 44
logos/mythos distinction, 27, 36, 154, 201, 203, 230, 237, 256, 259, 260
Luhmann, 213

Mabbott, 219
MacCormick, 4, 11, 13, 16–18, 30–1, 55, 65–7, 73–4, 79, 81, 84–8, 90, 99, 105–6, 111–13, 117, 121–4, 132, 136, 141, 147, 157, 175, 198, 200, 204–5, 214–16, 223–4, 229, 249, 252, 259, 265
madman argument, 224
underpinning reasons of law, 20, 205, 212, 215, 224, 265
Malcolm, 199
Mansfield, Lord, 100
Marcic, 19
Marshall, 121–3, 147
Marxism, 22, 156
neo-Marxism, 176
post-Marxism, 157
meaningful silences, 28
mens rea, 82
Merkl, 41, 47, 51, 83, 182, 206, 211
meta-legal, 227, 229
metaphysics, 24–9, 32–9, 160, 201, 203, 231, 235, 237, 239, 256, 258, 260, 266–7
preconceptual and prelogical preconditions of, 33–4, 35–7
see also prelogical
methodology, 16–17, 29–39, 144–8, 176–7, 200–1, 212–14
and repeatability, 29
legal methodology, 201, 203, 229, 231, 259
methodological anarchism, 73, 108, 116, 185
see also Feyerabind
self-effacing method, 27
Micklitz, 245
Miettinen, 135
Mill, 219
Montesquieu, 3, 56, 78, 80, 116–17, 240, 246
Montesquieuén dream or orthodoxy, *see* Montesquieu
Moore, 20
morality, 20, 54–5, 58–9, 62, 107, 165–8, 188
morality of aspiration, 159–60, 166, 190, 193, 254
morality of duty, 166
"morality that makes law possible", *see* Fuller, internal morality of law
Morawetz, 199
moving classification system, 93, 117, 246
multi-level structure of law, *see* levels of analysis
Museum of Normativity, 199

Nagel, 194
natural law, 19, 75, 106, 114, 117–19, 174, 180, 182–3, 193, 199, 205, 223
Nazi Germany, 4–5
negligence, 89, 92
Nino, 47
norm:
customary norms, 211
legal norm, 41–2, 78, 105, 260
legal norm constitution, 21, 153–4, 260–1
legal norm types, 54, 56–62
precedent norm, 59–63
varieties of, 58–63

norm/fact distinction, 27, 36, 154, 201, 202, 203, 215, 221–31, 234, 260–1
"normative in the small", 27
Nöth, 238

obiter dictum, 12, 31, 62, 68, 88, 108, 123, 129, 154, 250, 253
  see also ratio decidendi
Olbrechts-Tyteca:
  universal audience, 217–18
Oliphant, 68–9, 118
Olsson CJ, 138, 172
ontology, 27, 32–3, 37, 201, 203, 208, 229, 231, 259
  shift to epistemology, 226–9
order of things, 28, 33–6, 155, 194, 203, 231, 233–5, 238, 255–9, 266
  see also Foucault
ordinary language, 244
outweighability, 74, 117, 134
overruling, 73, 116
  sub silencio, 74
Oxford school of ordinary language, 9, 11, 20, 28, 34, 39, 55, 144, 164, 201, 265

paradigm, *see* concepts, cluster concepts
paradigm case, *see* judicial analogy, paradigm case model
parliamentary sovereignty, 210
Pattaro, 79
Patterson, 23, 67, 94, 199
Paulson, 207
Peczenik, 17–18, 106, 111, 148, 161, 180, 184, 187, 189, 204–5, 213–15, 222, 224, 229, 259, 265
  legal source norms, 211–2, 265
  levels of legal justification, 220–1
  moral/political background reasons, 20, 211–2, 224
  validity of law, 211–12
Peirce, 87
Perelman:
  universal audience, 217–18
performative contradiction, 160, 190–1, 254
persuasive precedent, 111–2
phenomenology, 22, 176
philosophy of law, *see* legal philosophy
Pietlià, 66
Plato, 25–7, 33, 236–7
  khōra, 27, 236–7, 256
policy:
  as Trojan horse for ideology, 176
  see also legal policies, principles
political liberalism, 3
politics, 54, 107
porous legality, 61–2
positivism:
  case-law positivism, 141
  critical legal positivism, 156
  judicial positivism, 78, 117–18
  logical positivism, 19
  see also analytical positivism, legal positivism
post-analytical philosophy of law, 21, 32, 255
Pound, 69, 102, 124
practical discourse, 54, 179, 187–8, 195, 217, 265
pragmatism, 102, 131
  American legal pragmatism, 17
  judicial pragmatism, 177
  legal pragmatism, 123, 126
  pragmatic instrumentalism, 117–19
precedent, 11–14, 16, 30, 65
  binding force, levels of, 71–2, 111
  definition of, 66
  determinants of the binding force of, 112, 172
  departing from, 73–4, 94, 116–17, 134, 137
  how to read, *see* reading the law
  inconsistencies in, 130–1
  lines of, 128, 130–1, 133
  overload of, 81, 130
  strings of, 148
  relation of theory to practice, 262–4
  shortage of cases, 82
precedent-based law:
  syntagmatic/paradigmatic elements, 239, 241–2, 245–6
precedent-following, 21, 31, 59, 65–7, 78, 95, 143–8, 153–4, 248, 249–55, 260–1, 262–7
  comparative study, 121–48, 252
  judicial signification, *see* judicial signification
  legitimacy for, 165, 168–75, 253
  opposing ideologies of, 126, 131
  systemic dynamics of, *see* systemic dynamics
precedent-identification, 21, 31, 59, 95, 111, 137, 143
precedent ideologies, 11, 14–17, 21, 29, 31, 152, 191, 193, 240, 250–1
  categories of, 61
  cluster of ideological fragments, 145–7
  comparative study of, 121–48, 252
  counter-ideologies to, 105–8
  ideological fragments of, 68–76, 144, 160–2, 251–2
  method of argumentation in, 115–16
  models of, 67–108, 250–1
  outline of models, 76–8, 250–51
  theoretical rationale, 117–19
  see also judicial reference, judicial legislation, judicial exegesis, judicial analogy, systemic construction, judicial revaluation
precedent-norm, 65

operative precedent-norm conception, 109–10
precedent-norm individuation, 70–1
precedent-recognition:
formal definition of, 163–4
predictability, 170–1
prediction theory of law, 104
predictivists, 118
pre–legal discourse, 54, 58, 60, 63, 71, 77–8
preliminary ruling, 79
prelogical, 21, 31, 33–5, 153–4, 157, 160, 201–2, 230–1, 237, 249, 253, 258, 260–1
principles, 117
principle/policy distinction, 55
see also legal principles
prior court, 80–3, 173, 184, 209, 242–3
original intentions, 84–90
relationship with subsequent court, *see* subsequent court/prior court
professors of law, 78–9
see also legal scholars
property law, 124
prospectivity/retroactivity, 72, 75
proto-norms, 55–8, 60, 183, 250
quasi-transcendental, 27, 33, 37, 203, 236, 239, 256, 259

radical displacement, 247–8
radical dissimilarity, 245
radical questioning (method of), 21, 32, 34–5, 37, 255, 265
radical undecidability, *see* Derrida
Radin, 107
Rasmussen, 80, 173, 210
ratio decidendi, 11–13, 58–63, 68–9, 71–2, 74–6, 78, 80–1, 83, 85–91, 93–4, 99–100, 104, 109–111, 113–16, 118, 122, 124, 126, 129, 131–3, 136–8, 140–2, 147–8, 152, 161–2, 174, 239–42, 244, 246–7, 252, 263
ascription of meaning-content to, 242–6
definitions of, 85–6, 102, 123
deontic mode of, 69–70
distinquished from *obiter dicta*, 12, 31, 65, 67–8, 109, 123, 142, 151, 153, 161, 253
plurality of, 85
role of prior/subsequent court, *see* prior court, subsequent court
rationalization, 68–9
rational reconstruction, 7–8, 30–1, 144, 164, 255, 262
descriptive and normative elements in, 31
Rawls, 217–19
veil of ignorance, 217–19
reading the law, 38–9, 53, 264–7
how to read precedent, 113, 122, 142–3, 145, 162, 174, 239, 249–55, 262–3
Rechtstaat, 101, 105, 156
Reid, Lord, 122
relentless questioning:
method of, 29, 32, 34–5, 37–8, 201, 228, 265
retroactivity, 165, 170
Richterstaat, 101, 105, 210
Riggs v. *Palmer*, 43, 46, 96–9
Rorty, 235
Ross, 7–8, 12, 14–15, 17–18, 21, 67, 142, 146, 154, 160–1, 163–4, 170, 175–7, 181, 195, 199, 222, 250–1, 255, 265
judge's normative ideology, 6–8, 11, 14, 67, 152, 160–2, 177, 195, 222, 250, 265
scheme of interpretation, 6–7
Rousseau, 25
Ruiz Miguel, 79, 112
rule of law, 21, 160 , 191, 193
for precedent following, 165, 168–75, 194, 253
rule of recognition, 201
norm/fact character of, 202, 221–9
recognition of, 201, 221
see also Hart, rule of recognition
rule/principle distinction, 42–7, 49–63, 97
binary/graded, 204
rules, 21, 60, 103–4, 124
abstracted rule, 93, 95, 124
defeasible legal rule, 53, 56–8, 61–3, 66, 70, 74, 103, 110, 111, 117, 183
meta–rules, 148, 151, 155, 174, 185, 187–9, 195–6
moral rules, 188
statutory/judicial origin distinguished, 84
ruling by reasons, ideology,135
Russell, 20
Ryle, 181, 212, 228

Sartor, 117
Saraviita, 138
Schauer, 47
Schermers, 80
Schlegel, 102
Schmitt, 5
seamless web of reasons, *see* Dworkin
Searle, 195–6, 198
Sein/Sollen distinction, *see* norm/fact distinction
self effacing self referentiality, *see* infrastructures
self-referentiality, 200–1, 246, 248, 266
semantic freeplay, 76–8
judicial hunch model, 105, 107–8, 114–16, 175, 185, 194, 240, 248
semantics:
judicial semantics, 9, 94, 115, 239–48
possible worlds semantics, 143, 161
semantic closure, *see* closure
semantic determinacy, 28
semantic open-endedness, 28

semiotics, 22
sense-differentiation:
 by latent signification structure, 244–5
 by radical alterity, 245–8, 266
 contextual sense-differentiation, 243–4, 246, 248
 systemic sense-differentiation, 246–8
separation of powers, 78, 127
separation thesis, 190, 223
Shakespeare, 101
signification, 14–5, 21, 24–5, 28, 32, 34, 37–8, 100, 115, 144, 153–4, 158, 160, 163, 202–3, 233–48, 253, 255–7, 258–61, 266–7
 structure, 103, 115, 244–5, 246–8, 266
Simpson, 85–8, 123
skating on thin ice metaphor, 38–9, 266–7
Smith, 91, 93
social institutions, 195–6
socialist legal systems, 5
social science, 30, 106
sociological jurisprudence, 4, 102
Spain, 79–80
 Constitutional Court, 112
speech act theory, 179, 185–7, 190, 195–6, 253–4
 abuses, 186–7
 illocutionary acts, 186
 locutionary acts, 186
 misfires, 186
 perlocutionary acts, 186
Spivak, 24, 26
special case thesis, 179, 187–91, 217, 265
standard norm, 199, 208, 229–31, 258
 absence of in law, 199
 see also Wittgenstein, standard metre
stāndige Rechtsprechung, 113, 133
stare decisis, 12, 13, 46, 60, 65–6, 76, 78, 102, 104–6, 117, 125, 134, 144, 148, 245, 248, 250, 252, 255
statute, 134, 137, 189
 general clauses, 5
 statutory interpretation, 94, 111, 115, 125, 141
 statutory law, 16, 124, 127–8
 statutory norms, 3, 10–13, 70–1, 94, 138, 168, 209, 213
Stone, 89
structuralism, 22, 176
stufenbau, 41, 43, 47–8, 51, 83, 182, 193, 206, 209, 211, 214
subsequent court, 125, 129–31, 173, 184, 242–3
 reconstructive task of, 90
subsequent court/prior court, 240
 roles, 72, 78, 80, 94, 100, 102
substantive approach, 78, 105–6, 114, 116, 125–6
 consequentialist model, 105–6, 147, 240
 rightness reasons model, 105–6, 145, 240
Summers, 4, 13, 16, 18, 21–2, 30–1, 47–9, 51–2, 56, 66–70, 73–4, 79, 81, 84, 102, 111–13, 118, 121–6, 132, 136, 141, 175, 249, 252, 255
 categories of legal formality, 47–9
systematicity in a set of precedents, 71, 75, 79–80, 81, 86–7, 94, 96–7, 99–101, 103, 110, 114–15, 251
 degree of, 110
systemic balance, *see* systemic congruence
systemic congruence, 171–3, 253
systemic construction, 78, 109–10, 114–16, 145, 147, 184–5, 251, 263
 underlying reasons model, 96–101, 135, 170, 240, 251
systemic dynamics, 111–15
systemic structure of a set of precedents:
 dynamic, 71–2
 static, 71
systems-theoretical approach, 213–14

tabula rasa situation, 218
Taruffo, 17, 79, 81, 113, 122, 129–32, 142
teleological construction of statutes, 94
Teubner, 196, 208, 213–14
textual analysis, 22–9, 35
textual criticism, 22–9
theoretical background, 74–6, 117–9
Timonen, 138–9
tort law, 124
tortoise, 189
 see also Achilles
Toulmin, 219
transcategorical context (i.e. transcategorical argument), 111–13, 136, 165, 171–2, 209–10, 262
 see also legal source doctrine
trashing, 24–5, 29, 37
Troper, 4, 13, 19, 79, 113, 122, 127
Tuori, 15, 152, 155–9, 255
 multi-layered structure of law, 155–9

Unger, 38, 175, 266
underlying reasons, *see* systemic construction
United Kingdom, 16, 113, 121–3, 148
 House of Lords Practice Statement, 122–3
United States (State of New York), 16, 113, 123–6
 contrast with UK, 123–4
 Court of Appeals of State of New York, 97–9, 145

Vaihinger, 207
validity, 36, 45, 47–8, 50, 54, 112, 179–83, 189–90, 196, 199, 201, 205–12, 265
 axiological validity, 182–3
 factual validity, 182–3

validity (*cont.*):
- systemic validity, 182–3
- validity claims, *see* Habermas, validity claims
- validity conceptions, 182
- validity of legal validity, 201, 204–15

view from nowhere, 194
view from the bench, *see* judges, view from the bench
von Wright, 30, 211

Wachtler, 84
Walter, 207
Weber, 8, 20, 30–1, 155, 176, 194
Weinberger, 198, 200, 206–7
Weltanschauung, 220
Western *épistémè*, 33, 38, 155, 158, 203, 230–1, 238, 255–7, 264, 266
Western ontology, 27, 230–1, 236–7, 256–8
Western philosophy, 22, 24, 26–8, 33, 36, 230, 235, 255–60, 264–7
Wiener Kreis, 19
Wilhelmsson, 245
Wilson, 38
Winch, 198
Wittgenstein, 6, 9, 20, 28, 32, 34–5, 37, 39, 93, 185, 197–9, 201, 217, 219, 222, 229, 256, 258, 260, 265–6
- domain of philosophy, 33–4
- Fliegenglas, 34
- infallible paradigm of identity, 233–5, 258
- philosopher's ladder, 33
- philosopher's spade, 229
- standard metre, 197–8, 222–3, 225, 231, 233, 257

Wróblewski, 10, 12, 14–15, 17–18, 21, 42, 67, 70, 161, 175–7, 180, 182–3, 185, 194–5, 216, 229, 250, 255, 259, 265
- ideologies of judicial decision-making, 3–6, 11, 76–7, 114, 154, 250
- levels of decision-making rationality, 215–16

Zeno, 198